Drive Around

Brittany

& Normandy

YOUR GUIDE TO GREAT DRIVES

Titles in this series include:

For further information about these and other Thomas Cook publications, write to Thomas Cook Publishing, PO Box 227, The Thomas Cook Business Park, 18 Coningsby Road, Peterborough PE3 8SB, United Kingdom.

Drive Around

Brittany

& Normandy

The best of the glorious coastline of Brittany and Normandy, plus the region's historic abbeys and churches, its châteaux, museums, markets, food, wine, traditions and scenery

Christopher and Melanie Rice

Thomas Cook
Publishing

www.thomascookpublishing.com

Published by Thomas Cook Publishing,
a division of Thomas Cook Tour Operations Limited
Company Registration No. 1450464 England
PO Box 227
The Thomas Cook Business Park
18 Coningsby Road
Peterborough PE3 8SB
United Kingdom

Telephone: +44 (0)1733 416477
Fax: +44 (0)1733 416688
E-mail: books@thomascook.com

For further information about
Thomas Cook Publishing, visit our website:
www.thomascookpublishing.com

ISBN 978-1-84157-739-5

Text: © 2007 Thomas Cook Publishing
Maps and diagrams:
City and road maps: © Thomas Cook Publishing
City maps supplied by RJS Associates
Road maps supplied and designed by
Lovell Johns Ltd., OX8 8LH
Road maps generated from Collins Bartholomew Digital Database © Collins Bartholomew Ltd, 1999

Series Editor: Diane Ashmore
Production/DTP Editor: Steven Collins
Written and researched by: Christopher and
Melanie Rice

Update research by: Mick Sinclair
Driving information: Michael Hafferty

About the authors

Christopher and Melanie Rice have travelled throughout Europe and have written numerous travel guides and articles, including books on Russia, the Czech Republic and Eastern Europe, Turkey, Berlin, the Algarve and islands in the Dodecanese. They discovered Brittany and Normandy while living on the south coast of England where they formed a lasting relationship with the cross-channel ferry. Since then their horizons have been widened to include Breton cuisine, culture and politics. Christopher and Melanie are also well-known children's authors with more than 30 titles to their credit.

Acknowledgements

The authors would like to thank Brittany Ferries, Eurostar, Françoise Martin du Nord of Les Aigles de Bretagne, Carine Verdier, Cécile Caous, Nelly Regnier, Philippe Van Kote, Armell Robic, Didier Llorca and the staff of all Offices du Tourisme who generously gave their time and expertise during the research for this book. Thanks also to our friends Erik, Robert and Monique.

Contents

About Drive Around Guides

Thomas Cook's Drive Around Guides are designed to provide you with a comprehensive but flexible reference source to guide you as you tour a country or region by car. This guide divides Brittany and Normandy into touring areas – one per chapter. Major cultural centres or cities form chapters in their own right. Each chapter contains enough attractions to provide at least a day's worth of activities – often more.

Ratings
To make it easier for you to plan your time and decide what to see, every area is rated according to its attractions in categories such as Architecture, Entertainment and Children.

Chapter contents
Every chapter has an introduction summing up the main attractions of the area, and a ratings box, which will highlight the area's strengths and weaknesses – some areas may be more attractive to families travelling with children, others to wine-lovers visiting vineyards, and others to people interested in finding castles, churches, nature reserves or good beaches.

Each chapter is then divided into an alphabetical gazetteer, and a suggested tour. You can select whether you just want to visit a particular sight or attraction, choosing from those described in the gazetteer, or whether you want to tour the area comprehensively. If the latter, you can construct your own itinerary, or follow the authors' suggested tour, which comes at the end of every area chapter.

The gazetteer
The gazetteer section describes all the major attractions in the area – the villages, towns, historic sites, nature reserves, parks or museums that you are most likely to want to see. Maps of the area highlight all the places mentioned in the text. Using this comprehensive overview of the area, you may choose just to visit one or two sights.

One way to use the guide is simply to find individual sights that interest you, using the index or overview map, and read what our authors have to say about them. This will help you decide whether to visit the sight. If you do, you will find plenty of practical information, such as the street address, the telephone number for enquiries and opening times.

Symbol Key

- ❶ Tourist Information Centre
- ❷ Advice on arriving or departing
- ❸ Parking locations
- ❹ Advice on getting around
- ❺ Directions
- ❻ Sights and attractions
- ❼ Accommodation
- ❽ Eating
- ❾ Shopping
- ❿ Sport
- ⓫ Entertainment

Practical information

The practical information in the page margins, or sidebar, will help you locate the services you need as an independent traveller – including the tourist information centre, car parks and public transport facilities. You will also find the opening times of sights, museums, churches and other attractions, as well as useful tips on shopping, market days, cultural events, entertainment, festivals and sports facilities.

Alternatively, you can choose a hotel, perhaps with the help of the accommodation recommendations contained in this guide. You can then turn to the overall map on page 10 to help you work out which chapters in the book describe those cities and regions that lie closest to your chosen touring base.

Driving tours

The suggested tour is just that – a suggestion, with plenty of optional detours and one or two ideas for making your own discoveries, under the heading *Also worth exploring*. The routes are designed to link the attractions described in the gazetteer section, and to cover outstandingly scenic coastal, mountain and rural landscapes. The total distance is given for each tour, as is the time it will take you to drive the complete route, but bear in mind that this indication is just for the driving time: you will need to add on extra time for visiting attractions along the way.

Many of the routes are circular, so that you can join them at any point. Where the nature of the terrain dictates that the route has to be linear, the route can either be followed out and back, or you can use it as a link route, to get from one area in the book to another.

As you follow the route descriptions, you will find names picked out in bold capital letters – this means that the place is described fully in the gazetteer. Other names picked out in bold indicate additional villages or attractions worth a brief stop along the route.

Accommodation and food

In every chapter you will find lodging and eating recommendations for individual towns, or for the area as a whole. These are designed to cover a range of price brackets and concentrate on more characterful small or individualistic hotels and restaurants. In addition, you will find information in the *Travel facts* chapter on chain hotels, with an address to which you can write for a guide, map or directory. The price indications used in the guide have the following meanings:

€   budget level
€€   typical/average prices
€€€   de luxe.

English Channel

Normandy

Paris

Brittany

FRANCE

Atlantic Ocean

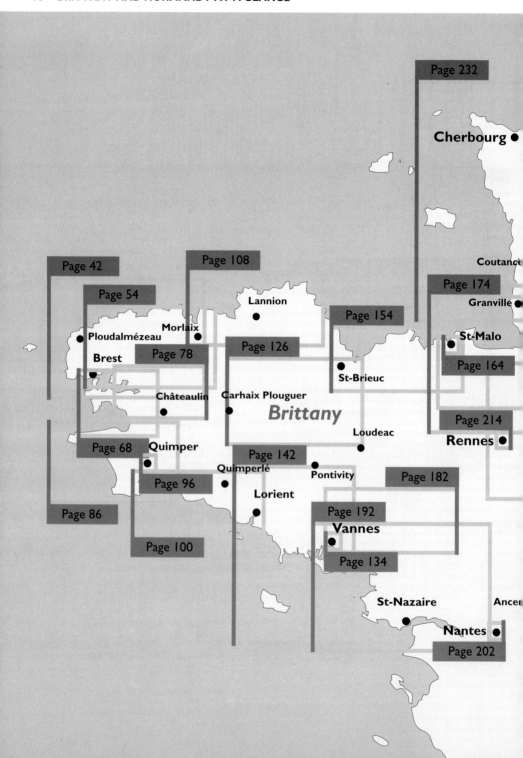

Page 232

Cherbourg ●

Page 42

Page 54

Page 108

Coutance

Page 174

Lannion ●

Granville ●

Morlaix ●

Page 154

St-Malo ●

Ploudalmézeau ●

Page 78

Page 126

Page 164

Brest

St-Brieuc ●

Châteaulin ●

Carhaix Plouguer ●

Brittany

Page 214

Rennes ●

Loudeac ●

Page 68

Quimper ●

Page 142

Page 182

Quimperlé ●

Pontivity ●

Page 96

Lorient ●

Page 192

Page 86

Vannes ●

Page 100

Page 134

St-Nazaire ●

Ancer

Nantes ●

Page 202

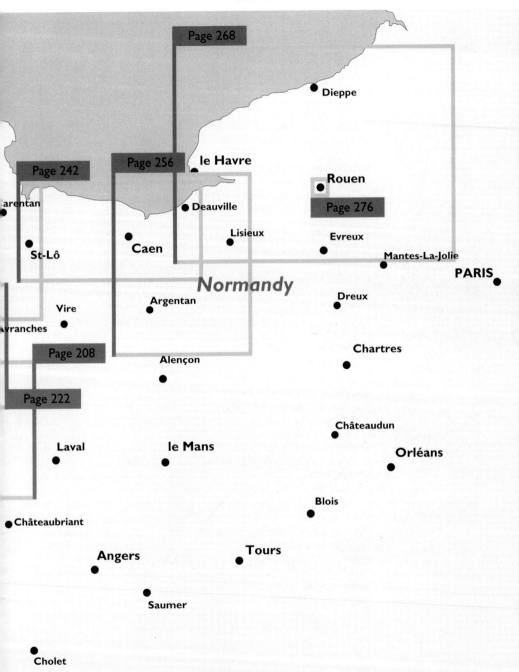

Page 268

Dieppe

Page 242

le Havre

Page 256

arentan

Deauville

Rouen

Page 276

St-Lô

Caen

Lisieux

Evreux

Mantes-La-Jolie

PARIS

Vire

Normandy

Argentan

Dreux

vranches

Page 208

Alençon

Chartres

Page 222

Châteaudun

Laval

le Mans

Orléans

Blois

Châteaubriant

Angers

Tours

Saumer

Cholet

Introduction

Brittany and Normandy are neighbours but with very different histories and traditions. In geological as well as human terms, Brittany is ancient – Carnac, in the Morbihan, may have been continuously inhabited longer than anywhere in the world and its prehistoric monuments, dating from around 5000 BC and as important as Stonehenge, are a major tourist attraction. Later, Brittany was settled by the Celts, and Breton culture (closely related to the Welsh, Cornish and Irish traditions) has survived more than four centuries of French domination. The Breton language is still spoken widely in the more remote areas and, throughout the region, the younger generation is once again developing a sense of Breton identity, although the separatist movement which hit the headlines in the 1970s and 1980s seems to have fallen out of favour. 'Normandy' was a Norse term coined by the Viking invaders of the 10th century and although the Scandinavians were quickly assimilated by the indigenous people, they left their mark in the ruthless determination so characteristic of the Normans, in their fierce martial spirit and their fondness for exploration and colonisation.

Most visitors will want to spend at least some time exploring the extensive coastline – 3500km in Brittany alone. The scenery is often rugged and dramatic, hence the large number of 'Côtes Sauvage' facing the Atlantic and the equally numerous and justly celebrated viewpoints out to sea – Cap Frehel and Pointe de Penhir, for example, or Pointe du Raz where the Druids are said to have buried their dead. The entire coast is heavily indented with coves, bays and river estuaries and it's here that you'll find the holiday resorts with their wonderful beaches. Some, such as Dinard and Trouville, have more than a whiff of the 19th century about them with showy villas and promenades, while others, la Baule being a spectacular example, have more in common with the Riviera. If you're looking for something more unspoilt, there are the sandy expanses of Plestin-les-Grèves or the Baie d'Audierne in Brittany, or in Normany, the dunes beyond Granville. Wherever you go the amenities (invariably first rate) are never very far away – everything from yacht clubs and watersports centres to golf courses and seafront restaurants.

Brittany is blessed with numerous offshore islands and you should allow for at least one boat excursion on your trip. The largest, Belle-Ile, was popular with writers and artists, but there's also Bréhat with its mild microclimate and luxuriant vegetation and the 365 islets in the Gulf of Morbihan, most now the private hideaways of French filmstars, perfume manufacturers and dress designers. If you're more keen on birdwatching than sunbathing and sightseeing, you should include the islands of Ouessant or les Sept Iles in your itinerary.

Normandy and Brittany both suffered during World War II but Brittany got off comparatively lightly – only Brest, St-Nazaire and St-Malo were heavily bombed. Fortunately Brittany's finest ornament, her picturesque medieval towns with their riverine ports, their ramparts and watchtowers, twisting cobbled streets of half-timbered or slate-hung houses and ancient churches are all intact. Dinan, Vannes, Quimper, Rennes, Vitré – you can take your pick; even St-Malo's walled city of sombre granite has been completely restored. Skilful restoration work has also preserved the best of the great architectural monuments of Normandy, the cathedrals, castles and abbey churches of Caen, Bayeux, Coutances, Rouen and Mont-St-Michel.

Inland Brittany was once covered by three great forests – Cranou, Brocéliande and Fougères – and you can still explore the vestiges around Huelgoat, Lac de Guerlédan and Paimpont. Alternatively you could follow the course of the Rance or the Vilaine or one of the other scenic waterways and estuaries that crisscross the countryside, possibly making an overnight stop in one of the flower-bedecked *villes fleuries*.

Below
The narrow streets of *Le Mont-St-Michel*

Both Normandy and Brittany are heavily agricultural, and as you drive you'll be able to enjoy the rolling farmland, studded with historic châteaux, half-timbered manor houses and farm buildings constructed from local granite or Cotentin stone. Many have rooms available for rent, while others have been converted into craft or cider museums. In Normandy you can also find out about Calvados and cheese-making. Eating and drinking in both regions is an undiluted pleasure. The coastal regions naturally specialise in seafood, and if you're an early riser you can watch the day's catch being brought ashore on its way to the dining table. When you've had your fill of oysters, mussels and crab, there are the specialities: *pré salé* lamb, carrying the salty tang of the coastal marshes; *andouilles* (chitterling); *canard à la Rouennais* (duck); and *poulet vallée d'Auge* (chicken), not forgetting the ubiquitous *crêpes* and the nourishing Breton stew *kig ha farz*.

Above
Medieval streets

Travel facts

Accommodation

In Brittany and Normandy you'll find a wide range of accommodation, in all price ranges, from campsites and converted farmhouses to luxury hotels and even châteaux. Bear in mind, however, that the main resorts are heavily booked at the height of the summer, especially during the French holiday season (mid-July to mid-August) and that in winter many hotels and campsites close – so be sure of getting what you want by booking in advance, especially if you're travelling with the family. Prices are generally higher in the fashionable resorts, in towns and around the channel ports.

There are dozens of hotel chains in France, offering a range of categories from 3- to 4-star to budget. The main chains are listed below:

Accor (incorporates Ibis, Mercure and Novotel) There is a central reservation number for these chains:
tel: (UK) 0870 609 0961;
tel: (USA) (800) 221-4542;
www.accorhotels.com

Best Western
tel: (UK) 0800 393130;
fax: (3902) 2901-3057;
(USA) 6201 W. 24th Parkway, Phoenix AZ 85016-2023, tel: (800) 780-7234;
fax: (602) 780-6099;
www.bestwestern.com

Campanile *tel: (France) 338 25 00 30 03; tel: (UK) 020 7519 5045;*
www.campanile.com

Choice Hotels
tel: (France) 08 00 91 24 24;
tel: (UK) 0800 444 444;
tel: (USA) (800) 424-6423;
www.choicehotelseurope.com

Hotels
French hotels are graded from 1–4 stars and 'luxury'. Unstarred establishments are cheap but have few facilities – always inspect a room before taking it. Tariffs are posted in reception and in every bedroom. Prices are quoted for a double room with two people sharing (not including breakfast) – check whether the 19.6 per cent VAT is included in the price. Single rooms are thin on the ground, so expect to pay for a double even if you're travelling alone. Most rooms have showers (cheaper than baths) but in smaller hotels there may be only one bathroom per floor. Breakfast often works out quite expensive – you'll find it more economical to eat out in a local café.

Reservations should be made in writing (letter or fax); you'll have to pay a deposit (usually the equivalent of one night or 25 per cent). If you cancel your stay after paying the deposit, the hotel may require you to pay the total cost of the reservation. If you call in person, tourist offices will make reservations for the coming week (for a small fee).

You will be expected to arrive at the hotel before 1900 and no room will be held beyond 2200. If you're planning to arrive later, make sure you inform the hotel in advance.

One of the best-known and most reputable groups of hotels is the Fédération des Logis de France *tel: (France) 01 45 84 83 84; www.logis-de-france.fr*. These are inexpensive, family-run hotels, often in attractive surroundings out of town. The restaurants are equally good value and usually feature regional specialities. They are classified by 'chimneys' (1–3).

Holiday Inn *tel: (France) 08 00 90 59 99; tel: (UK) 0800 405060; tel: (USA) (800) 465-4329; www.holiday-inn.com*

Mercure *tel: (France) 08 25 88 33 33; tel: (UK) 0870 609 0965; tel: (Canada/USA) (800) MERCURE; www.mercure.com*

Novotel *tel: (France) 08 25 01 20 11; tel: (UK) 0870 609 0962; tel: (Canada/USA) (800) NOVOTEL; www.novotel.com*

Relais et Chateaux *tel: (France) 08 25 32 32 32; tel: (UK) 0800 2000 00 02; tel: (USA) (800) 735-2478; www.relaischateaux.com*

Campsites

Campsites are graded from 1–4 stars. All have clean water, a refuse collection and a telephone; many have swimming pools, restaurants, children's play areas, camp shops and fabulous outlooks, depending on the price. Most sites have fixed tents, caravans or holiday bungalows on offer as well as free spaces for people bringing their own tent or caravan. Camping is very popular with the French, especially in southern Cornouaille, so book in advance. For more information, or to book, contact **Camping Plus Bretagne**, *BP 28, 29740 Plobannalec; tel: 02 98 87 87 86; fax: 02 98 82 21 19; www.campingplus.com*

Chambres d'hôtes

A green-and-white sign denotes *chambres d'hôtes* – accommodation in a private home, which could be anything from a château to a farm cottage. An evening meal is often included (*table d'hôte*) and you are expected to join in with the family. Rooms can be booked through local tourist offices, the French Tourist Office or through **Château Acceuil** *tel: 01 47 20 18 27; www.chateau-accueil.com* or **Bienvenue à la ferme** *tel: 01 53 57 11 44; www.bienvenue-a-la-ferme.com*. A large number of *Chambres d'Hôtes* establishments are represented by **Gîtes de France**, *59 rue St-Lazaire, 75439 Paris Cedex 09; tel: 01 49 70 75 75; e-mail: info@gites-de-france.fr; www.gites-de-france.fr*

Gîtes

A *gîte* is self-catering accommodation, often in a converted farmhouse or country cottage. Lists of the *gîtes* in the government-run scheme are available in *The Gîtes de France Handbook* or from the Internet – *www.gîtes-de-france.fr* – and are graded in 'ears of *Gîtes* wheat' (14). Traditionally they are booked by the week although some now offer weekends out of season. *Gîtes* can be booked via most travel agents or ferry companies, or via the owner direct. Gîtes de France publishes directories, and, for a small booking fee, will handle bookings for you – contact **Gîtes de France** (*see above*).

Airports

There are international airports at Rouen, Caen, Deauville, le Havre, Nantes, Quimper, Rennes and Brest for European flights. Those at Cherbourg, Dinard, Lannion, Vannes and St-Brieuc are for internal flights.

Children

Look out for the little puffin in a striped shirt and the greeting '*Salut les Enfants*' – this sign guarantees quality service and accommodation especially suitable for children. The French Tourist Board has awarded several resorts the accolade 'Station Kid' for their child-friendly

Opposite
Local seafood

facilities and activities (Fouesnant, Quiberon and Perros-Guirec appear in this book). Many other resorts, including Trouville in Normandy, also go out of their way to welcome children and babies with special menus, babysitting services and supervised beach clubs.

Climate

The mild climate in Normandy and Brittany means warm dry summers, but wetter winters. However, the Atlantic seaboard means you should expect some rain at any time. Average temperatures in the summer range from 20°C (in the north) to 24°C (in the south), while in the winter temperatures rarely drop below 8°C. For current national weather (in French) *tel: 892 68 00 00*; forecasts for each *département tel: 892 68 02* and add the number of the *département*.

Currency

The unit of currency, shared with many other European countries, is the euro, which officially replaced the French franc (FF) in 2002. A euro is worth about 6.5FF, and is divided into 100 cents (often called centimes, like the old one-hundredth of a franc). Many people, particularly in rural areas, still refer to prices in francs and you will often see both currencies displayed on price tickets.

There have been some problems with euro traveller's cheques, and it is usually better to carry these in US dollars or UK sterling currencies. Banks generally offer the best exchange rates.

Many banks have cash dispenser machines (ATMs) that accept foreign cards. Larger shops, hotels and petrol garages accept major credit cards, but France has a different chip and pin method of authorising card purchases to the UK – this means there can sometimes be difficulties. Take your passport with you and you may avoid the problem. Note that very few automatic 24-hour petrol pumps will accept anything other than French credit cards.

Customs regulations

There are no restrictions on goods brought to and from EU countries, provided they are for personal use (try to adhere to official guidelines: 10 litres of spirits, 90 litres of wine, 110 litres of beer and 800 cigarettes maximum). Goods purchased in duty-free shops are still subject to restrictions and visitors from outside Europe have to abide by stricter regulations – ask before you leave home. The import of weapons, drugs and pornography is prohibited.

Drinking

Left
Fishing boats, Concarneau

Tap water is safe to drink, but you may find the Breton mineral water Plancöet more refreshing. There's also apple and pear juice in

Electricity

The electric current is 220 volts (50Hz). Plugs should be circular with two round pins. Take an adaptor for non-continental appliances.

Entry formalities

Visitors from outside the EU require a valid passport. EU citizens need an identity card, but as the UK has no official identity card, British citizens should be in possession of a valid passport. Visas are not generally required for stays of less than three months, though nationals of certain countries, such as South Africa, do need to apply to the nearest French consulate before entering the country. Visa requirements no longer apply to holders of passports from the USA, Canada, Japan, Australia or New Zealand.

abundance. Cider is the popular local drink in Normandy and Brittany – the pear equivalent is Poiré (perry). Another by-product of the orchards is the strong apple-based brandy Calvados; Pommeau is a less alcoholic and refreshing mixture of Calvados and apple juice. Other local specialities include Benedictine, a sweet liqueur distilled in Fécamp (Normandy), and a real ale, unique to Brittany, called Coreff (brewed in Morlaix). There's also Warenghem whisky distilled near Lannion. The only wines that are truly local are those produced in the Muscadet region, near Nantes.

Eating out

Traditional mealtimes are 1200–1400 and 1900–2100. Restaurants are often pre-booked by French families for Sunday lunch, so be sure to reserve a table well in advance.

Bars and cafés sell snacks all day. It's often cheaper to stand at the counter and drink rather than sit on a terrace. *Salons de thé* are a more refined alternative if all you want is a light meal. *Crêperies* are everywhere, for pancakes and salads.

Restaurants and brasseries are comparable in terms of price and quality, but the latter stay open longer. Prices are generally posted outside and there is usually at least one fixed-price menu, often good value. *Servis compris* means that a service charge of 15 per cent has been included.

Most towns in Brittany and Normandy have a produce market so you can stock up on picnic fare. Delicatessens (*charcuteries*) also sell prepared dishes and salads. Other useful food outlets are bakers (*boulangeries*) and *pâtisseries* specialising in cakes and pastries.

Festivals

For folklore enthusiasts, the largest music festival in Brittany, attracting more than 4000 participants and up to 300,000 spectators, takes place in Lorient every August. Known as the Interceltic Festival, it presents a wide variety of folk and rock acts from all over the Celtic world (including Ireland, Scotland, Wales, Cornwall, Brittany and northern Spain). It's here that you're likely to see well-known performers such as Alan Stivell, a big name since the 1970s. To the right are some of the other festivals you might come across.

Food

Seafood is available everywhere in super-abundance. Oysters are a speciality of Cancale, the resorts of Baie du St-Michel and the villages of the Belon estuary; Courseulles is known for shellfish; Honfleur for shrimps; and Camaret and Douarnenez for lobster (served 'Armoricaine' in a rich hot sauce). A bowl of steaming *moules marinières* (mussels in wine sauce) often served with *frites* (chips) makes an appetising lunch. Sole, turbot, bass and mackerel, sardines and tuna

Festivals

Shrove Tuesday:
Granville – carnival and fair
Mid-May: **Coutances – Jazz sous les Pommiers**
Whitsunday and Monday:
Honfleur Seamen's Festival – blessing of the sea etc
6 June: **Normandy coast – D-Day Commemorations**
1–10 July: **Rennes Tombées de la Nuit – theatre and music festival**
2nd Sunday July: **Locronan – Troménie** *pardon*
Mid-July: **Dinan Fête des Remparts – medieval fair and celebrations**
Mid-July: **Bayeux – medieval festival**
3rd weekend July: **Fouesnant – Apple-tree festival**
17 July: **le Mont-St-Michel – pilgrimage crossing the mudflats from Gênets**
26 July: **Ste-Anne-d'Auray –** *pardon*
End July: **Quimper – Festival de Cornouaille – major Celtic festival**
2nd week September: **Lessay – Holy Cross cattle and animal fair**
Late October: **St-Brieuc – Rock Art Festival**
Late October: **Redon – chestnut festival**
December: **Falaise les Hivernales de Falaise – winter festival and market.**

also appear regularly on menus; other treats include salmon from the River Aulne and trout from the Monts d'Arrée.

Meat is traditionally served 'the Norman way', ie in cream sauces; pork in cider is also a popular dish. Look out for the succulent *pré salé* lamb (from sheep reared on the salt plains around St-Michel), *tripe à la mode de Caen, canard Rouennais* (duck from the Seine Valley), chicken from Rennes and the strong-flavoured Morlaix ham. Normandy produces the best cheeses, including Camembert, Livarot and Pont-l'Evêque.

Apples feature in turnovers, pastries, cakes and other desserts. *Crêpes* (thin pancakes) and *galettes* (the same only made with buckwheat) are served with every conceivable filling from cider, yoghurt and jam, to cheese, ham and eggs. Other specialities include Calvados-flavoured chocolates, butter cookies from Pont-Aven, Nantes' biscuits and stodgy puddings such as *far Breton.*

Health

There are no vaccinations specifically recommended for visitors to France. EU residents with a European Health Insurance Card are entitled to reciprocal health treatment – however, this will only meet part of your expenses and is no substitute for adequate health insurance. The card is available free from *www.ehic.org.uk*, by phoning *0845 606 2030*, or from post offices. American Express cardholders should apply to **Global Assist** *tel:* (call collect to US: *715 343 7977*) for any medical emergency. Pharmacies (marked with a green cross) will treat minor complaints. They will also direct you to a doctor or dentist.

Information

There are tourist offices (*Syndicats d'Initiatives* or *Offices de Tourisme*) in most towns. English is usually spoken and there is a comprehensive range of information on accommodation, local attractions, restaurants and other facilities.

Insurance

Adequate insurance is essential. Most package holiday companies offer policies, but you can make your own arrangements if you prefer. Some house contents and health policies cover losses and accidents abroad, so check your existing policies.

Maps

The best maps for drivers are the Michelin 1:200,000 maps of Brittany (No 230) and Normandy (No 231). Town plans are issued free by French Tourist Information and vary in their quality and usefulness. Most offices also have maps showing local footpaths with suggested routes.

Packing

Like the south coast of Britain, the climate is mild but there's a fair amount of rain so you'll need wet-weather gear. Also pack a warm jumper for boat trips and coastal walks. Remember to bring any prescribed medicines with you, also mosquito repellent. Most other items are generally available.

Novels set in the region

Les Chouans – Honoré de Balzac, the story of the rebellion set in Fougères. *Ninety Three* – Victor Hugo, also about the Chouan rebels. *The Three Musketeers* – Alexandre Dumas, scenes in Nantes and on Belle-Ile. *In Remembrance of Things Past* – Marcel Proust, scenes evocative of life in Normandy at the beginning of the 20th century (6 volumes). *Madame Bovary* – Gustave Flaubert, based on a real-life story from the Forêt de Lyons region. *Flaubert's Parrot* – Julian Barnes, novel based on Flaubert's life set in and around Rouen. *Contes de la Bécasse* – Guy de Maupassant, short stories set in le Havre and around the Cotentin peninsula.

Museums

Opening times and days vary according to season – some museums close altogether during the winter. Most have at least one closing day per week (often Mon or Tue) and relatively few remain open all day; the lunch hour falls from 1200–1400. If in doubt, check at the local tourist office.

Nature parks

There are four regional nature parks in the area covered by this book: the Parc d'Amorique and Grande Brière in Brittany and Marais du Cotentin et du Bessin and Parc de Brotonne in Normandy. They are run locally and aim to promote the local economy through crafts etc, while protecting the natural and cultural heritage of the region.

Opening times

As a general rule, food shops open *Mon–Sat 0800–2030*, other shops open *between 0900 (0930) and 1900 (1930)*. Bakers (*boulangeries*) open on *Sun mornings* too. Lunchtime closing is *1200–1400*, but supermarkets and shopping complexes stay open all day and sometimes later into the evening. Half-day closing is often Mon, but all these times are subject to seasonal variations.

Banks open *Mon–Fri 0900–1200, 1400–1600*. Some open *Sat morning, some close Mon*. They usually close early the day before a public holiday.

Postal services

Postcards and letters are charged at the same rate for all EU destinations, with delivery within a few days. Stamps are available in newsagents and tobacconists. Airmail rates for letters to other destinations are much higher and items have to be weighed at a post office (indicated by a PTT sign). Letter boxes are yellow. The stylised 'bird' symbol and the words 'La Poste' are universally used on post boxes, post office ATMs and the Post Office itself.

Books about the region in French

La Bretagne de A à Z – Jakez Gaucher (Coop Breizh). *La musique bretonne* – Roland Becker, Laure le Gurun (Coop Breizh). *La cuisine des Îles* – Françoise Buisson (published privately). *Premier vocabulaire Breton* (trilingual) – Béatrice Jouin (Éditions Ouest-France).

History books

A Distant Mirror: The Calamitous 14th century – Barbara Tuchman. *Citizens* – Simon Schama, a history of the French Revolution. *Overlord* – Max Hastings, history of D-Day and the Battle of Normandy.

Art and architecture

La Route des Peintres en Cornouaille (Groupement Touristique de Cornouaille) – edition in English. *Impressionism* – World of Art Library, Thames and Hudson. Éditions Ouest-France produce an extensive series of books on towns and architectural sights in Brittany, many translated into English. French Tourist Information publish a number of very useful leaflets and books on the sites, amenities and countryside of the regions, obtainable at local offices.

Left
Maison de Vannes

Public holidays

New Year's Day	– 1 January
Easter Sunday and Monday	
Labour Day	– 1 May
VE Day	– 8 May
Ascension Day	
Whitsunday and Monday	
Bastille Day	– 14 July
Assumption Day	– 5 August
All Saints' Day	– 1 November
Armistice Day	– 11 November
Christmas Day	– 25 December

Public transport

Public transport is generally reliable and efficient. SNCF is the national rail system. Services are frequent and fares reasonable – Eurailpass, Flexipass and Saver Pass are all valid in France. SNCF also offers its own range of discounted tickets. Under-4s travel free on public transport, 4–11s travel half price. For more information contact Rail Europe *tel: (08705) 848848; www.sncf.com; www.raileurope.co.uk*. All train tickets must be validated with a date stamp in the orange automatic machines at the entrance to platforms. Rail maps and timetables are available at stations. TGV super-express services between large towns require reservations, especially at peak times. You are not allowed to take a bike on TGV services, only local trains (if in doubt look for the bike sign on timetables).

Buses, particularly in Brittany, cover more towns than the train network and are a cheaper way of getting around. The central bus station is often next to the rail station; route maps and timetables can be picked up here and from Tourist Information. Bikes may be taken on some bus services at the discretion of the driver.

Safety and security

Brittany and Normandy are safe places to holiday, but groups of tourists will always attract opportunist thieves. Beware of pickpockets, especially on public transport and in crowds – keep your money in a belt or other secure place and don't leave valuables lying about where they can be seen. Never leave luggage unattended. It is a good idea to have photocopies of your passport and records of your credit cards, traveller's cheques and insurance policies stored separately from the items themselves. If you do lose something, report it to the police immediately.

Emergency phone numbers: Police and ambulance *17*
                             Fire brigade *18*

Regional tourist authorities:

Regional tourist office (Brittany) *Comité Régional de Tourisme, I rue Raoul Ponchon, 35069 Rennes; tel: 02 99 28 44 30; fax: 02 99 28 44 40; www.brittanytourism.com*

Regional tourist office (Normandy) *Le Doyenné, 14 rue Charles Corbeau, 27000 Evreux; tel: 02 32 33 79 00; fax: 02 32 31 19 04; www.normandy-tourism.org*

Côtes-d'Armor
Comité Départemental de Tourisme, Maison du Tourisme, 7 rue St Benoît, 22046 St-Brieuc; tel: 96 62 72 00, fax: 96 33 59 10; www.cotesdarmor.com

Finistère
Comité Départemental de Tourisme, 11 rue Théodore le Hars, 29014 Quimper; tel: 02 98 76 20 70; fax: 02 98 52 19 19; www.finisteretourisme.com

Ille-et-Villaine
Comité Départemental de Tourisme, 4 rue Jean Jaurés, BP 6046, 35060 Rennes, Cedex 3; tel: 02 99 78 47 47; fax: 02 99 78 33 24; www.bretagne35.com

Morbihan
Comité Départemental de Tourisme, BP 408, 56010 Vannes; tel: 02 97 54 06 56; fax: 02 97 42 71 02; www.morbihan.com

Loire-Atlantique
Comité Départemental de Tourisme, 2 allée Baco, BP 20502, 44005 Nantes Cedex 1; tel: 02 51 72 95 30; fax: 02 40 20 44 54; e-mail: loire-atlantiqueinfo@ loire-atlantique-tourisme.com; www.cdt44.com/fr

Shopping

Some ideas for souvenirs and presents – traditional navy-and-white striped fishermen's jumpers (striped T-shirts are a cheaper alternative). Other warm and waterproof clothing.
Jewellery – Celtic crosses or triskele symbol.
Crafts – embroidery from Cornouaille; lace from Bayeux; pottery from Quimper; copperware, pewter and wood carvings from Lizio, Villedieu-les-Poêles and other craft centres.
Food and drink – Pont-Aven biscuits, chocolates from Nantes, Normandy cheeses, cider, mead, Calvados and Muscadet.
Music – tape/CD of Celtic music (eg Alan Stivell).
Books – Coop Breizh, *17 rue Penhoet* in Rennes, for everything on a Celtic and Breton theme.

Sport

You will find all the literature you need on sports and outdoor activities in tourist offices, for example: Golf Courses in Normandy, Watersports in Brittany etc.
Golf – Normandy has over 40 courses, most with more than 18 holes. There are also courses in Brittany, mainly on the Emerald Coast and in the big resorts.
Water sports – sailing, surfing, windsurfing, sand-yachting, canoeing, kayaking, diving and rowing are all available.
Other outdoor activities include fishing, walking, cycling and horse-riding.
The guide to the long distance footpaths marked by red and white posts – *sentiers de grand randonnée* (GR) – can be bought from tourist information or from the **Fédération Française de la Randonnée Pédestre** *14 rue Riquet, Paris; tel: 01 44 89 93 93; www.ffrp.asso.fr*

Telephones

Public call boxes are in plentiful supply and usually in working order. You'll probably need a phone card (*télécarte*) available from post offices, railway stations and *tabacs* in 50 or 120 units. Calls from a restaurant or hotel are usually subject to a surcharge. Cheap rates apply to calls made on Sundays, between 2230 and 0800 on weekdays or after 1400 on Saturdays.
For the operator, dial 13.
For directory enquiries, dial 12.
To call Paris, dial 16, then when the tone changes, 1 followed by the number you require.
To call France from abroad, dial 33, then the number, omitting the first 0. In France, just dial the number as shown, with no other codes necessary.

International calls can be made from most call boxes. To make an international call, dial 00 followed by the country code (44 for UK, 1 for US) then the number, omitting any initial 0.

Time

France is on Central European Time, 1 hour ahead of GMT; 6 hours ahead of US Eastern Standard Time; 9 hours ahead of Pacific Standard Time.

French summer-time begins on the last Sunday of March and ends on the last Sunday in October.

Tipping

Service charges (15 per cent) are automatically added to hotel and restaurant bills; it's at your discretion whether you leave an additional tip in restaurants (a couple of euros will suffice). Taxi drivers, doormen and petrol pump attendants etc may be tipped, again at your discretion.

Toilets

Public toilets can be found at shopping centres, petrol stations etc. Standards vary; however, facilities in cafés, restaurants, hotels and museums are usually very good. *Messieurs* – men; *dames* – women.

Travellers with disabilities

Facilities for travellers with disabilities have improved in recent years, particularly in the main resorts. However, it's a different story once you venture into rural areas. Local police may be sympathetic to the parking needs of people with limited mobility, but there is no national policy, while the steep cobbled streets in some medieval towns may make life difficult. More information can be obtained from **Association France-Handicaps**, *9 rue de Luce-de-Lancival, 77340 Pontault-Combault; tel: 01 60 28 50 12*, who publish a French-language tourism guide; also in French are the government website: *www.handicap.gouv.fr*, and the more practical *www.apf.asso.fr*

Calvados *Le Comité Départemental de Tourisme du Calvados 8 rue Renoir, 14054 Caen Cedex 4; tel: 02 31 27 90 30; www.calvados-tourisme.com*

La Manche *Comité Départemental de Tourisme, Maison du Département, Rond-Pont de la Liberté, St-Lô; tel: 02 33 05 98 70; fax: 02 33 56 07 03; www.manchetourisme.com*

Seine-Maritime *Comité Départemental de Tourisme, 6 rue Couronné, BP 60, 76420 Bihorel; tel: 02 35 12 10 10; fax: 02 35 59 86 04; www.seine-maritime-tourisme.com*

Above
Rouen: the Gros-Horloge

Driver's guide

Automobile clubs

Members of UK motoring organisations (AA or RAC) can extend their accident insurance and breakdown services to France. Both organisations offer a wide range of information and advice as well as suggesting itineraries and routes. *www.theaa.com* offers a free, turn-by-turn route map of your journey. See also *www.rac.co.uk www.viamichelin.co.uk*

Autoroutes

Most of the French autoroutes are toll roads. The commonest system of charging (*péage*) involves taking a ticket from a machine at the start of the toll section, which raises an automatic barrier. On leaving the system, or at an intermediate tollbooth, the ticket is presented and the amount to pay is displayed on an illuminated sign. Payment may be made in euros or by credit card. Signatures are not normally required. Traveller's cheques cannot usually be used for tolls. On autoroutes speed is sometimes automatically computed from time of entry and distance covered on arrival at the tollbooth. If a speeding offence is disclosed you may be prosecuted.

Accidents

You must STOP after any accident. You can be in serious trouble if you don't. Call 15, 17 or 18 to alert the Ambulance, Police or Fire Service as appropriate, or use the EU universal emergency number 112. On an autoroute or main road, use one of the bright orange free SOS emergency roadside telephones located at frequent intervals.

Give whatever aid you are capable of to any person injured or in peril. It is an offence not to do this if it lies within your ability. This applies whether you are driver, passenger or witness. Safeguard against a secondary accident. Hazard lights – warning triangle – signal to other traffic. Exchange details of vehicles, drivers insurance etc. (French cars display insurance details on a windscreen sticker.) Complete a 'European Accident Statement' form – ask your insurers for this before you leave, the French driver will almost certainly have one. This forms a factual record. It is not an admission of fault. Note as many details as you can. Photographs? Witnesses? If someone has been injured, you must inform the police. If you have damaged someone else's vehicle or property and you are unable to give the owner your details, you must inform the police. The police will not usually take details where an accident involves material damage only, unless there is evidence of an offence such as dangerous or drink driving. Inform your insurers as soon as possible.

Breakdowns

If you are on an autoroute, stop your vehicle on the hard shoulder, getting it as far to the right as possible. On ordinary roads, consider using the verge but beware of roadside ditches. Hazard lights on. Place a warning triangle at least 30m from the scene, visible from 100m away. (Remember, it can be very dangerous to walk on the hard shoulder of any motorway.) You and your passengers are probably safer out of the vehicle and well up the verge away from the traffic.

If you need assistance on an autoroute you must use one of the free roadside telephones to connect you with the police. You cannot arrange recovery yourself, even if you are a member of a breakdown service. No garage will send a recovery vehicle onto an autoroute without police permission. There is a fixed scale of charges. (€72 by day, €108 by night.) You may not carry out a DIY tow on an autoroute and you may only do so on an ordinary road for 'a few metres' in an emergency. Makeshift towing is strongly discouraged and usually voids French car insurance.

Documents

Members of EU countries and US citizens only need a valid national driving licence, but an international driving licence is essential for other nationals. Provisional licences are not valid and drivers must be over the age of 18. UK photo card licences are best. Paper licences are lawful but further proof of ID may be required. Registration papers (a logbook) and a letter of authorisation if the car is not registered in your name, insurance papers and Test Certificate (MoT) (originals – photocopies are not valid) and a nationality plate must be carried. The above documents must be produced at the time on request by police. An immediate fine may be imposed if they are not to hand. For UK drivers a 'Green Card' is not required in France for car insurance. Your certificate of insurance issued in Britain conforms to French legal needs. However, this is minimum legal cover. You should ask your insurers to extend your normal, full cover for use abroad for the period of your stay. Continental breakdown insurance is recommended. Should you visit the state of Andorra in the Pyrenees you will require a Green Card. Holders of US insurance must take out a European policy.

Above
Decorative tilework at Huelgoat

Continental breakdown insurance is strongly recommended and one phone call is all it takes to hand the whole problem over to multi-lingual operators who are experts in sorting things out.

Caravans and camper vans (Trailers and RVs)

France is probably the most 'camping and caravanning friendly' country in Europe and there are numerous attractive campsites from economical to de luxe in the area covered by this guide. Booking ahead is really only necessary in the height of the season. The Alan Rogers' campsite guides are very useful. *Camping sauvage* ('wild' camping) is completely banned. Camping in State Forests or any wooded area is virtually always prohibited because of the serious risk of fire. Overnight parking of motorhomes is frequently permitted (and often free) in the central square of smaller towns and villages where water and toilet facilities are available. There are no formalities about bringing a caravan into France if your stay is for less than six months.

Motorhomes and cars towing trailers have to pay a higher toll on autoroutes. Some caravanners use the facilities of the autoroute *aires de repos* (rest areas) for an overnight stop. This is quite lawful, as your autoroute ticket lasts for at least 24 hours. If you do this, you are advised to use common sense and stop in a well-lit spot, in view of passers-by. Thefts and break-ins are, unfortunately, not unknown.

Speed limits for cars towing trailers or caravans are the same as solo vehicles. Occasionally, there may be a reduced speed limit for caravans on long declines. This is to reduce the danger of instability when the caravan is being neither pulled nor braked but is 'floating' behind the towing vehicle.

If you intend driving in the Pyrenees or the Alps (and particularly if you are towing a trailer) you should remember that engine efficiency decreases with altitude, by about 10% per 900m. This can mean that a heavily laden non-turbo car just coping with the additional load at sea level, may not manage the incline as it climbs higher.

Driving in Brittany and Normandy

There are three classes of road – motorway (*autoroute* – A); main road (*route nationale* – RN or N); and secondary road (*route départementale* – D).

Major roads also have an E number in green indicating that they are part of the European route network. The French Ministry of Transport is in the process of transferring responsibility for some N roads to *Départements* and these will be reclassified as D roads.

Drinking and driving

The French limit is 50mg of alcohol per 100ml of blood and penalties increase sharply if an 80mg limit is exceeded. There is a determined campaign to reduce incidents of drinking and driving, and penalties are severe, with heavy fines and imprisonment. Random breath tests are common and you should not underestimate the powers of the police or the consequences of failing a test. A large fine may be demanded on the spot and your vehicle may be impounded until it is paid. Any disqualification is immediate. If you are the sole driver, you will be stranded and any 'get-you-home' insurance will be invalidated by reason of you having committed an illegal act.

Essentials

You *must* have a red warning triangle and hazard lights in case of accident, a headlight dip adjusted to the right, a first-aid kit and spare bulbs. You'll also need nationality (GB, IRL, etc.) plates (or a sticker, usually supplied with Channel crossing tickets), a torch, and a petrol container.

Petrol = *Essence*
Unleaded = *Sans plomb 95 and 98 octane*
4-star = *Super*
Diesel = *Gazole, Gasoil or Diesel*
LPG = *GPL*

Autoroutes are of excellent quality with frequent rest and service areas, offering the fastest means of covering long distances by car. The exit slip roads tend to have very tight curves and should be negotiated at much reduced speed, especially if towing a trailer or caravan. Both Normandy and Brittany are easily accessed by the Autoroute network. The A16–A29–A13–A84 connecting autoroutes lead from the short crossing ports of north-eastern France along the Channel coast into the areas covered by this guide. From the east, the A11 leads from Paris to Nantes, or via the A81 spur, to Rennes.

Routes Nationales and Départementales. Within Normandy and Brittany there is a good network of both RN and D roads. Whilst the Brittany peninsula is lacking in autoroutes there are many RN roads of virtual autoroute standard which have the additional benefit of being toll-free.

Like all popular areas, there can be traffic problems in the high season (mid-July to mid-August) when a lot of French people take their holidays. This is colloquially known as *'le grand départ'*. If you are able to avoid this period you will find the roads very much quieter.

Driving rules

Traffic drives on the right in France. A fundamental driving rule is that traffic from the right has priority at junctions. In practice, priority from the right applies mostly in towns and on rural roads. Main roads are clearly signed as such by a yellow and white diamond sign which is repeated every 5km, or the conventional triangle showing a broad vertical black stripe with a narrow horizontal line crossing it (*see page 29*). Junctions marked with a simple X, or not marked at all, are governed by the 'Priority from the Right' rule. Any unmarked junction in a town or village must be treated as subject to this rule.

The rule applies to *junctions* and does not mean giving way to vehicles coming out of lay-bys, driveways, garages, parking spaces, etc. You should, however, give way to buses moving away from a bus stop.

Traffic on roundabouts has priority and drivers entering the system must wait for a safe opportunity. Unfortunately, French drivers are very haphazard about signalling their intentions on roundabouts and care is needed.

Pedestrians have right of way when on marked crossings, but the practice of stopping for a pedestrian waiting to use a crossing is unknown. If you decide to display such courtesy, remember that following drivers may not anticipate your action.

Fuel

Service stations are open all day but are normally closed on Sundays and public holidays. If a public holiday falls on, say, a Thursday, it is common practice to take the Friday off as well, rather than spoil a good weekend. This can mean that petrol stations are closed for four

Fines

The police/gendarmes have wide powers to impose on-the-spot fines for a variety of motoring offences. Speed checks are frequent and merciless. Payment must be in cash and should you not be able to pay there and then, for instance if the banks are closed and there is no ATM nearby, your vehicle and your passport may be impounded until you do. The fine is, in fact, a part payment (amende forfaitaire) and you may receive notification of a higher penalty later. At present such extra fines cannot be enforced abroad but EU legislation is being contemplated to make this possible.

Speed-trap detection devices are illegal, whether in use or not. The device is invariably seized and a heavy fine imposed.

In practice, if you drive sensibly, you are no more likely to be stopped or prosecuted in France than any other country. It is the consequences of such a prosecution that should be considered, especially when you are on holiday.

'Inforoute'

If your car radio is equipped with RDS this will work in France, interrupting radio programmes with road news flashes (in French). You may also receive traffic news on 'Inforoute' on 107.7 MHz FM. These low-power transmitters cover the motorway routes and provide local up-to-date traffic reports, in French.

days, especially in the country. In rural areas petrol stations can be few and far between, especially on départementale roads.

Fuel is cheapest at big supermarkets in out-of-town retail parks (Centre Commercial) and, not surprisingly, most expensive on motorways. Until the changeover of British credit cards to those incorporating a 'chip' is complete, 24-hour automatic pumps which require a credit card and PIN number, are very unlikely to work with British issued cards due to incompatible computing systems. Keeping the fuel tank well-filled is good practice.

Information

You should take an up-to-date map with you. Changes in road numbers and motorway interchanges can booby-trap old editions. The Michelin 1:200 000 'yellow' maps are ideal. Free Bison Futé (Crafty Bison) maps showing alternative routes using secondary roads to avoid traffic problems, are available from the French Government Tourist Office or information offices in France. These routes are well signposted, make a pleasant change from main roads and are a great help in avoiding the predictable traffic problem zones. If you want to be a 'Crafty Bison' yourself, you could try taking an early or late lunch and stay on the road between 1200 and 1400. The French drop everything for lunch and the roads become much quieter.

Parking

Street parking problems are the same the world over and at the height of the season, it can be difficult to find a space in the larger cities. In the smaller towns and villages the problem is not nearly as acute and tourists are well catered for.

There is some free parking in Disc Parking zones, where the bays are marked out in blue. Purchase a disc (Disque de stationnement) at petrol stations or supermarkets. Setting your arrival time on the disc automatically displays the expiry time in a cut-out window. Meter or ticket parking follows the usual pattern. Very often parking is free 1200–1400. These times are displayed on the ticket machine.

If parking in the street, you must park facing the direction of travel, i.e. on the right. It is, in any case, bad practice to park on the left, as you may drive off forgetting to move to the correct side of the road.

It is illegal to leave a vehicle parked in the same place for more than seven days, and a lesser time in some cities. Obstructive or illegal parking, especially in cities, often results in the offending vehicle being uplifted and taken to a pound. Foreign number plates will not save you.

Some parking zones work on the basis of parking on the odd-numbered side of the street for the first fortnight of a month (1st–15th) and on the even-numbered side for the second. A special sign indicates the entry to the zone. (See page 29.) Changeover time is between 2030 and 2100 on the last day of each fortnight.

Lights

All traffic must use headlights in rain or poor visibility. Right-hand-drive cars must have their headlight beam modified to prevent dazzle. This can take the form of masking off part of the headlamps (which unfortunately reduces the light output) or stick-on optical beam deflectors which cause the headlight to dip to the right. Some vehicles which have quartz-iodine headlamps cannot be modified in these ways and you should check with the car dealer. Driving with defective lights can result in a fine. The fine is less likely if you can remedy the defect right away. It is a legal requirement to carry a spare set of bulbs. Motorcycles must display headlights at all times.

Mobile phones

The use of a hand-held phone when driving is specifically forbidden. The use of hands-free phones is strongly discouraged. The only safe and legal way for the driver to use a mobile is to stop and switch off the engine beforehand.

Seat belts

Wearing of seat belts for front and rear passengers is compulsory when the vehicle engine is running. Children under 10 must occupy the rear seats but an infant up to 9 months may travel in the front seat if secured in an approved rear-facing seat, *but not if a passenger air bag is fitted.*

Security

Sensible care should be taken, particularly where vehicles are left for long periods in vulnerable places such as tourist site car parks. Do not leave items on view inside the car, even if you know they are of little or no value, a potential thief does not.

In the large cities it is wise to keep car doors locked and windows up, if in slow-moving traffic or while stationary at traffic lights, as thieves on motorcycles occasionally reach inside to steal valuables. If hot weather means you must have the window open, be sure that handbags, wallets, cameras etc. are well out of sight and reach and, above all, never on a passenger's lap.

Should you have the misfortune to become a victim of crime, your insurers will require you to report the circumstances to the police and obtain a record that you have done so. In the country go to the *Gendarmerie* and in larger towns the *Commissariat de Police*.

Speed limits

Autoroutes – 130kph (110kph in rain). If windscreen wipers are needed it's 'raining'.
Dual carriageways – 110kph (100kph in rain)
Other roads – 90kph (80kph in rain)
All built up areas – 50kph on roads between the entrance sign to a town and departure sign (place name crossed with diagonal bar).
There's a 50kph limit on any road when visibility is less than 50m.
Drivers with less than two years' experience must not exceed the 'rain' speed limits even in fine weather.

Road signs

All major routes are clearly signed; even most minor roads have their destinations and route numbers marked. International European traffic signs are used throughout France

accôtement non-stabilisé – soft verge
aire – rest area
cédez le passage – give way
chaussée déformée – uneven surface
défense de stationner/stationnement interdit – no parking
dépassement interdit – no overtaking
déviation – diversion
gravillons – loose chippings
passage protégé – right of way
péage – toll
poste d'essence – petrol station
priorité à droite – priority to traffic from the right
priorité aux piétons – give way to pedestrians

ralentir – slow down
rappel – reminder of previous restriction
renseignements – information
rives dangereuses – dangerous roadsides
route barrée – road closed
sens interdit – no entry
sens unique – one way
seulement riverains – residents only
sortie de camions – HGV exit
stationnement gratuit – free parking
stationnement interdit – no parking
stationnement payant – paid parking
toutes directions – route for through traffic
un train peut en cacher un autre – one train may hide another
virage – bend
vous n'avez pas la priorité – you do not have priority

FRENCH ROAD SIGNS

 Ⓐ
You have Priority at *all* junctions on this road.

 Ⓑ*
You have Priority at *next* junction. (Note: important difference with A.)

 Ⓒ*
Be prepared to *Give Way* to traffic from right at next junction.

End of Priority road.

'Give Way'.

*Signs B and C may indicate a junction from either side, not necessarily a full crossroads.

You do not have Priority. *Give Way* at roundabout.

Signs attached to traffic lights are valid only if lights are OFF or yellow light is flashing.

Flashing yellow light = Proceed with caution. *Give Way* to traffic on right.

 BERGERAC
The red border on a town sign *means start of 50km/h limit.* If surmounted by 'Priority' sign (as here), you are on the Priority road through the town.

PARKING

Disc Parking.

Parking on payment at meter.

Entry to zone where Parking is allowed first fortnight on odd-numbered side of street – second fortnight on even-numbered side.

WARNINGS

Risk of black ice.

Snow chains obligatory.

Switch on Headlights.

Minimum distance between vehicles.

 Itinéraire Bis
Alternative Route

Déviation
Diversion

Frequently found at tunnels

Getting to Brittany and Normandy

Brittany Ferries tel: (UK)
08703 665 333; (France)
0825 828 828;
www.brittanyferries.com
Portsmouth to Caen
(6 hrs) and St Malo
(8 hrs 45 mins), Poole to
Cherbourg (4 hrs 15 mins
or 2 hrs 15 mins by fast
ferry), Plymouth to Roscoff
(6 hrs), and Cork
(Republic of Ireland) to
Roscoff (14 hrs).

P&O Ferries tel: (UK)
08705 980 333; (France)
0825 120 156;
www.poferries.com
Dover to Calais (1 hr
15 mins).

Condor Ferries tel: (UK)
0870 243 5140; (France)
0825 135 135;
www.condorferries.co.uk
Poole to Cherbourg (4 hrs
35 mins), Portsmouth
to Cherbourg (5 hrs
30 mins), Weymouth to
St Malo (5 hrs 15 mins).

LD Lines tel: (UK) 08700
428 4335; (France) 0825
304 304; www.ldlines.co.uk
Portsmouth to Le Havre
(7 hrs 30 mins).

Norfolkline tel: (UK)
0870 870 10 10; (France)
03 28 28 95 50;
www.norfolkline.com
Dover to Dunkirque
(1 hr 45 mins).

Irish Ferries tel: (UK)
08705 17 17 17; (France)
01 56 93 43 40; (Republic
of Ireland) 0818 300 400;
www.irishferries.ie
Rosslare to Cherbourg
(19 hrs 30 mins) and
Roscoff (17 hrs).

Ferries

The ferry is still the most popular way to take a car to France, so booking ahead is strongly recommended, especially in high season. Cross-channel passenger and car ferries, hovercraft and the SeaCat (catamaran) leave from various points along the south coast of England, also from Ireland. There's an equally good choice of destination ports: four in Normandy and two in Brittany.

Flying

The choice is between scheduled flights, packages with rail link-ups or fly-drive schemes. Although the major international airlines fly only to the major cities, such as Paris or Nice, some smaller airlines have flights between UK and Brittany/Normandy, including: **Ryanair** tel: (UK) 0871 246 0000; (France) 0892 555 666; www.ryanair.com, with flights from London (Stansted) to Dinard and Nantes. **Air France** and **Brit Air** tel: (UK) 0845 0845 111; (France) 0820 820 820, offer flights between London (Gatwick) and Nantes, with onward connections to Brest.

To get to Brittany and Normandy from the US it is necessary to fly to Paris before continuing your journey by train or car. (From Paris it's a 4½-hour drive to Rennes.)

Coaches

If you are not planning to take your own car, coaches are a much more economical way of travelling long distances than taking the train, but the journey times are longer. **National Express Eurolines** (tel: (UK) 08705 808080; www.eurolines.com) run coaches from London to Caen (12 hours), Le Havre (12 hours) and Rouen (11 hours) in Normandy and to Nantes (14 hours), Rennes (12 hours) and Vannes (18 hours) in Brittany.

Rail services

Eurostar trains link London (Waterloo International) with Paris (Gare du Nord) via the Channel Tunnel – journey time 3 hours. Travellers to Brittany and Normandy can change at Lille for connecting services; alternatively there are frequent TGV services from Gare Montparnasse in Paris to Rennes, Nantes, Quimper and Brest.

Rail companies

For more information contact **Eurostar** *tel: (UK) 08705 186 186; www.eurostar.com;* **BritRail** *tel: (USA) 1-877-677-1066; www.britrail.com;* **SNCF** *tel: (UK) 08705 848 848; (France) 0892 353 535; www.sncf.com;* or **Eurotunnel** *tel: (UK) 08000 969 992; (France) 03 21 00 61 00; www.eurotunnel.com*

For up-to-date details of long-distance bus, ferry and rail services, consult the *Thomas Cook European Rail Timetable,* published monthly.

If you are planning to take your car through the Tunnel, the entrance is off the M20 at junction 11A just outside Folkestone. After boarding, the journey time is 35 minutes to Sangatte, just outside Calais. One advantage of this route is that fares are charged per car, regardless of the number of passengers. The service is operated by Eurotunnel.

British Rail and SNCF (French Rail) offer a through-ticket service. Tickets can be bought from any British station to any French station via any ferry route. Contact British Rail travel centres or High Street travel agents for more details. Discounted tickets are available for students and people under 26.

From Calais and Boulogne to Normandy

From Calais or Boulogne-sur-Mer it is just over 200km to Rouen (*see page 276*), from where you can explore the delights of the wooded Seine Valley (*see page 268*) and the Normandy coast (*see page 242*). The route to Rouen can be covered in under three hours using motorways and trunk roads. This alternative route via Dieppe takes longer (242km; allow a whole day), but passes through a number of delightful villages and coastal towns.

Calais' most famous landmark is the Hôtel de Ville (*place du Soldat-Inconnu*) built in Flemish Gothic style in the 1920s. In front is Auguste Rodin's famous bronze statue, the *Burghers of Calais*, which honours six citizens who surrendered themselves to the English in 1347 in order to prevent a massacre. From Calais the D940 coastal road goes to **Boulogne-sur-Mer**, via Cap Blanc-Nez, Cap Gris-Nez, Wissant, Audresselles and Wimereux. Boulogne, enclosed by ramparts, is home to **Nausicaa €€**, the biggest aquarium in Europe (*boulevard Ste-Beuve; tel: 02 21 30 98 98; www.nausicaa.fr; open daily 0930–1830, 1930 in summer*).

From Boulogne, continue on the D940 inland to Etaples, at the mouth of the River Canche, and then on to its more up-market neighbour, **Le Touquet-Paris-Plage**. Le Touquet is full of elegant turn-of-the-century hotels, nightclubs and casinos, whose architecture can be admired by taking a stroll along the seafront promenade.

From here stay on the D940, heading south, past the seaside resorts of Stella-Plage and Merlimont-Plage to Berck-sur-Mer. Here the D940 heads inland, skirting Rue, to Le Crotoy, before looping round the Somme Bay to **St Valéry-sur-Somme**, from where it continues to **Eu**. Pretty St Valéry was William the Conqueror's last port of call before he crossed the Channel to invade England, and Eu is where he married Mathilda of Flanders in 1050, in the castle that stood on the site of the 16th-century château that is now the Town Hall. The D940 continues along the north side of the River Bresle to Mers-les-Bains and Le Tréport. South of Le Tréport, the D940 joins the D925, which you follow all the way to **Dieppe**. To break your journey here, visit the **Cité de la Mer €€** (*37 rue de l'Asile Thomas; tel: 02 35 06 93 20; www.estrancitedelamer.free.fr; open daily 1000–1200 & 1400–1800*), which has displays of Channel sea-life and the workings of ships that ply the Channel waters.

From Dieppe, the N27 south will take you to Rouen (*see page 276*).

Above
Belle époque architecture in Nantes

Setting the scene

Breton beginnings

The first inhabitants of Brittany were hunter-gatherers living in caves in the Bay of Audierne about 400,000 years ago – a time when mammoths, bears and sabre-toothed tigers roamed the earth. But it was Stone-Age tribes from the Iberian peninsula who were probably responsible for the megaliths, mysterious stone monuments found in large concentrations in southern Brittany, especially near the prehistoric settlement of Carnac. Anthropologists continue to speculate over the whys and wherefores of the curious alignments, chambers and stone circles, although there is common agreement about their significance as places of burial and religious ritual.

The Celts

The Celts began arriving in Brittany in the 6th century BC. They were not only skilled potters and metalworkers but capable and efficient farmers with sophisticated agricultural implements, including scythes, harrows and wheeled ploughs. They called their country *Armor*, the Land by the Sea, as much of inland Brittany was still impenetrable forest. The Celts' tribalism was a source of division and enabled the Romans to drive them slowly but remorselessly to the fringes of Europe. The decisive moment came in 56 BC when the Veneti, the most powerful Breton tribe, was defeated at sea off the Gulf of Morbihan. The encounter was watched with grim satisfaction by the Roman general, Julius Caesar, who had no hesitation in putting the rebels to the sword.

As the Roman legions withdrew from northern Europe in the 5th century AD, a second wave of Celtic migrants headed for the shores of Armor from Wales and Cornwall. Many of their leaders were monks, and Christianity spread rapidly, thanks to the wholesale adoption of pagan customs and traditions, usually only thinly disguised. These early converts – St Malo, St Brieuc and St Lunaire – are still commemorated in the names of towns, while Brittany is itself a corruption of 'Little Britain', a term also coined during this period. As an aspiring nation, however, Brittany was a lost cause until Nominoë, a nobleman appointed governor by Charlemagne, broke away to establish the first independent Breton kingdom in 845 after defeating the Franks at the Battle of Redon.

The Breton flag

The ancient Breton flag, the Kroaz Du, consisted of a plain black cross on a white ground and was introduced by Pope Gregory VII in 1188 to distinguish Breton knights from their French counterparts during the Third Crusade. It continued to fly on Breton sailing vessels until the union with France in the 16th century. In 1923 a militant separatist, Morvan Marchal, came up with a new flag and it's this one you are likely to see in shop windows or carried during processions or pageants. It's composed of nine horizontal stripes, alternately black and white, with ermines on a white ground in the top left-hand corner. It's still illegal to fly either flag on public buildings.

The Breton language

Breton is the only Celtic language still spoken in continental Europe. Its closest relatives are Welsh and Cornish. Currently there are around 500,000 native speakers (compared with 400,000 Welsh speakers) and, after many years of official restrictions, Breton is once again being taught in schools. You're most likely to hear it spoken in the smaller, more isolated rural communities, roughly west of a line between Plouha (near St-Brieuc) and Questembert (east of Vannes). It's now fashionable to give children Breton names such as Tanguy (Zealous-Dog) and Armel (Bear-Prince). These were originally warrior titles, but Christian names including Ronan (after an Irish monk) or Enora (the wife of St Efflam) are also popular. Countless place-names, too, are of Breton origin; look out for the prefixes *ker* (village, house), *plou* (parish), *loc* (holy place), *lan* (heath) and *dol* (table), and for the suffix *-goat,* meaning forest. Breton is also used to describe features of the landscape – *aber* meaning estuary, for example, or *menhir,* the prehistoric standing stone. You'll also come across dual-language direction signs – Quimper/Kemper for example. If you're curious about the language, look out for Béatrice Jouin's booklet *Premier vocabulaire Breton* (trilingual), published by Editions Ouest-France, unfortunately without a pronunciation guide!

Legends and traditions

Breton culture is rich in legends and folk tales. It's an oral tradition, passed on from one generation to the next in poetry and song. For the Celts the written word was inexpressive, even dead – only monks wrote things down. Fairies, enchanters, mermaids, giants and korrigans (the 'little people', imps who live underground and get up to all kinds of mischief) are the common currency of Breton folk tales, the most famous of which, the Arthurian legends, also have roots in Wales and western England. In the Breton version the search for the Holy Grail takes place in the Brocéliande Forest (now the Fôret de Paimpont), and there's an 'Arthur's camp' in the woods near Huelgoat. Almost as well known is the story of the star-crossed lovers Tristan and Yseult (later immortalised by Wagner in his opera *Tristan and Isolde*) – there's an Ile Tristan near Douarnenez. If you're in Quimper you're bound to come across the legend of King Gradlon, his daughter Dahut, who later turned into a mermaid, and the lost city of Ys. Dahut's image is carved on the outside of numerous churches and there's a statue of Gradlon on Quimper Cathedral.

The Normans

The Vikings launched their first raids on the Seine and the Channel coast early in the 9th century. The incursions became steadily more frequent and prolonged until 911 when the French king, Charles the Simple, made a virtue out of necessity and invested their leader, Rollo, with the title Duke of Normandy. The following century marked the beginning of a golden age for the Normans. The conquest of England, one of the greatest military enterprises of medieval times, took place at the same time as the founding of the Kingdom of Sicily while, during the first Crusade, a Norman knight called Behemond gained a foothold in faraway Antioch. Norman government was ruthless but it brought a remarkable civilisation in its wake: the monasteries and cathedrals of Caen, Bayeux, Jumièges and Mont-St-Michel were important seats of learning as well as splendid architectural monuments.

William the Conqueror

Born in Falaise in 1028, William succeeded to the Duchy of Normandy at the age of eight. In 1051 he married a distant cousin, Mathilda of Flanders. Technically the union contravened church law and the pair were excommunicated, only being reconciled with the Church after they had agreed to build twin abbeys in Caen. Crowned King of England on Christmas Day, 1066, by Easter William felt secure enough to return to Normandy where he spent much of the remainder of his life. Conventionally pious, he had deserved a reputation for avarice and brutality. When the Domesday Book was compiled towards the end of his reign, the declining values of the estates through which he had passed on punitive raids 20 years earlier could still be traced. He died in 1087, after being thrown from his horse while campaigning in France.

The Hundred Years' War

In the age-old struggle for supremacy between the thrones of France and England, it was the role of Brittany to be a thorn in the side of the French. English troops were garrisoned in Breton towns, English ships were provisioned in the channel ports and Breton nobles championed the English cause as and when it suited. Brittany may have been an issue in the conflict but Normandy was the field of operations. In 1415, the new king of England, Henry V, renewed his claim on France and invaded the duchy. The fall of Harfleur and the magnificent victory at Agincourt put the English firmly in the driving seat; even after Henry's premature death in 1422 they were able to use Normandy as a springboard to advance on the Loire. It was at this point, when French fortunes were at their lowest ebb, that a young peasant girl from Domrémy emerged on the scene.

Joan of Arc persuaded the Dauphin of her divine mission to deliver France from the English and assumed overall command of the French armies. Within 15 months she had raised the siege of Orléans, regained control of the Loire valley and secured Paris. On 13 July, 1430 she was able to look on as Charles VII was crowned king in Reims Cathedral. If Joan's rise was dramatic, her downfall was spectacular. Captured by the Burgundian army at Compiègne in December she was sold to the English, Charles having refused to pay her ransom. The show trial which followed aimed to demonstrate that Joan's heavenly voices were inspired not by God but by the devil. Joan recanted but was tricked into relapsing. She died at the stake in Rouen on 30 May, 1431.

Anne of Brittany

The last independent ruler of Brittany, Anne succeeded to the Duchy in 1488 at the age of 11, only shortly after her father had been disastrously defeated in battle by the French. Brittany had been enjoying a golden age. Wealth derived from the cloth trade and from salt exports formed the basis of an extraordinary flowering of the arts – many of the Flamboyant Gothic churches and parish closes date from this period. Charles VIII saw his opportunity and married Anne in 1491. Physically unprepossessing – she was small and thin and walked with a limp – her intelligence and charm won the king over, so that what began as a dynastic alliance ended in a love match. When Charles died in 1498 leaving no heir, Anne agreed to marry his successor, but only after insisting on written guarantees of Brittany's independence. She died in 1514, genuinely mourned by her subjects, many of whom had met her on her travels through the duchy. But she had only succeeded in putting off the evil day when the French would achieve their long-term goal of formal union.

Below
Pleyben calvary

Parish closes

The parish close, an architectural monument, unique to Brittany, symbolised the passage from life to death. At first the typical close comprised little more than a church and a small cemetery enclosed by a perimeter wall. By the 16th century, however, several new elements had been added: a triumphal arch to represent Christ's victory over death; an ossuary containing the bones of parishioners exhumed from the increasingly crowded churchyard; and the calvary, a stone crucifix ornamented with dozens of animated figures depicting scenes from the Passion. The *closes* were funded by the parish council which employed local stonemasons, artists, sculptors and carpenters. A fierce rivalry developed between one community and the next as to which could build the finest monument. The church interiors, too, are a riot of colour, with brightly painted roof beams and elaborate altarpieces known as retables. Parish closes and wayside calvaries can be found all over Brittany, but the finest examples (St-Thégonnec, Guimiliau and Lampaul-Guimiliau) are in Finistère.

Above
Processional banner

Pardons

These solemn religious festivals, usually commemorating the feast of a local saint, are common to Normandy and Brittany. It's at the main event, the procession, that you're most likely to see women turned out in the traditional peasant costumes: embroidered dresses with decorative lace collars, starched aprons, and the elaborate headdress known as the coiffe. The focal point of the *pardon* is usually the parish church or, as in the case of le Folgoët, a chapel built in open countryside on the site of a miraculous apparition. Some *pardons*, such as that of Ste-Anne-d'Auray, have clear pagan origins. St Anne, the mother of the Virgin Mary, came into vogue during the reign of the popular ruler Anne of Brittany, but Ana was a Celtic goddess worshipped by the Druids as 'the mother of us all'. Similarly, at the Grand Troménie at Locronan, which honours the Irish missionary St Ronan, the faithful process around a hill held to be sacred since prehistoric times. Some *pardons* are associated with particular guilds or trades – that of St Yves at Tréguier, for example, is dedicated to lawyers and judges, while at Granville in Normandy the local bishop blesses the fishing fleet at the behest of the Corporations of the Sea. There's a sailor's *pardon* at Lamor-plages, a *pardon* of musicians in Gourin, of bikers in Porcaro, even of rabid dogs in Port-Blanc! If you're looking for a challenge, sign up for Tro Breizh, a marathon 30-day tour of the shrines of the seven founding bishops of Brittany. The 525km route extends from Dol-de-Bretagne to St-Pol-de-Léon and Vannes but be warned – you're expected to do it on foot not sitting behind the wheel.

Fest noz

A traditional Breton knees-up, the *fest noz* originated in the Middle Ages to celebrate a marriage or the gathering in of the harvest, but nowadays is just as likely to mark the arrival of the weekend. The entertainment includes folk dancing and singing, often to the accompaniment of a band of traditional musical instruments known as a *bagadou*. These are likely to include the *biniou* (bagpipes), the *bombarde* (a cross between an oboe and a bassoon), drums and a Celtic harp or two, as well as fiddles, flutes and anything else to hand. You'll see *festou noz* advertised in bars and restaurants. Everyone is welcome to party but you'll probably need to hire a cab or take the car, as most events are held out of town.

The Revolution

At first the French Revolution was welcomed with open arms in Normandy and Brittany, but by 1793 systematic attacks on religion, curbs on regional autonomy and the introduction of conscription stretched relations with Paris to breaking point. After a young woman from Caen, Charlotte Corday, assassinated the revolutionary ideologue Marat in his bath, terror became the order of the day in the two recalcitrant provinces. The worst atrocities were committed by Jean-Baptiste Carrier in Nantes where 13,000 oppositionists were executed in the space of just three months, many of them drowned in the Loire. Brittany subsequently became the focus of the counter-revolutionary movement known as the Chouannerie, but after two failed rebellions, in 1795 and 1799, the insurgents were forced to adopt guerilla tactics. Sporadic fighting continued until 1804 when the Chouan leader, Georges Cadoudal, was captured and executed in Paris after plotting to kidnap Napoleon.

Two of the greatest names in French literature set novels about the Chouan rebellion in the Breton border town of Fougères. Honoré de Balzac interviewed a number of survivors while he was researching *Les Chouans* in 1828. Fougères made an equally deep impression on Victor Hugo eight years later while he was working up material for his novel *Ninety-Three*. Hugo was already familiar with Revolutionary history. His father, a soldier and a staunch Republican, changed his name to Brutus during the Terror and took part in a number of massacres in the vicinity of Châteaubriant, near Nantes, where he met his future wife.

The Impressionists

A sailor's son, born in Honfleur in 1824, was one of the most important forerunners of the Impressionists. Eugène Boudin painted landcapes around Trouville, le Havre and the Pays de Caux. He believed in the importance of the first impression and that in order to create the right lighting effects, landscapes should be completed outdoors and not in the studio from a preliminary sketch.

In 1856 Boudin came across a young man from le Havre called Claude Monet and offered to teach him to paint. Boudin's theories about light had a profound and immediate effect on the 15-year-old: 'It was as if a veil had suddenly been torn from my eyes', he recalled later.

Monet was still accompanying Boudin on painting expeditions to the Normandy coast in the 1870s, sometimes staying with his erstwhile mentor at the Ferme St-Simon in Honfleur, together with Frédéric Bazille and Camille Pissarro. In 1874 Monet's trail-blazing *Impression – Sunrise* led contemptuous critics to dub him and his fellow painters Impressionists. Rough-mannered, moody and taciturn, Monet was passionately committed to his art and thought nothing of painting all day and in all weathers to capture 'the moment'. Desperately poor, he moved to Giverny in 1883 with his wife and six children and it was here, over the next 40 years, that he was to paint a series of great masterpieces. He died in 1926.

The Pont-Aven School

The beautiful but remote corner of Finistère near Pont-Aven became fashionable with artists in the 1860s as the railways opened up the countryside. By the time Paul Gauguin arrived in 1886 it was difficult to find a room in the local inn. Two years later Gauguin teamed up with Émile Bernard to evolve a style which became known as Synthetism. This two-dimensional approach used boldly contrasting colours in a non-naturalistic way to suggest ideas and symbolic meaning. Gauguin was particularly struck by the spirituality of peasant life and its close symbiosis with nature. His ideas struck a chord with more than a dozen artists including Paul Sérusier, Charles Filiger, Maurice Denis and others. Finding Pont-Aven increasingly claustrophobic he moved to le Pouldu in 1889, taking his leading disciples with him. Despite later revelatory experiences in the South Seas, Gauguin never forgot the profound artistic truths he had discovered while living in Brittany.

Architectural glossary

Apse	vaulted semicircular recess at the east end of the church.
Capital	decorated top of column.
Chancel	part of a church containing the main altar, choir and sanctuary.
Chevet	highly ornamented east end of French church.
Corbel	supporting piece of stone or timber used for carrying a beam, often decorated.
Crenellation	square indentation on battlement.
Dormer	brick or stone structure with gabled window projecting from sloping roof.
Flamboyant Gothic	elaborate style of church architecture, common in 15th-century France.
Flying buttress	brick or stone support for outside wall of building.
Gable	triangular section of wall between sloping ends of pitched roof.
Keep	main tower within the walls of a medieval castle.
Machicolation	opening in parapet through which missiles could be hurled.
Pepperpot	conical roof common on castle towers in 15th-century France.
Retable	ornamental screen behind altar, usually decorated with paintings or religious carvings.
Romanesque	architectural style of 9th to 12th centuries featuring rounded arches, thick masonry walls and massive, rounded columns.
Rood screen	decorated wood or stone partition at the entrance to the chancel.
Transept	arms of cross-shaped church set at right angles to the nave.
Vault	arch forming roof or ceiling.

Writers

Several episodes from Alexandre Dumas' swashbuckling tale *The Three Musketeers* are set in Brittany, mainly in Nantes and Belle-Ile. Marcel Proust was also a regular visitor to the island, but claimed to be put off by the smell of sardines. He is more closely associated with Normandy: Cabourg and Trouville were both models for the seaside town of Balbec in his masterpiece *À la Recherche du Temps Perdu (In Search of Lost Time)*. In fact Proust knew every inch of the Normandy coast, having spent numerous vacations there from boyhood on. The 19th-century novelist Gustave Flaubert was born in Rouen. His masterpiece *Madame Bovary* is set in the village of Ry and is based on the life story of Delphine Couturier, a doctor's wife who committed suicide in 1849. The short-story writer Guy de Maupassant, also a native of Normandy, was greatly influenced by Flaubert. Many of his stories are set in le Havre and around the Cotentin peninsula.

Right
The Abbaye de Hambye

Touring itineraries

Châteaux and fortresses

Day 1: **Château de Kerjean** – evocative of life in the 17th and 18th centuries (*see page 45*). **Château de la Hunaudaye** – scenes from medieval life are acted out within the walls of the ruined castle (*see page 163*).

Day 2: **Château de la Roche-Jagu** – the recently landscaped gardens are a horticulturist's delight (*see page 116*). **Fort la Latte** – superb views of the Côte d'Emeraude (Emerald Coast) from the old fortress (*see page 156*).

Day 3: **Château de Combourg** – meet the ghost in the home of a famous 19th-century writer (*see page 225*). **Château de la Bourbansais** – an added attraction here is the small zoo (*see page 174*).

Day 4: **Fougères** – a medieval castle, once defending the Breton Marches (*see page 210*). **Vitré** – a castle like Fougères but with a superb medieval town centre thrown in (*see page 211*).

Day 5: **St-Malo** – the castle and the walled town are both worth seeing (*see pages 164–73*). **Falaise** – birthplace of William the Conqueror; the magnificent keep dating from the 12th century has survived intact as have the storerooms and chapel (*see page 254*).

Day 6: **Château de St-Germain-de-Livet** – fairy-tale castle with frescoes and period furnishings (*see page 265*). **Château de Vascoueil** – there's a superb collection of modern sculpture in the grounds (*see page 273*).

Children

Day 1: **Bayeux** – most children learn about the tapestry in school, so why not take them to see the real thing (*see pages 242–5*). **Falaise** – the Museum of Automatons is equally entertaining (*see page 254*).

Day 2: **St-Malo** – the newly opened Aquarium will keep children occupied for hours (*see pages 164–73*); likewise the lake at **Villecartier** with its miniature boats (*see page 229*).

Day 3: **Trieux Valley** – a chance to travel on a real steam train (*see page 112*). **Perros-Guirec** – an opportunity to clamber over the rocks at a 'Station Kid' resort (*see pages 113–14*).

Day 4: **Pleumeur-Bodou** – set aside a couple of hours for the absorbing Telecommunications Museum (*see page 114*). **Menez-Meur** – follow the nature trail through the animal park (*see page 82*).

Day 5: **Landévennec** – the school museum gives children an insight into classrooms of the past (*see pages 71–2*). **Penmarc'h** – climb the 307 steps to the top of the Eckmühl Lighthouse (*see page 94*).

Day 6: **Quiberon** – another 'Station Kid' resort and one of the best in the region (*see page 149*). **Fouesnant** – enjoy the facilities in the Water Park (*see page 89*).

Day 7: **Malansac Dinosaur Park** – where the prehistoric age comes to life (*see page 188*). **Branféré Zoo** – real-life animals this time which can be stroked and fed (*see page 199*).

Day 8: **Josselin** – after the castle tour, there's the intriguing doll museum (*see pages 182–3*). **Lohéac** – the Automobile Museum will capture the imagination of young and old alike (*see page 184*).

Churches, abbeys and cathedrals

Day 1: **Rouen** – a magnificent Gothic cathedral, several medieval churches, one with an old plague cemetery (*see pages 276–81*). **Jumièges** and **St-Martin-de-Bouscherville** – ruined abbeys close to Rouen (*see page 273*).

Day 2: **Lisieux** – medieval cathedral and huge 20th-century basilica built in honour of St Thérèse (*see pages 261–2*). **Caen** – two great abbey churches founded by William the Conqueror (*see pages 246–7*). **Bayeux** – cathedral, restored after the war, successfully blending Romanesque and Gothic styles (*see pages 242–5*).

Day 3: **Coutances** – another cathedral, Norman Gothic architecture at its best (*see pages 235–6*). **Lessay** and **Hambye** – two abbeys worth seeing, one in ruins the other reconstructed (*see pages 239, 240*).

Day 4: **Mont-St-Michel** – magnificent fortified monastery with abbey church, crypts, cloisters, refectory and other historic buildings (*see pages 226–9*).

Day 5: **Kermaria-an-Iskuit** – chapel with 15th-century frescoes depicting a dance of death (*see pages 121–2*). **Tréguier** – the cathedral spire is one of the finest in Brittany (*see page 118*).

Day 6: **Guimiliau, Lampaul-Guimiliau** and **St-Thégonnec** – the best of the parish closes (*see pages 54–8 and 64*).

Day 7: **St-Fiacre** – tiny parish church in Morbihan with splendid carved reredos (*see page 106*). **Ste-Anne-d'Auray** – venue for one of Brittany's best-known *pardons* (*see page 150*).

Right
St-Aubin-sur-Mer war memorial

D-Day landings

The following routes are designated 'Normandie Terre Liberté' – look out for the signs.

Day 1: **Overlord – The Assault**: From Bénouville and the Pegasus Bridge, past the beaches of Juno, Sword and Gold, to Arromanches and Bayeux, the first French city to be liberated (*see pages 248–9*).

Day 2: **D-Day – The Onslaught**: From Coleville-sur-Mer past Omaha Beach and Pointe du Hoc to St-Lô and Carentan where American troops joined with those coming ashore from Utah Beach (*see page 253*).

Day 3: **Objective – A Port**: From Carentan, through Ste-Mère-Église to Ste-Marie-du-Mont and Utah Beach, then on to Cherbourg, a vital base for landing equipment and supplies (*see pages 234–5*).

Day 4: **Cobra – The Breakout**: From Cherbourg through the Cotentin Peninsula to Coutances, past the battlefield of Mont Castre, la Chapelle-en-Juger and Roncey to Avranches, which was finally liberated on 31 July (*see pages 222–4*).

The Lighthouse and Beacon Trail

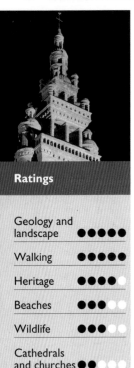

Ratings

Geology and landscape	●●●●●
Walking	●●●●●
Heritage	●●●●
Beaches	●●●
Wildlife	●●●
Cathedrals and churches	●●
Children	●●
History	●●

For medieval cartographers this remote region was *Finis Terrae* ('the end of the world'); to the Bretons it was *Penn-Ar-Bed* ('the beginning of land'). This most westerly part of France is where Celtic traditions are preserved and where the Breton language is most widely spoken.

There are more than a hundred lighthouses and beacons on the Finistère coast, not surprising given the number of natural hazards, from sea fogs and squalls to reefs and treacherous currents. Away from the headlands the 'lighthouse trail' follows a more tranquil course around the shallow, silted estuaries known locally as *abers*. Seaweed is big business here, with therapeutic as well as industrial uses, and seaplant stores, health clinics and thalassotherapy centres abound. The climate, warmed by the Gulf Stream, is a definite plus – even on the outlying islands of Ouessant and Molène it's surprisingly mild, and palms, cacti and eucalyptus all flourish in Roscoff's aptly named Jardin Exotique.

BREST

ℹ Brest Tourist Information *Place de la Liberté; tel: 02 98 44 24 96; e-mail: contact@brest-metropole-tourisme.fr; www.brest-metropole-tourisme.fr*

🏛 Océanopolis €€€ *Port de Plaisance du Moulin Blanc; tel: 02 98 34 40 40; www.oceanopolis.com. Open Apr–early-Sept, 0900–1800; rest of the year, 0900–1700 (Sun & holidays 1000–1800).*

An important naval base since the days of Cardinal Richelieu in the 17th century, Brest was almost totally destroyed by Allied bombing during World War II. Today it is the home of the French Atlantic Fleet and a European leader in oceanography and marine technology.

The **Rade de Brest** covers an area of more than 150sq km and is one of the most impressive natural harbours in the world. A long promenade known as the Cours Dajot, built by naval convicts, offers fine views of the harbour and roadstead, but for a more complete orientation you should take a boat cruise from the Pleasure Port. The commentary is in French but you'll have no difficulty making out the military harbour and shipping lanes, the aircraft carrier *Charles de Gaulle* (still under construction) and the nuclear submarine base. The Port de Plaisance is also the embarkation point for the Crozon Peninsula, as well as the site of Brest's one undisputed tourist attraction, **Océanopolis**.

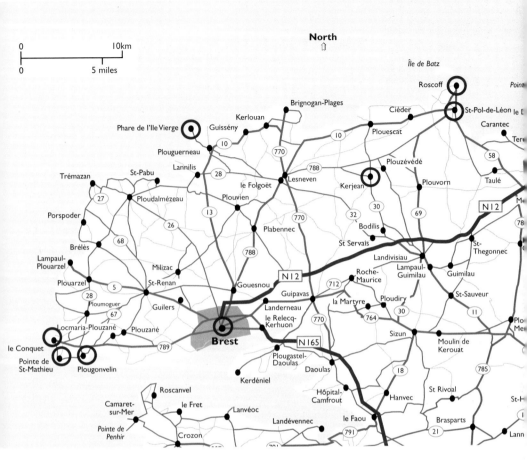

North

0 ——————— 10km
0 ——————— 5 miles

Île de Batz

Roscoff   Point

Brignogan-Plages   Cléder   St-Pol-de-Léon   le L

Kerlouan   Carantec

Phare de l'Île Vierge   Guisseny   10   Plouescat   Ter

Plouguerneau   10   770   Plouzévédé   58

Trémazan   St-Pabu   Lannilis   28   Lesneven   Plouvorn   Taulé

Porspoder   27   Ploudalmézeau   Plouvien   Kerjean   30   69   N12   M

Brélès   68   26   13   Plabennec   770   32   Bodilis   78

Lampaul-   788   St Servals   St-   St-Thegonnec

Plouarzel   Milizac   Landivisiau   Lampaul-   Guimiliau

Plouarzel   St-Renan   Gouesnou   N12   Roche-   Guimiliau   Guimilau

28   Ploumoguer   712   Maurice   St-Sauveur

67   Guilers   Guipavas   la Martyre   Ploudiry   11   Plo

Locmaria-Plouzané   Plouzané   Landerneau   770   764   30   Me

le Conquet   789   le Relecq-   Sizun   Moulin de

Brest   Kerhuon   Kerouat

Pointe de   N165   18   785

St-Mathieu   Plougonvelin   Plougastel-   Daoulas

Roscanvel   Daoulas   Kerdéniel   St Rivoal   St-H

Camaret-   le Fret   Hôpital-   Hanvec   1

sur-Mer   Lanvéoc   Camfrout   le Faou   Brasparts

Pointe de   Landévennec   791   21   Lann

Penhir   Crozon

Société Maritime Azénor *Port de Plaisance du Moulin Blanc; tel: 02 98 41 46 23; e-mail: azenor.brest@wanadoo.fr; www.azenor.com.* Cruises around the Rade de Brest; ferry to Presqu'île de Crozon (le Fret): *departs Brest May, June & Sept 0930, 1230, 1740 (Sun and holidays 0830, 1000, 1230, 1745); July and Aug 0830, 1000, 1230, 1745 (Sun and holidays 1000, 1740).*

Created with a view to making oceanology accessible to the general public, this vast scientific theme park sets out to replicate a complete marine environment. With the help of models, 3-D films, computer graphics and a variety of 'hands-on' experiences specifically with children in mind, you'll learn about the movement of the oceans, shipping and navigation, marine pollution, sea birds and coastal flora and fauna. There are fish tanks, the largest open-air aquariums in Europe and a seal pool. All the exhibitions are regularly updated and two new pavilions are planned, which will be devoted to the polar and tropical regions.

Accommodation and food in Brest

Almost nothing remains of the old town of Brest and the architecture of its post-war successor is drearily functionalist and almost wholly lacking in character. For this reason most visitors prefer to stay in the neighbouring resorts of le Conquet or Plougonvelin.

Place de la Liberté (24-hours). Parking along main roads is marked *payant* – put money in the ticket machines (maximum two hours).

Amour de Pomme de Terre €€ *23 rue des Halles Saint Louis; tel: 02 98 43 18 51.* From the weird and wonderful to the plain and simple, every dish is based around the humble potato.

Le Ruffé €€ *1 bis, rue Yves Collet; tel: 02 98 46 07; fax: 02 98 44 31; e-mail: le-ruffe@wanadoo.fr; www.restaurateurs-pointe-bretagne.com.* Classy seafood in an unpretentious setting.

Le Conquet

ℹ Le Conquet Tourist Information *Parc Beauséjour; tel: 02 98 89 11 31; fax: 02 98 89 08 20; e-mail: tourisme@ leconquet.fr; www.leconquet.fr*

Boats – Ouessant l'Evasion (Finist' mer) *Tel: 02 98 89 16 61; boats: www.finist-mer.fr.* Regular departures to Ouessant.

See also **Ile d'Ouessant** – page 53.

Market day is Tuesday.

This small, refreshingly uncommercialised resort makes an excellent base for touring the north coast of Finistère. Quaint grey stone fishermen's cottages lead down to the quay where fishermen unload pots of crab, lobster and crayfish and passenger ferries set out for the island of **Ouessant**. It's only a 20-minute walk from the port via the Croäe footbridge to the **Anse des Blancs Sablon**, a beautiful stretch of white sand sheltered by the Kermovan peninsula. There are superb views of the bay from the distinctive crenellated lighthouse at the tip of the grassy spit.

Accommodation and food in le Conquet

Hôtel Pointe St-Barbe € *Tel: 02 98 89 00 26; fax: 02 98 89 14 81; e-mail: hotelpointesaintebarbe@wannado.fr; www.hotelpointesaintebarbe.com.* Hotel overlooking the harbour with an excellent restaurant serving local cuisine.

Le Relais du Vieux Port € *1 quai de Drellach; tel: 02 98 89 15 91; www.lerelaisduvieuxport.com.* Reasonably priced restaurant with sea views.

Right
Fishing boats at le Conquet

CHATEAU DE KERJEAN

Château de Kerjean €€ *5km southwest of Plouzévéde; tel: 02 98 69 93 69; www.chateau-de-kerjean.com. Open July and Aug, daily, 1000–1900; June and Sept, Wed–Mon, 1400–1800. Other times of the year variable.*

This 16th-century country house, described by Louis XIII in 1618 as 'one of the most beautiful houses' in his kingdom, typifies the late flowering of Breton Renaissance architecture. It belonged to the Barbier family which acquired much of its immense fortune from the church. (When Pope Paul III was asked to fill the benefices left vacant on the death of Louis Barbier's uncle, he is said to have asked whether all the priests of Brittany had died on the same day.)

Set in its own 20-hectare grounds and surrounded by a moat and ramparts, the château certainly impresses. The 45-minute conducted tour (plus audio-visual show) provides an entertaining, though rather stilted commentary on the history of the house and its treasures, most of which are imported. The furniture dates mainly from the 17th and 18th centuries and includes handsome, intricately carved box beds, grain chests, linen presses and sideboards. Also interesting are the kitchens with their original chimneys (used as bread ovens) and copper cooking utensils. The château is also used for exhibitions on Breton history and contemporary art and culture.

PHARE DE L'ILE VIERGE

Vedettes des Abers € *Tel: 02 98 04 74 94. Departures from Lilia, Aber Wrac'h and Pont-de-Perros, daily between March and December. Times vary according to tides.*

The 'Lighthouse of the Virgin Isle' is a slender, cylindrical granite tower on an islet at the mouth of the Aber Wrac'h estuary. Completed in 1902, it is the tallest lighthouse in Europe at 82.5m, dwarfing its predecessor which still stands nearby. It's an exhausting climb of 397 steps to the top, but worth it for the panoramic views of the Finistère coastline. Round trips to the lighthouse leave from Pont-de-Perros, Port-de-Lilia and Aber Wrac'h.

Lighthouse walk

One of the oldest French lighthouses still in operation, le Stiff was built on the Ile d'Ouessant in 1695 by the ubiquitous military architect Vauban. With the dramatic increase in shipping in the channel early in the 19th century the need for a larger spread of warning signals became apparent. Today 30 lighthouses, 85 turrets, 44 navigation stations and 240 buoys guide ships through the hazardous waters of Finistère. The 'lighthouse walk' – a well-signed coastal footpath between Brest and Portsall – is tailor-made for beacon-spotters. For leaflets describing the individual lighthouses en route call in at the tourist office.

POINTE DE ST-MATHIEU AND PLOUGONVELIN

ⓘ Plougonvelin Tourist Information
Boulevard de la Mer L Trez Hir, Plougonvelin; tel: 02 98 48 30 18; fax: 02 98 48 25 94; e-mail: tourisme@ plougonvelin-fr.com; www.plougonvelin-fr.com

Ⓗ Fort de Bertheaume €
(son-et-lumière €€€) *Tel: 02 98 48 26 41. Open July and Aug, daily, 1000–1900; June, Sept & Oct, Wed and Sun only, 1400–1830.*

Opposite
Roscoff's fishing harbour

According to legend, the ship carrying the relics of St Matthew from Egypt was in danger of foundering off the Finistère coast when the panic-stricken sailors held up the saint's skull in an attempt to pacify the elements. At once the storm subsided and they were able to land safely. A monastery was founded on the spot in the 6th century and later rebuilt. Today the ruins of the 16th-century Benedictine abbey are flanked by two modern towers – one a naval radar station, the other a 19th-century lighthouse (open to the public) from where there are superb views of the **Ile d'Ouessant**, the Pierres Noires Causeway, the Molène archipelago and the **Crozon Peninsula**.

The nearby resort of **Plougonvelin** has all the usual amenities, including a watersports station on the main beach. The **Fort de Bertheaume** is open to the public. While its position is still clearly a commanding one, it takes some imagination to picture the imposing nature of the fort as it would have been when completed by the esteemed 17th-century French military engineer, Vauban (1633–1707), a close confidant of Louis XIV and, daringly, an advocate of taxing the rich. There's a small maritime museum in the blockhouse from where a bridge leads across to the fortified island, a magnificent setting for sound-and-light shows during the summer.

Accommodation and food in Pointe St-Mathieu and Plougonvelin

Camping de Bertheaume € *Route de Perzel; tel: 02 98 48 32 37.* Delightful site with panoramic views across the Brest estuary.

Chalet de Vacances Saint Yves €€ *Rue du Cleguer, Plougonvelin; tel: 02 98 48 32 11.* Selection of spacious and well-equipped chalets, sleeping up to six people.

Hostellerie de la Pointe St-Mathieu €€ *Pointe St-Mathieu; tel: 02 98 89 00 19; fax: 02 98 89 15 68; www.pointe-saint-mathieu.com.* This hotel, built alongside the ruins of the abbey, has an excellent restaurant and a brasserie for lunch.

ROSCOFF

ⓘ Roscoff Tourist Information *46 rue Gambetta; tel: 02 98 61 12 13; www.roscoff-tourisme.com*

Ⓟ Quai Charles de Gaulle; rue Brizeux.

There's a lot more to this versatile port than the car-ferry terminal. The ships' nails and miniature galleons carved on the walls of the 16th-century parish church of **Notre-Dame-de-Croas-Batz** are reminders of the town's colourful maritime past. The ornamental cannons on the tower point towards England, the old enemy, which burnt the original settlement to the ground in the 1400s. The lantern-turreted belfry is among the finest of its kind.

CFTM boats *Tel: 02 98 61 78 87*, **Armein** *Tel: 02 98 61 77 75. Regular sailings to Île de Batz.*

Cycle Fily *By the car park at the lighthouse; tel: 06 72 10 25 71; e-mail: location.velos@wanadoo.fr. Open July and Aug; rest of the year groups only.*

Notre-Dame-de-Croas-Batz *Rue Louis Pasteur. Open daily, 0900–1200, 1400–1900.*

Les Viviers € *Boulevard Ste-Barbe; tel: 02 98 61 19 61; e-mail: viviersderoscoff@wanadoo.fr; www.viviersroscoff.com. Open Mon–Fri, 0900–1200, 1530–1630.*

Roscoff has always made its living from the sea. By the 17th century many of the town's merchants were moonlighting as buccaneers, frustrating English customs officers who tried without success to stem the illegal traffic in wine and brandy. Clustered around the church are the former **corsairs' houses**, magnificent granite mansions with monumental chimneys, elaborate skylights, fanciful gargoyles and transom windows. One of the best examples is the so-called **Maison de Marie Stuart**, although the house has no connection with the Queen of Scots who visited Roscoff as a five-year-old in 1548.

From the garden of the 17th-century **Chapelle Ste-Barbe** there are good views of both the old port and the deep-water harbour at Bloscon. It's only a stone's throw from the chapel to the fish farm **les Viviers**, where you can watch the fishermen unloading vast quantities of crab, lobster and crayfish.

From the quai d'Auxerre boats leave for the **Ile de Batz** and the **Cairn de Barnenez** – alternatively there are round cruises of the Bay of Morlaix.

Musée des Johnnies € *Chapelle Ste-Anne; tel: 02 98 61 25 25; fax: 02 98 61 25 48; e-mail: maisondesjohnnies@ wanadoo.fr. Open mid-June– mid-Sept, 1000–1200, 1500–1800, reduced hours Feb–mid-June.*

Jardin Exotique de Roscoff €€ *Tel: 02 98 61 29 19; e-mail: jardin_grapes @wanadoo.fr. Open Nov, Feb & Mar, daily, 1400–1700; Apr–June, Sept & Oct, daily, 1030–12.30, 1400–1800; July and Aug, daily, 1000–1900.*

Entertainment *June–Aug includes music and folklore, Breton dancing, arts and crafts, concerts, circus. Contact tourist office for details.*

The main shopping area is behind the old port (rue Gambetta, rue Jules Ferry). The Wednesday morning market has fresh foods.

Thalado 'Comptoir des Algues' *5 rue Victor Hugo; tel: 02 98 69 77 05. Open Mon–Sat, 0900–1200, 1400–1900. Sea plant store selling related health products, cosmetics etc; also seaweeds exhibition.*

In 1899 Louis Bagot founded France's first thalassotherapy centre and spa at **Roc Kroum**, turning Roscoff into a major health resort. There's a beach here with sand-yachting, surfboarding and sailing facilities, or you may prefer the dunes at **Perharidy** where there's a swimming pool.

Vegetables are almost as plentiful in Roscoff as shellfish. One of the town's streets, rue des Johnnies, honours the band of local entrepreneurs who for more than a century travelled regularly to England to sell onions door-to-door, a practice which died out in the 1930s. There's a **Musée des Johnnies** if you want to find out more. Gardening enthusiasts will enjoy the **Jardin Exotique** at Roc Hievec on the southeast edge of town which has more than 1500 species of subtropical plants from the southern hemisphere including cactus, eucalyptus and proteaceous shrubs.

Accommodation and food in Roscoff

Le Bellevue €€ *Rue Jeanne d'Arc, boulevard Ste-Barbe; tel: 02 98 61 23 38; fax: 02 98 61 11 80; e-mail: hotelbellevue.roscoff@wanadoo.fr.* Small *logis* with unrestricted sea views from the terrace restaurant.

Camping du Manoir de Kerestat €€ *Manoir de Kerestat; tel: 02 98 69 71 92. Open Apr–Oct.* There are panoramic sea views from this site (32 places), located in the grounds of an historic manor house.

Les Chardons Bleus €€ *4 rue Amiral Réveillère; tel: 02 98 69 72 03; fax: 02 98 61 27 86; www.chardonsbleus.fr.st.* Centrally situated hotel restaurant serving seafood.

Grand Hôtel Talabardon €€€ *27 place Duthiers; tel: 02 98 61 24 95; fax: 02 98 61 10 54; e-mail: hotel.talabardon@wanadoo.fr; www. talabardon.com.* Traditional hotel in the old part of town with modern, comfortable rooms. The restaurant specialises in seafood dishes.

Hôtel des Arcades €€ *15 rue Réveillère; tel: 02 98 69 70 45; fax: 02 98 69 12 34; e-mail: lesarcadesroscoff@wanadoo.fr; www.hotel-les-arcades-roscoff.com. Open from Easter to the end of Sept.* Seafront hotel with panoramic terrace restaurant.

Seaweed

The north of Finistère is the most concentrated site for sea plants in the world with more than 800 varieties. Washed clean by the Gulf Stream and free from the effects of urban and industrial pollution, the algae here are unusually pure. Seaweed harvesting is now a thriving commercial business with medicinal, dietary, cosmetic, culinary and industrial applications. You can find out more about the processing at one of several farms open to the public – there are tastings too. A good place to start is the sea-plant store Thalado 'Comptoir des Algues' in Roscoff.

St-Pol-de-Leon

**ⓘ St-Pol Tourist
Information** *Place
de l'Evêché; tel: 02 98 69 05
69; fax: 02 98 69 01 20;
e-mail: tourisme.st.pol.de.leon
@wanadoo.fr;
www.saintpoldeleon.fr*

ⓟ Place M Colombe,
near the Kreisker
tower.

**ⓒ Hôtel-Restaurant
le Passiflore** € *28
rue Pen-ar-Pont; tel: 02 98
69 00 52. On the road
leading to the station. The
restaurant is closed on
Sunday evenings.*

This pleasant little market town lies at the heart of a rich agricultural region known as the Golden Belt (Ceinture d'Orée). St-Pol refers not to the Apostle but to a local Breton saint, Paul the Aurelian, who became the first bishop and whose remains are buried in the **Cathedral**. Inspired by its namesake in Coutances (Normandy), the nave has a cool, ethereal beauty. It dates from the 13th and 14th centuries and was constructed using Caen limestone rather than the customary granite. Some of the medieval stained glass has survived in the transepts. The large bell next to the reliquary of St-Pol is rung during *pardons* in the hope of curing pilgrims of headaches and other ailments. Down the hill from the cathedral is the slender spire of the **Chapelle du Kreisker**, model for countless others in Brittany but unrivalled in its grace. You can climb the 169 steps to the parapet for breathtaking views of the sea and surrounding countryside.

There are sandy **beaches** all along the coast, from Kersaliou, on the road to Roscoff, to Carantec. St-Anne is the most crowded but has the best facilities (bars and restaurants, as well as watersports and a sea water swimming pool). Children like fishing in the rock pools for periwinkles, shrimps, crabs and mussels. **Carantec** is a resort in its own right and a rather attractive one. You can leave your car to take a short walk through the pines to **Pointe de Pen-al-Lann**, from where there are views across to the island fortress of **Taureau**, built to ward off the English. **Ile Callot** is linked to the mainland by a causeway, accessible at low tide. It's a lovely spot popular with fishermen and there are beaches here too.

Above
Collecting seaweed to use as
fertiliser

Above
The Ile de Vierge lighthouse

Suggested tour

Total distance: 159.5km (282.5km with detours).

Time: 3 hours' driving. Allow 6 hours for the main route, 10 hours with detours to Aber Wrac'h and Château de Kerjean. Allow an extra day for a trip to Ile d'Ouessant and to Roscoff and St-Pol-de-Léon; half a day to see the port at Brest. Those with limited time should concentrate on the coast between Plougerneau and le Conquet.

Links: The route can be reached by the D58 or N12 from Morlaix (*see page 59*) and the Côte de Granit Rose (*see pages 108–25*).

Take the D85 from **Plougonvelin** to the junction with the D789.

Detour: Take the D789 to visit **BREST ❶**. Leave the town on the D134 to Bourg-Blanc, then turn on to the D38.

Cross the D789 and pick up the D67 to St-Renan. From here take the D38 through the villages of Milizac, Bourg-Blanc and St-Jaoua to **le Folgoët**. The name means 'Fool's Wood', from the legend of Saloün, a simpleton who lived in the forest. After his death, a lily, symbolising the Virgin Mary, is said to have sprung from his mouth and the place

Ⓩ Compagnie Maritime Penn Ar Bed *Tel: 02 98 80 80 80; www.pennarbed.com.* Daily ferry services from Brest and le Conquet to Ouessant (one or more daily from each). In June, July and Aug there is an increase in departures from le Conquet and one service from Camaret at 0845 (not Sun).

Finist' Mer *Tel: 02 40 69 40 40; www.finist-mer.fr.* High-speed ferries from le Conquet, Camaret and Lanildut during the summer.

Finist'Air *Tel: 02 98 84 64 87; www.finistair.fr.* Two flights daily from Brest.

has been venerated ever since (le Folgoët is still the focus of an annual *pardon* on the first Sunday in September). The fountain by the east wall of the church is fed by the spring where Saloün used to drink. The basilica boasts the finest bell tower in Brittany and a superb rood screen carved from local granite. Alongside the church is the 15th-century manor house of le Doyenne and a pilgrim's inn.

Detour: Leave le Folgoët on the D788. Just beyond Lanhouarneau take the next two right forks then continue to the **CHATEAU DE KERJEAN** ❷.

Take the D770 north from le Folgoët through Lesneven to **Brignogan-Plages**, a small resort with a huge sandy bay flanked by six rocky coves reminiscent of the Pink Granite coast. There is also a menhir, an 8m-high megalith Christianised by the Celts by the addition of a cross. Return to the junction with the D10.

Detour: Turn left and take the D10 to **Plouescat**, the first resort of any size outside Roscoff. This stretch of coast is famous for its beaches, notably Kernic Bay. The supervised beach at Porsmeur is ideal for young families while Porsguen is the place to head for if you're into watersports (including kayak and pedalo hire). In the town itself the 17th-century market hall is worth visiting for its high-timbered roof with sturdy oak supports. From Plouescat continue on the D10 to **ROSCOFF** ❸ and **ST-POL-DE-LÉON** ❹.

Turn on to the D10 and continue westwards to **Plouguerneau**, a centre for commercial seaweed gathering. The harvest is celebrated with a festival every August. Leave the town on the D32, turning right immediately on to the lane which follows the bank of **Aber Wrac'h**. The Abers (from the Celtic word for valley) are flooded river estuaries, characterised here by shallow silted waters and low-lying rocky banks with a dusting of heather. At Pellan turn on to the D28 which bridges the *aber* on the way to Lannilis.

Detour: Turn right on the D128 to **Aber Wrac'h**, a small resort and yachting centre with several good sandy beaches. From here boats leave three times daily to the lighthouse on **Ile de Vierge**. The road continues along the Baie des Anges. A viewing platform points out the old defences of the Wrac'h estuary: the island ruins of the Cézon Fort (operational 1685–1889) and Ile aux Américains, established as a seaplane base in 1917 to defend the estuary from German U-boats. At the end of the road footpaths crisscross through the sand dunes of **Ste-Marguerite**, a pleasant walk on a sunny day. Return to Lannilis.

The D28 crosses **Aber Benoît**, then follows the south bank of the estuary for 5km. Turn right at the signs for Dunes de Corn-ar-Gazel from where there are views of the islands of the Benoît estuary and the Ste-Marguerite peninsula.

L'Azou € *8 Rue Général Leclerc, Plouescat, tel: 02 98 69 60 16. A small hotel serving excellent French cuisine. Fish specialities.*

Hôtel-restaurant Les Voyagers €€ *16 rue St-Yves, St-Renan; tel: 02 98 84 21 14; fax: 02 98 84 37 84; e-mail: hotel.restaurant-des-voyageurs@wanadoo.fr.* Conveniently situated in the old heart of the town, this hotel has an excellent restaurant with fish specialities.

Capitain Crèpes €€ *Aber Wrac'h; tel: 02 98 04 82 03.* Deservedly busy crêperie in the port area, delicious pancakes and also strong on seafood.

Lampaul has a few shops selling necessities, but they tend to be expensive.

Follow the coast road past the harbour of Portsall to **Trémazan** where the ruined keep of a 13th-century castle stands guard over a magnificent beach, the first in a sequence of extensive sandy bays fringed by dunes. From here you should also be able to see the Corn Cerhai lighthouse and the Roches de Portsall. This is where the oil tanker *Amoco Cadiz* broke up in 1978 with disastrous ecological consequences for over 200km of the French coast.

From Trémazan a designated '*route touristique*' follows the shoreline past the rocky coves and village resorts of Argenton, Porspoder and Melon. Just before Lanildut turn right to the **Rocher du Crapaud** – good for photographing the picturesque **Aber Ildut**, the official boundary between the Atlantic and the Channel.

After Lanildut continue to Brélès, then turn right on the D28 towards Plouarzel. Turn right again on to the D5 for the attractive **Grève de Gouérou**, then follow the coast road to Trézien. Turn right to the lighthouse at **Pointe de Corsen**, the most westerly point of mainland France. Return to the D28 and continue to **LE CONQUET** ❺ from where boats leave to **ILE D'OUESSANT** ❻. Take the D85 to **POINTE DE ST-MATHIEU** ❼.

Above
The scenic north Brittany coast

Le Musée des Phares et Balises
€€ Tel: 02 98 48 80 70. Open Apr and May, daily, 1400–1830; June–Sept, 1030–1830; Oct–Mar, Tue–Sun, 1400–1600.

Hôtel Fromveur
€€ Lampaul; tel: 02 98 48 81 30; fax: 02 98 48 85 97. The restaurant in this hotel specialises in island cuisine, using local produce such as lamb and seaweed.

Ecomusée de Ouessant €
Tel: 02 98 48 86 37. Open Apr and May, Tue–Sun, 1400–1700; June–Sept, 1030–1830; Oct–Mar, Tue–Sun, 1400–1700.

Getting out of the car

Ile d'Ouessant

Boats leave from Brest, le Conquet and Camaret on the Crozon Peninsula, often stopping briefly at the smaller island of **Molène**. When the fog descends or the wind picks up, the channels here can be extremely hazardous. On a clear day you can relax as the ferry negotiates a course between the reefs with the help of dozens of buoys and beacons.

The landing point is by the old lighthouse of **le Stiff** (open to the public). There is a bus service from here to the 'capital' Lampaul, or if you want to see more of the island, you can hire a bike at the ferry terminal. In **Lampaul** itself there's a sprinkling of hotel-restaurants, cafés and shops, but you might prefer to take a picnic on to the clifftops. Head for the dramatic coast by the **Créach lighthouse** where the waves pound mercilessly against the jagged tooth-like rocks. The beacon of the lighthouse is one of the most powerful in the world, casting a beam 80km out to sea. The machine room has been converted into **Le Musée des Phares et Balises** (Museum of Lighthouses and Beacons). On the road back to Lampaul you could call in at the **Ecomusée de Ouessant** at Niou Uhella, two rural cottages furnished with wood salvaged from shipwrecks and painted blue to win protection from the Virgin Mary. Costumes, farm implements and other exhibits evoke life on the island in the 19th century.

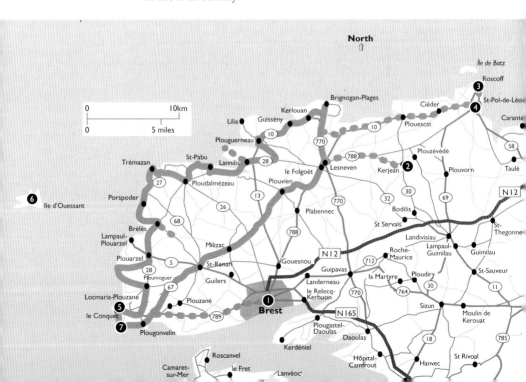

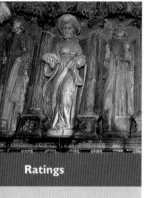

Parish closes

Ratings

Architecture	●●●●●
Art	●●●●●
Cathedrals and churches	●●●●●
Scenery	●●●●○
Food	●●●○○
Geology and landscape	●●●○○
History	●●●○○
Children	●●○○○

These remarkable architectural monuments, dating mainly from the 16th and 17th centuries, bear witness to a vernacular religious fervour derived from a twin obsession with death and eternal salvation. The *Enclos Paroissiaux* are found all over western Brittany, but the best examples are concentrated in the Elorn valley and the foothills of the Monts d'Arrée, once prosperous communities which had grown fat on the profits of the cloth trade.

The typical close comprises a triumphal arch to mark the transition from the secular to the sacred worlds, an ossuary where the bones of dead parishioners were exhibited after being exhumed and a calvary decorated with vividly sculpted figures representing the stages of Christ's Passion. The church interiors provide a colourful addition to the ensemble with their brightly painted statues and altarpieces. Each community tried to out-rival the others in the splendour and artistic invention of its close.

Abbaye de Daoulas

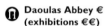 **Daoulas Abbey €
(exhibitions €€)**
21 rue de l'Eglise;
tel: 02 98 25 84 39;
www.abbaye-daoulas.com.
Open daily, 1030–1830 (last
admission 1730).

Founded in around AD 500, this ancient abbey fell into disuse at the time of the Viking invasions; it was rebuilt in the 12th century and flourished until the Revolution. The oldest part of the abbey to survive is the Romanesque cloisters, although some of the other buildings have been restored and are now used for ethnographic and other exhibitions. In the grounds a medieval herb garden has been painstakingly re-created using contemporary records; each of the thousand plants is carefully labelled to explain its culinary, medicinal or cosmetic uses.

Guimiliau

The most memorable feature of Guimiliau's parish close is its extraordinary calvary. Dating from 1581 to 1588 it is composed of almost 200 animated granite figures, arranged in a series of dramatic

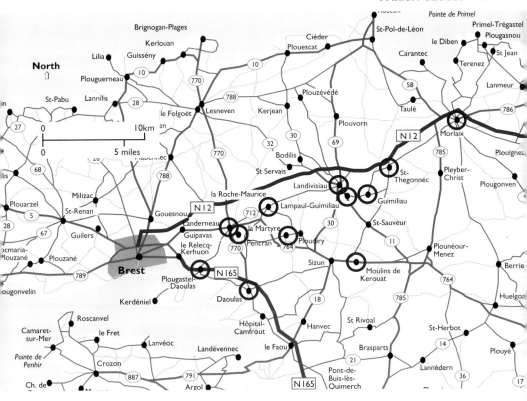

tableaux representing scenes from the life of Christ. Most are easily identifiable. On the side nearest the church for example you should be able to find St Peter cutting off the ear of the servant Malchus and the Agony in the Garden, while on the west side Christ rises from the dead over the sleeping bodies of his guards. Look just above the Last Supper for a spirited rendering of the Breton morality tale of Katell Gollet (Katherine the Damned), a young girl dragged off naked to hell by fearsome demons for desecrating the sacred wafer then concealing her sin in confession.

There are more miniature stone dramas crammed into every available recess of the porch. Once again they represent biblical stories, from the Temptation of Eve in the Garden of Eden to the Birth of Christ. One of the most attractive of these vignettes depicts Noah becoming drunk after cultivating the vine (above eye level, right hand side). Statues of the Apostles fill the niches on the inside of the porch while above the Renaissance pediment is a representation of the local patron saint, Miliau, King of Cornouaille.

The interior of the church, currently being restored, contains some wonderful carved ceiling beams, a magnificent 17th-century organ by an Englishman called Thomas Dallam and a sumptuous oak baldacchino (canopy) over the baptismal font. The ossuary, in classical style, dates from 1648.

LAMPAUL-GUIMILIAU

◐ Hôtel Restaurant de l'Enclos €€ *Route de St-Jacques; tel: 02 98 68 77 08.* This friendly hotel has a popular restaurant serving excellent local cuisine. Booking essential for Sunday lunch.

Thanks to the Counter-Reformation practice of installing altarpieces to instruct the congregation in the mysteries of the faith, the interior of the church at Lampaul-Guimiliau is ablaze with colour. Delicately sculpted groupings of polychrome or gilded figures, often in high relief, are surrounded by florid capitals and other ornamentation. The best example is the Passion Altarpiece to the left of the chancel – although this is mostly the work of Flemish craftsmen, Breton carpenters added the frame of columns wreathed with whorls of vine leaves in the 17th century. The most original work of art, however, is the superb rood beam at the entrance to the sanctuary. Beneath the figures of Christ on the cross, the Virgin and St John, sculpted miniatures tell the story of the Passion – you can just about make them out, starting with the Agony in the Garden on the far left. The figures on the reverse side are the sybils, pagan prophetesses reinvented and given Christian attributes in line with contemporary fashion.

Other treasures include a pietà in the north aisle and – a real rarity – fragments of the original medieval stained glass, pieced together and reassembled in the left window, near the Passion Altarpiece.

As an architectural ensemble the close at Lampaul-Guimiliau is rather disappointing, although the designers can hardly be held

Above
Lampaul-Guimiliau calvary

Right
Lampaul-Guimiliau church: decorated gable

responsible for the truncated tower, struck by lightning in 1809, or for the damaged figures on the calvary (c1530). It's a pity that the triumphal arch with its splendid baroque balusters had to be sandwiched between the ossuary and the perimeter wall.

LANDERNEAU

ℹ Landerneau Tourist Information *Pont de Rohan, BP 164 29800; tel: 02 98 85 13 09; fax: 02 98 05 13 09; e-mail: ot@landerneau.com; www.tourisme-landerneau-daoulas.fr.* Information on local boat trips, bike tours, walks and events. Very helpful, friendly staff.

Ⓟ Quai de Léon, rue de la Tour d'Auvergne.

A pretty market town standing at the mouth of the Elorn estuary, Landerneau has good shopping and is a convenient touring base for exploring the Monts d'Arrée and the parish closes, although the choice of accommodation is limited. For more than five centuries, Landerneau was an important port, its quays lined with sailing vessels trading in flax, linen, hemp and the famous Logonna and Kersanton building stones. The focal point of the town is the **Pont de Rohan** which, with the Ponte Vecchio in Florence, has the distinction of being the last inhabited bridge in Europe (it dates from 1510). It's the perfect spot for lunch, once you've photographed the black swans swimming under the stone parapets. Apart from the bridge, the only real sights are the tall, undeniably handsome **town houses** dating from the 16th and 17th centuries. The best known are the Maison de Rohan at the end of the bridge (note the sun dial) and Maison de la Duchesse Anne on place Général de Gaulle. There's a market on the quai de Léon on Tuesday and Friday mornings and all day Saturday – you'll find the farmhouse cheeses irresistible. The Comptoir des Produits Bretons on the opposite side of the river (quai de Cornouaille) is an excellent place to shop for Celtic heritage and Breton crafts.

Accommodation and food in Landerneau

Le Clos du Pontic €€ *Rue du Pontic; tel: 02 98 21 50 91; fax: 02 98 21 34 33; e-mail: clos.pontic@wanadoo.fr; www.clos-pontic.com.* Quiet hotel a little out of town; clean, comfortable rooms but lack-lustre ambience.

Hotel l'amandier €€ *53–55 Rue de Brest; tel: 02 98 85 10 89; fax: 02 98 85 34 14.* Fine hotel restaurant with good selection of regional fare.

Ibis Landerneau €€ *Route de Lesneven; tel: 02 98 21 85 00; fax: 02 98 21 67 61.* Set in a 10-hectare wooded park, this modern hotel is perfectly situated for touring the parish closes.

Restaurant de la Mairie €€ *9 rue de la Tour d'Auvergne; tel: 02 98 85 01 83; fax: 02 98 85 37 07; www.restaurantdelamairie.com.* Comfortable restaurant in the town centre serving Breton specialities.

Restaurant Le Rohan €€ *11 pont du Rohan; tel: 02 98 85 30 51.* Lovely spot on the bridge; wholesome Breton cooking, welcoming atmosphere.

LANDIVISIAU

While a busy and likeable cattle-market town of around 9000 people, Landivisiau nonetheless has little to detain the visitor except for the low key, high quality art exhibitions housed in a picturesque old house now functioning as the **Espace Culturel**. Despite the building's aged exterior, the spacious and well-lit interior provides a stimulating setting for exhibitions of painting, sculpture and photography, mainly focusing on Breton artists and themes. The space was donated by sculptor Lucien Prigent whose work is represented in the permanent collection. Even if the artworks fail to appeal, the park is a fine backdrop to a stroll.

MORLAIX

The coming of the railway changed the face of Morlaix forever in 1861 with the construction of the monumental granite **viaduct** which still bisects the town and looms over the Flamboyant Gothic spire of **Eglise St-Melaine**. It's an impressive piece of architecture and the lower level is open to visitors for views of the town and port.

There are few specific sights in Morlaix but there's plenty of enjoyment to be gained from strolling through the traffic-free streets that climb the steep hill from place des Otages, especially rue Ange de Guernisac and place des Halles. Look out for the statues of grotesques and saints that decorate the half-timbered houses on Grand Rue. The **Maison de la Duchesse Anne** in rue du Mur is an opportunity to see the interior of one of these Gothic residences known as a 'lantern-house' because of the skylight in the central hall. The magnificent spiral staircase leading to the upper storeys is 11m high and adorned with carvings of saints. At the end of rue du Mur is the **Church of St-Mathieu**, unremarkable except for a Madonna and Child made in Cologne around 1400. This ingenious piece of sculpture opens to reveal tiny carvings of the Trinity and painted scenes from the life of Christ.

Morlaix's location at the point where the rivers Jarelot and Queffleuth flow into the bay was the secret of its prosperity. The high point was in the 18th century when the town enjoyed a lucrative income from textiles, jewellery and the sale of butter and tobacco. Morlaix also served as a base for the local corsair fleet. For more about the history of Morlaix call in at the **Musée des Jacobins**. Located in former convent buildings where the five-year-old Mary, Queen of Scots, stayed in 1548 on her journey from Roscoff to Paris, the museum also exhibits paintings by modern Breton artists.

La Maisons des Vins, on place de Viarmes, stocks a good selection of French wine. **Joué Club** on rue de Paris is good for children's presents. **La Vieille Maison**, is a craft and souvenir shop on place des Otages.

Visit the **Coreff Brewery**, founded in Morlaix in 1985 by two Frenchmen after tasting real ales in Wales. They produce a range of bottled beers and a draught ale available fairly widely in Brittany.

Accommodation and food in Morlaix

Morlaix has a good selection of restaurants including one or two from the former French colony of Morocco, specialising in couscous and *tajine* dishes. Also worth investigating are the late-night bars in the

Opposite
The Moulins de Kerouat

tiny back streets off rue du Mur where local bands perform. If you are looking for a room, the port has several hotels as well as restaurants and bars.

Brasserie de l'Europe €€€ *place de Emile Souvestre; tel: 02 98 88 81 15; fax: 02 98 63 47 24; e-mail: contact@brasseriedeleurope.com; www.brasseriedeleurope.com.* Rich choice of traditional fare but it is seafood dishes that form the heart of the menu at this elegant eaterie.

Café de L'Aurore € *17 rue Traverse; tel: 02 98 88 03 05; www.aurorecafe.com.* Atmospheric spot for breakfast or lunch that later in the day turns into a pub with a formidable array of Breton beers.

Crêperie l'Océane €€ *2 rue de la Villeneuve; tel: 02 98 15 24 02; e-mail: creperieloceane@aol.com; www.creperieoceane.com.* Fluffy omelettes and sprightly salads are among the meals served overlooking Port de Plaisance.

La Dolce Vita € *3 rue Ange de Guernisac; tel: 02 98 63 37 67.* Pizzeria with Italian menu near the viaduct.

L'Europe €€ *1 rue Aiguillon; tel: 02 98 62 11 99; fax: 02 98 88 83 38.* Traditional hotel in the centre of town with 60 comfortable rooms and a helpful staff.

Le Marakech € *1 Venelle du Four St-Melaine; tel: 02 98 88 37 87. Open 1200–1400, 1900–2230 (Sun lunch only).* Friendly restaurant serving *tajine* and other Moroccan specialities, including full-bodied red wines.

Hôtel du Port € *3 quai de Léon; tel: 02 98 88 07 54; fax: 02 98 88 43 80; e-mail: info@lhotelduport.com; www.lhotelduport.com.* This hotel, overlooking the port, has no restaurant but some self-catering facilities.

Hotel le roi d'Ys € *8 place des Jacobins; tel: 02 98 63 30 55.* Inexpensive rooms, the cheapest lack bathrooms, but good value in a rewarding location.

MOULINS DE KEROUAT

Moulins de Kerouat €€
Commana; tel: 02 98 68 87 76. Open Mar–June, Sept–end Oct, Mon–Fri, 1000–1800, Sun, 1400–1800; July and Aug, daily, 1100–1900.

An entertaining window on to village life in the 19th century, this abandoned hamlet of 15 buildings near **Sizun** (*see page 63*) has been completely restored as an *ecomusée* (ecomuseum). The **mills of Kerouat** (and much else besides) were owned by the wealthy Fagot family – merchants, farmers and horse-breeders as well as millers. One of their number, Jean-Marie Fagot, rose to become Mayor of Commana in 1830. Apart from the overseer's house with its typical bourgeois furnishings, there are workmen's cottages, barns, stables, a tannery, a bread oven and a fully operational water mill, complete with millstone and mechanical gears. Children are especially welcome and there's plenty of space for them to run around.

Parish closes for enthusiasts

Milin an Elorn €€
Landivisiau Road, la Roche Maurice; tel: 02 98 20 41 46; www. creperiemilinanelorn.com. An attractive restaurant in an old mill on the banks of the Elorn, serving crêpes and grills.

Milin Kerroch € *Sizun; tel: 02 98 68 81 56; www.milinkerroch.com.* Cheap and cheerful *crêperie* in a converted water mill.

La Martyre

The oldest parish close, La Martyre dates from the 1450s. The triumphal arch has a Flamboyant balustrade surmounted by a small calvary. The façade of the ossuary (1619) is carved with macabre motifs while in the porch Ankou (death) appears wielding a mace and a severed head. The Breton inscription reads 'Death judgement, cold hell: let man think on these things and tremble.' The 15th-century chancel screen is lit by 16th-century stained glass.

Pencran

The 14th-century belfry contains one of the oldest bells in Finistère, 'Marie', cast in 1365. The church was restored in the 18th century but retains some original features – the porch (1552) is decorated with scenes from the Old Testament and an orchestra of angels. Inside are 15th- and 16th-century statues and a magnificent Deposition sculpture (1517) to the left of the high altar.

La Roche Maurice

The elegant belfry with its slender spire is a fine example of 16th-century Léon architecture and heralds more beautiful workmanship in the church. The stained-glass window in the apse dates from 1539 and depicts scenes from the Passion and Resurrection; it has retained its vivid colours despite its great age. Equally eye-catching is the rood screen with carved statues of popes and apostles and a canopy of grotesques, swirls and other ornamentation. The ossuary dates from 1639 – the medallions on the façade represent a variation of the *danse macabre*, with Ankou (death) above the water stoup, threatening *'Je vous tue tous'* (*I kill you all*).

Sizun

The splendid triple-arched gateway, surmounted by a calvary, dates from 1585–8 as does the ossuary, an equally imposing building, now a local museum exhibiting miscellaneous religious and household items. The church's interior decoration is 17th- to 18th-century. Look for the carved crocodile heads on the roof beams, contrasting with the angels which adorn the purlin (horizontal roof timbers).

Accommodation and food in Moulins de Kerouat

Auberge du Vieux Château € *La Roche Maurice; tel: 02 98 20 40 52; fax: 02 98 20 50 17.* As its name suggests, this small restaurant is near the castle. Good-value lunches, but only opens in the evenings in the height of the season.

Le Clos des 4 Saisons €€€ *2 rue de la Paix, Sizun; tel: 02 98 68 80 19; fax: 02 98 24 11 93; www.restaurant-4saisons.com.* A hotel catering specifically for the needs of fishermen.

Left
Lampaul-Guimiliau church: decorated altar

PLOUGASTEL-DAOULAS

Musée de la Fraise et du Patrimoine €€€ *Tel: 02 98 40 21 18; e-mail: contact@musee-fraise.org; www.musee-fraise.org. Open July and Aug, Mon–Fri, 1000–1230, 1400–1830; Sat and holidays, Mon–Fri, 1000–1200, 1400–1800; rest of the year, Mon–Fri, 1000–1200, 1400–1800.*

Famous for its strawberries, this rather ordinary town lies at the heart of a remote peninsula in the Rade de Brest. Following a devastating outbreak of plague in 1598, the chastened citizens commissioned one of the finest calvaries in Brittany, with more than 180 carved figures. Look for Christ emerging from the tomb on the base and the two thieves, watched over by an angel and a devil respectively. The church is vividly decorated with numerous painted wooden altarpieces. While you're here you should also consider visiting the **Musée de la Fraise et du Patrimoine**, a new local history museum with excellent displays on everything from strawberry cultivation to scallop trawling. On the first floor is a colourful exhibition of traditional Breton costumes.

ST-THEGONNEC

Enter the close through the highly ornamented (some would say over-elaborate) triumphal arch and the first thing that strikes the eye is the magnificent calvary, built by the stonemasons of Landerneau in 1610. It was the last of its kind. All the conventional elements are here, from the Passion scenes on the platform to the crucifixion, but the sculptors have added imaginative touches of their own, for example the pair of angels collecting every last drop of Christ's precious blood.

The ornamentation on the ossuary (1676–82) is a splendid example of the late French Renaissance style, with Corinthian columns, alcoves and canopies flanked by caryatids, dragons and other motifs. Inside is the moving *Entombment* by Jacques Lespaignol (1702).

Sadly the church was badly damaged by fire in the summer of 1998 and is undergoing extensive restoration. Most of the statuary and the sumptuous alterpieces which adorned the chapels at the east end have been moved for cleaning and repairs. The magnificent pulpit on the other hand has survived intact and you can admire the detail of the carved reliefs by the Lerrel brothers from Landivisiau. Images of the village patron, St Thégonnec abound: in the Holy Sacrament reredos (south aisle), for example, he appears in typical guise as a bishop, a wolf harnessed to a cart by his feet. According to legend the saint forced the wolf to pull the cart after it had eaten his donkey.

Accommodation and food in St-Thégonnec

Auberge St-Thégonnec €€ *place de la Mairie; tel: 02 98 79 61 18; fax: 02 98 62 71 10; e-mail: auberge@wanadoo.fr; www.aubergesaintthegonnec.com.* A modern hotel with clean comfortable bedrooms and an attractive garden. The restaurant is particularly good.

Suggested tour

Festival des Arts dans la Rue takes place in Morlaix on *Wednesday evenings in July and August.* Actors, circus clowns, poets and other entertainers take to the streets of the centre.

Chateau de Penhoat €€
Plouneour Menez; tel: 02 98 78 05 82. Open May–mid-Sept, Wed and Sun, 1400–1800.

Total distance: 119km (145km with detours).

Time: 2 hours' driving. Allow 8 hours for the main route, 9 hours with detours. Those with limited time should concentrate on the section between Landernau and Morlaix.

Links: This central route lies between the Côte de Granit Rose (*see pages 108–25*) and the shores of northwestern Finistère, while to the south are the Monts d'Arrée and the Aulne Valley (*see pages 78–85*).

Leave **MORLAIX ❶** heading south on the D712 then turn left on to the D785 which passes through **Pleber-Christ**, a village with a small parish close and a triumphal arch dedicated to the dead of World War I. The local pub sells Coreff, a tasty real ale brewed in Morlaix. Christian Blanchard and Jean-François Malgorn were inspired to make their own beer after visiting Wales.

Continue towards **Plounéour-Menez** where you can visit the grounds of the 16th-century chateau of **Penhoat**. Turn right on to the D111, then take the left fork to the hilltop village of **Commana**. There are several fine 17th-century polychrome altarpieces in the church and an elaborate canopied font carved with statues of the Five Virtues. From Commana head south, crossing the D764 to **Mougau-Bian**. This was the site of prehistoric tomb building – a 'covered alleyway' of five roof slabs supported by 28 upright stones with faint scratchings of spears and arrows carved on the inside.

Below
Sizun: the ossuary chapel

⓫ Maison de la Rivière, de l'Eau et de la Pêche € *Moulin de Vergraon, Sizun; tel: 02 98 68 86 33; e-mail: maison-de-la-riviere@wanadoo.fr; www.maison-de-la-riviere.fr. Open June and Sept, Mon–Fri, 1000–1200, 1400–1700, Sun, 1400–1700; July and Aug, daily, 1000–1900; Oct–May, Mon–Fri, 1000–1200, 1400–1700.*

Maison de la Rivière € *Barrage du Drennec, Sizun; tel: 02 98 68 86 33. Open July and Aug, 1000–1900; June and Sept, Mon–Fri, 1000–1200, 1400–1800, Sun, 1400–1700.*

Return to the D764 and head west past the **MOULINS DE KEROUAT** ❷ to **SIZUN** ❸. Follow the signs from the village 1km to the **Maison de la Rivière, de l'Eau et de la Pêche**, a small museum but worth a stop if you're at all interested in fish and fishing. **Maison de la Rivière** at the Drennec dam (6km east) has related information on lake and river management.

From Sizun take the D18 for about 5km before turning right after the signs to St-Eloy. After passing under the E60, turn right to **Hôpital Camfrout**, a pretty village with an old stone bridge, the 'Pont-Coz', and a 17th-century church built from local Kersanton stone (the west front is one of the finest examples of Renaissance architecture in Brittany). There are a number of options here. You could go for a walk in the woods at **Bois du Gars** or drive down one of the tiny side roads to explore the shoreline – the marshes at **Traon**, for example, or the ancient fishing port of **Kerascöet**, where two old sailing boats (classed as historical monuments) make leisurely sorties along the coast. Returning to Hôpital Camfrout, cross the river, then turn left towards Logonna Daoulas. The road follows the Camfrout, passing the abandoned quarries of **Kersanton**, now covered with brambles, ash trees and willows. This was once the source of the malleable, fine-grained granite used in Breton churches from the 14th century onwards and specially suited to intricate stone carving. At **Lagonna-Daoulas** there are panoramic views across the Faou estuary to the Landevennec Forest in one direction and Pointe de Rostivec and the Rade de Brest in the other. From **Pointe du Château** you can see the quarries at Roz where the ochre-coloured Lagonna stone is still extracted.

Take the D333 to **DAOULAS** ❹ to visit the abbey, then turn right on to the D33 to **PLOUGASTEL-DAOULAS** ❺. Leave on the D29.

Detour: After crossing the E60 turn left and drive on for 2km to **St-Jean**, where an elegant chapel with a graceful spire overlooks the River Elorn. The grassy bank is a nice spot to picnic. Return to the D29.

After 6km, turn right following the signs to **Dirnon**. The church here is dedicated to St Nonne, a young religious girl said to have been raped by a prince and forced to take refuge in the forest at Talarmon where she founded a hermitage at a place which became known as Diri-Nonn (the oaks of Nonne). A chapel to the right of the church contains her tomb which dates from 1450. From Dirnon take the D770 to **LANDERNEAU** ❻, leaving on the scenic D764. Then take the left fork to **LA ROCHE MAURICE** ❼ and the ruins of the former castle, described by the 19th-century novelist, Gustave Flaubert, as 'a true burgrave's castle, a nest of vultures on the summit of a mount'. Abandoned at the end of the 17th century the walls have gradually been dismantled and used by local builders.

Detour: From la Roche Maurice take the small road climbing in a southerly direction to Kermarice and **PENCRAN** ❽. Continue to la Croix Neuve, then turn east on to the D57 to **LA MARTYRE** ❾ and the parish close at **Ploudiry**.

From Ploudiry return to la Roche Maurice, then continue through the Elorn Valley to **LANDIVISIAU** ❿. Leave town on the D11 and follow the well-signposted 'Circuit des Enclos' to the parish closes at **LAMPAUL-GUIMILIAU** ⓫, **GUIMILIAU** ⓬ and St-**THEGONNEC** ⓭. Leave St-Thégonnec on the D712 to return to Morlaix.

Also worth exploring

The D769 follows a beautiful course along the bank of the **River Queffleuth** south from Morlaix to the edge of the Monts d'Arrée. The D11 crosses the main road at le Plessis (after 13km). To the west, lying in a valley is the **Abbaye du Relec**. The monastery buildings and chapterhouse lie in ruins but the 16th- to 17th-century church with its Romanesque transept has survived and a staircase leading to the monks' dormitory is a reminder of its past. To the east of the D769 is the **Cloître St-Thégonnec** and the 300-hectare nature reserve of moorland, marshes and craggy rocks. This is the habitat of hardy breeds such as Dartmoor ponies and Nantes cows, while carnivorous plants grow round the edges of the peat bogs. Botanic walks can be arranged from mid-June–mid-Sept (*tel: 02 98 79 71 98*).

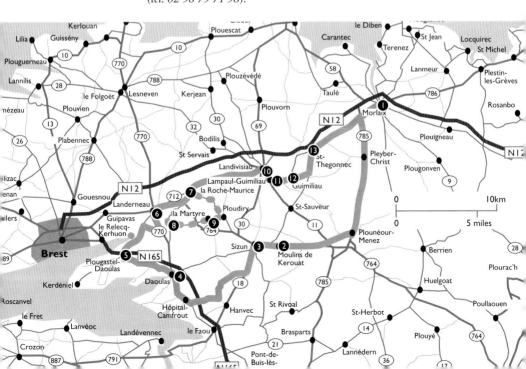

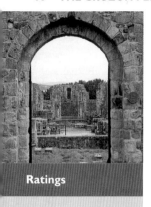

The Crozon Peninsula

Ratings

Beaches	●●●●●
Scenery	●●●●●
Walking	●●●●●
Watersports	●●●●●
Children	●●●●○
Food	●●●●○
Geology and landscape	●●●●○
Heritage	●●●○○

You could take in virtually the whole of the Crozon Peninsula in a day but to do it justice you'll need to spend at least a night or two in one of the resorts. Morgat and Camaret are popular choices and provide a nice contrast – one, a laid-back seaside village with a first-rate beach, good windsurfing and boat excursions to the caves across the bay; the other, a traditional fishing port with mouth-watering quayside restaurants and bracing clifftop walks.

If you're out in the car, pack your swimming things because there are beaches all along the south coast. (Pentrez plage is a gem.) There are plenty of opportunities to wander off the beaten track in search of that perfect headland view – Cap de la Chèvre takes some beating.

For a complete contrast in scenery, head for the heath-covered slopes of Ménez-Hom (the highest point on the peninsula) or to the verdant forest of Landévennec on the banks of the River Aulne.

ARGOL

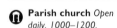 **Parish church** *Open daily, 1000–1200.*

Musée des Vieux Metiers Vivants (Living Crafts Museum) €€ *Tel: 02 98 27 79 30. Open June and Sept, Tue, Thur, Sun, 1400–1730; July and Aug, daily, 1000–1200, 1430–1800 (closed Sat, Sun, Mon am).*

Musée du Cidre €€ *La Ferme de Kermarzin, Route de Brest; tel: 02 98 27 35 85; www.musee-cidre-bretagne.com. Open daily, 1000–1200 (July and Aug, 1000–1300), 1400–1900.*

In the hamlet itself there's a **parish close** with an elegant triumphal arch. Emerging incongruously from the pediment is an equestrian statue of the legendary Breton king, Gradlon, originally from a medieval calvary. If the **church** is open the 16th-century frescoes of St Barbara and St Catherine are worth tracking down. The open-air **Musée des Vieux Metiers Vivants** organises demonstrations of

traditional crafts including spinning, basket weaving and cloth-making (during the summer only). The **Musée du Cidre**, located in farm buildings on the Route de Brest, explains all about cider production and beekeeping. There are tastings in the *crêperie* and there's a shop selling not only cider and apple juice, but apéritifs, *chouchenn* (mead), honey and fruit pastries. The carthorse is an added attraction!

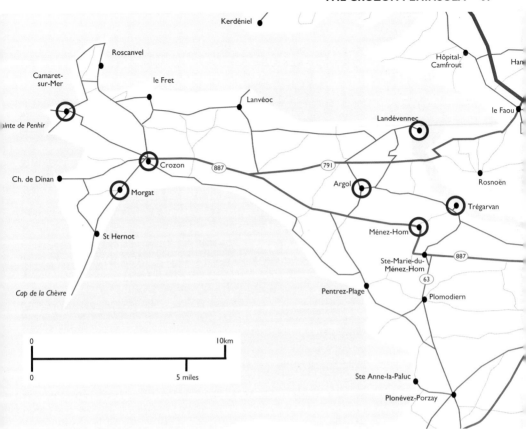

CAMARET-SUR-MER

Camaret-sur-Mer Tourist Information 15 quai Kleber; tel: 02 98 21 93 60; e-mail: ot.camaret@wanadoo.fr; www.camaret-sur-mer.com

As you would expect from a lobster-fishing port, the seafood restaurants in Camaret are cheap and plentiful. A leisurely stroll around the harbour will bring you to the Sillon – a short causeway with a jetty at one end. This is where the American inventor, Robert Fulton tested the world's first submarine in 1801 and it's also where you'll find Camaret's two 'sights'. The dour-looking chapel of **Notre-Dame de Rocamadour** dates from the 17th century and is a stopover for pilgrims even today – there's a *pardon* every September and a ceremonial blessing of the sea. Just beyond the chapel is a miniature pink fortress, the **Château de Vauban**. Named after the famous 17th-century military engineer, it was first called into service in 1704 when it withstood the assaults of the combined English and Dutch fleets under William of Orange. A small museum holds temporary art exhibitions.

There's a beach of sorts near the Sillon but the marshy **Anse de Dinan**, on the way to Crozon, has a more attractive setting. An enjoyable short drive over heathland takes you to the **Pointe de**

Opposite
Parish close, Argol

Vedettes Sirènes *Tel: 02 98 26 20 10.* Runs regular trips to the Tas de Pois.

Penn-Ar-Bed *Tel: 02 98 80 80 80; www.pennarbed.fr.* Operates a summer ferry service to the isles of Sein and Ouessant.

In summer there's a daily fruit and vegetable market on place St-Thomas. Clothes and flowers are on sale on the 2nd and 4th Wed of each month at the market on place Charles de Gaulle.

Commercial art galleries In the 19th century the charms of the old port were a draw for French painters and today's local artists will appreciate any interest shown in their work. You'll find their galleries and studios all over the village, but especially around the main square, place St-Thomas.

Above
The lobster-fishing port of Camaret-sur-Mer

Penhir, a well-known beauty spot. Tall white cliffs of armorican sandstone extend into the sea to the rocky outcrops known as the Tas de Pois (now a bird sanctuary). The views are superb and if you're feeling energetic you can scramble down the path to the grassy platform, the Chambre Verte. If you prefer there are boat cruises here from Camaret.

Accommodation and food in Camaret-sur-Mer

Hôtel de France €€ *Quai G Toudouze; tel: 02 98 27 93 06; fax: 02 98 27 88 14.* The first-floor restaurant serves excellent sea food platters and *homard l'Armoricaine* (lobster).

Hôtel du Styvel € *Quai du Styvel; tel: 02 98 27 92 74; fax: 02 98 27 88 37.* Hospitable, harbour-front hotel. Prices in the restaurant are hearteningly competitive. Seafood specialities.

Hôtel Vauban € *4 quai du Styvel; tel: 02 98 27 91 36; fax: 02 98 27 96 34.* Some of the rooms in this friendly, welcoming hotel (with restaurant) have sea views.

La Voilerie € *Quai G Toudouze; tel: 02 98 27 99 55.* The set-price dinners in this fish restaurant are excellent value for money.

CROZON

ℹ Crozon Tourist Information
Boulevard de Pralognan (near the Gare Routière); tel: 02 98 27 07 92; e-mail: ot.crozon.morgat@ wanadoo.fr; www.crozon.com

🚲 Bike hire: Nature Evasion *2B rue Garn an Aod; tel: 02 98 26 22 11.*

🛏 Hôtel Moderne €€ *61 rue Alsace-Lorraine; tel: 02 98 27 00 10; fax: 02 98 26 19 21.* Tastefully furnished *logis* with a good restaurant specialising in fish dishes.

🚗 Garage: Combot *Rocade Nord; tel: 02 98 27 10 40.*

Pharmacy *33 rue Alsace; tel: 02 98 27 10 19.*

A market is held every 2nd and 4th Wed. For a good range of shops look in rue Alsace-Lorraine and the other streets off the main square.

The steady flow of through-traffic from le Fret, Morgat and other resorts on the peninsula fails to spoil the charm of this busy little village which always seems to have an up-beat feel. Tourists come here mainly to stock up on provisions or to hunt for souvenirs, and Crozon is at its best on market days when the square in front of the church fills with stalls selling seafood delicacies, fresh fruit and vegetables, cheeses, yoghurt, Breton produce, leather goods and cheap souvenirs.

There are no sights as such but there is one curious item in the **church (Eglise St-Pierre)**. The altarpiece of the 10,000 Martyrs draws on a popular medieval legend. During the reign of the Emperor Hadrian (2nd century AD) the people of Armenia rose up against the occupying Roman army. Many of the soldiers took fright and fled but 10,000 stood their ground and, after an angel had appeared to them in their sleep on the eve of battle, won a stunning victory. Afterwards their tribune defied his commanding officer and refused to sacrifice to the gods. As a punishment he and his men were cruelly abused before being crucified on Mount Ararat. The retable, an oak tryptych with naive figures in polychrome relief probably dates from the 16th century. The 24 panels tell the story. On the left are the preparations for battle, the central panels begin with the appearance of the angel and end with scenes of torture, reminiscent of the humiliations endured by Christ, while those on the right culminate with the crucifixions.

LANDEVENNEC

🅜 Musée de l'Ancienne Abbaye
€€ Tel: 02 98 27 73 34; fax: 02 98 27 79 57; e-mail: abbaye.landevennec @wanadoo.fr; www.abbaye-landevennec.cef.fr. Open mid-June–end Sept, Mon–Sat, 1000–1900, Sun, 1400–1900; rest of year, 1400–1800.

This sheltered promontory at the confluence of the River Aulne and the Rade de Brest is one of the prettiest spots in Brittany. It was in the 5th century that the Welsh monk, St Guénolé, founded an **abbey** here and the remains are still the main attraction (follow the sign marked *Ruines de l'ancienne abbaye*). What you see today are the walls and foundations of the 13th-century nave and chancel – the rest is still being excavated. Here and there, traces of the church's 9th-century predecessor have survived – some of the capitals for example, decorated with Celtic motifs. Next to the abbey is the **museum** with an exhibition on the history of the abbey and the archaeological finds. There are models showing how the appearance of the site changed, some tiles removed from a Gallo-Roman hypocaust and a wooden sarcophagus weighing 170kg and made from a single hollowed-out oak trunk. The skeleton inside is thought to belong to one of the ancient princes of Cournouaille. A small Benedictine community still serves the village.

Follow the sign marked *Nouvelle abbaye* if you wish to see the simple church and/or visit the shop selling books, CDs of plain chant and other religious music, fruit grown by the monks and more. From the graveyard of the 17th-century **parish church** there are views across the River Aulne to the **Daoulas peninsula**.

Accommodation and food in Landévennec

Having seen Landévennec you may be tempted to stay the night. It's better to book a room in advance as demand is heavy in season. There are two hotels:

Hôtel Beauséjour €€ *Place de la Mairie; tel: 02 98 27 36 99; fax: 02 98 27 33 38; e-mail: hotel-beausejour-landevennec@wanadoo.fr.* Pleasant, good-value hotel in the centre of the village with a restaurant.

Hôtel St Patrick € *Rue St-Guénolé; tel: 02 98 27 70 83.* Small attractive hotel with simply furnished but comfortable rooms.

MENEZ-HOM

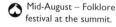

Club Celtic de Vol Libre *Tel: 02 98 81 50 27; e-mail: club@vol-libre-menez-hom.com; www.vol-libre-menez-hom.com.* Paragliding from Ménez Hom – beginners welcome.

Mid-August – Folklore festival at the summit.

Rising to a height of 330m, the isolated peak of Ménez Hom marks the end of the Presqu'Ile de Crozon. From the viewing table at the top the ragged outline of the peninsula stretches westwards, flanked by the Brest Estuary and Douarnenez Bay; to the east you can see across to the Monts d'Arrée and to the Montagnes Noires beyond the River Aulne.

On fine days paragliders float down to the gorse heath below the mountain and if you are around in mid-August you can join in the folklore festivities on the summit.

MORGAT

Morgat is the most popular beach resort on the Crozon Peninsula and with good reason. Fine white sand fills the crescent of the sheltered bay, ending in the pines of Beg-ar-gador. There is good, safe swimming and the watersports include sailing, windsurfing

**ⓘ Morgat Tourist
Information** *Place
d'Ys; tel: 02 98 27 29 49;
www.crozon-morgat.com/
toul-boss. Open only in
season.* Other times, try
the office in Crozon.

ⓡ Vedettes Rosmeur
*Tel: 02 98 92 83 83;
www douarnenez-
croisieres.com.* 90-minute
voyages around the
grottoes, and fishing trips.

Boat trips operate from
July–Sept only, starting
around *1000 in July and
Aug and 1430 in Sept.*
Departure times vary
according to the tides.

ⓝ Centre Nautique
*Port de Plaisance; tel:
02 98 16 00 00; e-mail:
cncm@cncm.asso.fr;
www.cncm.asso.fr.* Surf
board hire and other
watersports.

ⓐ Crapato Bicyclo
*2 place d'Y's;
tel: 06 88 71 72 22.*

and canoeing. If you get tired of lying on the beach there's a bracing cliff walk over rocky heathland and past clusters of white fishermen's cottages to **St-Hernot**. Local boat firms run regular excursions to the **grandes et petites grottes**. The larger caves, beyond Beg-ar-gador, include Ste-Marine, the 'devil's chamber' and the grotte de l'Autel (Cave of the Altar), 80m deep and 15m high with walls that glitter like gemstones. 'Chimneys' lead to the clifftops at various points, where hermits would set out to rescue shipwrecked sailors. Cruises last 45 minutes but you should allow three to four hours because of the tides. Pleasure boats also sail to the Cap de la Chèvre.

Back in Morgat itself the evening entertainment includes the **Mardis de Morgat**. Starting at about 2100 every Tuesday these open-air concerts are held just behind the main beach. Recent performers have included Irish folk singers and acts from the Caribbean, Peru and Mozambique as well as Brittany. If you prefer something a bit more active, there's a disco next to the tourist information office (behind the Grand Hôtel).

Accommodation and food in Morgat

Camping Les Bruyeres € *tel: 02 98 26 14 87; e-mail: camping.les.bruyeres @presquile-crozon.com; open mid-May–mid-Sept.* Spread across three very green hectares and 2km from the Morgat beach.

Les Échoppes €€ *24 quai de Kador; tel: 02 98 26 12 63.* Inventive seafood dishes presented in a little stone cottage; very popular and worth booking ahead.

Right
Morgat beach and caves

Hôtel de la Baie €€ *46 boulevard de la Plage; tel: 02 98 27 07 51; fax: 02 98 26 65; e-mail: hotel.delabaie@presquile-crozon.com.* Another likely option across the road from the beach, with a sea-facing restaurant.

Hôtel de la Plage €€ *42 boulevard de la Plage; tel: 02 98 16 02 16; fax: 02 98 16 01 65; e-mail: hotel-de-la-plage@presquile-crozon.com.* Modern, comfortable rooms, some with sea views, others overlooking the pool. The restaurant also overlooks the sea. Some noise from late-night revellers on the front.

Julia € *43 rue de Tréflez; tel: 02 98 27 05 89; fax: 02 98 27 23 10.* Traditional hotel in a secluded setting but not far from the beach and village. Restaurant and sea views.

Restaurant Pizzeria della Spiaggia €€ *Boulevard de la Mer; tel: 02 98 27 27 49.* Bustling restaurant serving salads and grills as well as pizzas. A good vantage point for listening to concerts on Tuesdays but you'll need to book.

Breton desserts

The *crêpe*, the *galette* and the *Far Breton* are just some of the mouth-watering desserts you will encounter during your stay in Brittany. They all have one ingredient in common, butter, all the more flavoursome if it carries the added tang of sea salt. *Far Breton* is a richly textured flan made with a creamy batter and filled with prunes or raisins (sometimes the flavour is enhanced with a dash of rum or cinnamon). *Konign-amann*, literally 'butter-cake' was invented in Douarnenez in 1865. This flaky pastry made with sugar and almonds is served warm – crisp on the outside it should melt in the mouth. *Crêpes* (pancakes) are usually sweet – fillings may include jam, ice cream or syrup. The lace-like *crêpe-dentelle* (originally from Quimper) is a more delicate variant. *Galettes*, on the other hand, are coarser and made with buckwheat. These savoury pancakes shouldn't be confused with the shortbread biscuits of the same name which are a speciality of Pont-Aven. If you develop a taste for them, they are sold in packets in supermarkets.

TREGARVAN

There are beautiful views of the River Aulne from this pretty hamlet, almost in the shadow of Ménez-Hom, but the main attraction for visitors is the **Musée de l'Ecole Rurale**. The old village school, its playground shaded by lime trees, finally closed in the 1970s but the classroom has now been restored to its turn-of-the-century appearance with plain white walls, blackboards and rough wooden benches, complete with inkwells and writing slates. There are photographs of the school as it was and background information (in French) on

Musée de l'Ecole Rurale €€

Tel: 02 98 26 04 72;
e-mail: musee.ecole.bretagne
@wanadoo.fr; www.pnr-
armorique.fr/fr/expositions/
ecole_rurale.html. Open mid-
Feb–June, Sun–Fri, 1400–
1800; July and Aug, daily,
1030–1900; Sept, daily,
1400–1800; Oct and Nov,
Sun–Fri, 1400–1700;
Dec–mid-Feb, Mon–Fri,
1400–1700.

subjects such as handwriting, discipline, playground games and Sunday school. Much is also made of the systematic attempts to suppress the Breton language which was spoken at home by almost all of the children at that time.

Suggested tour

Total distance: 136km (164km with detours).

Time: 2½ hours' driving. Allow 5 hours for the main route, 7 hours with detours.

Links: The peninsula can be reached from the Aulne Valley (*see pages 78–85*) on either the D887 or the D791.

From **CAMARET** ❶ take the D8 to **CROZON** ❷. Leave Crozon on the scenic coast road, passing through the hamlets of Rostolonnec and le Veniec to Lespiguet. After a right turn, the road climbs steeply, before dropping to **Trez-Bellec plage**, the first in a succession of stunning coves and beaches culminating in the long tongue of golden sand at **Pentrez-Plage**. Turn left at the end of the beach, then left again for **St-Nic** and a handsome church with a pierced belfry and some original 16th-century stained glass.

Take the D109 to the junction with the D887. Turn right, then left on to the narrow 2km-long road climbing to the summit of **MENEZ-HOM** ❸ from where there are sweeping views of the peninsula.

Return to the D887 turning left, then left again on to the D47 at **Ste-Marie-du-Ménez-Hom** – the balconied belfry dominates the parish close and is a useful landmark. Follow the D47 round the side of the

Right
Argol church and calvary

◐ Hôtel de la Mer
    €€ *Plage de Pentrez,*
St-Nic; tel: 02 98 26 50 55.
Small comfortable hotel
with sea views.

⑪ L'Escapade €€
    Route de Châteaulin,
*Telgruc-sur-Mer; tel: 02 98
27 72 79.* Smart
restaurant, specialising in
fruits-de-mer (seafood).

mount, then turn left on to the D60 to enjoy superb views across the wooded slopes of the River Aulne.

Detour: The signposts after 2km point to the hamlet of **TREGARVAN ❹** and (just off the road on the right) the **Musée de l'Ecole Rurale.**

Continue west on the D60 to **ARGOL ❺** , then double back as far as the turning to **LANDEVENNEC ❻** . Take the small winding road down through the forest to the chapel at **le Folgoat.** According to a medieval legend, a white lily inscribed with the words 'Ave Maria' appeared miraculously on the grave of a hermit who once lived in the forest. It's a tranquil spot where the sunlight filters through the trees on to a grassy bank beside a stream and is ideal for a picnic if others haven't already had the same idea.

From the chapel continue up the hill, turning right on to the D60 in the direction of Landévennec with the River Aulne below. There was a naval base here in the 19th century – a plaque reminds visitors of an inspection by the Emperor Napoléon III and his consort Eugénie in 1858. The battleship recalls the harbour's strategic importance during World War II.

Leave Landévennec on the D60 and after 3.5km, turn right to **le Loch**, a delightful inlet in the Aulne estuary with steeply wooded banks and a rocky beach. Continue west along the coast, turning right at Maison Blanche on to the D63 to **Lanveoc** and **le Fret,** a small boat-building and fishing community and the first port of call for visitors to the Crozon Peninsula arriving from Brest. Cormorants, terns, herons and other seabirds regularly feast on the young fish in the sheltered bay.

From le Fret take the D55 to the junction with the D355. Turn right and follow the coast road through Roscanvel to **Pointe-des Espagnols**; the name commemorates a small Spanish invading force which occupied the headland for six weeks in 1594 during the Wars of Religion.

Continue on the D355 down the wilder, west side of the peninsula. The remnants of discarded military bunkers protrude here and there from the gorse and blackthorn while, at the narrowest point by Quélern, the road passes the ruins of Vauban's 17th-century defences. The overwhelming impression, however, is of the glittering Atlantic merging seamlessly with the horizon.

Maison des Mineraux € *Route du Cap de la Chèvre, St-Hernot; tel: 02 98 27 19 73; e-mail: maison-de-mineraux@wanadoo.fr; www.maison-des-mineraux.org. Open July–mid-Sept, 1000–1900; rest of the year, Sun–Fri, 1000–1200, 1400–1700.*

Also worth exploring

The southern limb of the Crozon Peninsula is more isolated but by no means devoid of natural beauty. Take the D308 to the **Pointe du Dinan** where the rocky outcrop known as the 'Château' can be reached via a narrow footbridge spanning a natural arch in the cliff (a head for heights is called for).

Return on the D308, then turn right and head for **Cap de la Chèvre** where the bell-heather has a spellbinding purple hue and from where the views of the Baie de Douarnenez and the Cornouaille peninsula are spectacular. The 700-million-year-old cliffs are featured in the **Maison des Mineraux** at **St-Hernot** with its remarkable collection of fluorescent stones. Take the D887 back to Crozon.

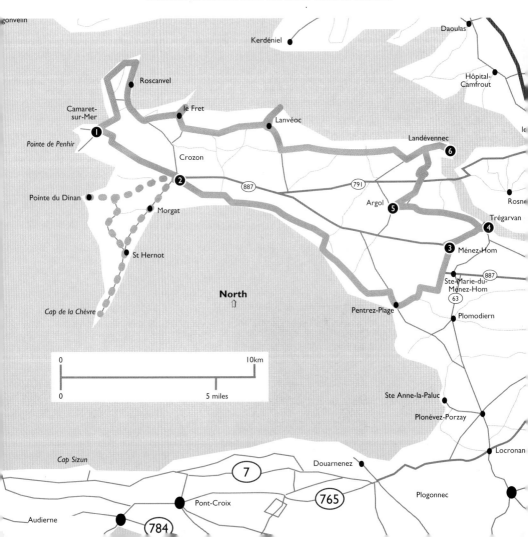

The Aulne Valley and the Monts d'Arrée

Ratings

Outdoor activities	●●●●●
Scenery	●●●●●
Angling	●●●●○
Walking	●●●●○
Children	●●●○○
Geology and landscape	●●●○○
Wildlife	●●●○○
Cathedrals and churches	●●○○○

This route takes in the serene Aulne estuary, gateway to the Rade de Brest and crosses the southern slopes of the Monts d'Arrée, hills eroded over time and now reduced to toothy granite ridges – the presence of quartz explains the proliferation of the Breton word roc'h (meaning 'quartz'). From the 'peaks' such as Roc'h Trévezel there are stunning views towards the coast.

There is no obvious touring base but picturesque Huelgoat is convenient both for exploring the Monts d'Arrée and the Forêt de Huelgoat, the remains of a primeval forest once said to have spread the length of Brittany. All kinds of activities are possible here from hiking and cycling to horse riding, canoeing and fishing. The magnificent River Aulne rises in the undulating countryside to the south of Huelgoat and threads a course towards the pretty town of Châteaulin, a favourite spot with anglers in spring when the river teems with trout and salmon.

CHATEAULIN

 Châteaulin Tourist Information *Quai Cosmao; tel: 02 98 86 02 11; fax: 02 98 86 38 74; www.chateaulin.fr*

Right
River Aulne

The River Aulne takes on a different aspect at Châteaulin where its canalised banks are lined with shady stone quays. It's a sleepy sort of place, a mecca for anglers who come every spring for the salmon fishing – trout are also found in abundance. Of the medieval castle which used to stand on the little hill above the town only the **Chapelle Notre-Dame** has survived. Its appearance was considerably altered in the 17th and 18th centuries but it still makes a good photograph. There's a restrained triumphal arch, a 15th-century calvary and a row of pretty cottages just outside the enclosure.

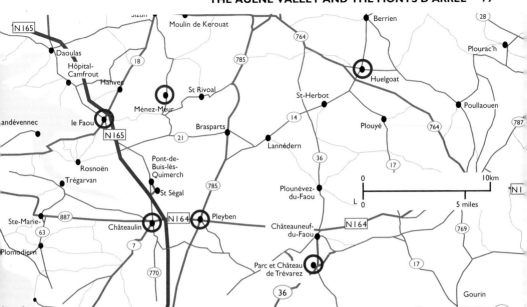

Accommodation and food in Châteaulin

Hôtel Au bon Accueil €€ *Avenue Louison Bobet; tel: 02 98 86 15 77; fax: 02 98 86 36 25; e-mail: bon-accueil@caramail.com; www.bon-accueil.com.* It's worth putting up with a little bit of noise from the road for the lovely waterside setting. Downstream from Châteaulin.

Hôtel Le Chrismas € *33 Grand' Rue; tel: 02 98 86 01 24; fax: 02 98 86 37 09.* Reasonably priced *logis* where the restaurant does a good line in country cooking.

Le Faou

ⓘ Le Faou Tourist Information *10 rue du Général de Gaulle; tel: 02 98 81 06 85; www.mairielefaou.fr*

This picturesque town at the mouth of the River Aulne once made its living supplying timber from the Cranou forest to the shipyards of the Brest Arsenal. There are few signs of life on the quayside today; instead, visitors can contemplate the serene beauty of the estuary, seen to best advantage at high tide. The local landmark is the slender lantern tower of the **Eglise de St-Sauveur**, completed in 1647. Many of the **corbelled houses** lining the high street (rue du Général de Gaulle) date from the same period or even earlier. There's a beautifully presented exhibition on the town's domestic architecture in one of the houses off place de la Mairie (town hall). Sadly, there are no surviving traces of the 11th-century castle built by Morvan du Faou, Vicomte de Cournouaille – the Mairie now occupies the site. If you happen to be in le Faou around 15 August there's a *pardon* just down the road at Rumengol (there are similar celebrations the weekend after Whitsun).

Accommodation and food in le Faou

Brasserie les Halles € *3 place des Fusillés; tel: 02 98 81 00 55.* Snacks, sandwiches, ice creams and simple lunches such as moussaka, chicken, and mussels and chips.

Hôtel de Beauvoir €€€ *11 place aux Foires; tel: 02 98 81 90 31; fax: 02 98 81 92 93; www.hotel-beauvoir.com.* On the same square as le Relais (below) this establishment is a little more expensive although there's not much to choose between them.

Le Relais de la Place €€ *7 place aux Foires; tel: 02 98 81 91 19; fax 02 98 81 92 58.* Excellent value *logis* opposite the Mairie (town hall), with a good restaurant.

Ty An Arvorig €€ *1 place des Fusillés; tel: 02 98 81 91 17.* Enterprising restaurant serving grills, pizzas, *fruits de mer* (seafood) etc. Try the *magrét de canard aux épices* (spiced fillet of duck breast) or the *espadon à la Bretonne* (swordfish à la Breton).

HUELGOAT

🛈 **Huelgoat Tourist Information** *Moulin du Chaos; tel: 02 98 99 72 32.* Maps, information on riding, fishing etc and a list of holiday homes in the area.

🏛 **Jardin de l'Argoat** *55 rue des Cieux; tel: 02 98 99 71 63; www.m-retraite-huelgoat.com.* Themed gardens, open-air concerts and tearooms.

🍯 **Miellerie de Huelgoat** *5 Route de la Roche Tremblante; tel: 02 98 99 94 36; www.presquile-crozon.com/miellerie-de-huelgoat. Open daily, 0900–1900* (1-hour tour). Discover the secrets of honey production and sample the produce.

Fishing, canoeing, cycling and horse riding are all on offer in the ancient Forest of Huelgoat, but for most visitors the hiking trails are the main attraction. Pick up a route map from the tourist office in the pretty lakeside village, pack a picnic then head straight for the woods (there are car parks at various points along the D769A as it follows the bends and twists of the magical Silver River – Rivière d'Argent). The Armorican tribes recognised the strategic value of the hilly, densely wooded terrain long before the arrival of Caesar's legions and as late as the 19th century unwary visitors were likely to encounter wolves, stags and even the occasional wild boar. Disaster struck in October 1987 when a great hurricane wreaked havoc on the beeches, oaks and pines but recovery is now well under way.

The forest has inspired its fair share of legends. During the Revolution a soldier escaping from Chouan rebels took refuge in a cave. When his pursuers saw him standing in the red glow of a fire, pitchfork in hand, they confused him with the devil and took to their heels. Since then the cave has been known as the **Grotte du Diable**. Both the river bed and the forest floor are littered with piled-up boulders such as the **Chaos du Moulin**, worn smooth by erosion and covered with moss and lichen. The **Roche Tremblante** (Trembling Rock) weighs in at more than 100 tonnes – but you can make it budge (so they say) if you lean on the right spot. From the **Ménage de la Vierge** (Virgin's Kitchen), where the boulders are said to resemble pots and pans, the **Sentir des Amoureux** (Lovers' Path) leads to another unusual rock formation, the **Mare aux Sangliers** (Boars' Pool) and the site of an important Roman hill fort, **Camp d'Artus.** Roman it may be but the name derives from Roi Artur, or King Arthur, of whom (one of many) legends holds that he passed through the local forest before being tempted to explore a dark cave, therein meeting his death. South of the river the **Promenade du Canal** follows the route of a waterway constructed in the 19th century to service the silver-bearing lead mines beyond la Mare aux Fées (follow the signs to la Mine).

There's little worth seeing in Huelgoat itself apart from the **Jardin de l'Argoat**, a botanical garden with more than 1000 species of plants, including giant-leaved rhododendrons, a rose garden and a landscaped arboretum. The project was the brainchild of the local hospital director who wanted to play his part in rescuing endangered plants.

Accommodation and food in Huelgoat

Camping Municipal du Lac € *Near the hotel (see below); tel: 02 98 99 78 80.*

Hôtel-Restaurant du Lac € *12 rue Général de Gaulle; tel: 02 98 99 71 14; fax: 02 98 99 70 91.* This 'no frills' lakeside hotel serves good food.

Below
Huelgoat

MENEZ-MEUR

Domaine de Ménez-Meur €€
Tel: 02 98 68 81 71; fax: 02 98 68 84 95; e-mail: menez.meur@pnr-armorique.fr; www.pnr-armorique.fr/fr/expositions/menez.html. Open July and Aug, 1000–1900; Mar, Apr, Oct & Nov, Wed and Sun, 1300–1730; May, June & Sept, 1000–1800; Dec–Feb, 1300–1700.

The 400-hectare estate at Ménez-Meur, **Domaine de Ménez-Meur,** has been transformed into a delightful wildlife park. A 1½-hour nature trail leads visitors through attractive woodland and there are information points explaining the flora and fauna. Enclosures contain wild boar, fallow deer, ponies, wolves and domesticated rare local breeds such as the Breton Pie Noire, Armorican cows and small Ouessant sheep. The Breton horse museum is also on the estate.

Right
Pleyben church

PLEYBEN

Crêpes Cozien 14 rue de l'Église; tel: 02 98 26 32 69. Open Mon–Fri, 1000–1200, 1330–1530.

Pleyben is unabashed about making its living from tourism. Apart from the usual cluster of craft and souvenir shops, two enterprises open their kitchens to visitors: **Crêpes Cozien** gives you the low-down on pancake making (mechanised and by hand), while at **Maison Châtillon,** you can watch the experts set to work on biscuits, florentines and chocolates.

○ **Maison Châtillon**
(confectioners) *46
place Charles de Gaulle;
tel: 02 98 26 63 77;
www.chatillon-chocolat.com.
Open daily during the summer.
Demonstrations and free
samples. Leaflet in English.*

○ **La Blanche
Hermine €€** *place
Charles de Gaulle; tel: 02 98
26 61 29.* On the main
square, this hotel
restaurant proffers tasty
traditional dishes.

Across the square is one of the most famous **parish close**s in Brittany. The star turn is the calvary, begun in 1555 and revamped in 1743 when the huge arched pedestal was added; the carvings tell the story of Christ's life from the annunciation to the crucifixion. The most unusual feature of the church, which has recently been cleaned, are the two belfries, one with a Renaissance dome, the other topped by a Gothic spire. Inside, the brightly painted roof beams add a splash of colour, along with the polychrome statues and the remarkable stained-glass window at the east end. The 16th-century ossuary (charnel house) houses a small museum which opens in the summer.

Parc et Chateau de Trevarez

○ **Parc et Château
de Trévarez €€**
*St-Goazec; tel: 02 98 26 82
79; e-mail: administration@
trevarez.com;
www.trevarez.com. Was due
to re-open in 2007.*

Known as the 'Pink Château' (actually red brick and grey Kersanton stone) this extravagant, neo-Gothic pile dates from the very end of the 19th century. It's not the château that's the attraction, however, but the 85-hectare park. Lose yourself among 12km of paths and avenues, decorated with fountains, waterfalls and cascades and enjoy the horticultural feast. The ever-changing seasonal displays include tulips, rhododendrons, azaleas, hydrangeas, fuchsias, hortensias and camellias. The former stables (state-of-the-art at the time they were built) are now used for temporary exhibitions. There are stunning views across the Aulne to Châteauneuf-du-Faou and the amenities include a children's playground and a teashop selling Breton cakes and other snacks.

The Basque connection

In September 1984 six members of Emgann, an organisation of militant Breton separatists, volunteered to 'adopt' a small group of Basque refugees from Guipuscoa who settled in Carhaix, Huelgoat, Châteauneuf-du-Faou and Fouesnant. Although Emgann had the support of local politicians, the national governments of France and Spain were alarmed and by 1987 all but one of the original community of Basques had either left Brittany voluntarily or been repatriated to Spain.

Undeterred, a secret network of Emgann members continued to receive refugees. Matters came to a head in 1992 when demonstrators took to the streets in Morlaix, Quimper and Lannion, following a heavy-handed police round-up of Basque sympathisers. The game of cat-and-mouse is still continuing, although the recent cease-fire by ETA (the Basque militant terrorist organisation favouring independence from Spain) may soon make the need for flight from the Basque country redundant.

Suggested tour

Total distance: 164.5km (170km with detours).

Time: 3 hours' driving. Allow 8 hours for the main route, 9 hours with detours. Those with limited time should concentrate on the stretch between Huelgoat and le Faou.

Links: The D785 from Roscoff or Morlaix links with the Aulne Valley route, or the N165 from Quimper.

Leave **CHATEAULIN** ❶ on the N164 heading east to **PLEYBEN** ❷. From Pleyben take the road south through Gars Maria and cross the River Aulne at Ti Men. At the junction with the D41 turn left to Croas-Brenn. Continue on the D41 to the hilltop village of Laz. Just outside on the D36 a car park allows drivers to stop and look down on the magnificent **Aulne Valley**. Follow the road through the Laz Forest to signs for the **Domaine de Trévarez** (on the left).

From the château take the D36 downhill to **Châteauneuf-de-Faou**, a pretty village nestling among the trees on the banks of the Aulne. Follow the river on the D117 to Spezet. Just before the village turn right to visit the **Chapelle Notre-Dame-du-Crann**. Dating from 1532 this typical Breton church is decorated with superb 16th-century stained glass depicting scenes from the life of Christ as well as an intricately carved shuttered altarpiece.

Take the D87 through St-Hernin, then turn left on the D769 to **Carhaix-Plouger**, a busy market town, but with little to detain visitors. From here the D769 climbs to **HUELGOAT** ❸ in the Monts d'Arrée. Take the D14 south to the square-towered church of **St-Herbot**, patron saint of horned cattle. You'll see tufts of cows' hair left as ex-votos on two small tables in front of the superb wooden chancel screen. Don't leave the church without lifting the seats in the choir to admire the imaginatively carved misericords. A few kilometres down the road the former priest's house belonging to the 16th-century church at **Locqueffret** is open as a tiny museum of rural parish life.

Continue through Lannédern, then turn on to the D21 to **Brasparts** where a small calvary includes St Michael 'patron of high places' killing a dragon. From Brasparts take the D785 north to the **Maison des Artisans**, where craftsmen demonstrate traditional country skills

ⓘ **Maison des Artisans** € *Ferme St-Michel; tel: 02 98 81 46 69. Open Jan–Mar weekends only, 1000–1900; Apr–Dec daily, 1000–1900.*

Maison Cornec € *St-Rivoal; tel: 02 98 81 40 99. Open July and Aug, Sun–Fri 1100–1900; June and Sept, 1400–1800.*

Above
Pleyben calvary

Auberge du Poher
*€ Route de Lorient,
Carhaix-Plouger; tel: 02 98
99 51 18. Attractive inn
offering local Breton
dishes.*

**Camping Penn ar
Pont** *€ Châteauneuf-
de-Faou; tel: 02 98 81 81
25; www.bretagnenet.
com/penn_ar_pont. Open
mid-Mar–mid-Oct. Site by
the Nantes-Brest Canal
with swimming pool and
boat rental.*

Hôtel Noz Vad *€€€
12 boulevard de la
Republique, Carhaix-Plouger;
tel: 02 98 99 12 12; fax: 02
98 99 44 32; e-mail:
aemcs@nozvad.com;
www.nozvad.com. Well-
appointed rooms and
slightly wacky décor in the
public areas; dependable
restaurant.*

including weaving, sculpting and pottery. From here you can drive to
the summit of **Montagne St-Michel**, which overlooks the Brennilis
reservoir and the notorious peat bog, Yeun Elez, so foul and dangerous
when the mists descend that it was known in Breton legends as
'Youdig', the entrance to hell.

Ten kilometres up the road is **Roc'h Trévezel**, the highest peak of the
Monts d'Arrée at 384m (Roc'h is the Breton word for quartz). It is a 15-
minute walk from the car park to the jagged rocks at the summit and
worth the climb for the splendid panoramic views over the Léon
plateau to Lannion Bay, the Rade de Brest and to the south, the
Montagnes Noires.

Return along the D785 to the junction with the D42, then turn right
to **St-Rivoal** and **Maison Cornec**, one of the region's more interesting
ecomuseums. The house belonged to a local wealthy farmer and has
been restored to its 18th-century appearance with the external
staircase leading to a hayloft, bread ovens in the courtyard and a
packed clay floor.

Detour: Turn right on to the D342 to the **Domaine de Ménez-Meur**.
Return to the D42.

Continue on the D42 past **Pen-ar-Hoat**, a hill in the **Forêt du Cranon**
which is ideal for walks and picnics. The scenic road passes through
Rumengol and ends at **LE FAOU ❹**. From here take the D770 back to
Châteaulin, a more diverting route than the E60.

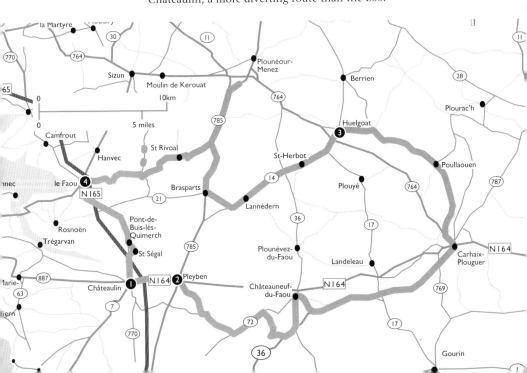

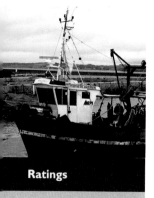

The Côte de Cornouaille

Ratings

Children	●●●●●
Heritage	●●●●●
Scenery	●●●●●
Wildlife	●●●●●
Beaches	●●●●○
Walking	●●●●○
Watersports	●●●○○
Cathedrals and churches	●●○○○
Entertainment	●●○○○

Cornouaille shares with its English counterpart, Cornwall, not only a common etymology but a similar coastal landscape and a geographical remoteness well suited to preserving customs and traditions. According to a medieval legend, this was once the kingdom of Gradlon, ruler of the lost city of Ys. It is also thought that the Druids settled here, embarking from the Baie des Trépassés to bury their dead on the remote island of Sein. The local flora and fauna are the main attraction of the wild and rugged coastline which boasts some of the most dramatic scenery in Brittany. Cornouaille is a paradise for birdwatchers – there are wildlife sanctuaries on the cliffs at Cap Sizun and down among the brackish lagoons of the Baie d'Audierne. The wooded inlets and river estuaries around the popular resorts of Bénodet and Pont-l'Abbé make up the other face of Cornouaille. This is Bigouden country, where you're most likely to see the distinctive towering headdress of the region.

BENODET

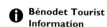 **Bénodet Tourist Information**
29 Avenue de la Mer; tel: 02 98 57 00 14; fax: 02 98 23 00 29; e-mail: tourisme@benodet.fr; www.benodet.fr

P Place du Meneyer, place J Boissel (near the tourist office), avenue de la Mer (Eglise Notre-Dame).

Market on Monday at 0900–1330, place du Meneyer.

This lively resort at the mouth of the River Odet is a port of call on the scenic route from Quimper to Concarneau and the Iles Glénan. Sheltered, south-facing beaches of fine sand offer the usual range of watersports and there's sailing on the lagoon at le Letty, with a restaurant for landlubbers. Some visitors find Bénodet over-commercialised but few of the complaints come from parents with children (the amenities include beach clubs with swings, trampolines and crèches). If you haven't time for the river cruise, take the short-hop passenger ferry to the picturesque little harbour at St-Marine. There are more beaches in the direction of Pointe de Mousterlin, the best spot for views, and there's life after dark at the casino or one of the discos. Bénodet really comes to life in July and August when the special events include jazz concerts on the beach, Breton evenings, regattas, circus acts and firework displays.

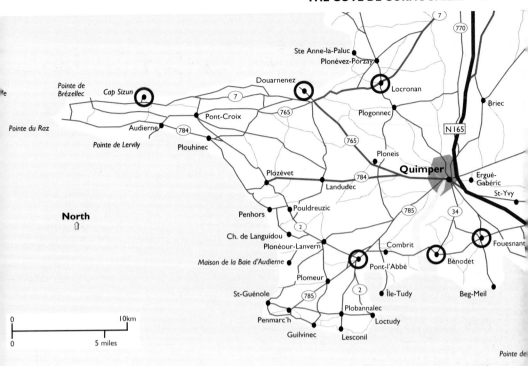

North

⇧

| 0 | | 10km |
| 0 | | 5 miles |

Boats: Vedettes de l'Odet 2 avenue de l'Odet; tel: 02 98 59 00 58; fax: 02 98 59 11 03; www.vedettes-odet.com

Bike hire: 5 avenue de la mer Charcot.

Taxis: ABC Cabs Tel: 02 98 57 00 44.

Accommodation and food in Bénodet

Les Bains de Mer €€ *11 rue de Kerguélen; tel: 02 98 57 03 41; fax: 02 98 57 11 07; e-mail: bainsdemer@portdebenodet.com; www.lesbainsdemer.com.* Interestingly designed mid-price hotel with its own swimming pool and seafood restaurant near the port and beaches.

Le Cornouaille €€ *62 avenue de la Plage; tel: 02 98 57 03 78; fax: 02 98 57 09 80; e-mail: info@la-cornouaille-hotel.com; www.la-cornouaille-hotel.com.* Exceptionally restful accommodations facing the beach; also offers spa treatments.

La Croisette Café €€ *3 avenue de l'odet; tel: 02 98 57 06 39.* Good spot for seafood with atmospheric river views.

CAP SIZUN

ⓘ **Maison du Site de la Pointe du Raz** (information) tel: 02 98 70 67 18; e-mail: contact@pointeduraz.com; www.pointeduraz.com

Pointe du Raz, at the western tip of this rocky peninsula, is the main tourist attraction. So many visitors come here (currently more than a million a year), that the authorities have introduced measures to protect and restore the environment: repairing damage to footpaths, dunes and heathland; replacing lost vegetation; and re-landscaping shops and car parks. The waves seethe and boil among the reefs 70m

Kermoor € *Plage du Loch, Plogoff; tel: 02 98 70 62 06; fax: 02 98 70 32 69; e-mail: kermoor.h.rest@ wanadoo.fr; www.hotel-kermoor.com.* With plain but comfortable rooms, this beachfront hotel specialises in seafood.

Réserve de Goulien € *Cap Sizun; tel: 02 98 70 13 53. Open 1 Apr–31 Aug daily.* Naturalists' tours on Mon, Tue & Fri in July and Aug.

below the headland, presenting a truly awesome spectacle when the wind gets up, while on calmer days you can see beyond la Vieille lighthouse to the Ile de Sein. **Pointe du Van**, to the north, is less dramatic but the cliffs are just as treacherous and there are fewer tourists, leaving you with the elements in a desolate and barren land. Between the two points is the crescent of the **Baie des Trépassés** (Bay of the Dead), so called because the Druids, who used the Ile de Sein as a burial ground, embarked from here – at least that's the latest theory. There's a sandy beach and dunes sheltering the wetlands of the Laoual Pool. If you're enamoured of this wild terrain and its birdlife, **Réserve de Goulien** is for you. Visits to the sanctuary begin in April, only a few weeks after the start of the nesting season, and continue to the end of August, when most of the birds have left for warmer climes. In the meantime the rocky crevices fill with guillemots, shags, fulmars, kittiwakes, ravens, choughs and gulls. If you're looking for somewhere to stay, there are a couple of hotels in **Plogoff**, on the south coast of the peninsula.

DOUARNENEZ

Douarnenez Tourist Information *2 rue du Dr-Mével; tel: 02 98 92 13 35; fax: 02 98 92 70 47; e-mail: info@douarnenez-tourisme.com; www.douarnenez-tourisme.com*

For the perfect photo opportunity visit Douarnenez in the evening as the brightly painted fishing boats return to the haven of **Rosmeur** and dazzling white yachts head for the marina at **Tréboul**. If you're out and about early in the morning, don't miss the fish auctions in front of the canning factories on the quay, before taking a stroll through the maze of little streets behind the port to the market at **place Gabriel Péri**. There are good walks along the Plomarch path from Rosmeur to the

AFFIMEDIA

Bienvenue
Welcome

Parking is limited in the old centre. Try rue Henri Barbusse.

Boats: Vedettes Rosmeur *Port de Pêche; tel: 02 98 92 83 83 (Apr–June tel: 06 85 95 55 49). Trips to the seabird sanctuary at Cap Sizun and the Tréfeuntec sea caves (leaflets in English) or fishing trips.*

Musée du Bateau €€ *Place de l'Enfer, le Port-Rhu; tel: 02 98 92 65 20; www.port-musee.org. Open June–mid-Sept, daily, 1000–1900; Oct–Dec and Feb–mid-June, Tue–Sun, 1000–1230, 1400–1800.*

Below left:
Sign welcoming visitors to Douarnenez

pine-backed **Plage de Ris** and from Tréboul on the **Roches Blanches coastal path** to Pointe de Leydé. The beaches at Douarnenez are not safe for swimming, but there are sea-fishing trips and boat excursions along the coast, as well as a thalassotherapy spa.

The excellent **Musée du Bateau**, part of the waterfront Port Musée complex, contains a superb collection of fishing vessels and sailing craft, including flat-bottomed coracles, a Dutch *tjotter* and primitive rowing boats made from animal skins. Shipwrights, carpenters, sail- and rope-makers and other craftsmen are on hand to demonstrate their skills or, for a more hands-on experience, you can clamber aboard the steam tug *Saint Denys*, one of 50 boats moored in the **Rhu estuary**. A 19th-century **waterfront** has been re-created on the far side of the harbour.

Accommodation and food in Douarnenez

There's a good choice of fish restaurants and *crêperies* on the quayside at Port de Rosmeur and in the vicinity of the boat museum.

Hôtel Thalasstonic €€€ *Rue des Professeurs Curie; tel: 02 98 74 45 45; fax: 02 98 74 36 07; www.thalasso.com/hotel_douarnenez.* Smart hotel with restaurant and thalassotherapy spa.

Ty Mad €€ *Plage St Jean; tel: 02 98 74 00 53; fax: 02 98 74 15 16; e-mail: info@hoteltymad; www.hoteltymad.com.* Pristine hotel with sea views and restaurant.

FOUESNANT-LES-GLENAN

Fouesnant Tourist Information *5 rue Armour; tel: 02 98 56 00 93; fax: 02 98 56 64 02.*

Bike hire: Mécanique Loisirs *tel: 02 98 56 18 23 or* **Cycles Quilfen** *tel: 02 98 56 58 45.*

Les Balnéides €€ *Allée de Loc'Hilaire; tel: 02 98 56 18 19; fax: 02 98 56 63 05; e-mail: contact@ balneides.com; www.balneides.com*

Centre Nautique *(yachting marina) Tel: 02 98 56 01 05; e-mail: cn.fouesnant@wanadoo.fr; www.asso.ffv.fr/cn-fouesnant*

Fouesnant has won the accolade '*Station Kid*' for its beach clubs, playgrounds, family-friendly campsites and hotels with children's menus, babysitting services and other amenities. If it's too cold for the beach, the aqua-park **Les Balnéides**, just outside town, has saunas, jacuzzis and swimming pools with water cannons, mini-slides and a massive 75m chute. If you're here in mid-July there's the apple harvest festival – Fête des Pommiers – part-religious ceremony, part-bacchanal. (Fouesnant is the centre of a cider-producing area.)

Three kilometres away, at the end of a wooded inlet, is the 800-berth yachting marina at **le Forêt-Fouesnant**.

Getting out of the car

The tourist office in **Fouesnant** won the 1994 Crystal Stork award for quality nature trails. The walks take in the Polder of Mousterlin, the habitat of kingfishers, herons and warblers; the saltwater Lake of Penfoulic where Shetland ponies graze the coarse grass; the Dunes of Beg Meil; and the Fouesnant Forest.

There is a daily market in the covered halls by place Gabriel Péri.

Mid-July Fête des Pommiers (cider harvest celebration).

Accommodation and food in Fouesnant-les-Glenan

Auberge du Bon Cidre €€ *37 rue de Cornouaille; tel: 02 98 56 00 16; fax: 02 98 51 60 15; e-mail: contact@aubergeduboncidre.com; www.aubergeduboncidre.com.* Family-run hotel in the centre of Fouesnant with comfortable bedrooms and a good restaurant.

La Baguette d'Or €€ *Route de Quimper; tel: 02 98 56 62 15.* Takes the best local ingredients and fashions them into tasty Chinese- and Vietnamese-based dishes.

L'Espérance € *6 rue Charles de Gaulle, la Forêt-Fouesnant; tel: 02 98 56 96 58; fax: 02 98 51 42 25; www.esperance-foret-fouesnant.com.* Comfortable hotel in the centre of the village, near the church.

LOCRONAN

Locronan Tourist Information *Place de la Mairie; tel: 02 98 91 70 14; fax: 02 98 51 83 64; e-mail: locronan.Tourisme@ wanadoo.fr; www.locronan.org*

Strictly speaking, Locronan lies just outside the Cornouaille region but it's worth a detour to see the **Grand Place**, a stunning ensemble of dormer windowed Renaissance mansions, built originally for the cloth merchants who brought prosperity to the town. (If you've seen Roman Polanski's film adaptation of Thomas Hardy's novel *Tess of the d'Urbervilles* you may recognise the setting.) Now these elegant residences have been put to a more prosaic use as tearooms or craft shops – linen items are the local speciality. The **parish church** is dedicated to St Ronan, the 5th-century Irish missionary whose life story is related in carvings on the pulpit and whose tomb can be seen in the Chapelle du Pénity on the south side. A short walk down **rue Moal** will bring you to the delightful 14th-century chapel of Notre-Dame-de-Bonne-Nouvelle (Our Lady of Good News) with its small calvary and 17th-century fountain.

Right
Locronan

Locronan's **annual** *pardon*, known as the Petite Troménie, is held outside the town every July. Pilgrims process behind colourful parish banners to the top of a small hill in imitation of St Ronan who according to tradition came here every day to pray. The Grand Troménie is a larger-scale version of the same event, held every sixth year (the next is due in 2007).

PONT-L'ABBE

ℹ Pont-l'Abbé Tourist Information *Square de l'Europe; tel: 02 98 82 37 99; fax: 02 98 66 10 82; e-mail: info@pontlabbe-lesconil.com; www.pontlabbe-lesconil.com*

🏛 Le Musée Bigouden **€** *Donjon du Château; tel: 02 98 66 09 03. Open June–Sept, Mon–Sat, 0900–1200, 1400–1830.*

Ecomusée La Maison du Pays Bigouden €€ *Kervazégan (route de Loctudy); tel: 02 98 87 35 63. Open June–Sept, daily, 1000–1230, 1400–1830.*

The self-styled capital of Bigouden (roughly the region between the River Odet and the Bay of Audierne), Pont-l'Abbé was founded by the monks of Loctudy who built the first bridge across the river estuary (hence the name). The monks also built the castle, which dates originally from the 14th century and which now contains the tourist office and a local history museum with a predictable emphasis on Bigouden headdresses and costumes. If you're not interested in this kind of thing, the museum is best avoided as visits are by guided tour only. If you are, then you'll want to see (on the same ticket) the ecomuseum, **la Maison du Pays Bigouden**. This farm on the road to Loctudy has been restored to its turn-of-the-century appearance with period furniture in the house and farming tools and equipment in the outbuildings. Pont-l'Abbé's church, **Notre-Dame-des-Carmes**, has an unusual domed bell tower but is most remarkable for the 15th-century rose window over the high altar. From here, there's a pleasant walk along the towpath by the Monuments aux Bigoudens.

The lost city of Ys

Ys, ancient capital of the kingdom of Cournouaille, is a lost city, submerged according to legend somewhere in the Baie des Trépassés. Ys had been protected from inundation by a belt of dikes and locks to which only King Gradlon held the key. Unfortunately the king's beautiful daughter, Dahut, was seduced by the devil who had taken on human form to lead her astray. Satan duly persuaded Dahut to steal the keys to the sea defences and open the sluices, with predictable consequences. As Gradlon and his daughter fled the drowning city on horseback, a voice from the heavens revealed Dahut's crime and ordered her father to cast her into the sea as a punishment. Gradlon obeyed and the waters retreated, but while Cournouaille was saved, Ys was lost forever and Quimper became the new capital of Gradlon's kingdom. Since that time, so the story goes, sailors lost and confused by the treacherous Atlantic fogs have been lured to their deaths by the siren voice of a mermaid who is, of course, Dahut transformed.

Hôtel de Bretagne
€€ *24 place de la République; tel: 02 98 87 17 22; fax: 02 98 82 39 31.* Ideally situated on the main square, this is probably the best hotel in town, with tastefully furnished rooms and an excellent fish restaurant.

Suggested tour

Total distance: 188km (212km with detours).

Time: 4 hours' driving. Allow 8 hours for the main route, 10 hours with detours. Those with limited time should concentrate on the roads from Locronan to Pont Croix via Pointe du Raz.

Links: The N165 links the peninsula with Pont-Aven (*see pages 102–3*) to the south and Crozon and the Monts d'Arrée (*see pages 78–85*) to the north.

Leave **Quimper** (*see pages 96–9*) on the D63, crossing the Steir valley and the gently rolling countryside to **LOCRONAN** ❶. Continue on the D7 along the edge of the Nevet Forest to **DOUARNENEZ** ❷.

The D7 hugs the coast all the way to the end of the peninsula. There are various stopping places en route to enjoy the clifftop walks. Ten minutes' walk from the car park is the lighthouse at **Pointe du Millier**, overlooking Douarnenez Bay and the Cap de la Chèvre on the Crozon Peninsula. Alternatively, there are similar views from the **Pointe de Beuzec**. You may want to visit the nature reserve at **CAP SIZUN** ❸; otherwise drive straight on to **Pointe de Brézellec**. From **Pointe du Van** take the coast road around the **Baie des Trépassés** to **Pointe du Raz**.

From here take the D784 to **Audierne**. Tuna fishing used to be the main industry here but nowadays you're more likely to see yachts cluttering the harbour. Audierne is also the embarcation point for **Ile de Sein**, a remote Atlantic island with barren terrain and an 'edge of the world' atmosphere.

Detour: From Audierne take the small coast road to **St-Tugen**, a Gothic church with a superb porch, carved with lace-like tracery. The curiosities inside include a catafalque with statues of Adam and Eve at either end and a chimney with granite firedogs in the baptistery.

Detour: Take the D765 to **Pont-Croix**, a small town perched on a ridge above the River Goyen. Steep, cobbled streets lined with modest stone cottages lead from the tidal mill by the bridge to the 13th-century church at the top of the hill. The church's steeple served as a model for Quimper Cathedral. Note the elaborate gabling on the south porch, a marked contrast to the plain Romanesque interior.

From Audierne take the D784 to Plouhinec. Turn right after the church and take the coast road, gateway to the Bigouden. Turn right on to the D2 at Tréogat then take the D156 at Plonéour Lanvern to the **Maison de la Baie d'Audierne**, the visitors' centre in a nature reserve of dunes, water meadows, brackish lagoons and marshes. Leaflets describe the varied flora and fauna and binoculars are available for hire.

Left
Locronan

Hôtel de Bretagne
*€€ Beg Meil; tel: 02
98 94 98 04; fax: 02 98
94 90 58;
www.hotel-bretagne.com.*
Comfortable hotel with
swimming pool.

Le Goyen €€€ *Place
Jean-Simon, Audierne; tel: 02
98 70 08 88; fax: 02 98 70
18 77; e-mail: hotel.le.goyen
@wanadoo.fr;
www.le-goyen.com.*
Expensive, traditional
hotel with an excellent
restaurant. Set menus
available.

De La Plage €€ *21
boulevard Emmanuel Brusa,
Audierne; tel: 02 98 70 01
07; fax: 02 98 75 04 69.
Open May to September.*
Large hotel with excellent
views.

Return to Plonéour Lanvern, then take the D57, turning right at the
first crossroad to **Notre-Dame-de-Tronoën**, which boasts the oldest
calvary in Brittany (1450–60). Unfortunately some of the carvings on
the south side have weathered badly but the statues on the north side,
made of hardier Kersanton granite, have survived to depict episodes
from the birth of Christ. An annual *pardon* is held here on the third
Sunday in September.

Turn right after the calvary and continue along the coast road to the
Plage du Pors Carn where the waves rolling in from the Atlantic
make the beach a fun-boarders paradise. Driving into the fishing port
of St-Guénole you'll pass a number of megaliths and a small museum
of prehistory. Turn left to the **Phare d'Eckmühl** lighthouse at the tip
of **Pointe de Penmarc'h** – climb the 307 stairs for views across the
20km-long shingle beach of Audierne Bay towards Pointe du Raz.
From here take the D785 to Penmarc'h, then the D53 to Plobannaiec.
Take the D102 to **Loctudy** at the mouth of the Pont-l'Abbé estuary.
This fishing port has sheltered beaches on the river side, the best
swimming beaches on this stretch of coast.

Leave on the D2 for **Kerazan**, a 16th- to 18th-century manor house in
a large park. Several of the rooms are open to the public and there are

Right
Douarnenez: cockle boat

Manoir de Kerazan
€ 29750 Loctudy; tel:
02 98 87 40 40; e-mail:
kerazan.loctudy@wanadoo.fr.
Open mid–June–mid–Sept,
daily, 1030–1900; Apr–mid–
June and mid–end Sept,
Tue–Sun, 1400–1800.

**Musée du Cidre
Bigouden** €€ Combrit; tel:
02 98 51 90 84. Open mid–
May–mid-Sept, Mon–Sat,
1000–1200, 1430–1900.

François Garrec Route
de Fouesnant; tel: 02 98 57
17 17; e-mail: pggarrec@
club-internet.fr;
www.garrec.com. Open July
and Aug, Mon–Fri, 0800–
1930; reduced hours rest of
year. Tours Tue, Thur and Fri
at 1100.

fascinating collections of Breton paintings, Quimper faience and ceramics by 18th-century artist Alfred Bea, as well as memorabilia belonging to the Astor family, the last private owners of the estate. The most unusual exhibit is Beau's 'Cello', the largest ceramic musical instrument in the world.

Continue on the D2 to **PONT-L'ABBE** ❹. Leave on the D44 to Botform-en-Combrit. The **Musée du Cidre Bigouden** at **Combrit** offers tastings as well as a guided tour of the orchard and presses. Cross the River Odet to **BENODET** ❺ and **FOUSENANT** ❻. At Bénodet, the **François Garrec** (previously at St-Evarec) can be visited. Traditional Breton delicacies, including *galettes*, *palets* and *kouign-amann* can be tasted and purchased.

Detour: Take the D45 to **Beg-Meil**, a small resort popular with families because of its large dune-backed beaches, rock pools and wooded coves.

Return to Fouesnant and take the scenic road through the **Fouesnant Forest** to St-Evarec. Turn left on to the D783 and return to Quimper.

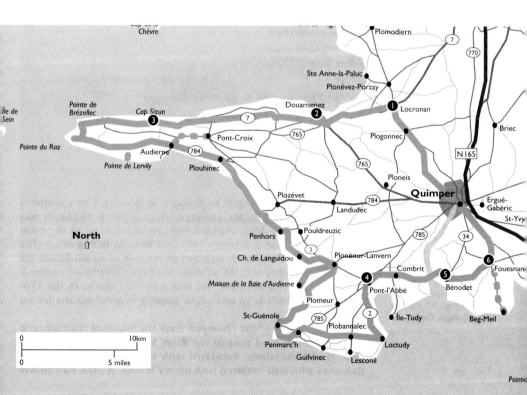

Quimper

Ratings

Architecture	●●●●●
Heritage	●●●●●
History	●●●●○
Cathedrals and churches	●●●○○
Food	●●●○○
Scenery	●●●○○
Art	●●○○○
Walking	●●○○○

Y ou won't find anywhere with more pride in its Breton roots than the ancient capital of Cournouaille. Founded by the legendary King Gradlon of Ys, Quimper derives its name from the Celtic word *kemper* meaning the confluence of rivers (in this case, the Steir and the Odet) and it's these two waterways that still give the town its character. Quimper is famous for its faïence. There's also a cathedral and a picturesque old town with lively waterside cafés where you can sample the local delicacy, *crêpes-dentelles*.

In the summer, pleasure boats leave the port for the Odet estuary where the wooded shoreline is broken here and there by the manicured lawns of stately manor houses. If you prefer you can take a stroll along the river bank or there are splendid views from the slopes of Mount Frugy opposite the town. If you arrive in July you could witness the Festival de Cornouaille, arguably the liveliest celebration of Breton culture in the region.

Sights

Aéroport de Quimper Cornouaille *Tel: 02 98 94 30 30.* Handles flights to and from Paris. You'll find it on the D785, about 7km from the town centre.

By car Quimper is on the N165 from Brest to Nantes (look for the exit signs *Quimper Centre*).

Old Quimper

The **Cathedral**, the largest in Brittany, is dedicated to Quimper's first bishop, St Corentin. An impressive Gothic building, it was completed in the 15th century with the exception of the twin lace-like spires, added between 1854 and 1856 to telling effect. The refinements of the medieval architecture can best be admired from the Jardin de l'Evêché, and the interior has been completely restored. Incidentally, when the nave was added to the chancel in the 15th century it was built at an odd angle, possibly to avoid marshy terrain near the river.

To see the heart of **old Quimper**, leave the towers of the Cathedral behind you and head towards the **River Steir**. In this pedestrianised area, feudal mansions, decorated with statues and caryatids, rub shoulders with half-timbered tradesmen's houses. A little watchtower

ℹ Quimper Tourist Information *Place de la Résistance; tel: 02 98 53 04 05; fax: 02 98 53 31 33; e-mail: contact@ quimper-tourisme.com; www.quimper-tourisme.com.* This busy office on the opposite bank of the Odet to the Old Town has lists of accommodation. The staff will help with hotel booking if required but queues often build up. The **passeport culturel** is an inclusive ticket to the main museums and the H-B Henriot faïence showrooms, and there's a free guided tour of the town included.

Ⓟ Cars are excluded from the Old Town. There is a large fee-paying car park (except 1200–1400) in front of the tourist office. Free parking is available at *place de la Tour d'Auvergne* (west), *place de la Tourbie* and *rue Rouget de l'Isle* (north), and *Allés de Locmaria* (south).

Ⓑ Boats: Les Vedettes de l'Odet operate cruises on the River Odet from *April to September* single or return. A one-way trip lasts 75 minutes. From *mid-July to August* the same company operates several daily services to the Îles Glénan. *Services are reduced Apr–June and during Sept, and do not run during winter. Tel: 02 98 57 00 58; www.vedettes-odet.com*

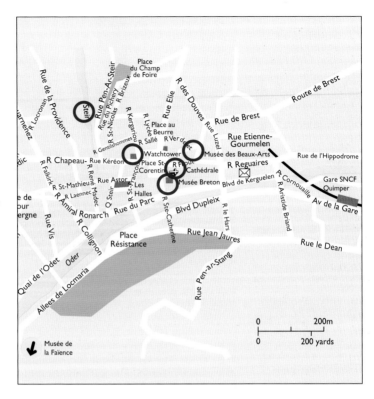

at the end of **rue Kéréon** guards the approaches to Pont-Médard over the River Steir and is a reminder that Quimper was once a fortified city – you can see remains of the town walls on **rue des Douves**.

Museums

There are three museums in Quimper worth considering. The **Musée Départmental Breton** in a splendidly revamped former bishop's palace. The displays cover everything from archaeological finds to mosaics, stained glass, faïence, costumes and furniture. Before leaving, check out the exquisite spiral staircase in the Rohan Tower, part of the original 16th-century palace.

The strong suit of the **Musée des Beaux Arts** in the Town Hall is 19th- and 20th-century Breton painting – street scenes, landscapes and domestic subjects. Don't miss drawings by the illustrator Gustav Doré, the room devoted to Picasso's friend, Max Jacob (a native of Quimper), and works by the French landscape artists Camille Corot and Eugène Boudin, who trained Monet.

On the opposite bank of the River Odet is the **Musée de la Faïence**. The exhibition, in an old pottery factory, gives the low-down on an industry which is still thriving today. Approximately 500 pieces from

⊕ Musée Départmental Breton €€ *Rue du Roi Gradlon; tel: 02 98 95 21 60. Open June–Sept, daily, 0900–2100; Oct–May, Tue–Sat, 0900–1200, 1400–1700, Sun, 1400–1700.*

Musée des Beaux-Arts €€ *40 place St-Corentin; tel: 02 98 95 45 20; Open July and Aug, daily, 1000–1900; Sept–June, Wed–Mon, 1000–1200, 1400–1800. (Also closed Sun morning from Nov–Mar.)*

Musée de la Faïence €€ *14 rue Jean-Baptiste-Bousquet; tel: 02 98 90 12 72; www.quimper-faiences.com. Open mid-Apr–Oct, Mon–Sat, 1000–1800.*

⊕ Festival de Cornouaille (*3rd–4th Sun in July*). More than 200 events and attractions including singing, dancing, concerts, Celtic games, costume parades, puppet shows, tastings, exhibitions and a host of other celebrations. *Tel: 02 98 53 53 53; e-mail: contact@ festival-cornouaille.com; www.festival-cornouaille.com* or contact tourist information.

Semaines Musicales *tel: 02 98 95 32 43; www.semaines-musicales-quimper.org* (August). Concerts of mainly classical music by French and international artists.

the collection are on show at any one time – not only plates but painted statues, figurines, globes, clocks, musical instruments and a variety of commemorative items. Visitors learn about the styles of the individual artists and craftsmen, manufacturing techniques and how they evolved over time and the minerals used to

create the distinctive blue, green and yellow pigments. After viewing the exhibition you may want to browse in the showrooms of the H-B Henriot faïencerie next door.

Other things to see and do in Quimper

If the weather's fine you could take a **boat trip** on the enchanting River Odet. The setting is idyllic, although the crowds can begin to pall in high season. Alternatively, in July and August there's also a daily sailing to the Iles Glénan.

Die-hard landlubbers might prefer a walk in the woods. Why not shop for a picnic in the covered market near the cathedral, then head across the river to **Mont Frugy** from where there are splendid views of Quimper and the surrounding countryside?

Outside town there's the **Parc du Château de Lanniron**, the former summer residence of the bishops of Quimper with magnificent 17th-century terraced gardens leading down to the River Odet.

A walk through Quimper

Start from Quimper's main square, **place St-Corentin**. The large building next to the **cathedral** dates from the 16th to 19th centuries and was the bishop's palace.

Walk up **rue Elie Fréron**. Turn left into **rue du Guéodet** passing the Maison des Cariatides, a 16th-century mansion which takes its name from the caryatids and other contemporary statues decorating the façade; the house is now a popular *crêperie*. Turn right at rue des Boucheries then right again on to **rue du Sallé** and **place au Beurre**, where in medieval times peasants from the outlying villages came to sell butter and honey cakes. Return to rue Elie Fréron and the cathedral.

Faïence is sold at the showrooms of **H-B Henriot** *rue Haute* (closed weekends) and at outlets throughout the town, including **L'Art de Cornouaille** *12 place St-Corentin.* Embroidered napkins and tablecloths, as well as faïence, are on sale from **François Le Villec** *4 rue du Roi Gradlon.*

Les Halles *rue St-François* is a covered fruit and vegetable market just a short walk from the cathedral, with a butcher and delicatessen.

Take the shopping street **rue Kéréon** to **Pont Médard**. Cross the bridge where windowboxes of geraniums are reflected in the placid waters of the **River Steir**. **Place Terre au Duc** belonged to the Dukes of Brittany and was the secular centre of town – the site of the law courts, the prison and a large market. Some of the oldest houses can be found here.

At the end of the square, cross the bridge into rue Astor, then turn immediately right into **quai du Steir** which leads down to **rue du Parc** and the **quai de Odet**.

Accommodation and food

In the summer, quality, reasonably priced accommodation is at a premium in Quimper and if you're camping you should certainly book in advance. There's a surprising dearth of hotels in the centre of town and, as prices are generally on the steep side, it might be worth considering one of the cheaper, if rather characterless establishments nearer the railway station.

L'Ambroisie €€€ *49 rue Elie Fréron; tel: 02 98 95 00 02; fax: 02 98 95 88 06; www.ambroisie-quimper.com. Closed Mon.* Creative workings of traditional Breton cuisine help make this stylish and fashionable restaurant one of the best stops in town.

An Poitin Still € *2 avenue de la Libération; tel: 02 98 90 02 77.* Irish 'pub' near to the railway station. Serves food and celebrates the region's Celtic roots with music on Friday nights and some Wednesdays.

Café de l'Epée €€ *14 rue de Parc; tel: 02 98 95 28 97, 02 98 64 37 73.* Stylish spot for Quimper's fashionable faces; drawn by the social caché and the extensive, good quality menu.

Hôtel de la Gare €€ *17 avenue de la Gare; tel: 02 98 90 00 81; fax: 02 98 53 21 81; www.hoteldelagarequimper.com.* The plain but tidy rooms overlook a central courtyard; downstairs is a bar and a simple restaurant.

Hôtel Gradlon €€€ *30 rue de Brest; tel: 02 98 95 04 39; fax: 02 98 95 61 25; www.hotel-gradlon.com.* One of the better hotels in Quimper, the Gradlon has tastefully furnished modern rooms and a convenient location on the edge of the old town. No restaurant.

Le Jardin de l'Odette €€ *39 boulevard de Kurguélen; tel: 02 98 95 76 76.* Luxuriate in the art deco surrounds overlooking the river and choosing from a range of temptingly-priced, creative fare.

Orangerie de Lanniron € *South of Quimper, towards Bénodet; tel: 02 98 90 62 02; fax: 02 98 52 15 56; www.lanniron.com.* The best campsite in the area with tennis courts, swimming pool and other amenities, but you must book ahead.

The artists of Pont-Aven

Ratings

Art	●●●●●
Food	●●●●●
Scenery	●●●●●
Outdoor activities	●●●●○
Walking	●●●●○
Cathedrals and churches	●●●○○
Children	●●●○○
Wildlife	●●●○○

With the coming of the railways in the 19th century, hitherto remote parts of Brittany became accessible almost overnight. The traditional way of life and untamed scenery of southern Finistère and the Cornouaille peninsula proved especially appealing to artists. Americans began arriving in Pont-Aven as early as the 1860s but it was Paul Gauguin and his French disciples who really put the town on the map. There's still no Gauguin museum in Pont-Aven but you can see paintings by the other leading members of the school. More to the point, the scenery that inspired them has changed surprisingly little over the last hundred years. For devotees of Breton art *La Route des Peintres en Cornouaille*, a useful brochure compiled by the local tourist board, helps visitors discover the landscapes and settings that still inspire artists today and points them to the galleries and museums where the paintings are exhibited.

CONCARNEAU

ⓘ Concarneau Tourist Information *Quai d'Aiguillon; tel: 02 98 97 01 44; fax: 02 98 50 88 81; e-mail: OTSI.concarneau@ wanadoo.fr, www.ville-concarneau.fr*

 Quai d'Aiguillon or quai Pénéroff.

There are good views of this busy fishing port and its river from the Pont du Moros on the D783. Like St-Malo (*see page 164*), the old town, known here as the **Ville Close**, is built on an island, linked to the rest of Concarneau by a bridge near quai Pénroff. Inside, it's a tight squeeze in the often congested streets and alleyways, lined with the predictable mixture of souvenir shops, art galleries and *crêperies*. The only way to escape the melée is to go for a walk on the massive granite **ramparts** built in the 14th century and strengthened by the French military engineer Vauban in the 17th century. Near the Tour du Major is the excellent **Musée de la Pêche** where you can clamber aboard a 34m trawler, the *Hémérica*, for a good insight into the none-too-comfortable life of an Atlantic fisherman.

Outside the Ville Close **boat excursions** leave from the marina for Quimper or the Iles de Glénan. There are good beaches to the north and south of the town.

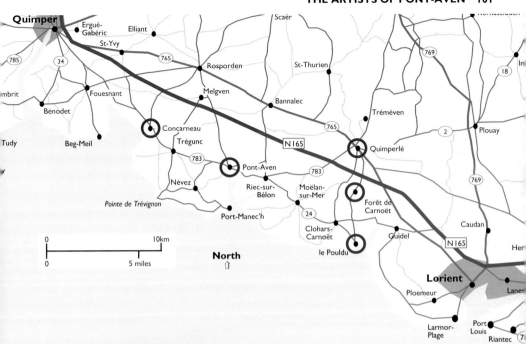

Musée de la Pêche
€€ *3 rue Vauban*
(Ville-Close); tel: 02 98 97
10 20; e-mail:
museedelapeche@wanadoo.fr.
Open July and Aug, daily,
0930–2000; Sept–Dec and
Feb–June, daily, 1000–1200,
1400–1800.

Market day is *Friday*
on quai Pénéroff, but
the covered market halls
are open every morning.

Accommodation and food in Concarneau

La Coquille €€€ *Quai du Moros; tel: 02 98 97 08 52; fax: 02 98 50 69 13; www.lacoquille-concarneau.com.* Delightful restaurant on the fisherman's quay with views of the Ville Close. Serves first-rate fish and seafood.

Hôtel de l'Océan €€ *Plage des Sables Blancs; tel: 02 98 50 53 50; fax: 02 98 50 84 16; e-mail: hotel.ocean@wanadoo.fr; www.hotel-ocean.com.* Comfortable modern hotel overlooking the beach.

Hôtel les Océanides €€ *3 rue du Lin; tel: 02 98 97 08 61; fax: 02 98 97 09 13; e-mail: lesoceanides@online.fr; www.lesoceanides.free.fr.* Good value *logis* with restaurant.

Des Ramparts €€ *31 rue Théophile Louarn; tel: 02 98 50 65 66; www.creperie-les-remparts.com.* Dependable *crêperie* in the heart of the Ville Close with good soup dishes, *crêpes*, and general Breton fare.

FORET DE CARNOET

There are numerous parking areas around the edge of the forest.

This 810-hectare stretch of forest bordered by the River Laïta lies just to the south of Quimperlé. Footpaths radiate from the information shelter at the edge of the wood and, either here or at the tourist office in Quimperlé, you can pick up a booklet with maps outlining suggested walks of between 5 and 10km. The forest has been planted with a mixture of deciduous trees and conifers: oaks, beeches and chestnuts, Norwegian pines, Sitka spruces, Japanese larches and Californian sequoias. The topography includes unusual rock formations such as the 'bishop's pulpit', as well as brooks, streams, ravines and the ruins of an old castle associated with the Bluebeard legend, and if you're looking for a place to picnic you'll be spoilt for choice.

PONT-AVEN

Pont-Aven Tourist Information *5 place de l'Hôtel de Ville; tel: 02 98 06 04 70; e-mail: ot.pont.aven@wanadoo.fr; www.pontaven.com*

Boat trips: Les Vedettes Aven-Bélon *Quai Botrel; tel: 02 98 71 14 59.* Excursions to Port-Manec'h or Port-Belon.

On the first Sunday of August the Fête de Fleurs d'Ajoncs (Golden Gorse Festival) commemorates the turn-of-the-century folk singer, Théodore Botrel. It is a celebration of costume, song, dance and Breton customs.

One memory you'll take away from this idyllic spot is the sound of rushing water, bubbling and foaming over the smoothed stones of the river bed; another is the sight of fellow tourists massing on the granite bridge or converging on the old watermill still in working order. Pont-Aven trades mercilessly on its links with the artist Paul Gauguin, who founded the 'Pont-Aven School' in the 1880s, urging fellow 'daubers' to 'paint what you see, not what is there'. The Brittany of clogs, lace headdresses and archaic piety that fascinated Gauguin has all but vanished; not so the enchanting countryside that inspired so many paintings.

You'll find leaflets detailing the various woodland walks and art trails at the tourist office. You can, for example, follow the banks of the Aven past derelict mills, manicured river gardens and old washhouses to the sleepy port at the head of the tidal estuary – no longer trading in wine and cereals but a haven for pleasure craft. From here you can sail directly to the fishing harbour at Port-Manec'h or join the more leisurely excursion rounding the estuary to Port-Belon, famous for its oysters. (Schedules vary according to the tide.) Canoes and kayaks are also available for hire.

Right
Mill at Pont-Aven

Musée de Pont-Aven €€ *Place de l'Hôtel de Ville; tel: 02 98 06 14 43. Open July and Aug, daily, 1000–1900; Apr–June, Sept & Oct, 1000–1230, 1400–1830; Mar and Nov–Jan, 1000–1230, 1400–1800.*

Galerie Dominique C *24 rue du Général de Gaulle; tel: 02 98 09 13 59. Figurative paintings and sculpture chiefly from contemporary French artists.*

Galerie du Bois d'Amour *8 rue de la Belle Angéle; tel: 02 98 06 16 28; e-mail: chantale.jouet@ galerieduboisdamour.com; www.boida.chez.tiscali.fr. Paintings, glass, ceramics and sculpture. Frequent visiting exhibitions.*

To follow in the footsteps of the artists, climb the wooded hillside of the **Bois d'Amour** with its shimmering canopy of beeches and chestnuts, to the open ground beside the 16th-century **chapelle de Trémalo**. Inside is the gaunt Christ figure which inspired Gauguin's *Le Christ Jaune* (1889); note, too, the roof beams decorated with painted grotesques and gaping dragon heads. On the way down you may find a suitable place to picnic – surprisingly few tourists stray far from the beaten track.

The **Musée de Pont-Aven** opened in 1986 to coincide with the centenary of Gauguin's first visit, although there are surprisingly few works here by the master himself (most have gone abroad). What you will find are paintings, prints and drawings by other leading members of the group, notably Emile Bernard, Paul Sérusier, Maurice Denis and Emile Jourdan, as well as a solitary canvas by the Impressionist master, Claude Monet (*Faiaises à Ouessant*). In fact, Gauguin and his admirers rejected Impressionism in favour of Synthetism – a daring neo-primitivist style of bold, flat outlines and brilliantly contrasting colours, toned down with a dull, matt finish. Temporary exhibitions feature each of the artists in turn and there are documents and old photographs illustrating life in Pont-Aven at the time.

Apart from its artists, the town is also renowned for the delicious butter biscuits known as *galettes de Pont-Aven*.

Accommodation and food in Pont-Aven

Sadly, Madame Gloanec's boarding house where Gauguin used to stay because it was cheap, is now a newsagents. From June–Sept, reasonably priced rooms are like gold dust and if you haven't booked ahead you may well end up staying some way outside town (not necessarily a bad thing). The staff in the tourist office do their best to help. Best value all round is the **Hôtel des Ajoncs d'Or** €€ in the main square (place de l'Hôtel de Ville) *tel: 02 98 06 02 06; fax: 02 98 06 18 91*. There are two equally attractive, but pricier establishments on the road leading down to the port: **Hôtel des Mimosas** €€€ *tel: 02 98 06 00 30; fax: 02 98 06 01 54* and **Hôtel La Chaumière Roz-Aven** €€€ *tel: 02 98 06 13 06; fax: 02 98 06 03 89; e-mail: rozaven@wanadoo.fr*. All these places have reliable restaurants.

Eating out is not a problem and needn't cost an arm and a leg if you shop around.

La Campagna €€ *40 rue du Général de Gaulle; tel: 02 98 06 03 35. Pizzeria.*

Le Moulin du Grand Poulguin €€ *2 quai Théodore Botrel; tel: 02 98 06 02 67; fax: 02 98 06 08 55. Crêperie and pizzas.*

Moulin de Rosmadec €€€ *Centre of town; tel: 02 98 06 00 22; fax: 02 98 06 18 00. Haute cuisine, and if you're very lucky you may even find a room here.*

Le Talisman €€ *4 rue Paul Sérusier; tel: 02 98 06 02 58*. Dependable *crêperie* with a nice garden. *Closed November and Sundays outside season.*

La Taupinière €€€ *Route de Concarneau; tel: 02 98 06 03 12; fax: 02 98 06 16 46*. Caters for the discerning gourmet.

Paul Gauguin

Born in 1848, Gauguin spent part of his childhood in Lima, Peru, before sailing round the world as a merchant seaman. He then worked as a stockbroker on the Paris Bourse before suddenly abandoning his career at the age of 35 to take up painting, to the dismay of his wife who eventually left him, taking their five children, the furniture and Gauguin's precious collection of modern art with her. In 1888 he went to stay with Van Gogh in Arles, but the two didn't get on – it was during this period that the Dutch artist cut off his ear. In between his two seminal journeys to Tahiti, in 1891 and 1895, Gauguin visited Brittany for a second time, but got into a fight with some fishermen after they had insulted his mixed-race girlfriend. In 1900, the art dealer, Ambroise Vollard, financed Gauguin's final move to the Marquesas islands where he died from the effects of advanced syphilis at the age of 55.

LE POULDU

Made famous by the artists of the Pont-Aven School, who decamped here in the winter of 1889, le Pouldu is a small resort now characterised by holiday homes and campsites. The long south-facing beach, much-beloved by Gauguin lies beyond the sheltered port on the Laïta estuary. Purists should know that the place where the artists actually stayed is now the Café de Plage; **Maison Marie-Henry** has been faithfully reconstructed next door, however, even down to the wall paintings left as part-payment – a white goose by Gauguin and an angel by Charles Filiger.

QUIMPERLE

ℹ Quimperlé Tourist Information *45 Place St-Michel; tel: 02 98 96 04 32; e-mail: ot.quimperle@wanadoo.fr; www.quimperletourisme.com*

℗ *(Lower Town) rue Ellé, rue Brémond d'Ars; (Upper Town) place des Ecoles, place Jean-Jaurès, place des Anciens Haras.*

Quimperlé is two towns rolled into one. The island formed by the rivers Ellé and Isole before they merge to become the Laïta is known as the **Basse Ville** (Lower Town). Its chief monument is the **Eglise Ste-Croix**, all that remains of the monastery founded in the 11th century by Benedictine monks. Only the apse and the crypt are genuinely Romanesque – the rest of the church had to be rebuilt after the bell tower fell in, in 1862. **Rue Dom Morice** is a picturesque cobbled street of half-timbered houses with a small local museum, the **Maison des Archers** at No 7. In the adjoining rue Brémond d'Ars you'll find an unusual 17th-century staircase which originally belonged to the law courts. Cross the River Isole by the Pont Salé and you're in the equally

⚫ In July and August free outdoor concerts are held from time to time on place St-Michel (Upper Town). Ask at the tourist office for details.

pretty **Haute Ville** (Upper Town). Dominating the main square (place St-Michel) is the **Eglise Notre-Dame-de-l'Assomption**, a Gothic church dating from the 13th to 15th centuries. Also known confusingly as St-Michael's, it's as imposing as Ste-Croix but more authentic and it's here that the locals come for mass on Sundays. The church's treasures include a 15th-century font and a wooden statue of Our Lady.

Accommodation and food in Quimperlé

Auberge de Toulfoën € *La Plaine; tel: 02 98 96 00 29; www.auberge-toulfoen.com.* Equally handy for Quimperlé and the Forêt de Carnoët, this country inn has a few comfortable rooms as well as a restaurant. (If you plan to eat here on Sundays you'll need to book.)

Hôtel 'Le Brizeux' €€ *7 quai Brizeux; tel: 02 98 96 19 25.* Central location on the banks of the Laïta. There's a bar downstairs and a dependable restaurant upstairs specialising in fish dishes; the set menu is good value.

Right
Quimperlé

Suggested tour

Total distance: 150km (196km with detours).

Time: 3 hours' driving. Allow 8 hours for the main route, 11 hours with detours. Extra half days should be allocated to explore the main towns. Those with limited time should concentrate on the stretch between Quimperlé, Pont-Aven and Concarneau.

Links: The N165 crosses this route between the Cornouaille peninsula (*see pages 86–95*) and the Monts d'Arrée (*see pages 78–85*).

Leave **QUIMPERLE** ❶ on the D22 to the village of Plouay, and once there turn left on to the D178 to **Kernascléden** where the superb parish church is definitely worth getting out of the car for. Built in 1453 by the Rohan family, its flamboyant Gothic exterior – slender tower, rose windows, pinnacles and carved gables – is matched by fine wall paintings in the chancel depicting the Virgin's life and by a graphic depiction of hell and all its torments in the south transept. The latter shows the journey to the after-life, beginning with impalement on the sharp branches of a barren tree until a horned devil oversees the troubled souls being transferred to one of three steaming cauldrons (where they are relentlessly boiled). From Kernascléden take the D782 to **le Faouët**, an attractive town nestling in the valley between the rivers Ster-Laer and Ellé. Stretch your legs here to see the 16th-century covered market in the main square and the paintings of Breton life in the art gallery, a former Ursuline convent.

Detour: Head north from le Faouët on the D790, turning right at the signs to **St-Barbe**, a chapel built into a crevice on a rocky hillside overlooking the Ellé valley. For views climb the 78 steps to the church. Return to le Faouët.

Take the D790 south to **St-Fiacre** where the church has an unusual belfry with two pencil-like turrets flanking the decorated steeple. Inside there's a superbly carved Flamboyant rood screen dating from 1480. The brightly painted Biblical scenes facing the nave are fairly conventional, but look round the back and you'll find lively depictions of four of the deadly sins. After St-Fiacre join the D6 heading south, cross the D769 and turn on to the D222. Follow the signs to **Roches du Diable**. Just before the road crosses the River Ellé there is a right turn to a car park. From here it's a 15-minute walk to the Devil's Rock, a sheer cliff above the Ellé.

Musée du Faouët €
1 rue de Quimper, le Faouët; tel: 02 97 23 15 27; e-mail: musee.du.faouet@ wanadoo.fr. Open June–Oct, Wed–Mon, 1000–1200, 1400–1800. Twentieth-century paintings inspired by Brittany and the rural way of life.

Manoir de Kernault €€
3km from the Kervidanou turning on the N165; tel: 02 98 71 90 60. Open mid-Feb–mid-Dec, Sat, Sun & public holidays, 1400–1730; July and Aug, daily, 1000–1230, 1400–1900.

Huîtrières du Château de Bélon €€ *M. De Solminihac, Port de Bélon, Riec-sur-Bélon; tel: 02 98 06 90 58. Open daily, 1100–1300, 1530–1800.*

Above
The pretty town of Pont-Aven

Domaine de Kerstinec €€€ *Riec-sur-Bélon (route de Moëlan-sur-Mer); tel: 02 98 06 42 98; e-mail: kerstinec@online.fr; www.hotelbelon.online.fr.* Sampling oysters in the delightful Louis XV dining-room is an aesthetic as well as gastronomic delight.

Les Moulins du Duc €€€ *Moëlan-sur-Mer; tel: 02 98 96 52 52; fax: 02 98 96 52 53; www.hotel-moulins-du-duc.com.* Spoil yourself in this converted mill with excellent restaurant.

Continue through Lounolé to the D790, turning left to Quimperlé. Take the D783 across the N165. At Kervidanou, the **Manoir de Kernault**, a beautifully restored Breton manor house, holds exhibitions and events including a horse festival in July. At other times of the year there are carriage rides through the attractive grounds.

Take the D783 to **PONT-AVEN** ❷ , then continue west to **CONCARNEAU** ❸ . Return to Pont-Aven.

Detour: Take the D77 south to **Névez**. Turn right to Pointe de Trévignon where there are views from the abandoned fort of La Forêt Bay in one direction and the dunes, ponds and scattered communities of the Névez in the other. Take the D1 coast road through **Kerascoët**, where householders still maintain their thatched roofs, to **Port-Manec'h**, a small estuary resort with a sheltered beach. Return to Pont-Aven on the D77.

From Pont-Aven take the D783. At **Riec-sur-Bélon** turn on to the D24, following the Bélon river which is famous for its oyster beds. You can sample these delicacies at the farm, **Huîtrières du Château de Bélon**, or at one of a number of small restaurants in the villages dotted about the estuary. Continue to **LE POULDU** ❹ . Leave on the D49 to pass through the beautiful **FORET DE CARNOET** ❺ on the way back to Quimperlé.

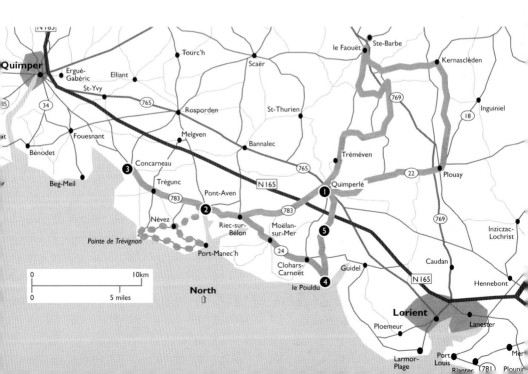

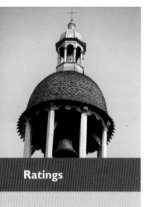

The Côte de Granit Rose

Ratings

Beaches	●●●●●
Cathedrals and churches	●●●●●
Children	●●●●●
Scenery	●●●●●
Walking	●●●●●
Watersports	●●●●●
Geology and landscape	●●●●○
Wildlife	●●●●○

It's taken nature more than 300 million years to mould the giant boulders of the 'pink granite coast' into the weird and wonderful shapes which have made them into today's tourist attraction. You can see them in splendid isolation on Trégastel beach, coralled into a nature park at Ploumanac'h or gaping from the undergrowth in the Traouïéro Valley.

If the boulders fail to win you over, then the man-made attractions of the resorts are sure to entice. Perros-Guirec has everything from discos and hydrotherapy, to beach clubs and tennis courts. If you want to get away from it all, head for the windswept beaches of the Corniche de l'Amorique, the sand-yachters' paradise, or inland to one of the scenic châteaux. There are boat trips to the islands off the coast: gannets cling to the rocks of the bird sanctuary at Les Sept-Iles, while the microclimate of the Ile de Bréhat smiles on subtropical beaches.

ABBAYE DE BEAUPORT

 Abbaye de Beauport €€
Paimpol (off road to Plouha); tel: 02 96 55 18 55; fax: 02 96 55 18 56; e-mail: abbaye.de.beauport@ wanadoo.fr; www.abbaye-beauport.com. Open mid-June–mid-Sept, daily, 1000–1900; other times, 1000–1200, 1400–1700.

The appeal of this ruined abbey lies in its romantic clifftop setting overlooking the Anse de Paimpol. Founded in 1203 by Count Adam de Goëlo, whose family gave their name to this stretch of coastline, it became a popular stopover with pilgrims en route to the Spanish shrine of Santiago de Compostela. The monks laboured in the fields, tending their apple orchards, growing medicinal plants and grazing sheep on the salt meadows, but much of the abbey's wealth derived from sister foundations in England. Deprived of this source of income by the Reformation, it fell into decline. Visitors are shown the remains of the 14th-century church, the cloisters, the refectory, the Gothic chapterhouse and the guesthouse where visiting pilgrims would have stayed. The 'Duke's room', formerly the monks' living quarters, is now used for making traditional Breton cider. Footpaths lead from the abbey grounds down to the sea and are well worth exploring.

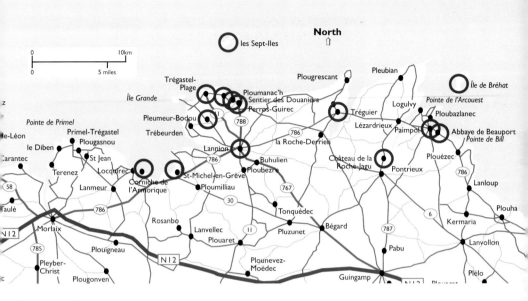

ILE DE BREHAT

ℹ Bréhat Tourist Information Tel: 02 96 20 04 15; fax: 02 96 20 06 94.

📞 Vedettes de Bréhat Tel: 02 96 55 79 50; www.vedettesdebrehat.com. Ferry service (€€) from Pointe de l'Arcouest near Paimpol. *Departures every hour July and Aug, every 2 hours at other times.* The earliest summer crossing is at *0830* and the last boat back leaves Port-Clos at *1945*.

If it looks enchanting as the ferry departs from **Pointe de l'Arcouest**, Ile de Bréhat more than lives up to expectations. It's a lovely place where the low-lying topography ensures a mild climate and plenty of dry, sunny weather. Consequently, the southern part of the island is enveloped in subtropical vegetation – oleander, mimosa, fig trees and palms. Cars are outlawed but it's only an hour's walk from one end of the island to the other. The best of the beaches is Grève de Guerzido; after drying off you could take a picnic into the woods at Bois de la Citadelle (follow the signs to the camping site). For real peace and quiet, though, you'll have to head north, crossing the bridge that looks out across the Baie de la Corderie. It's wilder and windier beyond this point and there are dramatic coastal views from the weathered rocks at Paon lighthouse.

CORNICHE DE L'ARMORIQUE

This enchanting stretch of coastline has marvellous beaches and equally stunning estuarine scenery. At **St-Efflam** and **Plestin-les-Grèves**, choppy seas and expanses of flat, hard-packed sand are especially suited to surfboards and wave-skis, while the beaches to the west and east of **Locquirec** are favoured by swimmers. There are sweeping views from the windswept headland at Marc' Sammet in one direction and the jagged pinnacle of le Grand Rocher in the other.

Right
Sand yachting on the firm sands
at Locquirec

St-Efflam is named after an Irish hermit who landed here in AD 470 – a
forlorn-looking chapel marks the spot. You can see his tomb in the
restored 16th-century church at Plestin where he founded a monastery
(the recumbent effigy dates from 1576). Between Plestin and the resort
of Locquirec is the tiny port of Toul-an-Hery – on the beach are the
ruins of Roman baths dating from about AD 50 (Thermes du Hogolo).
The buildings were occupied by local fishermen towards the end of
the second century AD and later abandoned. The estuary of the River
Douron is rich in flora and fauna, especially bird life. Wigeons and
oystercatchers are a common sight here.

Accommodation in Locquirec

Grand Hôtel des Bains €€€ *15 rue de l'Eglise; tel: 02 98 67 41 02; fax:
02 98 67 44 60; e-mail: hotel.des.bains@wanadoo.fr; www.grand-hotel-des-
bains.com.* Smart hotel in a superb setting.

LANNION

ⓘ Lannion Tourist Information 2 quai d'Aiguillon; tel: 02 96 46 41 00; fax: 02 96 37 19 64; e-mail: infos@ot-lannion.fr; www.ot-lannion.fr. Guided tours of the town available.

Ⓟ Quai de Viarmes (near tourist office), rue de Tréguier.

Ⓒ Boat trips on the Leguer estuary depart from Pont de Viarmes (200m from Post Office), round-trip 1½ hours. Ask at tourist information for departure times or tel: 02 96 46 41 00 (L'Amarine).

ⓘ Eglise de Brélévenez
Open daily, 1000–1200, 1430–1800, except during services.

Ⓒ The main shopping area is just off place Général Leclerc, with a market lower down the hill.

Ⓒ Annual organ festival; tel: 02 96 37 07 73. July and Aug.

Trégor festival of photography – June.

This prosperous town, straddling the banks of the River Léguer, is the administrative capital of the Trégor region and an important centre of the French telecommunications industry – you'll see the research centre as you drive in from the north.

Lannion is a good touring base for accessing the resorts of the Pink Granite Coast and the Baie de Lannion, while pleasure boats explore the 7km-long Léguer estuary, the habitat of herons, cormorants, sheldrakes and other birds. If you prefer to take the car, the D88 affords views of the estuary at **Loguivy-lès-Lannion** (just outside the town) and a little further downstream at **le Yaudet**, where a chapel looks out over the bay.

Lannion itself is a busy place during the daytime, although it quickly empties out after dark so don't expect much in the way of night-life. Start by climbing the 140 or so steps to the **Eglise de Brélévenez** with its landmark granite tower. Founded by the Knights Templar in the 12th century, the present church dates from the 14th to 17th centuries. On entering look out for the stone water stoop, once used for measuring tithe wheat. Little survives of the original Romanesque crypt, but the 18th-century Entombment scene is worth a look.

The town is a good place to shop, especially for lace. While you're out and about you'll also see some striking examples of 15th- and 16th-century half-timbered houses with intricately carved caryatids and other embellishments – slate roofs were introduced as a precautionary measure, in place of the once-traditional roofing of thatch, following a disastrous fire in 1593.

Accommodation and food in Lannion

Arcadia €€ *Route de Perros-Guirec; tel: 02 96 48 45 65; fax: 02 96 48 15 68; www.hotel-arcadia.com.* Modern hotel on the road to Perros-Guirec with heated swimming pool, bar and garden terrace.

La Clé des Champs €€ *1 rue Hingard Huellan; tel: 02 96 48 45 78.* Locally popular *crêperie* with many well-priced dishes.

La Gourmandine €€ *rue Cie Roger Barbé; tel: 02 96 46 40 55.* Friendly eatery specialising in grilled dishes and *crêpes*.

Ibis Lannion €€ *30 avenue de Général de Gaulle; tel: 02 96 37 03 67; fax: 02 96 46 45 83; www.ibishotel.com/ibis/fichehotel/fr/ibi/3401/ fiche_hotel.shtml.* Comfortable if slightly impersonal business-oriented hotel that reduces its rates at weekends.

Le Tire-Bouchon €€ *8 rue de Keriauley; tel: 02 96 37 91 20. Closed Sunday.* French cuisine with Breton nuances and a 'no fries, no ketchup' guarantee.

PAIMPOL

ⓘ Paimpol Tourist Information *Place de la République; tel: 02 96 20 83 16; fax: 02 96 20 73 96; e-mail: tourisme@ paimpol-goelo.com; www.paimpol-goelo.com*

Ⓡ Le Trieux Steam Railway July–Aug trains depart from Paimpol, in mid-morning, some include a 40-minute stop at Traou-Nez and all stop for around 2 hours in Pontrieux.

No service Mon or Tue. €€. *Further information/ reservations tel: 08 92 39 14 27; www.vapeurdutrieux.com*

Ⓜ Musée de la Mer € *Rue de Labenne; tel: 02 96 22 02 19; www.museemerpaimpol.com. Open daily, 1030–1300; mid-June–Aug, 1400–1830; rest of year, 1400–1800.*

Ⓒ Hôtel-Restaurant Le Repaire de Kerroc'h €€ 29 quai Morand; tel: 02 96 20 50 13. *Harbour-front establishment with comfortable rooms, swimming pool and restaurant specialising in fish dishes.*

Pleasure craft now outnumber fishing boats in Paimpol's twin harbours but this is a port with a great seafaring tradition. In times gone by up to a hundred sailing vessels would set out from Paimpol on the arduous, often hazardous voyage to the fishing grounds off Iceland. Not all the crews returned – the headland where the women traditionally gathered to welcome their menfolk is still known as the **Croix des Veuves** (widow's cross).

Models of historic sailing vessels and other nautical memorabilia are on display in the undemanding **Maritime Museum (Musée de la Mer)** – if you're here in season, the admission ticket also allows you on board an old schooner known as *Le Mad Atao*. Otherwise there's not much to do in Paimpol – the port itself is disappointing. If you are moving on, take the scenic route to **Pointe de l'Arcouest**, a small creek from where boats depart for **Ile de Bréhat**.

Getting out of the car

The Trieux Railway
In days gone by the River Trieux was a major waterway for transporting flax, hemp, fish, cereals and other produce. The pretty estuary can still be explored by boat – hire a canoe or kayak in Pontrieux or take the pleasure cruiser from **Pointe de l'Arcouest** near Paimpol – but for children, train buffs and other romantics the steam railway is an all but irresistible alternative.

Three blasts on the stationmaster's whistle and it's full steam ahead for locomotive 230.G as it makes for the pine forest of Penhoat-

Above
Paimpol harbour

Lancerf and **Traou-Nez** where there is a 40-minute halt to sample the local produce (*crêpes bretonnes* and a bowl of cider). The local manor house, La Maison de l'Estuaire, was the scene of a famous murder in the 1920s – Guillaume Seznec was sentenced to 32 years' penal servitude for killing a government official although doubts remain to this day about his guilt. From Traou-Nez the train continues to wind its way between the river and the forest, crossing the viaduct over the Leff from where visitors can gaze up at the magnificent **Château de la Roche Jagu** (*see page 116*). Journey's end is **Pontrieux**, a charming town of freestone and half-timbered houses. The best example is known locally (for reasons that remain a mystery) as la Tour Eiffel.

PERROS-GUIREC

ⓘ Perros-Guirec Tourist Information *21 place de l'Hôtel de Ville; tel: 02 96 23 21 15; fax: 02 96 23 04 72; www.perros-guirec.com*

ⓟ Behind Plage de Trestraou, Plage de Trestrignel; near place de l'Hôtel de Ville.

ⓗ Eglise St-Jacques *Open daily, 0800–1200, 1400–1830.*

ⓒ Centre Nautique *Tel: 02 96 49 81 21; e-mail: centrenautique@ perros-guirec.com. Open daily in season. Catamarans, windsurfing, kayaks, surfboards.*

The biggest resort on the Côte de Granit Rose, Perros-Guirec is also the liveliest with beach clubs, discos, a cinema, casino and hydrotherapy and fitness centre (Centre de Thalassothérapie). Life revolves around the two town beaches: Plage de Trestraou, with a **Centre Nautique** for watersports enthusiasts, and Plage de Trestrignel – both are safe for swimming and ideal for parents with young children. Other sports catered for here include tennis, golf and horse riding.

Perros-Guirec is also a good jumping-off point for excursions. Boats leave Plage de Trestraou for a tour of the bird sanctuary at **les Sept-Iles** (*see page 117*) or you could take a one-hour round trip to **Ploumanac'h** (*see page 114*) on the tourist train. There is only one tourist attraction as such, but the **Eglise St-Jacques** is a 'must see'. The hexagonal domed cap and steeple were grafted on to the squat Romanesque tower in the 17th century and give the church an unusual appearance. The Romanesque nave is almost perfectly preserved – look for the biblical sculptures on the pillars. Within the Gothic chancel arch a magnificent rood beam, dating from the 15th century, supports painted statues of the crucified Christ, the Virgin and St John. The church's other treasures include a Romanesque stoup, a 16th-century pietà and other painted images of the saints.

Accommodation and food in Perros-Guirec

Les Feux des Iles €€ *53 boulevard Clemenceau; tel: 02 96 23 22 94; fax: 02 96 91 07 30; e-mail: feuxdesiles2@wanadoo.fr; www.feux-des-iles.com.* Excellent French cuisine in a room with a view.

Hôtel de la Mairie € *28 place de l'Hôtel de Ville; tel: 02 96 23 22 41; fax: 02 96 23 33 04; e-mail hoteldesrochers@wanadoo.fr; www.hoteldelamairie-perrosguirec.com.* Good-value hotel near the tourist office.

Hôtel des Rochers €€€ *Port de Ploumanac'h; tel: 02 96 91 44 49; fax: 02 96 91 43 64; e-mail: hoteldesrochers@wanadoo.fr; www.hotel-des-rochers.com.* Food fit for gourmands.

Opposite
Pink granite boulders at
Ploumanac'h

Manoir du Sphinx €€€ *67 chemin de la Messe; tel: 02 96 23 25 42; fax: 02 96 91 26 13.* Imposing 19th-century mansion with sea views.

Trestraou Camping € *89 avenue du Casino; tel: 02 96 23 08 11; fax: 02 96 23 26 06; e-mail: campingtrestraou@voila.fr; www.trestraou-camping.com.* 180 places, a stone's throw from the beach and handy for all town amenities. *Open May–early Sept.*

Les Violettes €€ *19 rue du Calvaire; tel: 02 96 23 21 33.* Rooms in a pretty house just a few minutes' walk from the beach.

PLEUMEUR-BODOU

Musée des Télécommunications €€€ (special family tickets available, also all inclusive tickets with Planetarium). *Tel: 02 96 46 63 80; www.leradome.com. Open July and Aug daily 1100–1900; Apr, May, June & Sept 1100–1800; rest of year 1400–1700 (closed Sat).*

Planetarium de Bretagne €€ *Tel: 02 96 15 80 30; e-mail: contact@ planetarium-bretagne.fr; www.planetarium-bretagne.fr. Daily showings July and Aug on the hour 1100–1800; daily in Sept at 1500, 1600.*

On 11 July, 1962, the Radôme (radar dome) at Pleumeur-Bodou made telecommunications history when its 340-tonne antenna received the first TV images from the USA via the Telstar satellite. Even decades later, Pleumeur-Bodou remains the home of the French telecommunications industry. Very much 'hands on' in its approach, the ambitious, highly imaginative **museum** introduces visitors to all the major technological advances in the field over the last 150 years and will be appreciated by young and old alike. Highlights include an imaginary journey from the deck of a modern cable ship to the SCARAB submarine robot, the opportunity to take a close look at a real satellite and to relive the launch of an Ariane rocket.

More than 60m high and with a diameter of 64m, the Radôme could easily contain the Arc de Triomphe, but its synthetic rubber outer casing is only 2mm thick. Inside there is a 30-minute sound-and-light show about the antenna and the historic Telstar mission (usually in French). The nearby **Planetarium de Bretagne** is one of the largest in Europe; some of the shows are in English and German.

PLOUMANAC'H

Ploumanac'h Tourist Information *Place du Centre. Off season contact the tourist office at Perros-Guirec (see page 113).*

P The car park for the Parc Municipal is at the end of rue A. Fournier.

This small resort is especially popular with young families who come here to scramble over the rocks and shrimp in the pools at low tide. The main bay is called St-Guirec, named after the Welsh monk said to have landed here in the 6th century (an oratory containing a granite statue of the saint occupies a lone rock at the edge of the bay). Beach cafés, shops and restaurants are all in plentiful supply, while boats leave from the port on fishing trips and excursions to the **Sept Iles** (*see page 117*).

A walk, or a very short drive inland, leads to the pink-granite chapel of Notre-Dame-de-la-Clarté, erected by a local nobleman in the 16th century to honour a vow made to the Virgin after his ship had become stranded in fog.

St-Guirec et de la Plage €€ *Tel: 02 96 91 40 89; fax: 02 96 91 49 27; e-mail: hotelsaint-guirec@wanadoo.fr; www.hotelsaint-guirec.com.* Attractively decorated in pastel shades, this hotel offers sea-view rooms and a decent restaurant. Closed in winter.

A walk in the Traouïéros

The variegated and colourful scenery of the Grand Traouïéro (Traouïéro being the Breton word for valley), near **Ploumanac'h**, can be enjoyed by following the designated nature trail. Allow 3 hours for the 2.5km-long walk. Sturdy shoes are recommended.

Start from the old tidal mill at the mouth of the Grand Traouïéro and cross the D788, taking the side turning opposite. After about 600m a footpath leads off to the right. The path follows the river through a deciduous wood of oaks and chestnuts, now recovering from the devastation of the 1987 hurricane. Giant boulders protrude from the undergrowth at precarious angles or lie strewn across the forest floor, sometimes forming caves or hollows. The flora of the valley is also unusual: high levels of humidity have created a microclimate in which ferns, mosses and lichens flourish together with more than 150 varieties of fungus and, in spring, bluebells, lesser celandine and other woodland flowers.

CHATEAU DE LA ROCHE-JAGU

Château de la Roche-Jagu €€ **(park free)** *Tel: 02 96 95 62 35; e-mail: parcdelarochejagu@cg22.fr. Open July and Aug, daily, 1000–1900; Apr–June and Sept–Nov, 1030–1230, 1400–1800. Guided tours take an hour. Restaurant by the gate.*

Less flamboyant than the average Breton château, la Roche-Jagu occupies a commanding position above the wooded banks of the Trieux river. Some original Renaissance features have been preserved, including the chimneys and the spacious fireplaces, but the interior itself is unfurnished. The main hall is used for exhibitions during the summer, often on Celtic themes.

The park was devastated by the 1987 hurricane and has been completely re-landscaped by Betrand Paulet, a specialist in medieval gardens. Thousands of trees including willow, hazel and mountain ash have been replanted and vines are now cultivated on the slopes of the partly restored ramparts. Other innovations include a herb garden and a palm grove, symbolising the discovery of the Orient by the crusading knights. Paulet also exploits the natural beauty of the valley, employing terraces, cascades and waterfalls to striking effect.

ST-MICHEL-EN-GREVE

This small, unassuming resort overlooks one of Brittany's finest beaches, la Lieu de Grève. There are sweeping views of the 4km crescent of golden sand from the parish church of St Michael the Archangel which boasts one of the few maritime cemeteries in Europe. Apart from the 17th-century church and its polychrome statue of St Michael slaying the dragon, there's little to see in the village itself. Down on the beach, swimmers should take advantage of any incoming tide; otherwise it's a trek of anything up to 2km out to sea. For volleyball enthusiasts and sand-yachters, however, la Lieu de Grève is a paradise.

There's a pleasant walk from the village along the coast to **Grand Rocher,** a rocky mound, some 80m high, offering panoramic views. This is a protected natural site with pine forests and caves inhabited by several species of bat.

Back in the 19th century la Lieu de Grève was a wild and desolate place. Travellers were held to ransom by the notorious Yann Ar Moch (John the pork butcher) and torn apart by wild dogs if they refused to pay up. None of the bodies of Yann's victims was ever found; as he boasted after his capture – the Lieu de Grève was 'the best kept cemetery of all'.

SENTIER DES DOUANIERS

The remarkable 'coast guards' path' rounds the headland between **Ploumanac'h** and Trestraou beach in **Perros-Guirec.** The stretch between Pors-Kamor and Pors-Rolland has been designated a municipal park to preserve the distinctive pink granite boulders that characterise this part of the coast. Many of the rocks have been given names – the 'witch', the 'rabbit', 'Napoleon's hat', the 'tortoise' and so on – but you may need to use your imagination to see the resemblance.

LES SEPT-ILES

Boats: Les Sept-Iles en Vedettes runs daily boat tours to the islands, departing from plage de Trestraou, Perros-Guirec (*Mar to Oct*). *Tel: 02 96 91 10 00 for reservations/additional information.*

The archipelago of seven low-lying islets off the coast of **Perros-Guirec** is one of France's most important bird sanctuaries. Thirteen different species make their nests here between March and September, including black-backed gulls, razorbills, guillemots, shags, terns, kittiwakes, puffins and oystercatchers. On the island of Rouzic there is also a small colony of grey seals and, at the last count, 13,000 pairs of northern gannets.

For ecological reasons, visitors are only allowed on one of the islands, so if you want to see the birds at close quarters you'll need to bring binoculars. Half-day cruises depart from Perros-Guirec every day in season. Visitors disembark on Ile aux Moines for a short stop of about 40 minutes – time enough to inspect the old gunpowder factory, the lighthouse and the ruined fort, built in 1740 on the orders of Louis XV to deal with smugglers and marauding pirates. Discounting the ornithologists and the lighthouse keeper, Les Sept Iles are uninhabited due to the harsh conditions in winter. Even the hermit monks who tried to settle in the 15th century were soon forced to return to the mainland.

TREGASTEL-PLAGE

P By the aquarium, boulevard du Coz-Porz.

aquarium Aquarium Marin de Trégastel €€
Boulevard du Coz-Pors; tel: 02 96 15 38 38; www.aquarium-tregastel.com. Open Apr–June and Sept, daily, 1000–1200, 1400–1800; July and Aug, daily, 1000–1900; Oct and school winter holidays, 1400–1700.

Like the boulders of Sentier des Douaniers, the grotesques of Trégastel also have names: 'the skull', 'King Gradlon', even 'the stack of *crêpes*'. Coz-Pors is the livelier of the two beaches with a children's club, windsurfing and other watersports facilities, as well as a salt-water swimming pool and fitness centre. The caves beneath the granite outcrop at the far end of the beach are now an **aquarium** with lobsters, crayfish, bass and conger eels from Breton waters, including fish from the Mediterranean. A 30sq-m model of the coast with film and commentary explains the action of the tides. Outside, steps lead to a statue of Père Eternal (God the Father), a reminder that the caves once served as a chapel.

Accommodation in Trégastel-Plage

Bellevue €€€ *20 rue des Calculots; tel: 02 96 23 88 18; fax: 02 96 23 89 91; e-mail: Bellevue.Tregastel@wanadoo.fr; www.hotelbellevuetregastel.com.* Smart, comfortable hotel with beautiful garden and sea views.

Hôtel de la Mer €€ *Plage de Coz-Pors; tel: 02 96 15 60 00; fax: 02 96 15 31 11; e-mail: hoteldelamer.tregastel@laposte.net.* Small, modern hotel looking out on to a popular beach.

TREGUIER

i Tréguier Tourist Information 67 rue Ernest Renan; tel: 02 96 92 22 33; fax: 02 96 92 95 11; e-mail: ot-pays-de-treguier@wanadoo.fr; www.paysdetreguier.com

P Place de la République, rue Dr Carrel, Port.

market Market every Wednesday in the central square and the port.

This charming hillside town, overlooking the Jaudy and Guindry rivers, was founded in the 6th century by the Welsh monk Tugdual. It is better known as the last resting place of St Yves, patron saint of lawyers, who is still commemorated in an annual *pardon*.

Tréguier Cathedral dates mainly from the 14th and 15th centuries and can stand comparison with any in Brittany. Look up from the delicate stone tracery of the south porch to the Flamboyant Gothic window and the unusual spire, added in the 18th century. (The perforations – designed to improve wind resistance – give it a moth-eaten appearance.)

Inside, beneath a recess in the vaulted nave of pink granite, crowds still gather around the tomb of St Yves to light candles and make other votive offerings. The tomb in the adjoining chapel belongs to Jean V, Duke of Brittany. Also worth looking out for are the wood carvings on the Renaissance choir stalls, polychrome statues dating from the 13th to 17th centuries, a bronze reliquary containing the skull of St Yves, and the cloisters from where there are good views of the Hastings tower, the only part of the original Romanesque cathedral to survive.

Tréguier has its fair share of half-timbered houses – the finest examples are on place des Halles. Equally picturesque is rue St-Yves and the former choir school of La Psalette, dating from 1447. In the centre of place du Martray is a statue of Ernest Renan, noted philosopher and historian whose *Life of Jesus* denied the divinity of Christ, causing a sensation when it first appeared in 1863. The beautiful 16th-century house where Renan was born is now a museum and is worth a look, even if you don't wish to venture in. It's a short walk from here to the old port on the banks of the River Jaudy; in medieval times there were boat-building yards here as well as a lively trade in wine, cereals and cloth. On the other side of town is the wooded Bois du Poète (once part of the bishop's garden); there is a picnic area here overlooking the Guindy. You may also notice the religious monument known as the Calvaire de la Protestation, erected in 1904, one year after the statue to Renan, by indignant Catholics hostile to his views.

Just outside Tréguier is the attractive village of Minihy-Tréguier. During the annual Grand Pardon of St Yves on the third Sunday of May there is a colourful procession from Tréguier Cathedral to the chapel of the Manor of Kermartin, the birthplace of the great man.

Below
Tréguier Cathedral

Musée des Arts et Traditions Populaires € *Square Fichet-des-Grèves, Binic; tel: 02 96 73 37 95. Open July and Aug, daily, 1430–1800; mid-Apr–May and Sept, closed Tue.*

Jardin Zoologique de Bretagne €€ *www.zoo-tregomeur.com. Café, picnic area, children's playground and facilities for babies. Due to re-open mid-2007.*

Saint Yves

When Yves de Kermartin was 14 years old, in 1267, his parents sent him to study at the University of Paris. After graduating in philosophy, theology and canon law he returned to Brittany in 1280 and began practising as a judge in the church courts at Rennes. Recalled to serve in his native Tréguier by the local bishop, Yves was ordained a priest and was eventually appointed rector of Louannec. Following the death of his parents, he turned the family estate over to the poor and infirm for use as a hospice. Yves' saintly reputation stemmed largely from his willingness to champion the cause of widows, orphans and other disadvantaged without charging a fee. He was canonised by Pope Clement VI in 1347, only 44 years after his death.

Accommodation and food in Tréguier

L'Auberge du Trégor € *3 rue St Yves; tel: 02 96 92 32 34.* Seafood specialities. English spoken.

Crêperie des Halles € *16 rue Renan; tel: 02 96 92 39 15.* Pancakes made the traditional Breton way. Specialities include crab and mussels in cream.

Hôtel L'Estuaire € *Sur les Quais; tel: 02 96 92 30 25; fax: 02 96 92 94 80.* Reasonably priced rooms and splendid estuary views. Restaurant.

Poissonnerie Moulinet € *2 rue Ernest Renan; tel: 02 96 92 30 27.* Reasonably priced fish restaurant with takeaway service.

Also worth exploring

The French Tourist Board has signposted a clifftop route known as the **Circuit des Falaises** which follows the Goëlo Coast west of St-Brieuc (the Goëlo were medieval counts). A procession of stark windswept headlands – Pointe de Bilfot, Pointe de Minard and Pointe Berjule – leads inexorably to the cliffs at Plouha, the highest in Brittany at 104m and the nesting ground for large seabirds such as the shag, fulmar and raven.

St-Quay-Portrieux is a lively family resort with good beaches, a large new marina and a plentiful supply of cafés, restaurants, bars and discos. Tourism has not blighted the charming little port of **Binic** to the south where a small museum recalls the perilous voyages to the coast of Newfoundland undertaken by local fishermen in the 19th century.

Inland from Binic is the **Trégomeur wildlife park** (Jardin Zoologique), where big cats, antelopes, kangaroos, ring-tailed lemurs and other exotic animals exist in the microclimate peculiar to this sheltered valley. The park is due to re-open in improved form in mid-2007.

It's worth going out of your way to see the magnificent artwork in two 15th-century churches. The walls of **Kermaria-an-Iskuit** (Our

Left
Tréguier town gate

Lady, restorer of health), west of Plouha, are covered with frescoes depicting a *danse macabre* in which skeletons and corpses lead a motley crew of kings, cardinals, ploughboys and peasants to meet their maker. At **Notre-Dame-du-Tertre** in **Châtelaudren** (the ancient capital of Goëlo), another medieval artist has set to work with a vengeance, juxtaposing episodes from the Bible with scenes from the lives of St Marguerite, St Fiacre and Mary Magdalene on 132 brilliantly coloured ceiling panels.

Suggested tour

Total distance: 150km (180km with detours).

Time: 3 hours' driving. Allow 8 hours for the main route, 12 hours with detours. (If you have children you might find yourself spending longer at the Pleumeur-Bodou museum or the Amoripark.) Extra half days should be allocated for excursions to the islands. Those with limited time should concentrate on the coast between Tréguier and Locquirec.

Links: This route links with Morlaix (*see page 59*) and the Parish closes in the west (*see pages 54–67*).

From **PAIMPOL** ❶ take the D789 north to the Ploubazlanec Peninsula; outside the village a neat row of plaques commemorates the 2000 fishermen who lost their lives at sea between 1852 and 1935. Take a right turn here for the fishing port of Porz-Aven and **La Croix des Veuves**. Return to the D789 and continue to **Pointe de l'Arcouest** where ferries embark for the idyllic **ILE DE BREHAT** ❷. To continue the drive take the road down the west side of the peninsula to the suspension bridge at Lezardrieux.

Detour: After crossing the bridge, turn south on to the D787 for **LA ROCHE-JAGU** ❸. Return to the D786.

Take the D786 to **TREGUIER** ❹. From here follow the coast road on to the windswept Plougrescant Peninsula, also known as the Côte des Ajoncs from the gorse which gilds the heathland in spring and summer. Just outside **Plougrescant** is the church of St Gonery, the wooden steeple balanced at a jaunty angle on the 10th-century tower. Follow the signs to **Pors-Hir** where you'll see a photogenic granite cottage wedged between two gigantic boulders. After enjoying the fine sea views at Point du Château, continue round the coast to **Port-Blanc**. Perched on a rocky outcrop in the bay is a tiny 16th-century watchtower. Several kilometres beyond the sandy beach at Trévon-Tréguignec is the junction with the D6. Turn right here for **PERROS-GUIREC** ❺. Leave the town on the D788, the remarkable coastal road known as the **Corniche Bretonne**. You can park your car at one of a number of designated viewing points and look down on the busy resorts of **PLOUMANAC'H** ❻ and **TREGASTEL** ❼.

Rochers €€€ *Plage St-Guirec, Ploumanac'h; tel: 02 96 91 44 49; e-mail: hoteldesrochers@ wanadoo.fr.* This exclusive hotel/restaurant overlooking the coast serves rich seafood dishes, including lobster. Booking essential.

Forum de Trégastel *Plage du Coz-Pors; tel: 02 96 15 30 44; fax: 02 96 23 86 65; www.forum-tregastel.com. Open daily.* Sauna, Jacuzzi, gymnasium, fitness suite, aquagym, relaxation and ionisation room and pool with fountains, underwater jets etc.

Just offshore (and linked to the mainland by a causeway) is **Ile Grande**, the tiny island where Joseph Conrad wrote his novel *The Nigger of the Narcissus*. **Trébeurden**, a popular resort with several good sandy beaches, is famous for Père Trébeurden, an eroded rock resembling the head of a giant. Leave the town on the D6. At **PLEUMEUR-BODOU** ❽ turn left on to the D21, then right to visit the telecommunications museum. Return on the D21 to **LANNION** ❾.

Detour: 20km south of **Lannion** on the D767 is **Amoripark**, a compulsory stopover for families with young children. The amusements here include indoor and outdoor swimming pools, pedal boats, trampolines, inflated castles, a small farm and mini-golf among other activities. You will also find a picnic area, café and restaurant.

From Lannion the D88 follows the estuary of the River Léguer. After **ST-MICHEL-EN-GREVE** ❿ take the D786 to **St-Efflam**, then the **CORNICHE DE L'ARMORIQUE** ⓫ (D42 becoming D64) as far as Moulin de la Riys. Turn right here and continue along the scenic coast road – a designated *'route touristique'*. After about 7km turn left to the village of **St-Jean-du-Doigt** – St John of the Finger, named after a relic of St John the Baptist kept in the church. The parish close has an exquisite Renaissance fountain with stone carvings depicting the baptism of Christ.

Return to the coast road, passing through **Plougasnou** on the way to **Pointe de Primel**, a beautiful promontary with commanding views of the Baie de Lannion. To the east are the sands of **Primel-Trégastel bay**, to the west the fishing ports of **le Digbden** and **Terenez**. Continue southwards to Kergaradec where a right turn leads to the small Kernéhélden peninsula and the 6500-year-old **Tumulus de Barnenez**, a burial chamber 72m long, comprising two stone mounds encircled by terracing. For safety reasons most of the chambers and passages inside are sealed.

Also worth exploring

This route introduces some of the inland villages, châteaux and sights of the region. South of Lannion on the D88 is **Ploumillau** and the 17th-century **church of St-Milliau**. It contains some wonderful artwork including painted wooden panels illustrating scenes from the Life of Christ and a macabre statue of Ankou, the Breton representation of death, wielding in one hand a scythe to cut down the living and in the other a spade to bury them. Continue on the D88, then turn right on to the D38 to Lanvellec and the imposing **Château de Rosanbo**. The rooms, decorated in the traditional Breton style with Trégorrois furniture, include a magnificent 18th-century library, while the garden, designed by Achille Duchêne, features one of the longest arched hornbeam hedges in France.

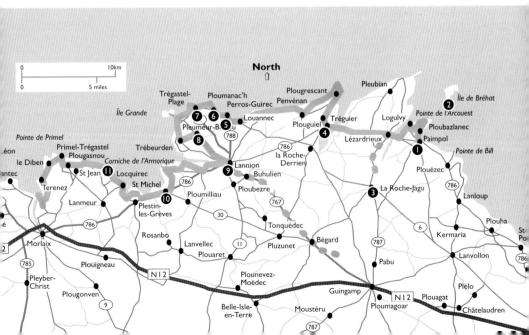 **Château de Rosanbo** €€

Lanvellec; tel: 02 96 35 18 77; www.rosanbo.net. Open Apr, May, June, daily, 1400–1700; July and Aug, daily, 1100–1830; Sept and Oct, Sun, 1400–1700. Guided tours of castle take approximately 45 minutes.

Château de Kergrist

€€ Ploubezre; tel: 02 96 38 91 44. Open June–Sept, daily, 1100–1830; Easter and May, weekends, 1400–1800.

Château de Tonquédec

€ Tonquédec; tel: 02 96 47 18 47. Open July and Aug, daily, 1000–2000; Apr–June and Sept, daily, 1500–1900; Oct, Sat and Sun, 1400–1800.

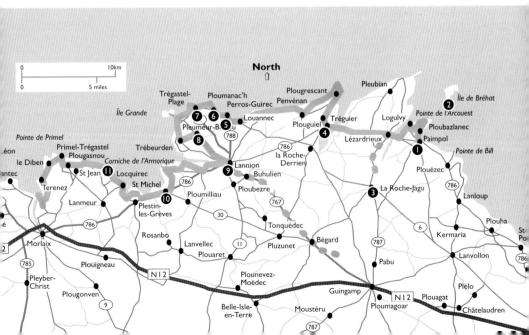 **Chambre d'Hote Anne and Greg** €€

Bell-Isle-en-Terre; tel: 02 96 43 09 94; e-mail: greane@wanadoo.fr; www.biet.info. Cosy, British-run bed and breakfast inn with three rooms.

From Lanvellec take the D22 to the picturesque town of **Belle-Isle-en-Terre**, a good place to stop for lunch. As the D22 leaves the town it follows the River Légeur through the beeches and oaks which mark the edge of the **Forêt du Coat an Hay**. At the D31 turn north to the hamlet of Pen-an-Stang. Take the right fork, then, just before the N12 turn right on to the D712. The first turning on the left is the steep road to **Menez-Bré**. This isolated hill, shimmering with gorse throughout the summer, rises to a height of 150m above the Trégor plateau. There are magnificent views on a clear day from the chapel of St Hervé on the summit.

Return to the D31 and continue heading north to Pluzunet to join the D30. At the junction with the D11 turn right and, after 1km, right again to visit **Kergrist**, a 16th-century château with an attractive garden and an outlook on the Monts d'Arrée. The next right turn on the D11 leads to the impressive ruins of the **Château de Tonquedec** – the curtain walls and towers still dominating the Léguer valley as they have done for 800 years.

After leaving the castle, return in the direction of the D11, then follow the signs to the village of **Kerfons** where the beautiful 15th-century chapel contains an exquisite wooden rood screen with intricate carvings of the saints. From Kerfons return to the D11 and follow the signs to Lannion.

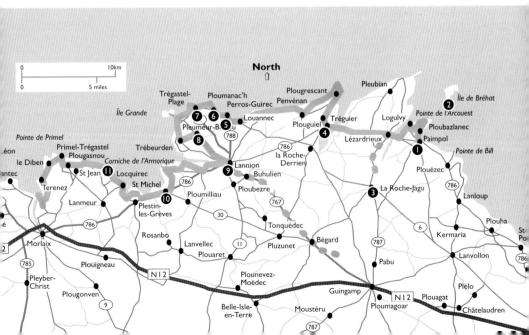

The Lac de Guerlédan

Ratings

Heritage	●●●●●
Outdoor activities	●●●●●
Scenery	●●●●●
Wildlife	●●●●●
Walking	●●●●○
Children	●●●○○
History	●●●○○
Markets	●●●○○

From the ancient Forêt de Quénécan, still teeming with bird and animal life, to the spectacular gorges created by the Daoulas and Blavet rivers – Lac de Guerlédan is surrounded by stunning landscapes. There are hiking trails past abandoned watermills, wayside chapels, fountains and attractive picnic areas, and other attractions include watersports at le Rond Point or Beau Rivage, an industrial museum at les Forges des Salles, a ruined abbey and lock at Bon-Repos and the inland resort of Mûr-de-Bretagne, where you'll find hotels, campsites and *pensions*.

Lac de Guerlédan was created in the 1930s when the dam finally killed off the declining goods traffic on the Nantes-Brest Canal. This impressive waterway was created early in the 19th century by Napoleon. Two towns in one, Pontivy has a castle, historic houses, a colourful market and a 'new town' built by Napoleon as a military base and regional capital with imposing avenues which still bear the names of his victories.

ABBAYE DE BON REPOS

Abbaye de Bon Repos (shows €€€)
Tel: 02 96 24 82 20; e-mail: abbaye@bon-repos.com; www.bon-repos.com. Open mid-June–mid-Sept, daily, 1100–1900; rest of the year groups only.

Founded in 1184 by Vicomte Alain de Rohan, this Cistercian monastery has had a chequered history. Rebuilt in the 14th century, it was given another face-lift in the 18th before being ransacked and partly demolished during the Revolution. Renovation began in 1986 and is continuing with European funding, and help from various local sponsors. During the summer the main façade of the abbey provides a suitably imposing backdrop for a sound-and-light pageant. There's a fruit and vegetable market on Sunday mornings and organised walks from the information point.

LES FORGES DES SALLES

This fascinating open-air museum of local industrial history occupies a former iron-and-steel works at the edge of the Fôret de Quénécan. The

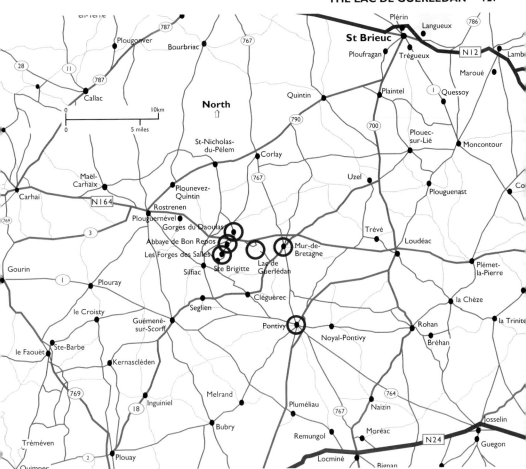

Les Forges des Salles €€
Tel: 02 96 24 90 12;
www.lesforgesdessalles.com.
Open July and Aug, daily,
1400–1830;
other times by prior
arrangement only.

village comprises more than 30 buildings in a verdant setting among ponds and garden terraces, the neat row of blacksmiths' cottages a reminder that this was once a community as well as a factory. One of the cottages has been restored to its 19th-century appearance and you can also visit the imposing iron-master's house, the smithy, the smelting furnaces, the joiner's workshop, the village school, the canteen and the accounts office.

GORGES DU DAOULAS

The gorges suffered severe deforestation during the devastating storm of 1987, but today young birch trees are again springing up among the tangle of gorse and heather and the site has lost none of its drama as the River Daoulas rushes through the jagged cliffs of schist and quartzite to join the Blavet at the bottom of the valley.

Lac de Guerledan

ℹ **Mur-de-Bretagne Tourist Information** *Place de l'Église; tel: 02 96 26 31 37; fax: 02 96 26 35 31.* In summer there are also information points at St-Aignan (La Maison de Pays), Gouarec (ancienne gare) and Bon-Repos.

🏊 All kinds of sports and leisure activities are catered for. The best places to swim around the lake are Caurel (Beau Rivage), Rond-Point du Lac, Landroannec (Mur-de-Bretagne), Anse de Sordan and Roc'h Trégnanton (St-Gelven). There's an indoor swimming pool with sauna and solarium at le bout du pont Plélauff, Gouarec; *tel: 02 96 24 86 15.*

For watersports (skiing, windsurfing, canoes, kayaks, pedalos, boats) head for Beau Rivage (Caurel) or le Rond-Point (Mur-de-Bretagne or contact tourist information).

There are tennis courts in Caurel, Cléguerec, Mur-de-Bretagne, St-Aignan and horse riding at Chevaux du Lac, Trevejean, Mur-de-Bretagne. Details from local tourist offices.

The 400-hectare reservoir between Gouarec and Mûr-de-Bretagne is the largest artificial lake in Brittany and boasts some of the region's finest inland scenery. Constructed between 1923 and 1930, the **Barrage de Guerlédan** (open for guided tours *tel: 02 97 27 51 39*), is 45m high, 206m long and sufficiently strong to hold back 110,000 cubic metres of water. Windsurfing, canoeing and other watersports are organised from **le Rond-Point** at the eastern end of the lake. The holiday complex at **Beau-Rivage** offers water-skiing, swimming, mini-golf, pedalos and a children's play area, as well as camping and hotel accommodation. Guerlédan is equally well suited to hiking and country walks. To the south is the **Forêt de Quénécan**, the remains of primeval woodland known as the Argoat. It extends for more than 3000 hectares and supports beeches, oaks, pines, yews and holly, as well as around 70 species of nesting birds, deer and wild boar.

St-Aignan is a good starting point for walks; in the 15th-century church there are beautiful medieval wood carvings of the Trinity and the Tree of Jesse. At the edge of the forest is a little creek known as the **Anse de Sordan** with a restaurant overlooking the lake and places to picnic. Another good picnic spot is by the lock-keeper's house at the **Ecluse de Bon-Repos** where an old corbelled bridge spans the Blavet river.

Accommodation and food in Lac de Guerlédan

Anse de Sordan €€€ *Tel: 02 97 27 52 36. Open Apr–Oct.* Fish restaurant with set menus as well as à la carte dishes. Camping and canoe hire.

Camping Nautic International €€ *Route de Beau Rivage, Caurel; tel: 02 96 28 57 94; fax: 02 96 26 02 00; e-mail: contact@campingnautic.fr.st; www.campingnautic.fr.st. Open Apr–Sept.* Luxury campsite on the shores of the lake with swimming pools, tennis, video etc.

Hôtellerie de l'Abbaye de Bon-Repos €€€ *Bon-Repos-en-St-Gelven; tel: 02 96 24 98 38; fax: 02 96 24 97 80. Logis* with restaurant, terrace and a wonderful setting overlooking the canal and the forest.

Le Relais du Lac €€ *Caurel RN 164; tel: 02 96 67 11 00; fax: 02 96 67 11 09; e-mail: relaisdulaccaurel@wanadoo.fr.* Reasonably priced rooms and family restaurant near the lake.

Getting out of the car

Distance: 10.2km.

Time: 3 hours.

This lakeside walk starts behind the 15th-century church in **St-Aignan**. Leave the village and take the little path to the right, then continue towards the **Barrage** with views of the dam and the Guerlédan

Opposite
Chapelle Ste-Suzanne, Mur-de-Bretagne

Boats: For excursions on the lake, *tel: 02 96 28 52 64; www.guerledan.com*

lock. Follow the sloping, stony path along the side of the hill to the lakeside, then into the forest as far as the chapel at Ste-Tréphine (1897), which stands on the site of Castel Finans, an ancient fortified camp. There's a picnic area here. Continue through the forest, then, about 100m beyond the chapel, turn left down the hill to see the St-Trémeur fountain before returning to the main path. From here there are more views of the lake and the holiday complex of Beau-Rivage on the opposite bank. Head now for the Maison de la Nature, then take a left to the hamlet of la Carrière Botlan. Continue as far as the water tower then take a sharp right and follow the signs back to town.

Mur-de-Bretagne

Situated just off the N164, this pleasant holiday resort makes a good touring base for the Lac de Guerlédan area and is especially handy for the facilities at le Rond-Point. Apart from the Barrage there's nothing of importance to see except the 16th-century **Chapelle Ste-Suzanne** which lies just outside the town in a pretty woodland setting. Inside, the 18th-century painted ceiling has now been restored but it was the chapel's location which captivated Camille Corot, the 19th-century artist.

Accommodation and food in Mur-de-Bretagne

Auberge Grand'Maison €€ *1 rue Léon le Cerf; tel: 02 96 28 51 10; fax: 02 96 28 52 30; www.auberge-grand-maison.com.* Classy village inn with an enterprising restaurant. Some of the rooms are on the small side.

Les Blés d'Or € *17 place de l'Eglise; tel: 02 96 26 04 89. Closed Mon.* Reliable *crêperie* near the tourist office, popular with visitors and locals alike.

Rond-Point du Lac €€ *Tel: 02 96 26 01 90. Open mid-June–Sept.* Large municipal campsite with excellent facilities.

PONTIVY

This cheerful market town is steeped in history. Founded by Ivy, a monk who built the first bridge over the River Blavet in the 7th century (hence Pont-Ivy), it became the ancestral seat of the Rohan family in 1485 when Viscount Jean II built the castle at the north end of town. Under Napoléon, Pontivy became the military and administrative capital of Brittany. An imposing new town, Napoléonville, was grafted on to the old one and Pontivy's strategic importance increased with the construction of the Nantes–Brest canal.

A long avenue connects Pontivy with its most illustrious landmark. The **Château de Rohan** dates from the 15th to 18th centuries; it's a formidable structure with ramparts 20m high, two massive stone bastions and a dry moat. Some of the rooms inside the castle are used for temporary exhibitions. In the **Old Town**, the half-timbered cloth merchants' houses on the pedestrianised **rue du Fil** and **rue du Pont** are well worth a look. Number 14 rue du Pont belonged to the Sénéchal, the keeper of the Rohan family's estates; Renaissance in style, it dates from 1577. The house was also a meeting point for pilgrims heading for the Spanish shrine of Santiago de Compostella, hence the shell emblem sculpted on the façade (shells were worn as a badge of pilgrimage). Between the two streets is the market square, **place du Martray**. Vegetables are sold here every day and there's a fruit and flower market on Mondays. A little lower down, on place Anne de Bretagne, is the **Basilica of Notre-Dame-de-Joie**. Commissioned in 1536 by the bishop of Cornouaille (another scion of the Rohan family),

Above
The market town of Pontivy

THE LAC DE GUERLEDAN

Information *61 rue
Général de Gaulle; tel: 02 97
25 04 10; fax: 02 97 27 87
09; www.bfi.fr/pontivy.*
Guided tours set out from
this former leprosy
hospital in July and Aug.
The helpful staff also has
lists of accommodation
and information on hiking,
horse-riding, bike hire and
cycle routes.

P Place Aristide Briand
(New Town), Palais
des Congrès (near the
tourist office).

**Château des
Rohan** € *Tel: 02 97
25 04 10. Open July and
Aug, daily, 1030–1900; rest
of the year, Mon–Sat,
1400–1800.*

Market every Monday
on place du Martray
and place Aristide Briand.

**Canoe and kayak
hire:** Base
**nautique de
Toulboubou** *Tel: 02 97
25 09 51.* **Fishing:
Maison de la Pêche** *Ilôt
des Récollets; tel: 02 97 25
39 06.*

**Bike rental: M
Lamouric,** *1 rue
Clémentel; tel: 02 97 25
03 46.*

Eté Musical: Jazz,
folk and classical
concerts at various
locations in July and Aug.

The **Pardon of Notre-
Dame-de-Joie** takes
place on 12 Sept or the
nearest Sun following.

the church was originally dedicated to St Ivy but took its new title in
1696 when an outbreak of dysentery abated following appeals to the
Virgin Mary. There's an annual *pardon* in September.

Napoléon designed the **New Town** on a grid pattern with broad,
tree-lined avenues and spacious squares. The architecture, though, is
austere and lacks the easygoing grace and charm of its older
counterpart. Typical examples are the **Mairie** (Town Hall) and the
Maison Napoléonienne on rue Carnot. Tellingly, the main square,
now **place Aristide-Briand**, was originally a parade ground.

Accommodation and food in Pontivy

Hôtel l'Europe €€€ *12 rue François Mitterrand; tel: 02 97 25 11 14; fax: 02
97 25 48 04; e-mail: contact@hotellerieurope.com; www.hotellerieurope.com.*
Very well-appointed and decorated with a profusion of colourful flowers;
stylish restaurant.

Hôtel le Porhoët €€ *41 rue Général de Gaulle; tel: 02 97 25 34 88; fax:
02 97 25 57 17.* Comfortable rooms with easy access to the Old Town.

La Pommeraie €€ *17 quai du Couvent; tel: 02 97 25 60 09; fax: 02 97 25
75 93. Closed Sun evenings and Mon.* The best of Breton cuisine drawing
on the finest agricultural produce.

Suggested tour

Total distance: 104km (154km with detours).

Time: 2½ hours' driving. Allow 6 hours for the main route but an
additional 3 hours if you intend to stop at any of the points around
the Lac de Guerlédan. Those with limited time should concentrate on
Pontivy and the area around the lake.

Links: The D700 links this central route to St-Brieuc (*see page 158*) in
the north, while the D767 from Pontivy heads south to Vannes (*see
pages 134–41*).

Leave **PONTIVY ❶** on the D764 heading north to the church at
Stival. Take a look at the 16th-century murals of St Mériadoc in the
choir; the saint was reputed to cure headaches and deafness by ringing
a large bronze bell over the heads of his patients! The fine stained glass
by Jehan le Flamant has also survived from the 16th century.

Turn right on to the D15 passing through Cléguérec on the way to
Silfiac, then pick up the D764 again to **Rostrenen**, a pretty
market town built on a hillside. From here take the D31 to **Kergrist
Moëlou**, where the barrel-vaulted ceiling of the imposing 16th-
century church is decorated with portraits of the lords and ladies of
Rostrenen and their families. Turn on to the D87. After a few

kilometres boulders protrude from the undergrowth on either side of the road, heralding the approach of **Gorges de Toul Goulic** and the village of Trémargat. Turn right to the car park from where it's only a ten-minute walk down the steep slope to the point where the River Blavet disappears beneath the boulders.

Take the D87 to **Lanrivain** where the small parish close has a calvary with unusually large stone figures, then follow the D50 across the delightful Faoudel valley to St-Nicolas-du-Pélem. Turn south on to the D5, then take the D95 at Trozulon to Laniscat. From here the D44 passes through the **GORGES DU DAOULAS ❷**. Continue to the junction with the N164 and turn left. After crossing the River Daoulas turn right to the **ABBAYE DE BON REPOS ❸** then follow the D15A to **LES FORGES DES SALLES ❹**.

Detour: The small lane to the hamlet of Ste-Brigitte (10km there and back) offers views of the placid Lake Fourneau on one side and the beech and spruce trees of the **Forêt de Quénécan** on the other.

At Les Forges des Salles take the right fork through the ancient Forêt de Quénécan. After 4km a left turn leads to the Anse de Sordan, a small lakeside beach with views of **LAC DE GUERLEDAN ❺**. If it's too wet for a woodland picnic, there's a popular, if expensive, fish restaurant here. Return to the D15B and continue to **St-Aignan** near the **Barrage de Guerlédan**.

Heading south, take the D35 to **MUR-DE-BRETAGNE ❻**, then the D767 south to Neulliac. The D125 will bring you to **St-Gérand** where nine locks control the water levels of the Nantes–Brest Canal.

Continue past the lakes, pines and chestnut groves of the **Forêt de Brangvily** to **Rohan**, an old town that prospered in the 19th century with the canal trade. Today this picturesque waterway is redundant but forms an attractive ensemble with the lock and the 16th-century chapel of Notre-Dame-de-Bonne-Encontre.

From Rohan take the D2 through **Noyal-Pontivy** where the church has an elegant 15th-century belfry. St Noyale, decapitated by a frustrated Armorican chief whose advances she had refused, is depicted in the stained glass, head in hand. Like St Mériadoc (*see page 131*), she is reputed to cure headaches.

Continue on the D2 to Pontivy.

● Hotel de Rohan €€ 15 place de la Mairie, Rohan; tel: 02 97 51 54 04. Central hotel with restaurant serving gourmand *menus du terroir* as well as cheaper tourist dishes.

L'Argoat € 22 place Pobeguin, Cléguérec; tel: 02 97 38 01 18. Couscous and paella are the specialities here; there is also a takeaway service.

● Maison de la Chouannerie et de la Révolution € 4 place de la Carrière, Moncontour; tel: 02 96 73 49 57. Open June–mid-July 1000–1230, 1430–1830; mid-July–Aug 1000–1830; Sept 1000–1230, 1400–1800.

● Moncontour Market every Monday.

Quintin Market every Tuesday.

Above
Bon Repos

ⓘ Moncontour Tourist Information *4 place de la Carrière; tel: 02 96 73 49 57; fax: 02 96 73 53 78.*

Quintin Tourist Information *6 place 1830; tel: 02 96 74 01 51.*

**ⓘ Château € ** *Tel: 02 96 74 94 79; e-mail: chateaudequintin@club-internet.fr. Open July and Aug, daily, 1000–1830; June and Sept, daily, 1030–1230, 1400–1800; Apr, May & Oct, weekends only, 1400–1700.*

☾ Hôtel du Commerce €€ *2, rue Rochonen; tel: 02 96 74 94 67; www.hotelducommerce.st.fr. Slightly overbearing décor but well-placed. Dependable restaurant.*

Also worth exploring

The road through the hills and valleys of the Forêt de Lorge, north of Mûr-de-Bretagne, makes an attractive drive. The two main centres are the feudal towns of Moncontour and Quintin – both prospered from the boom in the linen industry in the 17th and 18th centuries.

Picturesquely situated on a rocky cliff at the confluence of two rivers, **Moncontour**'s granite terraced houses and steep alleyways rise to the triangular place du Penthièvre and the 16th-century church of St-Mathurin which retains its splendid stained glass. In the **Maison de la Chouannerie et de la Révolution** above the tourist information office you'll find vivid tableaux, re-creating Moncontour's role in the French Revolution. If you happen to be in town on the last Sunday of August, there's all the fun of a medieval fair.

Quintin is a larger town with elegant granite mansions, half-timbered houses and an attractive landscaped park overlooking the River Gouët. The Basilica of Notre-Dame is worth a look. There's a relic of the Virgin's belt (a trophy brought back from Jerusalem by the crusading knights), four water stoups made from huge Javanese shells and a 14th-century font. The **château** dates from the 13th century. There is a guided tour (in French) of the furnished rooms and temporary exhibitions of decorative arts.

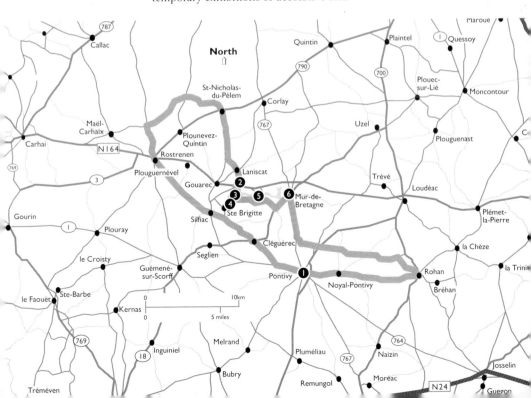

Vannes

Ratings

Architecture	●●●●●
Boats	●●●●●
Food	●●●●●
Heritage	●●●●●
Markets	●●●●●
Cathedrals and churches	●●●○○
Entertainment	●●●○○
Children	●●○○○

This historic town takes its name from the Veneti, a tribe of Celtic seafarers who lost out to the Roman legions of Julius Caesar in the first century BC. During the Middle Ages Vannes was the capital of the kingdom (later the duchy) of Brittany and the Breton parliament continued to meet here long after the Treaty of Union with France was signed in 1532 – the signing ceremony took place in the Château Gaillard, now the Archaeological Museum.

Still one of the liveliest towns in Brittany, Vannes likes to promote its maritime image, even though its commercial prosperity now relies mainly on high-tech industries. The port is the gateway to the Gulf of Morbihan but there are enough attractions in Vannes itself to merit a stay of a day or two. The only drawbacks are the crazy one-way systems skirting the town, and the crowds, which can begin to pall in peak season.

ℹ Vannes Tourist Information *1 rue Thiers; tel: 02 97 47 24 34; fax: 02 97 47 29 49; e-mail: info@tourisme-vannes.com; www.tourisme-vannes.com*

⇄ From Brest, Quimper and Lorient take the N165; from Rennes, take the N166 and N24. Then follow the signs for *Centre Ville.* A number of hotels are also signposted.

🅿 Place de la République or the Port (also handy for the tourist office).

Vieu Vannes

In days gone by Vannes was a fortified city and a 600m stretch of the original ramparts, complete with gates and machicolated watch-towers, still runs along the banks of the little stream known as the Marle. Behind the town walls are clusters of brightly painted half-timbered houses dating from the 15th and 16th centuries with slated overhangs and gabled windows – **place Henri IV** has some of the best examples. The preacher St Vincent Ferrier breathed his last at **No 17 place Valencia** in 1419 – the decorated stone supports were added during the Renaissance, together with the little statue in the niche. In the summer this square is a regular haunt of buskers. On the corner with rue Rogue is the **Maison de Vannes** with its pair of cheeky wooden sculptures known as 'Vannes and His Wife'. There's a lively market on Wednesday and Saturday mornings in and around **place des Lices**, originally an open field used for tournaments and executions. The medieval market took place indoors at **la Cohue**, a

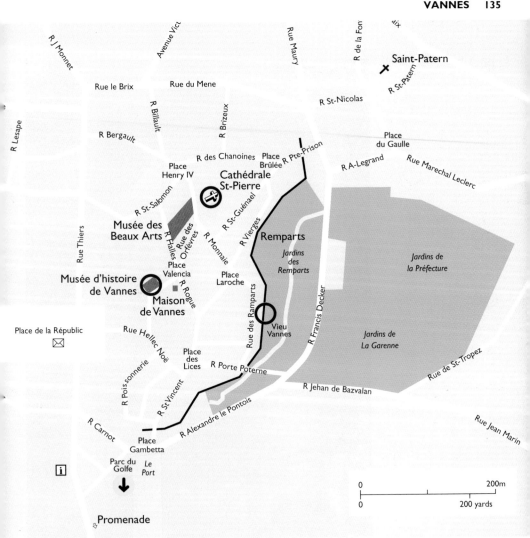

Map of Vannes showing streets including Rue le Brix, Rue du Mene, Rue Maury, R de la Fon, Saint-Patern, R St-Paterm, R St-Nicolas, R J Monnet, Avenue Vict, R Billault, R Bergault, R des Chanoines, Place Brûlée, R Pte-Prison, Place du Gaulle, R A-Legrand, Rue Marechal Leclerc, Place Henry IV, Cathédrale St-Pierre, R Brizeux, R St-Salomon, R Halles, Rue des Orfevres, R Monnaie, R St-Guénael, R Vierges, Remparts, Jardins des Remparts, Jardins de la Préfecture, R Lesape, Rue Thiers, Musée des Beaux Arts, Place Valencia, Place Laroche, Musée d'histoire de Vannes, Maison de Vannes, R Rogue, Rue des Remparts, Vieu Vannes, R Francis Decker, Jardins de La Garenne, Place de la Républic, Rue Hellec Noë, Rue de St-Tropez, Place des Lices, R Porte Poterne, R Jehan de Bazvalan, R Pois-sonnerie, R St-Vincent, R Alexandre le Pontois, R Carnot, Place Gambetta, Rue Jean Marin, Parc du Golfe, Le Port, Promenade, 0 200m, 0 200 yards

**Musée des Beaux
Arts** €€ *9 and 15
place St-Pierre; tel: 02 97 01
63 00. Open mid-June–Sept,
daily, except bank holidays
1000–1800; Oct–mid-June,
daily, except bank holidays,
1330–1800. Guided tours
of the old town take place
on certain days during
May–Sept (for times enquire
at the museum). English
commentary is available.*

wonderful 13th-century building that later served variously as a
prison, a parliament in exile, a revolutionary tribunal and a theatre. It
is currently the **Musée des Beaux Arts** with temporary exhibitions on
the history of the town and a collection of Breton paintings, drawings,
engravings and sculptures.

Cathédrale St-Pierre

Architects have been tinkering with Vannes Cathedral for more than
700 years – and it shows. The exterior is impressive enough, especially
the 13th-century north tower overlooking place St-Pierre. Inside
though, where the mélange of styles is more obvious, it's a different
story: note the extraordinary giant pillars crowned by urns at the nave

⊙ Boat excursions:
Vannes is the most convenient touring base for exploring the **Golfe du Morbihan**. Boats leave from the Gare Maritime, 1.6km from place Gambetta, at the far end of the Promenade de la Rabine. The most popular excursions are to Ile d'Arz and Ile aux Moines.

Several companies run excursions round the Gulf of Morbihan and ferries to the offshore islands:

Compagnie des Iles (*tel: 02 97 46 18 19*); *e-mail: cie-iles@wanadoo.fr; www.compagniedesiles.com* advertises Gulf cruises with commentary and optional stop-overs on Iles aux Moines and Ile d'Arz.

Navix (*tel: 08 25 13 21 00*); *e-mail: info@navix.fr; www.navix.fr* offers tours of the Gulf, with stops at Ile aux Moines and Ile d'Arz; alternatively, more expensive lunch and dinner cruises around the 42 islands depart from Vannes, Port Navalo, Locmariaquer, Auray and La Trinité-sur-Mer.

ⓘ Trésor de la Cathédrale € *Open June–Sept, Mon–Sat, 1030–1800; Oct, Mon–Fri, 1400–1800.*

Above
Porte St-Vincent

Opposite
The riverside lavoirs (wash houses) in Vannes

crossing. You'll find evidence of the local cult of St Vincent Ferrier in the gloomy 19th-century paintings in the north transept and in the rotunda chapel where the preacher is buried. The mummified finger of Blessed Pierre Rogue, guillotined for his beliefs during the Revolution, is exhibited for veneration in the 15th-century Chapelle du Rosaire. Behind the high altar is the **Trésor de la Cathédrale** (treasury) where you can see a fine collection of gold-worked chalices, monstrances, ciboria and other precious religious objects dating back to the Middle Ages. Pride of place belongs to the exquisite 13th-century wedding chest decorated with painted scenes of knightly romance.

ⓘ Musée d'histoire de Vannes € 2 *rue Noé; tel: 02 97 01 63 00. Open mid-June–Sept, 1000–1800.*

Aquarium de Vannes €€ *Tel: 02 97 40 67 40; www.aquariumdevannes.com. Open July and Aug, daily, 0900–1900; Apr, June & Sept, daily, 1000–1200, 1400–1830; Oct–Mar, Wed–Sun, 1400–1800.*

Jardin aux Papillons €€ *Tel: 02 97 40 67 40; www.jardinauxpapillons.com. Open July and Aug, daily, 1000–1800; Apr, May, June & Sept, 1400–1800.*

Captaine d'un Jour €€ *Tel: 02 97 40 40 39. Call for hours or ask at the tourist office.*

Musée d'histoire de Vannes

Housed in the Château Gaillard, a magnificent 15th-century mansion with painted roof beams on one floor and 17th-century wood panelling on another, is one of the world's finest collections of artefacts from the Stone, Bronze and Iron ages. All the finds, which include axe-heads, swords, rings, necklaces, ingots, engraved knife sheaths, urns and cineraries come from sites in Morbihan. Among the museum's other treasures are ceramics, statues and mosaics from the Gallo-Roman period, medieval jewellery boxes, Aubusson tapestries, 17th-century paintings and an assortment of weapons.

Parc du Golfe

There are three excellent attractions within the confines of this leisure complex on the edge of Vannes, near the Gare Maritime. Sharks, giant groupers, piranhas, electric eels and a 2.5m-long saw fish are among the prize exhibits of the **Aquarium de Vannes** which boasts the best collection of tropical fish in Europe, a kaleidoscope of colour with each of the 50 or so tanks re-creating its own discrete marine environment.

Equally eye-catching is the **Jardin aux Papillons** where thousands of butterflies from exotic locations (including Madagascar, New Guinea and the Philippines) flutter randomly among banana and coffee trees, sometimes landing in the cupped hands of visitors. You can watch chrysalises develop in the hatchery and there are terrariums for observing crickets and – if you're not squeamish – giant trap-door spiders.

Insights into the long maritime history of Vannes can be acquired from **Captaine d'un Jour**, a still-evolving conceptual museum with models and reconstruction spread across a 600-sq m space.

The Parc du Golfe also has one of the largest bowling alleys in France, as well as pool and snooker tables (open daily).

Accommodation and food

Vannes suffers from a dearth of good quality accommodation and in season the hotels in the centre of town may be fully booked for days at a time. If you don't want to reserve a room in advance, it may be worth considering staying in one of the smaller resorts on the Gulf. In Vannes itself the harbour-front hotel on place Gambetta, **Le Marina** €€ *tel: 02 97 47 00 10; fax: 02 97 47 00 34* is the first to show *complet* (full) signs.

Hôtel Manche Océan €€€ *31 rue Colonel Maury; tel: 02 97 47 26 46; fax: 02 97 47 30 86; e-mail: info@manche-ocean.com; www.manche-ocean.com.* Lacks character but the rooms are comfortable and it's only a short walk to the old town.

Left
Old timbered houses in Vannes

⊙ There's a general market every Wednesday and Saturday morning with a number of stalls selling Breton produce, including honey, cakes, salted butter and *lait ribot* (sour milk). There's an equally good fish market every morning (Tue–Sat) in the hall on place de la Poissonnerie.

Business Corner 8 *rue de Closmadeuc* produces personalised T-shirts (you provide the photo, design and text).

Clipper 16 *rue St-Salomon; www.clipper-marine.com* sells ornaments and gifts on a nautical theme.

◐ **Festival de Jazz à Vannes (July)** International and local artists.

Fêtes d'Arvor (mid-August) Three days of celebrations including folklore events, processions, competitions, fireworks etc.

Fêtes historiques de Vannes (July) Sound-and-light show based on key events in Breton history. Further information from the tourist office.

St Vincent Ferrier

Born in Valencia of a Spanish mother and an English father, St Vincent Ferrier was a Dominican friar who toured Europe as an itinerant preacher healing the sick. His reputation as a miracle worker earned him extraordinary popularity but he was also a firebrand whose revivalist sermons led not only to mass conversions, but to frenzied acts of violence against the Jews and other minorities. A confessor to popes, St Vincent played an important role in ending the Great Schism between Rome and Avignon. When he died in 1419 while preaching in Brittany the people of Vannes refused to hand over his body and he was eventually buried in the cathedral.

Mercure Aquarium Hotel €€€ 19 *rue Daniel Gilard Le Parc du Golfe; tel: 02 97 40 44 52; fax: 02 97 63 03 20. A quality logis,* handy for the port as well as the entertainment complex.

Just outside Vannes on an attractive little peninsula in the Gulf of Morbihan is **Hôtel le Roof** €€€ *Presqu'île de Conleau; tel: 02 97 63 47 47; fax: 02 97 63 48 10; e-mail: leroof@clubinternet.fr*

Restaurants cluster in the pedestrianised streets off place Henri IV and down by the port (place Gambetta, rue St-Vincent). In July and August if you see somewhere you like during the day, book a table.

Brasserie des Halles € 9 *rue Des halles; tel: 02 97 54 08 34; fax: 02 97 47 80 64.* Good location for an eat-and-run snack or a longer lunch, all at attractive prices.

Le Commodore €€ *rue Pasteur; tel: 02 97 46 42 62. Closed Sun; dinner only Mon and Sat.* Hard to better for fish and seafood fare, and atmosphere.

Le Dragon d'Or € 25 *rue Maréchal Leclerc; tel: 02 97 42 59 21.* Chinese and Vietnamese cuisine, good value.

Le Grain de Sel €€ 13 *rue des Halles; tel: 02 97 54 37 41; e-mail: denis.schmid@free.fr.* Predominantly Breton fare in an atmospheric setting.

A walk through Vannes

Start at **place Gambetta** ❶, a crescent framed by hotels and pavement cafés, constantly thronging with visitors. Yachts are berthed along the canalised river which leads from here to the port and the Gare Maritime. Enter the old town by the **Porte St-Vincent** ❷, then follow the little street to the right until you come to **rue A le Pontois** ❸. To your left are the ramparts, built over the foundations of 4th-century Roman walls. Beneath the **Porte Poterne** ❹, a row of timber-framed wash houses dating from the 17th century overlooks the Marle stream. Continue along **rue Francis Decker** ❺, from where there are fine views of the town and the **Jardin des Remparts** ❻ (originally the moat) with its colourful flowerbeds. At **Porte-Prison** ❼, another of the town gates, turn left into place Brûlée, then continue down **rue St-Guénael** ❽ past the cathedral to **place St-Pierre** ❾. Turn right into **place Henri IV** ❿ then take **rue St-Salomon** ⓫, turning left on to **rue des Halles** ⓬, which leads past the medieval market of **la Cohue** ⓭. Continue into **Place Valencia** ⓮, then take **rue R Rogue** ⓯ into **place des Lices** ⓰. From here follow **rue St Vincent** ⓱ and a line of beautiful 17th-century mansions back to the port.

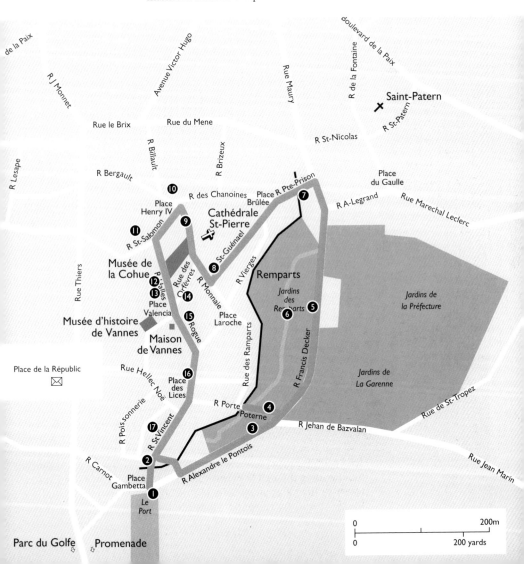

The Gulf of Morbihan

Ratings

Archaeology	●●●●●
Heritage	●●●●●
Scenery	●●●●●
Boats	●●●●○
Children	●●●●○
Watersports	●●●●○
Beaches	●●●○○
History	●●●○○

It's said that there is one island in the gulf for every day of the year – an exaggeration, but a pardonable one. Morbihan means 'little sea', an apt description of this vast, sheltered lagoon measuring 20km across and 15km from the Atlantic to the most distant shoreline. The landscape is not dramatic but impressionistic and varies with the tides. For most of the time the sea laps benignly around the scattering of low-lying rocks and wooded islets, but as the waters recede they reveal a mass of mudbanks interwoven with numerous river channels.

The gulf has been inhabited since prehistoric times and Carnac can lay claim to being one of the world's oldest human settlements. No one should visit the region without taking a look at the mysterious standing stones and burial chambers either here or at Locmariaquer, and the gulf island of Gavrinis.

The beaches in the gulf are better suited to crabbing and shrimping than swimming, and exploring the shoreline on foot can be rewarding. The local tourist office will suggest itineraries, alternatively you can work out your own route using the 120km of signposted footpaths.

ARRADON

This unassuming village, just off the D101 from Vannes to le Bono, merits a look, especially on market days (Tue and Fri) when there's an enticing variety of local produce on sale as well as souvenirs (the hand-painted wooden boats are a bargain). The tourist office produces fact sheets with ideas for walks (maps included) – definitely worth considering as the natural beauty of the area is best appreciated on foot. It's only a five-minute drive to the beach which is safe for swimming as long as you don't mind wading through large quantities of seaweed. There are few places to eat in the village, especially at lunchtime, so a picnic is definitely the best bet if you're planning to spend the day here.

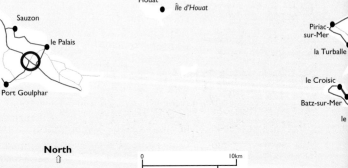

ℹ **Tourist Information**
2 place de l'Eglise,
Arradon; tel: 02 97 44 77
44; fax: 02 97 44 81 22;
e-mail: info.tourisme@
arradon.fr; www.arradon.com

A walk around the Pointe d'Arradon

Distance: 6km.

Time: 2 hours.

Leave place de l'Eglise at the corner of 'Les Logodens' restaurant, then take rue St-Vincent Ferrier to the Chapelle Ste-Barbe. Turn left just after the chapel, then left again along the little Chemin de Ste-Barbe. Go right at the Chemin des Bernaches, which leads down to the sea, and you'll come to the Tour St-Vincent. At low tide follow the footpath along the water's edge, at other times take rue de la Tour Vincent, which joins rue St-Vincent. At the next junction, bear left across the Kérat estate, then take the steps down to the beach. Continue as far as the oyster fisherman's hut, then go back up the steep Kérat path to the **Manoir de Kérat**. Turn left to rejoin rue St-Vincent, then left again, taking the path which leads across the boat park and behind the Les Vénettes hotel. Then follow a low wall to the slipway at the far end of the **Pointe d'Arradon** from where there are views of l'Ile aux Moines (south), l'Ile Irus (west) and the Pen er Men coastline (northwest).

Return to the Pointe footpath and continue between the villas, crossing the parking area, then go left to the bay of Pen Meil. Follow the bay as far as the ruined mill, **Moulin du Paluden**, then climb back on to rue du Paluden. Turn right along the Kervérho footpath. Cross the road leading to the Pointe then turn left on to rue de Pratmer. Take the left fork, rue de la Mairie, in the direction of the church clock tower.

AURAY

🚢 **Goélette St-Sauveur**
€ Promenade du Loch;
tel: 02 97 56 63 38. Open
Apr–Sept, daily, 1030–1230,
1430–1900.

🌙 **Hôtel le Marin** € 1
place du Rolland; tel: 02
97 24 14 58; fax: 02 97 24
39 59; e-mail:
contact@hotel-lemarin;
www.hotel-lemarin.com.
Small, cheap hotel next to
the quai Benjamin Franklin.

Picturesque Auray is a town of two parts. On one side of the River Loch lies the **Quartier St-Goustan**, the old port with cobbled streets and 15th-century half-timbered houses. The American ambassador Benjamin Franklin stayed at No 8 **place St-Sauveur** (now a *crêperie*) in 1776 while on a mission to enlist France's support in the War of Independence from England. The quay named in his honour can be seen to best effect from the Promenade du Loch opposite where a reconstructed schooner, *Goélette St-Sauveur*, is now a museum of local history. Across the medieval stone bridge is the **upper town**, built around a covered market and the 17th-century church of St-Gildas with its fine Renaissance porch. Just to the west of the town, on Kerléano Hill, is a small domed **mausoleum.** This is the burial place of Georges Cadoudal, a local leader of the Chouans (so called because of their signal – the cry of a screech owl). Nine hundred and fifty-three members of this secret society were executed in Auray after a failed insurrection in 1795. Cadoudal escaped to continue his struggle against the Revolution even to the point of plotting to kidnap the Emperor Napoleon. This reckless act brought about his downfall – he was captured and shot in Paris in 1804.

BELLE-ILE

Belle-Ile Tourist Information *Quai Bonnelle, le Palais; tel: 02 97 31 81 93; fax: 02 97 31 56 17; e-mail: contacts@belle.ile.com; www.belle-ile.com*

Bike hire: Velo Fun *34 avenue Carnot Le Palais; tel: 02 97 31 57 48.*

Citadelle Vauban *€€ Le Palais, tel: 02 97 31 84 17. Open July and Aug, daily, 0900–1900; Apr–June, Sept & Oct, daily, 0930–1800.*

Flaubert and Proust, Monet and Matisse, the actress Sarah Bernhardt, King Edward VII, Karl Marx and, latterly, President Mitterand – Belle-Ile has enchanted them all. The island has also been the subject of historical romance: Alexandre Dumas set part of *The Three Musketeers* here following an incident in 1661 when the Marquis de Belle-Ile, Nicholas Fouquet, was arrested by D'Artagnan and his swashbuckling companions on the orders of Louis XIV. Belle-Ile is renowned for its scenic beauty, but before rushing off to enjoy it you should call in at the tourist office for information about the activities on offer (everything from drives and coastal walks to golf, tennis, horse riding, canoeing, surfing and sea fishing).

Belle-Ile's strategic importance (it was highly prized by the English, who occupied it for two years before swapping it for Menorca in 1763) necessitated the building of fortifications. The walls enclosing the main port of **le Palais**, though remarkable enough, date only from the 19th century. Incoming visitors are more likely to be struck by the magnificent **Citadelle**, begun early in the 16th century and completed by Vauban around 1690. The fort was abandoned long ago but it has been well preserved and you are free to explore more or less everything you see: casemates, storerooms, bastions, blockhouses, dungeons and labyrinthine passageways. Belvederes look out on to the sea and there's a small museum on the history of the island.

About 9km from le Palais is **Sauzon**, arguably the prettiest spot on Belle-Ile. The port lies at the mouth of a long estuary and there are two-star camping facilities nearby. You can watch the boats bobbing about in the marina or dine on crab and lobster caught by the local fishermen.

One of the best vantage points on the island is **Pointe des Poulains** with its views of Quiberon, Houat, Hoedic and the Rhuys peninsula. Fort Sarah Bernhardt honours the famous French actress who came here for more than 30 years – the point was her favourite spot and it was here that she would have liked to have been buried.

If you pick up the coastal footpath near **Grotte de l'Apothicairerie**, an enormous vaulted cavern invaded by the sea (take care descending the steps), you can follow it all the way to the islet-studded harbour at **Port Goulphar**. This is the Côte Sauvage, the most impressive stretch of Belle-Ile's 100km coastline. From the nearby **lighthouse** (Grand-Phare) there are good views of the dune-backed sands at **Plage de Donnant** (unsafe for swimming) and the Needles at **Port-Coton**.

Cormorants nest in the rocky crevices of Belle-Ile's southern seaboard and curlews, gannets, terns and choughs (a rarity elsewhere) also make an appearance.

Bathing is safest in the vicinity of Locmaria where there are five beaches, including **Port-An-Dro** and **Grandes Sables**, 2km of the purest white sand. If you don't want to venture too far from le Palais, **Plage de Bourdardoué** is your best bet.

Accommodation and food on Belle-Ile

Moderately priced accommodation is hard to come by in le Palais, but there's plenty of choice in the smaller resorts.

Camping A La Source € *Sauzon; tel: 02 97 31 60 95; fax: 02 97 31 63 52; www.belleile-lasource.com.* Campsite just outside Sauzon.

Hôtel Atlantique €€ *Quai de l'Acadie, le Palais; tel: 02 97 31 80 11; fax: 02 97 31 81 46; e-mail: contact@hotel-atlantique.com; www.hotel-atlantique.com.* Medium-sized hotel near the citadel.

Le Goëland €€ *3 quai, Le Palais; tel: 02 97 31 81 26.* Both the ground-level brasserie and the upstairs restaurant are deservedly popular.

Hôtel Le Phare €€ *Sauzon; tel: 02 97 31 60 36; fax: 02 97 31 63 94.* Scenic hotel with terrace restaurant.

Below and opposite
Prehistoric sites near Carnac

L'Odysséé €€€ *Quai Vauban, le Palais; tel: 02 97 31 43 24.* Views of the Citadelle from the terrace of this traditional fish restaurant.

CARNAC

Carnac Tourist Information 74 *avenue des Druides; tel: 02 97 52 13 52; e-mail: accueiltourisme@carnac.fr; www.carnac.fr*

From Apr to Sept a tourist train links Carnac with la Trinité-sur-Mer, calling at the Alignements de Kerlescan, Kermario and le Menec. For times pick up a leaflet at the tourist office or look at bus stops at Carnac-Plage or in front of the Archéoscope in Carnac town; *tel: 02 97 24 06 29.*

Musée de Préhistoire €€ *10 place de la Chapelle; tel: 02 97 52 22 04; e-mail: info@ museedecarnac.com; www.museedecarnac.com. Open mid-June–mid-Sept, daily, 1000–1230, 1330–1900; mid-Sept–mid-June, 1000–1230, 1330–1800, closed Wed morning.*

The first humans arrived in Carnac more than 7000 years ago and they've been here ever since. A record? It may be. Certainly Carnac is one of the most important prehistoric sites in the world and it trades mercilessly on the fact. The **Alignements**, just outside Carnac Ville, are parallel rows of about 2700 monumental stones (menhirs), spread out over a distance of nearly 4km. Access is restricted although you can still get quite close to the Alignements de Kermario on foot. There are views of the Alignements du Ménec (the largest concentration of stones) from the **Archéoscope**, a rather tacky audio-visual centre otherwise best avoided. Driving into Carnac on the *route des Alignements* (D196) offers another good vantage point, providing you don't mind being held up in traffic. If what you've seen has whetted your appetite, take a look around the **Tumulus de St-Michel**, a large burial mound dating from around 3000 BC, with primitive chambers and passageways – not for the claustrophobic!

To get a proper historical perspective on Carnac and its earliest inhabitants, it's essential to visit the **Musée de Préhistoire**. The presentation is lively and imaginative and there are some wonderful finds: primitive tools including a polished axe-head made from jadeite and a bone awl, exquisite brooches and necklaces, bronze ornaments, pottery, coins and early examples of stone engraving. The voyage of discovery begins in the palaeolithic era, 450,000 years ago, and ends with the arrival of the Celts. The museum shop sells a variety of souvenirs, from books and imitation jewellery to pencils and casts of some of the finds. There's nothing else to see in town but the **parish church** of St-Cornély, patron saint of horned cattle. His painted statue

Horse riding:
Centre Equestre
des Menhirs *Le Manio; tel:
02 97 55 73 45.*

Golf: Parc de Loisirs de
St-Laurent *St-Laurent-en-
Ploemel (18 holes); tel: 02
97 56 85 18.*

Tennis: Tennis Club de
Carnac *Avenue d'Orient
(10 hard courts); tel: 02 97
52 93 53.*

Cycle hire: Cyclo'Hiss
*93 avenue des Druides; tel:
02 97 52 75 08.*

Nightclubs: Le
Petit Bedon *108
avenue des Druides (open
2230–0400); tel: 02 97 52
11 62.* Cinéma Rex *21
avenue Miln; tel: 02 97 52
92 20.*

occupies a niche in one of the walls, along with paintings of the beasts he protects. The vaulted ceiling is also covered with paintings depicting the life of the saint.

The resort of **Carnac-Plage** is the town's other face. The main beach quickly fills up with guests from the surrounding hotels but there are alternatives to east and west, with more secluded coves further afield. The amenities include a yacht club, thalassotherapy centre, children's beach clubs, golf course, tennis courts, cinema, discos and nightclubs. Avenue des Druides, tucked away behind the seafront, is the place to shop and eat.

Accommodation and food in Carnac

Le Bateau Ivre €€€ *70 boulevard de la Plage; tel: 02 97 52 19 55; fax: 02 97 52 84 94.* Decorous hotel with comfortable rooms overlooking the sea (most with balconies), heated outdoor swimming pool and reputable restaurant.

Hôtel du Tumulus €€ *31 rue du Tumulus €€; tel: 02 97 52 08 21; fax: 02 97 52 81 88; www.hotel-tumulus.com.* Excellent *logis* near the Tumulus St-Michel with panoramic views of sea and megaliths, restaurant and heated outdoor pool.

La Plage/La Baie €€ *La Trinité-Sur-Mer; tel: 02 97 55 73 28 or 02 97 55 73 42; fax: 02 97 55 88 81; e-mail: camping@camping-la-baie.com; www.camping-la-baie.com.* Two camping sites just behind the beach with swimming pool, mini-golf, tennis. Reductions out of season.

Megaliths

No one really knows who raised the megaliths. These huge stone slabs are thought to date from between 5000 and 2000 BC when isolated groups of Stone-Age settlers, the predecessors of the Gauls, inhabited this remote area. In a 1979 experiment using wooden rollers, 260 people were required to raise a single 32,000kg stone. The amount of planning, social organisation and sheer physical effort involved in erecting thousands of these menhirs suggests that they must have been of great cultural significance.

Theories abound as to why the stones were erected. One suggests that they were part of a vast observatory used to predict the path of the moon; another for determining the best time for sowing and harvesting. More recently, scholars have argued that they may have been used as boundary posts to mark territory or that they symbolised a rite of passage to the afterlife, in much the same way as the Parish closes. Given the amount of time that has elapsed, it is unlikely that the key to the mystery will ever be found.

ISLANDS OF THE GOLFE DU MORBIHAN

L'Escale En Arz
€€ *Ile d'Arz; tel: 02 97 44 32 15; e-mail: hotel. escale.en.arz@wanadoo.fr; www.restaurant-escale.com.* Restaurant overlooking the jetty. A full meal will set you back a bit but snacks (crudités, chicken and chips etc) are also available and there's excellent chilled draught cider. Rooms available.

There are more than 300 islands in the Gulf. Many are little more than lumps of rock with a generous covering of vegetation while others – the exclusive preserve of French film stars and other glitterati – are exotic paradises. The two main destinations for pleasure cruises are **Ile d'Arz** and **Ile aux Moines**. On Ile d'Arz there's little for tourists apart from shell-strewn beaches, a campsite and a good fish restaurant handily situated near the jetty – **l'Escale En Arz**. If you decide to give Arz a miss it will give you more time on the largest of the islands, **Ile aux Moines**. To call it the 'pearl of the gulf' may be an exaggeration but it's an attractive place with markedly contrasting scenery and a microclimate similar to the Ile de Bréhat on the Granit Rose Coast. Camellias, hortensias, Judas trees and palms all flourish and add more than a dash of colour. There's an information point at the Port de Plaisance and shops, *crêperies* and other amenities 15 minutes' walk away in le Bourg. The nearest beach is only a stone's throw from the jetty, on the far side of the wooded hillock known as the Bois d'Amour, but you may find more seclusion at Plage du Goret, a tree-backed cove 25 minutes' walk from le Bourg. If you want to discover the rest of the island there are signposted walks to a number of local beauty spots and places of interest (ask for the *Perle du Golfe* brochure at the tourist office.)

Ile de Gavrinis is also open to tourists. Here the main attraction is the tumulus, the most impressive of Brittany's prehistoric funereal chambers on account of the fascinating whorls, spirals and other motifs carved on to the stones 5000 years ago. They have been found to match those of the Table des Marchands in Locmariquer and may once have formed part of the same menhir.

PRESQU'ILE DE QUIBERON

Quiberon Tourist Information *14 rue de Verdun; tel: 08 25 13 56 00; e-mail: quiberon@ quiberon.com; www.quiberon.com*

Getting around
From Apr to the end of Sept, daily, a tourist train leaves from the bus stop at place Hoche, Quiberon town on a 50-min tour of local places of interest. For times and further details, *tel: 02 97 24 06 29; www.petittrain-quiberon.com*

To call it 'the most beautiful peninsula in Europe' may be overstating the case but this skeletal finger of land, hanging on to the mainland by a thread, has much to recommend it. **Quiberon** town is the embarkation point for **boat excursions** to Belle-Ile, Ile de Hoedic and Ile de Houat, but it's also a lively seaside resort with a string of bars and hotels as well as a casino, thalassotherapy centre and beachfront cafés. The tourist train (*June to end of September*) is a good way to get orientated and won't eat too much into your day. Alternatively, take a stroll out to **Pointe-de-Conguel** for splendid views of Morbihan and the islands, or watch the yachts racing at Port-Haliguen.

The west coast of the peninsula, known with good reason as the **Côte Sauvage**, is awesome in rough weather when the sea detonates on impact with the cliffs and fierce winds carry the fall-out of spume and spray upwards, stinging the faces of passers-by. Shipwrecks, drownings and other misadventures are commonplace in these

Le Corsaire €€ 24 quai de Belle-Ile, Quiberon; tel: 02 97 50 42 69; fax: 02 97 50 27 61. As well as large helpings of excellent seafood, there are splendid waterfront views from terrace tables.

De la Criée € 11 quai de L'Océan, Quiberon; tel: 02 97 30 53 09. Cheap and informal. Fish dishes.

Fresh local produce is on sale on Saturday mornings in Quiberon town and Thursday mornings in St-Pierre.

Musée de Chouannerie € Tel: 02 97 52 31 31. Open Apr–Sept, 1000–1200 and 1400–1700.

Galion de Plouharnel €€ Isthme de Penthièvre; tel: 02 97 52 39 56. Open daily, 0930–1900.

Ste-Anne-d'Auray Costume Museum € Tel: 02 97 57 58 50. Open Mon–Sat, 1000–1200, 1430–1800, Sun, 1430–1800.

Ste-Anne-d'Auray History Museum € Tel: 02 97 57 64 05; www.musee-de-cire.com. Open Mar–15 Oct, daily, 0800–1900.

Ste-Anne-d'Auray Treasury € Tel: 02 97 57 58 50. Open Mon–Sat, 1000–1200, 1430–1800, Sun, 1430–1800.

Locmariaquer €€ Tel: 02 97 57 37 59. Open May–Sept, daily, 1000–1900; Oct–May, daily, 1000–1230, 1400–1700. Guided tours 45 minutes.

treacherous waters. Review the spectacle at a safe distance from the promontory at **Beg-er-Goalennec** or further north at **Pointe-du-Percho** where the rocks provide shelter for the surfers at **Portivy**. From here you can see the isthmus of **Penthièvre** with its windswept beach and fort, built in 1795 to guard the Lorient roadstead; the redoubts and casemates were later put to use by the Germans who executed 59 members of the Resistance here in 1944.

The northern gateway to the peninsula is **Plouharnel**, a modest resort with sandy beaches, oyster beds and a scattering of prehistoric remains. The **Musée de Chouannerie** tells the story of the pro-royalist Chouan rebellion which ended ignominiously on Quiberon in 1795, while a replica Spanish galleon houses a colourful museum of shell pictures. The sheltered **east coast** has the best beaches for swimming, notably the **sables blancs** near Penthièvre and the mini-resort of **St-Pierre-Quiberon**. The little port here, known informally as 'orange', takes its name from the *Prince d'Orange*, a merchant vessel which famously 'lost' its cargo of rum just as customs officers were about to board.

Suggested tour

Total distance: 56km (92km with detours).

Time: 1 hour's driving. Allow 4 hours for the main route, 6 hours with detours. Add extra days for boat trips round the gulf or to the island of Belle-Ile.

Links: The N165 passes the gulf on its way from Quimper (*see pages 96–9*) to Nantes (*see pages 202–7*).

Leave Vannes on the D101, turning left on the D101A to **ARRADON** ❶. Take the road west to le Moustoir, then bear left on to the D316 and follow the coast road around Kerdelen Bay to Larmor-Baden, the embarkation point for **Ile Gavrinis**. Continue on the D316 passing the Pen en Toule marshes where white stilts, redshanks and ringed plovers make their nests, then turn left on to the D101. Just before the bridge across the River Bono, take the right turning to the picturesque fishing village of **le Bono**, where you can watch the oyster farmers at work. Return to the D101 and **AURAY** ❷.

Detour: Take the D17 to **Ste-Anne-d'Auray**, the venue for one of Brittany's most famous *pardons*. Tradition has it that in 1623 St Anne appeared to a local farmer and directed him to a statue buried 900 years earlier. Pilgrimage is big business here, with over 30,000 visitors to the church, the small treasury, the history and costume museums and the Scala Sancta (a staircase leading from the square that pilgrims traditionally climb on their knees). In an altogether different vein is the sombre '**Monument aux Morts**', a 200m wall inscribed with the names of 250,000 Bretons who died in World War I.

Above
St-Cado

Leave Auray on the D28 heading south. At the junction with the D781 turn left to **Locmariaquer**, an important ancient site. Excavations here have revealed what may have been the world's largest standing stone at 20.3m. Known as le Grand Menhir Brise, it was damaged thousands of years ago according to the latest theory and now lies broken into four pieces. The most impressive of several dolmens (ancient burial chambers) in the vicinity is the Table des Marchands where you can still make out some of the ancient carvings.

Return on the D781 and cross the **Pont de Kerisper** from where there are magnificent views of the Crach estuary and the marina at **la**

Château de Suscinio €€
*Sarzeau; tel: 02 97 41 91 91.
Open mid Nov–Jan,
1000–1200, 1400–1700;
Feb, Mar and Oct–mid-Nov,
1000–1200, 1400–1800;
Apr and May, 1000–1200,
1400–1900; June–Sept,
1000–1900.*

**Musée des Artes, Métiers et Commerces
€€** *tel: 02 97 53 68 25;
fax: 02 97 53 98 34; e-mail:
musee.artsmetiers@
wanadoo.fr; www.musee-arts-
metiers.com. Open July and
Aug, Mon–Sat, 1000–1200
& 1400–1900, Sun,
1400–1900; June and Sept,
1400–1900.*

L' Auberge €€ *56
route de Vannes, Ste-
Anne-d'Auray; tel: 02 97 57
61 55; fax: 02 97 57 69 10;
www.auberge-larvoir.com.
Traditional inn with
excellent restaurant.*

Lautram € *Place de
l'Eglise, Locmariaquer; tel: 02
97 57 31 32; fax: 02 97 57
37 87. Open Apr–Sept.
Small comfortable hotel
with seafood restaurant.*

Port-Navalo is the main
resort of the peninsula
with glitzy restaurants,
hotels and good campsites,
for example **Port Sable**
*(tel: 02 97 53 71 98; e-mail:
portsable@arzon.fr)* and **le
Tindio** *(tel: 02 97 53 75 59;
e-mail: letindio@arzon.fr).*

**Hôtel Glenn Ar-
Mor €€** *27 rue des
Fontaines, Port Navalo; tel:
02 97 53 88 30; e-mail:
infos@glennarmor.fr;
www.glennarmor.fr.
Restaurant with seafood
specialities.*

Trinité-sur-Mer. Continue on the D781 to **CARNAC** ❸ and then to **Plouharnel**, where a restored Spanish galleon moored in Bego Cove is home to a colourful shell museum and souvenir shop.

Detour: Take the D781 west to the expansive **Etel Estuary**, popular with anglers and oyster breeders. Possibly the best spot to head for is **St-Cado**, a tranquil island with a scattering of houses and a 12th-century chapel, linked to the mainland by a footbridge. The stone 'bed' of the 6th-century saint is said to cure hearing problems.

Turn on to the D768 and cross the coastal strip to **Quiberon**, the embarkation point for **BELLE ILE** ❹, or the smaller islands of **Houat** and **Hoëdic**. 'Duck' and 'Duckling' are popular with visitors who appreciate the sandy beaches, sheltered coves, cliff walks and clusters of whitewashed fishermen's houses bedecked with flowers. Ferries take 40 minutes to get to Houat (the larger of the islands) and just over an hour to Hoëdic.

Also worth exploring

South of the Gulf of Morbihan, the **Rhuys Peninsula** has an unusually mild climate, supporting pomegranates, fig trees, even vineyards – this is the only wine-producing area in Brittany. The D780 follows the curve of the peninsula to its tip, where **Port-Navalo** lies just a few hundred metres from the Pointe de Kerpentin on the northern shore. Just south of the road are three of the main sights of the peninsula.

The **Château de Suscinio**, a splendid 13th- to 15th-century castle overlooking the ocean, was once the summer residence of the dukes of Brittany. After the Revolution, much of the stone was carried away by local builders, but the battlements have recently been restored and you can visit the banqueting hall, the chapel and the dukes' reception rooms. The reconstructed medieval tiled floors in the museum are quite stunning.

West of Sarzeau, off the D780 near Laugueven, the **Musée des Artes, Métiers et Commerces** is a fascinating museum of traditional Breton trades and crafts, filled with colourful window displays and intriguing shop interiors. The grocer's, chemist's, barber's and lace-maker's have all been painstakingly re-created and there's a shop with a dazzling array of posters, tins, boxes and other commercial souvenirs.

Further along the coast is **St Gildas Abbey** where the renowned medieval scholar, Pierre Abelard, served as abbot in 1126 during his exile from Paris. He was decidedly unimpressed by this 'wild country, where every day brings new perils' and when the incensed monks finally tried to poison him, he fled back to Paris and his beloved Héloïse. There's a Romanesque chancel and several old gravestones to see, including the 11th-century tomb of St Gildas behind the high altar.

North

The Côte d'Emeraude

Ratings

Beaches	●●●●●
Scenery	●●●●●
Watersports	●●●●●
Outdoor activities	●●●●○
Castles and châteaux	●●●○○
Children	●●●○○
Entertainment	●●●○○
Cathedrals and churches	●●○○○

The Côte d'Emeraude stretches from St-Malo to the Baie de St-Brieuc. The landscape is rugged for the most part and heavily indented with bays and coves, river estuaries and rocky peninsulas. It was the British and American property speculators of the 19th century who first saw the possibilities for mass tourism. Today the resorts of Dinard, St-Lunaire and le Val André, with their clifftop villas, casinos and seafront promenades have an undeniable period charm, although they're probably better suited to families than young people looking for a night on the town.

Whether you're driving, hiking or cycling, it's the coastal scenery that's the main attraction here – sometimes dramatic, as at Cap Fréhel; occasionally serene and always pleasing to the eye. If the weather is favourable you'll probably want to spend some time swimming or relaxing on one of the numerous beaches. Opinions differ over why this is called the Emerald Coast. Does it stem from the verdant countryside, the greenish hues of the sea or the six golf courses? Judge for yourself.

CAP FREHEL

Cap Fréhel Lighthouse *Tel: 02 96 41 40 03; usually open July and Aug, daily, 1400–1800 though hours can vary.*

This spectacular beauty spot is a 'must see'. Beyond the 160 hectares of unspoilt heath and moorland, sheer cliffs of schist and pink sandstone form a natural barrier to the advancing sea which lashes the reefs more than 70m below. There are panoramic views of the coastline from here, stretching all the way from the **Ile de Bréhat** in the west to Pointe de Grouin and the **Cotentin Peninsula** in the east. Cap Fréhel is also the habitat of many species of sea bird including guillemots, black-backed gulls, cormorants, ravens, herring gulls, kittiwakes and razorbills.

To enjoy the area, park your car near the lighthouse and climb the 145 steps to the gallery for equally rewarding views out to sea – visibility is 120km on a fine day. The lighthouse and its stunning setting have exercised the imaginations of local painters for decades; their efforts well represented in local galleries and souvenir shops.

Gr

Bill

up

North
⇧

0   10km
|————————————|
0   5 miles

Cap Fréhel   Rothéneuf   *Pointe du Gr*

Sables-d'Or-les-Pins   Paramé
Plouha   *Île de Cézembre* **St Malo**   Car
St-Quay-   Fort la Latte   355
Portrieux   Erquy   St-Lunaire Dinard
                    Fréhel   St Cast   St-Méloir-
786 Étables-   Pléneuf-Val-   St-Briac-   St Servan des-Ondes
sur-Mer   André   786   sur-Mer
Binic   Matignon   St-Jouan-   4   155
                              786   des-Guérets
laudren   St-Alban   Hénanbihen   Ploubalay   N137   Châteauneuf
Plérin   766   N176
St-Brieuc Langueux   786   Plancoët   Miniac-Morvan
Ploufragan Trégueux N12   Lamballe   Corseul   Pleudihen-   N137
          Maroué   sur-Rance
Plaintel   Quessoy   Dinan 794   St-Pierre-
                    N176   N176   Léhon   de-Plesguen
          N12   Jugon-les-Lacs

DINARD

ℹ **Dinard Tourist
Information** 2
*boulevard Féart; tel: 02
99 46 94 12; fax: 02
99 88 21 07; e-mail:
infos@ot-dinard.com;
www.ot-dinard.com*

🅿 Boulevard Féart (near
tourist office), place
du Marché, place de la
République.

Ⓠ Bus de Mer, ferry to
St-Malo; tel: 02 99 46
10 45. Apr–Oct, night
service in high season.
Leaves from the pleasure
port.

🎬 **Hitchcock Statue**
Place Maréchal Joffe.

Villa Eugenie *10 rue des
Français-Libres.*

Once a humble fishing village, Dinard acquired an opulent, even regal
air in the late 19th century when it was all the rage with American
and British visitors who attempted to outdo one another in the
grandeur of their clifftop villas. The French were quick to follow suit
and today these neo-Gothic residences are a valued attraction (guided
tours leave from the tourist information office). Dinard still attracts
the smart set and prices are higher than elsewhere on the coast,
although you can economise in restaurants by opting for one of the
fixed-price menus.

Most visitors head straight for the beach. There are three in Dinard
itself, all suitable for swimming. Windsurfing, kayaking and other
watersports are also available and if the weather isn't kind, the Plage
de l'Ecluse boasts a heated swimming pool. However, you won't find
much in the way of shops and snack bars on the promenade, so before
setting out it's probably a good idea to stock up at the market (Halles
de la Concorde).

Flanking the Plage de l'Ecluse are the headlands of Malouine and
Moulinet, offering wonderful views across to **St-Malo** (*see pages
164–73*) and the isles of **Grand Bé** and **Cézembre**. St-Malo makes an
ideal day-trip from Dinard and it's only ten minutes away by boat (it
will take you twice as long to drive there by car). Otherwise, Dinard
has few specific sights apart from those discovered simply by strolling
its streets. These include features such as the elegant four-towered Villa
Eugenie, built and named for the wife of Napoleon III (though she
never actually stayed in it) and, even more curious, a statue of film-

Market, les Halles de la Concorde, place du Marché; open every morning.

British Film Festival (October).

director Alfred Hitchcock. After dark Dinard may appear a little staid, unless you can afford a flutter in the casino. Easier on the pocket is a pre-dinner stroll along the Promenade de Clair de Lune (illuminated at night) with its garden backdrop of palms, eucalyptus and mimosa. The social calendar includes festivals devoted to ballet, classical music, theatre and film but the nearest disco is in **St-Lunaire** (*see page 160*).

Accommodation and food in Dinard

Altair €€ *18 boulevard Féart; tel: 02 99 46 13 58; fax: 02 99 88 24 49. Open all day.* Excellent hotel restaurant serving a variety of seafood and meat dishes.

Grand Hôtel €€€ *46 avenue George-V; tel: 02 99 88 26 26; fax: 02 99 88 26 27.* Dinard's most exclusive hotel offers many creature comforts.

La Plage €€ *3 boulevard Féart; tel: 02 99 46 14 87; fax: 02 99 46 55 52; e-mail: hotel-de-la-plage@wanadoo.fr.* Comfortable rooms and a good location close to Plage de l'Ecluse; also a restaurant.

Printania €€ *5 avenue George-V; tel: 02 99 46 13 07; fax: 02 99 46 26 32; e-mail: PRINTANIA.DINARD@wanadoo.fr. Open all day.* There are views of St-Malo from the terrace. Fish specialities include stuffed clams and grilled salmon. Rooms available.

La Vallée €€ *6 avenue George-V; tel: 02 99 46 94 00; fax: 02 99 88 22 47; e-mail: contact@hoteldelavallee.com; www.hoteldelavallee.com.* Attractive, reasonably priced *logis* close to the pleasure port.

FORT LA LATTE

Fort La Latte € *Tel: 02 96 41 40 31. Open July and Aug, 1000–1900; Apr–Sept, 1000–1230, 1400–1800; Oct–Mar, Sat, Sun & French school holidays, 1400–1730.*

Perched on a rocky spur overlooking **Cap Fréhel** (*see page 154*), the fortress stands in splendid semi-isolation from the mainland – the sea serves as a moat at high tide and is spanned by two drawbridges. Fort la Latte last saw action in 1957 when it was a film set for the swashbuckling Hollywood epic *The Vikings*, starring Kirk Douglas. In fact the keep dates only from the 14th century; 300 years later it was remodelled by Louis XIV's outstanding military engineer, Vauban, who built the gun emplacements above the outer curtain wall. Apart from film actors, the castle has accommodated English spies during the French Revolution, White Russians during World War II and the son of the deposed King of England, James II, known as the Old Pretender.

Fort la Latte is open for guided tours only. Visitors are shown the outer enclosures, the guardroom, the governor's living quarters, the chapel and the Tour de l'Echaguette, once used as a cannon ball foundry. From the parapet there are outstanding views of **Cap Fréhel** to the west and **St-Malo** and **Ile de Cézembre** to the east.

Right
Fort la Latte

LAMBALLE

ⓘ Lamballe Tourist Information *Place du Martray; tel: 02 96 31 05 38; fax: 02 96 50 01 96; e-mail: otsi.lamballe@ netcourrier.com; www.lamballe-communaute.com*

Ⓗ Haras National € *Place du Champ de Foire; tel: 02 96 50 06 98; e-mail: promoharas@ wanadoo.fr; www.haraspatrimoine.com. Open mid-June–mid-Sept, 1030–1200, 1400–1730; rest of year, school holidays, Wed, Sat & Sun, 1400–1730. Tours in English during summer.*

Ⓒ Tour des Arc'hants €€ *2 rue Dr-Lavagne; tel: 02 96 31 01 37; e-mail: latourdargent @wanadoo.fr. Comfortable rooms and a reasonably priced restaurant.*

Lamballe is an attractive agricultural town built on a hillside overlooking the River Gouessant. Its best-known sight is the **Haras National** or National Stud, the second largest in France. Founded in the 17th century by Louis XIV's chief minister Colbert, the original purpose of the stud was to provide a ready supply of cavalry and artillery horses for the army. Nowadays it concentrates on breeding the sturdy and ever reliable Breton draught horses which are slowly coming back into fashion for economic and environmental reasons. The premises are spacious and imposing. Visitors are taken on a guided tour of the stables, the farrier's workshop, the carriage house, the riding school and the harness rooms. If your visit coincides with the first weekend after 15 August, visit the annual Horse Festival (for further details contact the tourist office).

The stud is only a few minutes' walk from place du Martray with its picturesque half-timbered houses. The oldest of them, the Maison du Bourreau (Hangman's House) dates from the 15th century and is now occupied by the tourist office and two small museums, one containing mainly costumes and headdresses, the other devoted to paintings by Mathurin Méhuet, a local artist born in 1882.

St-Brieuc

ℹ️ **St-Brieuc Tourist Information** 7 rue St-Gouéno; tel: 08 25 00 22 22; fax: 02 96 61 42 16; e-mail: info@ baiedesaintbrieuc.com; www.baiedesaintbrieuc.com

🅿️ Place de la Résistance, place Général de Gaulle.

🌀 Festival of Breton Music (July), Art Rock Festival (variable).

The administrative capital of the Côtes d'Amor region, St-Brieuc is a sprawling industrial town with an unprepossessing hinterland. The old quarter, on the other hand, is not without charm, and merits an hour or two's sightseeing, combined with lunch and a spot of shopping – head for the pedestrianised area near the tourist office (rue St-Gouéno).

The massive fortified towers of the **Cathedral of St-Etienne** date from the 13th and 14th centuries. No flight of fancy on the architect's part, they were there to protect the town's inhabitants as missiles could be hurled at the enemy from the parapets. The nave was rebuilt in the 18th century but is in harmony with the fine proportions of the Annunciation Chapel (right) and the superb choir, completed in just three years following a fire in 1353.

The streets adjacent to the cathedral are also worth exploring for their handsome half-timbered houses, notably the 15th-century Ribeault mansion on rue Fardel. On Wednesdays and Saturdays there's a market near place du Martray where you'll also find a shop selling gifts and handicrafts. The tourist office is well stocked with information on the Côtes d'Amor region.

Above
St-Brieuc Cathedral of St-Etienne

St-Cast-le-Guildo

Tourist Information *Place Charles de Gaulle; tel: 02 96 41 81 52; fax: 02 96 41 76 19; e-mail: saint.cast.le.guildo@ wanadoo.fr; www.ot-st-cast-le-guildo.fr*

Le Biniou €€ *Pen Guen; tel: 02 96 41 94 53.* This sophisticated fish restaurant overlooks the beach.

'The peninsula with seven beaches', as St-Cast is described in the brochures, is a modern resort with excellent sporting facilities, including an 18-hole golf course, tennis courts, sailing, riding and of course swimming (there's a heated seawater pool for rainy days). Orientation is initially something of a problem but becomes less so once you realise that St-Cast is not one, but several communities spread out across the headland. Most tourists hang out in les Mielles or near Pen Guen, the most sought-after of the beaches. To the west lies the old port of L'Isle, where the fishermen still land catches of scallops and clams which are the mainstay of the local restaurants. Not far from Pen Guen are the historic ruins of **le Guildo castle** which guarded the Arguenon estuary until the 17th century when it was demolished at the behest of Cardinal Richelieu who feared it might become a focus for revolt. The coastal path from Pointe St-Cast to Pointe de la Guarde offers some beautiful scenery as well as opportunities for birdwatching – guillemots especially but also scoter and brent geese – while the sweeping views of the Emerald Coast (all the way from St-Malo to Cap Fréhel) are spectacular.

Accommodation in St-Cast-le-Guildo

Hôtel Port-Jacquet €€ *32 rue de Port; tel: 02 96 41 97 18; fax: 02 96 41 74 82; e-mail: port.jacquet@wanadoo.fr; www.port-jacquet.com.* Very cosy and overlooking the harbour; good seafood restaurant.

Right
St-Cast-le-Guildo

St-Lunaire

This small seaside resort bears more than a passing resemblance to its grander neighbour, **Dinard** (*see pages 155–6*). It developed along similar lines at the end of the 19th century, thanks to a millionaire Haitian businessman who built the obligatory casino. Nowadays, St-Lunaire only really comes alive in high season (July and August) when French visitors arrive en masse, decamping on the two superb beaches, la Plage Lonchamps – 900m long and favoured by windsurfers – and the Grand Plage. Between them lies a rocky promontory known as the Pointe du Décollé. The clifftop walk through clumps of brushwood and bracken is especially invigorating in rough weather, when the sea pounds the headland and swirls around the Saut du Chat (Cat's Leap), the most famous of the numerous grottoes. It was these sea views which inspired the composer Debussy at the turn of the century. St-Lunaire itself lacks specific sights except for the **parish church**, the nave of which dates back to the 11th century. It contains the tomb of the saint from which the community takes its name.

Le Val-Andre

This pretty resort boasts one of the finest expanses of golden sand in Brittany – too much sand some might think at low tide, when

Tourist Information / rue Winston Churchill; tel: 02 96 72 20 55; fax: 02 96 63 00 34; www.val-andre.org

the sea threatens to disappear over the horizon. Le Val-André grew out of the little village of Pléneuf in the 1880s and the architecture (elegant villas for the most part) takes a leaf out of Dinard's book. It's a restful place, worth considering for an overnight stay. Apart from tennis, golf and swimming, nature walks are the most obvious forms of relaxation. To the east of the promenade are the limestone cliffs of Pointe de Pléneuf, where human remains dating back 200,000 years have been discovered. There are views from here out to the **Ile du Verdelet** bird sanctuary, and if you have brought binoculars you may be able to see cormorants nesting. La Guette, the headland to the west of the promenade, looks on to St-Brieuc Bay. From here it's only a short walk to the old fishing port of **Dahouët**; pleasure boats leave from here bound for the **Ile de Bréhat**. If you're here on a Tuesday you'll be able to catch the local market at **Pleneuf-Val-André**, just south of the resort proper.

Accommodation and food in le Val-André

De la Mer €€ *63 rue Amiral Charner; tel: 02 96 72 20 44; e-mail: hdlm2@wanadoo.fr. Open daily.* Excellent French cuisine is served in this friendly, relaxed hotel restaurant; *moules marinières* is a speciality.

Below
St-Lunaire: Ile Pointe du Décollé

Hotel du Commerce € *2 place de Lourmel; tel: 02 96 72 22 48.* Small, inexpensive hotel. No restaurant, but plenty of choice nearby.

Getting out of the car

One of the most enjoyable ways to appreciate the scenic diversity of the Côte d'Emeraude is to take a boat trip. The Emeraude Line operates cruises between **Dinard** and **Cap Fréhel**, with views of the beaches of **St-Cast Bay** and the rocky promontory of **Fort la Latte**.

Boats also leave Dinard for the sea-bird haven of **Ile de Cézembre**. Sun worshippers will relish the south-facing beach (the warmest in the region) while the restaurant **Repaire de Corsaires** is a good spot for lunch.

Suggested tour

Total distance: 150km (215km with detours).

Time: 3 hours' driving. Allow 8 hours for the main route, 12 hours with detours. Those with limited time should concentrate on the coast between Fort la Latte and Erquy.

Links: This route borders the Côte de Granit Rose (*see pages 108–25*) to the west and the Rance Valley (*see pages 174–81*) to the east.

Campagnie Corsaire *Tel: 0 825 138 130; www.campagniecorsaire.com.* Boat trips along the coast to a variety of destinations, departures being most frequent during July and Aug.

Ile de Cezembre Sailings from Dinard, *July and Aug at 1230, returning at 1820 daily, weekly in Apr, May, June & Sept. Tel: 02 99 46 10 45.*

Leave **DINARD** ❶ on the D786 travelling west along the coast and you will pass through the resorts of **ST-LUNAIRE** ❷ and St-Briac-sur-Mer where the cliff road and bridge over the River Frémur offer good views of the estuary. On the opposite bank is **Lancieux** where the bell tower of the former church stands in splendid isolation in the centre of the village. Continue to Ploubalay.

Detour: At Ploubalay take the D168 eastwards for 1km to the 104m-high **water tower**. There are panoramic vistas of the Frémur valley and the Côte d'Emeraude from the viewing platform of the restaurant here. Return to Ploubalay.

After Ploubalay take the D786 towards Matignon and Cap Fréhel.

Detour: About 2.5km from Ploubalay turn right on to the D26 and the peninsula of **St-Jacut-de-la-Mer**. Nineteenth-century villas now encroach on the old port, once so isolated that the fishermen spoke their own dialect. Even today traditional activities such as mackerel fishing, mussel gathering and shrimping in the rock pools round **Pointe Chevrel** persist.

Return to the D768 and cross the River Arguenon, turning right on to the D19 and the resort of **ST-CAST-LE-GUILDO** ❸. Leave by the D13 and at Matignon rejoin the D786. Follow the shoreline of the **Baie de la Fréynaye**, turning right immediately after crossing the bridge over

Above
St-Briac-sur-Mer

Château de Bienassis €€ *Tel: 02 96 72 22 03. Guided tours mid-June–mid-Sept, Mon–Sat, 1030–1230, 1400–1830, Sun, 1400–1830.*

Château de la Hunaudaye €€ *Tel: 02 96 34 82 10; e-mail: chateau@la-hunaudaye.com. Guided tours mid-June–mid-Sept, 1030–1800; Apr–mid-June and mid-Sept–Oct, Sun, 1430–1800.*

the other(!) River Frémur. This attractive road hugs the bay all the way to **FORT LA LATTE** ❹ and **CAP FREHEL** ❺. Follow the D34 on to the other side of the peninsula and the scenery is even more stunning. Stop at one of the designated parking areas and you can look down on the dune-fringed sands of Pléherel-Plage or stroll through the pine woods behind la Ville Men. **Sables-d'Or-les-Pins** as the name suggests offers more pines and golden beaches; at low tide you can walk from here to the offshore islet of St-Michel. At the D786 turn right in the direction of **Erquy**, a bustling fishing port noted for its scallops. Here the D786 leaves the coast again, passing the 17th-century **Château de Bienassis** with rooms furnished in the style of Louis XIV. After **LE VAL-ANDRE** ❻ take the D791 to **LAMBALLE** ❼.

Detour: To visit the cathedral town of **St-BRIEUC** ❽, take the D786 from le Val-André to St-René, then the D712 westwards to avoid the congested bypass. Return to the driving route either via the busy N12 or the quieter D712 to Lamballe.

Leave Lamballe on the D28. This picturesque road winds through the **Forêt de la Hunaudaye.** Just before Pleven, a right turn leads to the ruined castle, its five towers clearly visible above the trees. (Medieval pageants are held here in July and August.) The D28 through Pleven offers views of the River Arguennon which assumes lakelike proportions at this point. Follow the road to **Plancoët**, a market town famous for its mineral water – you can sample it for free here.

Detour: South of Plancoët the D792 leads to **Jugon-les-Lacs.** Standing at the junction of three rivers – the Arguenon, the Rieule and the Rosette – this small resort with an artificial lake is popular with fishermen, yachters and watersports enthusiasts.

Return to Plancoët and pick up the D768 to la Villes Comte from where you can return to Dinard on the D168.

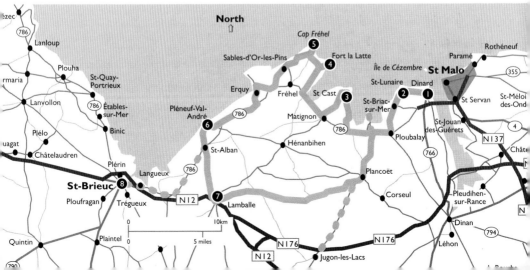

St-Malo

Ratings

Food	●●●●●
History	●●●●●
Architecture	●●●●○
Children	●●●●○
Entertainment	●●●●○
Heritage	●●●●○
Beaches	●●●○○
Scenery	●●●○○

This lively Channel port welcomes tourists with enthusiasm, and there's lots to do here. Apart from the sights (pride of place belongs to the château and the citadel) there are miles of beaches, parks, cinemas and plenty of late-night bars and restaurants, and the Grand Aquarium, a big hit with children.

St-Malo takes its name from the Welsh monk Maclow who became Bishop of Aleth (now St-Servan) in the 6th century. The sea-going Malouins earned a fearsome reputation as privateers, preying on any enemy vessel which dared to sail too close to the shores of their island fortress (the town has not always been joined to the mainland by a causeway). In 1590 it proclaimed itself a separate republic. The breakaway state only lasted four years but the money continued to flow in from the voyages of discovery and the slave trade. During World War II about 80 per cent of the town was destroyed by Allied bombing, but you'd hardly notice looking at St-Malo today. The only drawback is the heavy traffic around the ferry terminal.

Sights

i St-Malo Tourist Information

Esplanade St-Vincent; tel: 08 25 13 52 00; fax: 02 99 56 67 00; e-mail: info@ saint.malo-tourisme.com; www.saint-malo-tourisme.com. Closed Sun except during July and Aug; no accommodation booking service.

Château

Enter the citadel through the **St-Vincent Gate** and you will come face to face with St-Malo's formidable castle. Building began in 1395 and the massive keep, the walls 7m thick in places, was completed some 30 years later. Construction continued well into the 18th century when the barracks, now the **Town Hall (Hôtel de Ville)** were added.

The castle keep is now the **Municipal Museum (Musée d'Histoire de la Ville et du Pays Malouin)**. The exhibition, spread over three floors, focuses on the colourful history of this great seafaring community which some might regard as beginning with the St Malo-born explorer Jacques Cartier who, in 1534, crossed the Atlantic in just 20 days but subsequently failed to find a route through North America to Asia. The best sections are those dealing with the swashbuckling

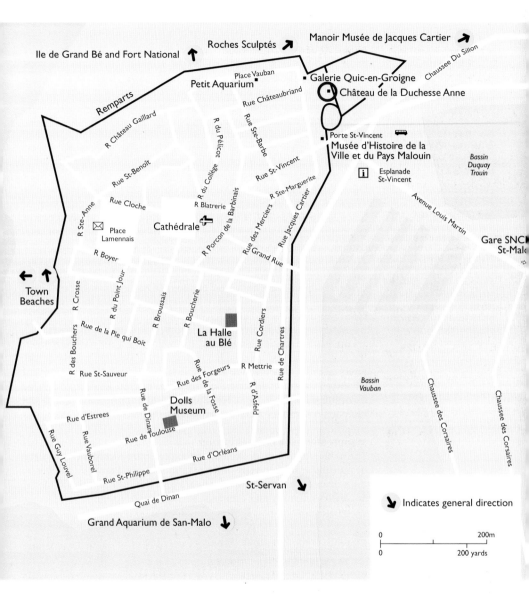

Ile de Grand Bé and Fort National

Roches Sculptés

Manoir Musée de Jacques Cartier

Chaussee Du Sillon

Place Vauban

Petit Aquarium

Galerie Quic-en-Groigne

Rue Châteaubriand

Château de la Duchesse Anne

Remparts

R Château Gaillard

Porte St-Vincent

Musée d'Histoire de la
Ville et du Pays Malouin

Bassin
Duquay
Trouin

Rue St-Benoît

R du Pélicot

R du Collège

Rue Ste-Barbe

Rue St-Vincent

Esplanade
St-Vincent

Rue Cloche

R Ste-Anne

R Blatrerie

R Porcon de la Barbinais

R Ste-Marguerite

Rue des Merciers

Rue Jacques Cartier

Avenue Louis Martin

Cathédrale

Place
Lamennais

Gare SNCF
St-Malo

R Boyer

Rue Grand Rue

Town
Beaches

R Crosse

R du Point Jour

R Broussais

R Boucherie

La Halle
au Blé

Rue Cordiers

Rue de Chartres

Rue de la Pie qui Boit

R des Bouchers

Rue St-Sauveur

Rue des Forgeurs

R Mettrie

R d'Asfeld

Bassin
Vauban

Chaussée des Corsaires

Chaussée des Corsaires

Dolls
Museum

Rue de la Fosse

Rue d'Estrees

Rue de Dinan

Rue de Toulouse

Rue Vauborel

Rue d'Orléans

St-Servan

Rue Guy Louvel

Rue St-Philippe

Quai de Dinan

Grand Aquarium de San-Malo

Indicates general direction

0   200m

0   200 yards

**Musée d'Histoire
de la Ville €€**

*Château de la Duchesse Anne;
tel: 02 99 40 71 57;
Open Apr–Sept, daily,
1000–1230, 1400–1800;
Oct–Mar, Tue–Sun,
1000–1200, 1400–1800.*

adventures of the corsairs and the lucrative trade with the Americas which of course included the profits of slave trading and piracy. It's a steep climb (169 steps) to the top of the tower but worth it for the bird's-eye view of the citadel and harbour. On the opposite side of the castle is the **Tour Quic-en-Groigne**. The tower's unusual name derives from a disdainful put-down by Queen Anne of Brittany of the local bishop: 'Whoever may complain, this is how it will be because it is my wish.' Her words were later carved into the stone.

Grand Aquarium
€€€ *La ville Jouan,
avenue du Général Patton;
tel: 02 99 21 19 02;
www.aquarium-st-malo.com.
Open July and Aug,
0930–2000; Apr–June and
Sept, 1000–1900; Feb, Mar
& Oct–Dec, 1000–1800
(closed most weekdays in
Jan and Dec).*

Fort National €
*Tel: 02 99 85 34 33;
www.fortnational.com.
Open mid-June–mid-Sept
daily for guided tours.*

**Manoir Musée de
Jacques Cartier €** *Rue D
McDonald Stewart, Limoelou;
tel: 02 99 40 97 73; fax: 02
99 40 82 63; e-mail:
Musee.Jacques.Cartier@
wanadoo.fr; www.musee-
jacques-cartier.com. Open
June–Sept, daily, 1000–1130,
1430–1800; rest of year,
Mon–Fri, guided tours only at
1000 and 1500.*

Grand Aquarium de St-Malo

From the moment it opened in 1996 the aquarium proved to be a great crowd pleaser and is currently Brittany's most visited fee-charging attraction. Located just outside the town, the complex includes a shop, bar, brasserie and free parking, not to mention 40 aquariums, reflecting the marine environments of all seven of the world's seas. Sharks, piranhas and giant turtles are among the thousands of tropical creatures on view and there are film shows in the 3-D cinema. Expect to queue for around half-an-hour in high season.

Ile de Grand Bé and Fort National

There are great views from these two island outposts, accessible only at low tide. To the French, Grand Bé is virtually synonymous with one of the nation's great literary figures (and a Malouin by birth), François-René de Chateaubriand, whose last wish was to be buried on the island. The trek to see his grave, marked by a plain granite cross, is so popular that queues sometimes form on the causeway. There's little else to do here but admire the view – you can see the entire Emerald Coast on a clear day. Take care to start back before the tide comes in or you may suffer the indignity of being rescued by the coastguard in full view of the locals, who gather on the beach precisely to witness this spectacle.

Fort National was constructed by Louis XIV's military engineer, Vauban, in 1689 to give added protection to the town – before the Revolution it was known as Fort Royale. Built from the hardiest Chausey granite, its greatest moment came in 1692 when it withstood a combined assault from the English and Dutch fleets. From the ramparts you can see as far as Dinard and the Rance estuary.

Manoir Musée de Jacques Cartier

The achievements of the celebrated explorer are nicely evoked in the beautifully restored, 16th-century farmhouse at Limoëlou which he once owned. The museum tells the story of how Cartier opened up the St Lawrence Seaway and claimed Canada for the French.

Jacques Cartier

Born in St-Malo in 1494, Cartier was already 40 when he went in search of the elusive Northwest Passage to Asia. After landing instead at Gaspé Bay in North America, he was welcomed by the indigenous natives who told him the place was called Canada (the Huron word for village). Cartier claimed the new territories for France and in 1535, still convinced that he would eventually find a northern route to the east, sailed up the St Lawrence river as far as Hochelaga, now Montreal. At this point he gave up on his quest and retired to a farm just outside St-Malo. He died in 1557.

Roches Sculptés €
*Tel: 02 99 56 23 95.
Open Apr–Sept, daily,
0900–1900; Oct–Mar,
1000–1200, 1400–1900.*

**Tour Solidor (Musée
International du Long-
Cours Cap-Hornier) €**
*St-Servan-sur-Mer; tel: 02 99
40 71 58. Open Apr–Sept,
1000–1200, 1400–1800.*

Fort de la Cité € *Tel: 02
99 40 71 57. Open for
guided tours Apr–June and
Sept–Nov, Tue–Sun, 1400,
1515, 1630; July and Aug,
daily, 1015, 1100, 1400,
1500, 1600, 1700.*

Rochers Sculptés

It was in 1870 that a priest called Abbé Fouré began sculpting figures into the granite rocks of the promontory at **Rothéneuf**, a labour of love that was to take 25 years. Today the 300 or so dragons, grotesques and other fanciful creatures are showing distinct signs of weathering and will eventually disappear altogether. Until then the abbé's masterwork will continue to draw the crowds. The site also contains a pottery shop, café and gardens.

St-Servan

The largest of St-Malo's suburbs is actually older than the town itself. St-Servan is an agreeable mini-resort with beaches, coastal walks and two museums. Overlooking the Rance estuary is the 14th-century **Tour Solidor**, now a museum tracing the history of the Atlantic clipper route around Cape Horn. The **Fort de la Cité**, on the opposite side of the Corniche d'Aleth, was founded in 1759 to defend St-Malo and the maritime commerce on the Rance. Its strategic importance was such that it later became a key element in the Atlantic defences of Nazi Germany. The projected artillery batteries, command posts and barracks were to have been linked by a subterranean narrow-gauge railway 1300m long. Building was still underway in August 1944 when, following a fierce battle, the occupying troops surrendered the 'fortified city' to the Americans. Visitors are shown a film then taken on a guided tour of the fort and museum **Mémorial 39/45**. If you're not keen on military history there's an interesting walk round the

Corniche d'Aleth from the ruins of the old cathedral to Sablons Bay with views of the lighthouse, the harbour, the port and the isles of Grand Bé and Cézembre.

Beaches

The town beach, **Plage de Bonsecours**, lies directly in front of the citadel. The facilities include an open-air swimming pool and a centre for watersports (Station Voile). If it's crowded here you'll find more room on the other side of the headland, where a 3km-long promenade links the **Grande Plage du Sillon** (also known as Casino Beach) with the **Plage de Rochebonne** at Paramé. Between the two is a hydrotherapy and fitness centre (Therme Marins). Further along the coast, beyond the villas at Minihic and the camping site (de Nielles), is the suburb of **Rothéneuf**. The main point of interest here is the **Rochers Sculptés** (*see page 167*), but there are also two beaches, the **Plage du Val** and the more sheltered **Plage du Havre**, with a backdrop of cliffs, pines and sand dunes.

Below
St-Malo ramparts

Entertainment

St-Malo is the liveliest town on the Emerald coast and, festivals aside, there's quite a bit to do in the evenings. Rue Jacques Cartier, just inside the town walls, is lined with pavement restaurants, or, if your penchant is pancakes, *crêperies* cluster around rue des Mercier. To eat out with sea views you'll have to go further afield – try St-Servan or the Grande Plage du Sillon. Facilities at the **Casino** € *Chausée du Sillon, tel: 02 99 40 64 00*, include bars, a brasserie and a disco. There are several other good nightspots: for atmosphere, **Le 109** € (*3 rue des Cordiers; tel: 02 99 56 81 09*) scores well, being a night-club with drinking and dancing in a 300-year-old-cellar. **Cunningham's** bar € *2 rue des Hauts-Sablons* puts on concerts and theme evenings and stays open until the wee small hours or there's the *craic* at **Le Shamrock** € *4 rue Boursaint; tel: 06 11 19 56 74;* and the impressive variety of beers at l'**Aviso** €, *12 rue de Point du Jour; tel: 02 99 40 99 08*.

Fruits de mer

Equally enjoyable on a sunny terrace overlooking the sea, or in the more expensive surroundings of a traditional French restaurant, a *plateau de fruits de mer* is a dish to be savoured. Arranged on a bed of seaweed and crushed ice, the classic seafood platter is accompanied by side servings of brown and white bread, home-made mayonnaise and butter. Small forks and 'winkle pins' are provided to help lever the fish from their shells.

Many French restaurateurs have signed up to a charter specifying exactly how a *plateau de fruits de mer* should be served and guaranteeing at least six different kinds of seafood (allowing for seasonal variations in the catch). There should be three from each of the following categories:

Crustaceans: crabs (spider, edible or velvet swimming crabs), Dublin Bay prawns, shrimps, scampi, lobsters and oysters.

Molluscs: clams (*praires* or *palourdes*), scallops, mussels, winkles, whelks and spinous squat lobsters.

Accommodation and food

While there is plenty of hotel accommodation in St-Malo, remember that this is a busy ferry port with thousands of through-passengers booking overnight stays in the town. Be sure, therefore, to reserve rooms in advance – the tourist office does not operate a booking service.

If the hotels in the walled town are full there are plenty of attractive alternatives in the suburban resorts of Paramé, St-Servan and Rothéneuf.

L'Atre €€ *7 Esplanade Commandant Menguy, St-Servan; tel: 02 99 81 68 39; fax: 02 99 81 56 18. Closed Wed, also Tue evenings out of season.* Restaurant offering *fruits de mer* and fish specialities.

Le Cassé €€ *2 Chaussée du Sillon, Plage du Sillon; tel: 02 99 40 64 00.* The casino's nautically-themed restaurant serves reasonably priced pizzas, salads and pâtés; also fixed-price menus.

Les Charmettes € *64 boulevard Hébert, Paramé; tel: 02 99 56 07 31; fax: 02 99 56 85 96; e-mail: hotel.les.charmettes@wanadoo.fr; www.hotel-les-charmettes.com.* Small, comfortable *pension* with sea views.

Duchesse Anne €€€ *place Guy la Chambre; tel: 02 99 40 85 33.* Probably the best and priciest eaterie in town, though the lunches offer a taste of top-class cooking at more reasonable cost.

Hôtel le Croiseur € *2 place de la Poisonnerie; tel: 02 99 40 80 40; fax: 02 99 56 83 76; e-mail: hotel.le.croiseur@free.fr.* Old town hotel offering clean, simply furnished rooms.

Hôtel de la Porte St Pierre €€ *2 place du Guet; tel: 02 99 40 91 27; fax: 99 56 06 94.* Pleasant *logis* close to the port and handy for the town beach.

La Korrigane €€€ *39 rue le Pomellec, St-Servan; tel: 02 99 81 65 85.* Smart hotel located in a mansion close to the sea.

L'Univers €€ *place Châteaubriand; tel: 02 99 40 89 52.* Patronised by locals as much as by tourists for the range of delectable fare, including oysters and excellent fish soups.

Le Valmarin €€€ *7 rue Jean XXIII, St-Servan; tel: 02 99 81 94 76; fax: 02 99 81 30 03.* Luxury accommodation in a former corsair's house.

Suggested tour

Any tour of St-Malo falls naturally into two parts: a circuit of the ramparts and a stroll through the cobbled streets of the citadel.

Ⓟ Parking isn't usually a problem although there are restrictions in August when it is advisable to leave your car outside the walled town on the Esplanade St-Vincent. Intra-muros parking spaces can be found behind the Plage de Bonsecours.

Steps lead up to the parapet of the **ramparts** by the **Tour Quic-en-Groigne**. From here there are views of the extensive beaches at **Paramé** and **Rothéneuf**. The defensive walls were originally built round the island-town in the 12th century. They were later improved and enlarged by Louis XIV's military architect Vauban, and were one of the few parts of St-Malo to survive the Allied bombing of 1944. Follow the ramparts to the Fort à la Reine and stop to look at the outlying **FORT NATIONAL**, then continue to Tour Bidouane from

Transport is needed to reach many of the sights outside the walled town. **St-Malo Bus** links the harbour with the suburbs of Rothéneuf and St-Servan (departs Esplanade St-Vincent).

Boats: The short-hop ferry to Dinard and cruises on the Rance or to the islands leave from Cale de Dinan beneath the ramparts. **Compagne Corsaire** *Gare Maritime*; *tel: 08 25 13 80 35.*

Below
One of the many beaches at St-Malo

where you can see the causeway leading to **ILE DU GRAND BE**. By the tower is a statue of St-Malo's best-known corsair. Robert Surcouf went to sea at the age of 14, took command of his own ship at 20 and made a fortune from the slave trade, before retiring at 36 to begin a second equally lucrative career as a shipping magnate. Cross **Porte des Champs Vauverts**, one of several gates opening on to the **Plage de Bonsecours**. On the beach below you can see remnants of the original 12th-century fortifications. A monument to the explorer Jacques Cartier looks out from the massive bulwark known as the Bastion de la Hollande towards the **Ile de Cézembre** and the beaches at **Dinard**. Stretching into the distance is the **Côte d'Emeraude** – you should be able to make out the **Pointe de-St-Cast** and **Cap Fréhel**. Continue past the Bastion St Philippe, then cross **Porte de Dinan**. The quay below is the departure point for the Dinard ferry while beyond is the **Fort de la Cité** and the estuary of the Rance. The final stretch of the ramparts, past the Bastion St-Louis, presents an unfolding panorama of St-Malo's inner **harbours** and extensive modern suburbs. You will also cross the ceremonial entrance to the citadel, known as the **Grande Porte**. There are steps down by the Porte St-Vincent.

🟡 La Halle au Blé (Corn Market) *Thur, Fri morning*.

🔺 *Mid-July–mid-Aug –* Festival de Musique Sacrée. Sacred music from Gregorian chant to Duruflé.

July (one week) – Folklores du Monde à St-Malo. Open-air celebration of folk music from around the world.

Late July–late Aug–Fridays in the walled town. International music of all kinds; also theatre.

From **Porte St-Vincent** ❶ cross place Chateaubriand to an area of souvenir shops, *pâtisseries* and restaurants. Take rue St-Vincent to the **cathedral** ❷. With the notable exception of the stained glass – the stunning windows by Jean le Moal cast colourful splashes of light on to the arches of the 13th-century chancel – there is little to detain you here. Turn left on to rue Porcon de la Barbinais. The street takes its name from the 17th-century sea captain, charged with protecting St-Malo's merchant fleet from marauding pirates. De la Barbinais was later captured in Algeria and offered his freedom if he could negotiate a peace treaty with France. When the terms were rejected by Louis XIV

he felt bound as a man of honour to return to his former captors who immediately ordered his execution. Continue along rue de la VIIe Boucherie to the Marché aux Legumes. Cross the square and walk down rue de la Fosse to the walls. The houses here date from the 18th century and were built by St-Malo ship owners – the neat rows of windows, chimneys and high roofs towering above the ramparts proclaiming their wealth to visitors arriving by sea. (The house at the

Above
The defences of St-Malo

corner of rue St-Philippe and rue de Dinan belonged to Surcouf.) From the **Porte de Dinan** ❸ take the main road back towards the centre. Turn left at place Brevet passing the 18th-century chapel of **St-Sauveur** ❹, then right at rue des Bouchers to the **Porte St-Pierre** ❺ and (beyond the wall) the **Plage de Bonsecours** ❻. From place du Guet take rue de la Pie Qui Boit, turning left on to rue Broussais. Pass the west end of the cathedral and turn right to the little network of old streets beyond rue du College: rue du Pelicot (No 5 is the only surviving house from the 17th century), Cour la Houssaye and rue de la Corne de Cerf. Return via rue Garangeau to place Châteaubriand.

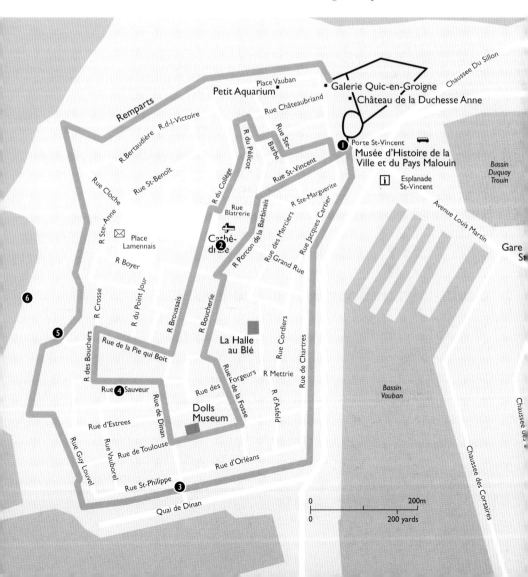

The Rance Valley

Ratings

Architecture	●●●●●
Heritage	●●●●●
History	●●●●●
Food	●●●●○
Scenery	●●●●○
Walking	●●●●○
Castles and châteaux	●●●○○
Cathedrals and churches	●●●○○

Back in the mists of time the original Rance Valley was inundated by the sea, 'drowning' the river and its tributaries and carving out characteristic fiord-like inlets. Today's tidal surges are harnessed by the vast Barrage de la Rance to generate hydroelectricity and the tidal power station (*usine marémotrice*) at la Richardais is a tourist attraction in its own right. Beyond the dam the now tamed river meanders below lush, gently sloping fields, interspersed with woodland and apple orchards. Further upstream the canal boats negotiate their way through the locks of the Ille-et-Rance waterway, the towpaths and bridges bedecked with geraniums, petunias and clematis. Dinan, with its castle, ramparts and picturesque half-timbered houses is one of the most beautiful medieval towns in France and an ideal touring base.

CHATEAU DE LA BOURBANSAIS AND ZOO

Château de la Bourbansais €€€
Pleugueneuc; tel: 02 99 69 40 07; e-mail: contact@ labourbansais.com; www. zoo-bansais.com. Open Apr–Sept, daily, 1000–1900; Oct–Mar, 1400–1800. Salon de thé, restaurant, picnic areas and a small children's playground.

The 16th-century château has been embellished by successive generations and is replete with pointed turrets and tent-roofed pavilions, but the grounds are the main attraction. A formal French garden opens out on to more than 100 hectares of parkland and a zoo comprising animals and birds from five continents, including kangaroos, dromedaries, macaws, flamingos and a panoply of wild cats. Inside the château are exhibitions of porcelain and 17th-century Aubusson tapestries. The kennels, with a pack of more than 80 hunting hounds, are also open to the public.

COBAC PARK

This entertaining fun park is designed specifically for the young but some of the activities may appeal to older visitors as well. Scattered

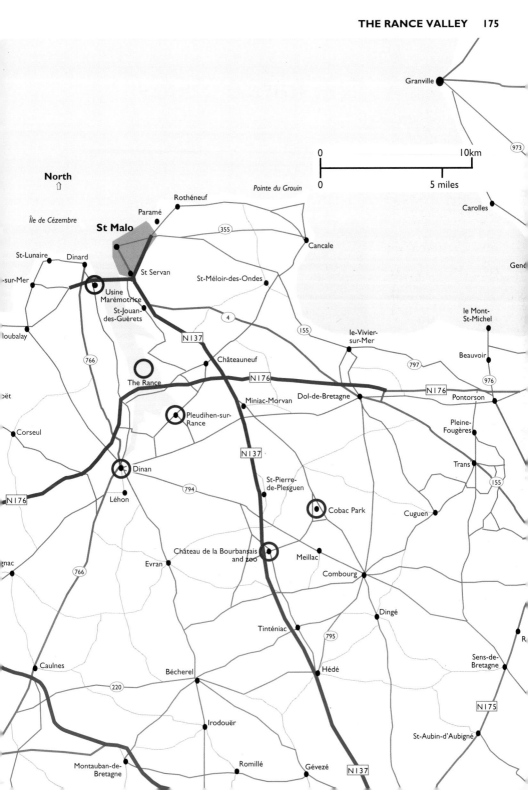

Cobac Park €€€
Route de Pleugueneuc, Lanhelin; tel: 02 99 73 80 16; www.cobac-parc.fr. Open July and Aug, 1000–1830, June, 1000–1800; Apr, May & Sept, weekends only, 1030–1800.

around the landscaped woodland site are swings and play equipment, go-karting, a swimming pool with water slide, mini-golf, a bird park, paddle boats, bouncy castles, a pony stables, a miniature train and a children's zoo. There are fast-food outlets as well as indoor and outdoor picnic areas on the site.

DINAN

Dinan Tourist Information *9 rue du Château; tel: 02 96 87 69 76; fax: 02 96 87 69 77; e-mail: info@dinan-tourisme.com; www.dinan-tourisme.com.* Guided themed tours of the town are available in season (not Sun or holidays); also combined museum ticket 'Les Clefs de Dinan' (includes entry to castle, Tour de l'Horloge and Maison du Gouveurneur).

P Below the viaduct (*rue du Quai*), place Duclos, place des Cordeliers, place St-Sauveur and the market squares place du Guesclin and place du Champs (*not Thur*).

The one-way trip to Dinard/St-Malo takes 2¼ hours, schedule depending on the tides. Return only possible by bus or train. Departures from the port with Compagne Corsaire. Boats with English commentary also make the short trip to Léhan.

Tour de l'Horloge *€ Rue de l'Horloge. Open Apr and May, 1400–1800; June–Sept, daily, 1000–1830.*

Above
Dinan

Discovering this perfectly-preserved medieval town is a sheer delight. Anyone driving into Dinan over the former railway viaduct (now the N176) will appreciate its strategic location high above the Rance Valley, likened by the novelist Victor Hugo to a housemartin's nest cleaving to a precipice. This location, coupled with the protection of powerful overlords, enabled Dinan to spawn a prosperous mercantile community trading in wool and cloth. Street names such as rue de la Lainerie (Woolshops Street) and place des Merciers (Haberdashers' Square) reflect this tradition.

Castle Museum €€
Rue du Château; tel: 02
96 39 45 20. Open
June–Sept, 1000–1830,
Oct–May, 1330–1730.

Maison du Gouverneur
€ 24 rue le Petit-Fort;
tel: 02 96 39 29 97. Open
June–Sept, daily, 1000–1900.

Market, Thursday,
place du Champ and
place du Guesclin.

Fête des Remparts
July; every two years.
Events with a medieval
theme including processions,
banquets and jousting.

Arvor €€ 5 rue
Pavie; tel: 02 96 39 21
22; fax: 02 96 39 03 09.
This former convent has a
central location near the
tourist office.

La Duchesse Anne € 10
place du Guesclin; tel: 02 96
39 59 76; fax: 02 96 87 57
26. Good-value hotel with
restaurant on the old market
square. Can be noisy.

Hotel d'Avagour €€
1 place du Champ;
tel: 02 96 39 07 49;
fax: 02 96 85 43 04; e-mail:
avagour.hotel@wanadoo.fr;
www.avagourhotel.com.
Situated in the heart of the
historic city, this hotel was
recently refurbished.

Hotel de France
€€ 7 place du 11
Novembre 1918; tel: 02 96
39 22 56; fax: 02 96 39 08
96. Well-positioned logis
with a seasonally varied
menu spanning roast duck
and crispy apple pancakes.

Castle and ramparts

The most accessible stretch of Dinan's 3km girdle of ramparts and watchtowers connects the neat flowerbeds of the **Jardin Anglais** with the **Tour du Sillon**. The sturdy **castle keep** (14th-century) was once separated from the rest of the town by a moat. You can visit the chapel, kitchen and guardrooms, before moving on to an exhibition on the life and history of the region in one of the towers.

Churches and monasteries

Between place des Merciers and the Jardin Anglais is the church of **St-Sauveur**. The superb Romanesque porch dates from the 12th century – note the intricate stone carving in the central arch and above, the figures of a bull and a lion. Inside, the history of the church can be read in its architecture – an uneasy transition from Romanesque to late Gothic. Beneath the gravestone in the north transept is the heart of the Breton warrior, Bertrand du Guesclin (*see page 178*).

The former **Franciscan monastery** in place des Cordeliers (13th century) was converted into a school shortly after the Revolution, but the original courtyard, chapterhouse and cloister have survived and are worth a look. From the quandrangle you can see the apse of Dinan's other main church, **St-Malo**, replete with flying buttresses and pinnacled side chapels. Concerts and recitals are often held here in summer.

Commercial heart

Colourful half-timbered houses, dating mostly from the 14th and 15th centuries, overhang the cobbled streets of the old town. Those around **place des Cordeliers** and **place des Merciers** were built with arcades, supported by massive wooden beams; here tradesmen would once have sold their wares. Near the latter is **rue de l'Horloge**, with its landmark steeple-topped clock tower. The clock dates from 1498 while the clangerous bell was presented to the town by Anne of Brittany in 1507. If you have the energy, climb the 158 steps for panoramic views of the town and surrounding countryside.

The port

The most impressive of the gate-towers is the monumental **Porte du Jerzual**. Through here lies the most picturesque street of all, **rue du Petit Fort**, a steep, cobbled roadway leading down to the port. Once an important thoroughfare, echoing to the clatter of carts crammed with leather, ships' timbers, cloth and wax bound for St-Malo, it is now a set-piece 'artisans' quarter' with workshops and galleries specialising in glassware, woodcraft and ceramics. In the stunning **Maison du Gouverneur** (15th century), weavers demonstrate the art of tapestry-making on a hand loom.

A walk through Dinan

Bertrand du Guesclin

Born in 1320, this brave Breton knight became a hero after distinguishing himself during the Hundred Years' War. It was said of him that 'there is none so ugly from Rennes to Dinant'. In 1359, during the siege of Dinan, Bertrand challenged the English knight Thomas of Canterbury to single combat after the invading army had broken a truce. The two combatants slugged it out on what is now place du Guesclin; Bertrand emerged victorious and eventually rose to be Constable of France. He died in 1380 and his heart is buried in Dinan.

This walking tour guides you through the main streets of Dinan's old town. Approach from the port, as visitors have done for centuries, climbing the steep and winding **rue de Petit-Fort** and entering the citadel through the **Jerzuel Gate**. Turn left and cross rue Haute-Voie to visit the **Church of St-Sauveur**. Behind the church, the **Jardin Anglais** opens on to a magnificent panorama of the port and the Rance Valley. Leave the gardens via the Promenade de la Duchesse Anne which follows the line of the ramparts in a southerly direction.

Continue along rue du Général de Gaulle to the **castle**, then cross place du Guesclin which commemorates the famous military hero. His equestrian statue now presides over the square. Turn right into rue Ste-Claire, then left into rue de l'Horloge. Just before the clock tower stop to look at the arcaded **Maison du Gisant** and the 14th-century tombstone discovered during a recent restoration of the house. At the end of rue de l'Horloge turn left into **place des Merciers**, stopping to admire the half-timbered houses here and in the adjoining streets – rue de la Cordoniere, rue du Petit Pain and la Mittrie.

Cross **place des Cordeliers** to Grand Rue Lainerie. On your left is the church of **St-Malo**, ahead the **Franciscan Monastery**. Take the intermediate street, rue Comte de la Garaye, then turn right on to Promenade des Grands Fossés. Follow the ramparts to the Tour du Gouverneur for more views of the town and the Rance Valley, before returning to the port.

PLEUDIHEN-SUR-RANCE

🏛 **Musée de la Pomme et du Cidre** € *Pleudihen-sur-Rance (near Mordreuc on D29); tel: 02 96 83 20 78. Open June–Aug, 1000–1900; Apr, May & Sept, 1400–1900.*

The **Musée de la Pomme et du Cidre** (apple and cider museum) is located on a farm in the heart of the Breton countryside. The exhibition covers all aspects of cultivation and distilling, including the different apple varieties, how diseases are treated, apple picking, cider presses and related trades (cooperage etc). There's a film show followed by a tasting. You can test your knowledge by looking around the orchard on your way out.

THE RANCE

The best way to explore the lower reaches of the Rance from Dinan is by boat. If you are on foot the rue du Quai follows the river to a towpath which winds its way scenically for another 7km before petering out. About 2km in the opposite direction is Léhon and the ruins of the former Priory of St-Magloire (accessible either by boat or on foot).

USINE MAREMOTRICE (BARRAGE DE LA RANCE)

Usine Marémotrice
La Richardais (access by the lock on the Dinard side); tel: 02 99 16 37 00. Open Tue–Sun, 1300–1900. No photography inside.

Château de Montmarin
€€ Pleurtuit, tel: 02 99 88 58 79. Open May–Sept, Sun–Fri, 1400–1900. For details of special displays contact tourist information in Dinan.

Kyriad Hôtel €€
14 rue des Genêts, la Richardais; tel: 02 99 46 69 55; fax: 02 99 88 16 16. This hotel near the dam has a seafood restaurant with two set menus.

Le Chateaubriand
€€€ Barrage de la Rance; tel: 08 00 03 58 00; e-mail: chateaubriand@ chateaubriand.com. www.chateaubriand.com. Dine in luxury while cruising down the Rance. Departures twice daily. Tours last 3½ hours.

Kerguelen € *26 rue Gougeonnais, la Richardais; tel: 02 99 46 66 76. Crêperie with a delicious choice of galettes.*

As early as the 12th century the powerful tides of the Rance estuary were harnessed to mill flour. At one time there were as many as 16 tidal mills in its lower reaches – the remains of one of them can still be seen at St-Suliac. Modern engineers, aware of the continuing value of 'blue coal' have constructed a hydroelectric station to dam the estuary at la Richardais. The Usine Marémotrice – the only one of its kind in the world – produces a staggering 600 million kilowatt hours of electricity per year. The dam is currently France's most popular industrial tourist attraction with an estimated 400,000 visitors annually.

Suggested tour

Total distance: 115.5km (140km with detours).

Time: 2½ hours' driving. Allow 6 hours for the main route but an additional 3 hours if you intend to take a detour to Cobac Parc or la Bourbansais zoo. Those with limited time should concentrate on the Rance Valley.

Links: This route is crossed by the N176 which links the Baie du Mont-St-Michel (*see pages 222–31*) to St-Brieuc and the Côte de Granit Rose (*see pages 108–25*). It also borders the Côte d'Emeraude (*see pages 154–63*).

The D12 leaves from the port of **DINAN ①** and heads north, winding its way through the villages on the west bank of the Rance Valley. **Taden** is the first point of access to the river – a 14th-century turret stands at the top of the slipway. This part of the towpath is popular with anglers who compete for fishing rights with coots and gulls. At la Hisse turn right just before crossing the railway where the road leads to the busy lock at **Ecluse du Chatelier**. Return to the D12 and continue northwards through the village of Plouër-sur-Rance, then take the D114 to le Minihic. For a good view of the upper reaches of the Rance, turn right on to the D5 1.5km after le Minihic towards **Cale de la Jouvente**. Rejoin the D114 for la Richardais. Just before the town look out for signs to **Château de Montmarin**, a former shipowner's mansion with a beautiful terraced garden on the banks of the Rance. **La Richardais** is the site of the hydroelectric power station, **USINE MAREMOTRICE ②**. After leaving the town, join the D168 crossing the top of the dam, then turn right on to the D117, a quieter road than the parallel N137 and with plenty of opportunities to stop for photographs. Beyond St-Jouan-des-Guérets the road crosses an inlet before passing the old **Beauchet tidal mill**, a nature reserve and a favourite haunt of egrets, herons, shelducks and other migrating birds. At **St-Suliac** the D117 turns south to climb Mont Garrot from

🅡 Maison du Canal €
Bazouges-sous-Hédé;
tel: 02 99 45 48 90. Open
July and Aug, daily,
1030–1230, 1330–1900;
Apr–June, Sept & Oct,
Wed–Mon, 1400–1800;
Nov–Mar, Sun, 1400–1800.
Information in English.

Château de Caradeuc
Park € Bécherel. Open July
and Aug, daily, 1200–1800,
reduced hours rest of year,
tel: 02 99 66 81 10.

🄲 Aux Voyageurs
Gourmandis €€ 39
rue Nationale, Tinténiac; tel:
02 99 68 02 21; fax: 02 99
68 19 58. A logis near the
canal quay with a small
garden and an excellent
restaurant serving fish
specialities.

Hôtel du Vieux Moulin
€€ La Vallé des Moulins,
Hédé; tel: 02 99 45 45 70;
fax: 02 99 45 44 86. The
stream tumbling through
the garden is just part of
the attractive surroundings
of this old inn. A delightful
spot for lunch.

🄼 L'Oree Du Parc
€€ 35 Bécherel-St
Pern; tel: 02 99 66 74 72;
fax: 02 99 66 86 20.
Traditional regional fare in
large amounts; just outside
Bécherel.

where there are more panoramic views. Cross the N176 and turn right on to the D29, heading towards the apple orchards of **PLEUDIHEN-SUR-RANCE ❸**. From here take the D48 eastwards to Miniac Morvan and join the D73, passing through the Forêt du Mesnil on the way to Lanhélin.

Detour: Take the D75 from Lanhélin to **COBAC PARC ❹**; another 12km along the same road will bring you to the château and zoo at **LA BOURBANSAIS ❺**.

Continue to Pleugueneuc then take the road south through the waterside village of **Tinténiac** to **Hédé**, a possible lunch stop. Just the other side of the village, at Bazouges-sous-Hédé, you can watch the boats negotiate the ladder of 11 locks – if you're interested the lock-keeper's house has been converted into a small but entertaining museum, the **Maison du Canal**, about the canal and its history. Return to Hédé and take the D221. Cross the N137 and turn first right then right again through the villages of les Iffs and Cardoc to the D27. Bibliophiles should make a beeline for the hillside town of **Bécherel** which boasts an amazing 16 bookshops as well as two bookbinders and a large second-hand market on the first Sunday of every month. From the **Thabor Gardens** in town or the terrace of the **Château de Caradeuc**, 1km to the west, there are superb views of the Rance Valley as far as Dinan. Follow the valley on the D68 to **Evran**, where the lock is ablaze with flowers in summer. From here take the D2 in the direction of Dinan. Just outside the town is the ruined priory of **St-Magloire** at **Léhon** where the restored 13th-century church contains the tombs of members of the Beaumanoir family. The adjacent convent buildings have recently opened as a small museum.

Also worth exploring

The Rance Valley west of Bécherel is also an area of great natural beauty. At Médréac take the small road to la Reculais, then turn left to Guitté and Caulnes. From Guitté a footpath leads along the river bank to the bridge at Néal; alternatively drive to Guenroc and the Barrage de Rophémel for good views.

Right
Road bridge over the Rance

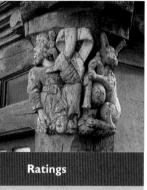

The Nantes-Brest Canal

Ratings

Heritage	●●●●●
Boats	●●●●○
Children	●●●●○
Architecture	●●●○○
Castles and châteaux	●●●○○
Food	●●●○○
History	●●●○○
Scenery	●●●○○

Three waterways, the Vilaine, the Oust and the Nantes-Brest Canal meet at Redon, an engaging maze of sluices, locks and towpaths with 19th-century shipowners' houses gracing the port. There are boat excursions from Redon along the Vilaine as far as la Roche-Bernard and the Arzal Dam in one direction and Beslé in the other. Boats also visit the local beauty spot, Ile aux Pies (Magpie Island); alternatively, you can hire a motor launch or canoe and work out an itinerary of your own.

Almost every town and village in the region lays claim to the title *ville (village) fleuris* and competition for the best floral decoration is fierce. You can be your own judge between Rochefort-en-Terre, Lizio, la Gacilly and Malestroit. Josselin's Musée des Poupées is one of a number of first-rate museums definitely worth investigating. If you're not bowled over by dolls, other subjects given the treatment include beauty products, classic cars, the prehistoric world and the French Resistance.

JOSSELIN

ⓘ **Josselin Tourist information** *Place de la Congrégation (by the castle); tel: 02 97 22 36 43; fax: 02 97 22 20 44; e-mail: ot.josselin@wanadoo.fr; www.josselin.com*

Ⓟ Place St-Martin, place A-de-Rohan (behind the basilica), rue de la Fontaine.

Right
Josselin town sign

The **château** has been in the hands of the Rohan family for more than 500 years already and they're still in residence. Three tent-roofed towers guarding the River Oust and a magnificent traceried façade overlooking the park are all that remain of the 15th-century building destroyed on the orders of Cardinal Richelieu in 1629. History buffs will want to see the table on which the Edict of Nantes was signed in 1598; otherwise the tour of the apartments with their paintings, *objets d'art* and ponderous furniture is unmemorable. Not so the **Musée des Poupées (Doll Museum)** in the former stables, a collection of more than 600 dolls

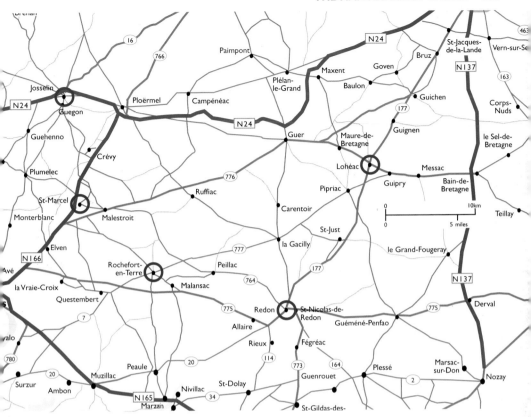

Castle and Doll Museum €€€ (Two separate tickets may be purchased. Guided tours of the castle last 45 minutes) *tel: 02 97 22 36 45.* Open mid-July–Aug, 1000–1800; June–mid-July and Sept, 1400–1800; Apr, May & school holidays, 1400–1800.

There is a market on Saturday.

Mid-July – Josselin Medieval Festival.

from all over the world, the oldest dating back to the 17th century. There are toys and games, too, to entertain the children.

Hemmed in between the castle and the hillside is the old town and the ancient basilica of **Notre-Dame-du-Roncier**. Founded in the 12th century, the church honours an even older legend of a peasant who found a statue of the Virgin in a bramble bush – Our Lady of the Brambles. Look in the south chapel for the tomb of the one-eyed Olivier de Clisson, called the Butcher – his trade mark was chopping off the arms and legs of his English opponents during battle. For good views of the château, cross the river to the picturesque little quarter of **Ste-Croix** with its 11th-century chapel.

Accommodation and food in Josselin

Hôtel du Château €€ *1 rue du Général de Gaulle; tel: 02 97 22 20 11; fax: 02 97 22 34 09; e-mail: contact@hotel-chateau.com; www.hotel-chateau.com.* Medieval building with dormer windows overlooking the river opposite the castle. Atmospheric dining hall.

Hôtel de France €€ *6 place Notre-Dame; tel: 02 97 73 61 93.* Attractive ivy-clad *logis* in the centre of town. Excellent restaurant.

LOHÉAC

Manoir de l'Automobile €€
Lohéac; tel: 02 99 34 02 32; fax: 02 99 34 05 01; www.manoir-automobile.fr. Open Tue–Sun, 1000–1300, 1400–1900.

Lohéac has a number of establishments catering for cars and their owners. There's a market on Saturdays.

Our long and passionate love affair with the internal combustion engine is celebrated at la Courneuve, near Lohéac, where the manor house and grounds have been converted into the fascinating **Manoir de l'Automobile,** with several hundred cars on show. Exhibits include vintage models from the beginning of the century, a prize collection of Alpines (including the Berlinette Tour de France A 108) and enough Ferraris, Lamborghinis and Porsches to set the heart of any collector or amateur enthusiast racing. In the adjoining **Chapelle des Moteurs** you can see a small exhibition of car engines while children will enjoy the scale models (more than 3000 in all). The museum shop sells everything from toy cars to key rings, posters, T-shirts and designer holdalls and there are films of car rallies and other events in the projection room.

Accommodation and food in Lohéac

Le Café du Village € *23 rue de la Poste; tel: 02 99 34 19 19; fax: 02 99 34 19 20.* Piano-bar with its own wine cellar. A few rooms available too.

Opposite
The Nantes-Brest Canal at Redon

La Gibecière €€ *28 rue de la Poste; tel: 02 99 34 06 14; fax: 02 99 34 10 37.* Family-run hotel and restaurant in the centre of the village.

REDON

Redon Tourist Information *Place de la République; tel: 02 99 71 06 04; fax: 02 99 71 01 59; e-mail: tourisme.redon@ wanadoo.fr; www.redon.fr.* An annexe is open in the port during the summer.

Musée de la Batellerie € *Quai Jean-Bart; tel: 02 99 72 30 95. Open mid-June–mid-Sept, 1000–1200, 1500–1800; 16 Sept–14 June, Sat–Mon, Wed, 1400–1800.*

This historic little town has a lot to recommend it: a wonderful location at the confluence of the Oust and Vilaine rivers; direct access to one of the loveliest stretches of the Nantes-Brest canal; and, down by the port (which once served Rennes), stately shipowners' houses dating back to the 18th century.

For more than 900 years the driving force behind this thriving riverine community was its abbey, and the monastic church, the magnificent **Eglise St-Sauveur,** is still the town's principal monument. In 1780 a disastrous fire destroyed part of the nave. The dispirited monks, lacking the means to restore it, left things the way they were with the result that the 14th-century bell tower stands in splendid isolation from the rest of the building. Architecturally it's the pointed lantern-tower over the transept crossing that's really remarkable – it dates from the 12th century and is one of the finest examples of Romanesque architecture in Brittany. The tower rests on a massive stone-vaulted cupola, supported in its turn by rounded arches and pillars with decorated capitals. Light floods in through the windows of the superb 13th-century choir. The elaborate baroque retable was installed at the behest of Cardinal Richelieu in the 17th century (the

Bike hire: M. Chedaleux Nicolas
44 rue Notre Dame; tel: 02 99 72 19 95. Parking is on quai Surcouf, rue Victor-Hugo (by the railway).

Vedettes Jaunes
Tel: 02 97 45 02 81;
fax: 02 97 45 00 41;
www.vedettesjaunes.com.
Runs boat excursions past la Roche Bernard to the Arzal Barrage (return journey by coach because of the tides) – 5-hour trip.

October – Mois du Maron (Chestnut festival). Typical events include a folk singing competition and a fair with street pedlars, lots of stalls and of course roasted chestnuts.

cloisters, now a school, are of the same period). Follow the avenue of chestnut trees around the back of the church for a better view of the chevet and flying buttresses.

To your left is the Vilaine, Redon's principal waterway, while at the end of quai St-Jacques are the lock gates and sluices of the Nantes-Brest Canal. Continue over the bridge and you'll arrive at the **port**. In days gone by cargoes of cloth, wine and spices were unloaded on the quayside and stored in the ground-floor rooms of the houses on quai Duguay Trouin. Other reminders of Redon's maritime past include the old customs barracks on rue du Jeu de Paume and the 17th-century salt warehouses on rue du Port. The **Musée de la Batellerie** recounts the history of Brittany's canals and the lives of its watermen with models, documents, photographs, various artefacts and a film – in French of course. Every Thursday in July and August **pleasure boats** leave from near the Croix des Marins for a day-long, 40km excursion downstream to the Arzal dam (return journey by coach). If you don't care to ride on the canal you're free to wander the tree-shaded towpaths into open country. Pack a picnic from the shops on the **Grand Rue** – the merchants' houses here are among the oldest in town. If you're eating out, *marrons* (chestnuts) are the local speciality – there's a month-long festival in their honour in October.

Accommodation and food in Redon

Bel Hôtel €€ *St-Nicolas-de-Redon; tel: 02 99 71 10 10; fax: 02 99 72 33 03; e-mail: bienvenue@bel-hotel.com; www.bel-hotel.com.* Comfortable new hotel with friendly staff. (On the Nantes road, the other side of the river.)

Chandouineau €€€ *1 rue Thiers; tel: 02 99 71 02 04; fax: 02 99 71 08 81.* Upmarket gourmet menus with enticing seasonal specialities.

Le France € *30 rue Du Guesclin; tel: 02 99 71 06 11; fax: 02 99 72 17 92; e-mail: lefrance@worldonline.fr; www.citotel.com/hotels/redon.htm.* Exceedingly comfortable town-centre hotel, overlooking the port. No restaurant.

L'Ile aux Grillades € *15 rue d'Enfer; tel: 02 99 72 20 40.* Grills and fish cooked on a wood fire. *Closed Sun & Mon.*

ROCHEFORT-EN-TERRE

ℹ️ Rochefort-en-Terre Tourist Information *Place des Halles; tel: 02 97 43 33 57; e-mail: ot.rochefortenterre@ wanadoo.fr; www.rochefort-en-terre.com*

🏛️ Château €€ *Tel: 02 97 43 31 56. Guided tours (1 hour) July and Aug, daily, 1000–1830; June and Sept, daily, 1400–1830; Apr, May & Oct, Sat–Sun and public holidays, 1400–1830.*

☕ Le Rucher Fleuri *Rue du Porche; tel: 02 97 43 35 78; e-mail: jean-francois.humeau@wanadoo.fr.* Spiced bread, honey cakes and other honey produce.

Candre Faience *Rue Candray; tel: 02 97 43 34 46.* Hand-crafted pottery and souvenirs.

This pretty little village perched on a ridge, the wooded slopes dropping away dramatically to the River Arz below, was once of great strategic importance. The **château** was destroyed during the Revolution and in the 19th century its picturesque ruins were a popular subject with artists. One of them, a wealthy American portrait painter named Alfred Klots, fell in love with the place and, in 1907, decided to restore it. (Klots is also credited with setting Rochefort on the road to becoming one of France's outstanding '*village fleuris*'.) The restoration, if not exactly authentic, is tastefully done. Only four rooms are open to the public. They're richly furnished with tapestries, paintings by Klots and his son, Trafford, and a collection of faïence madonnas. The views of the Gueuzon Valley from the terrace are outstanding. Below the château is the church of **Notre-Dame-de-la-Tronchaye**. According to legend a statue of the Virgin was found hidden in a nearby tree in the 12th century, apparently in an attempt to prevent it falling into the hands of the Norsemen – you'll find it in the south transept of the church, behind a wrought-iron grille. The local *pardon* is held on the Sunday after the feast of the Assumption (15 August).

In the summer the streets around place du Puits and rue du Porce are illuminated at night to show off their stone and half-timbered houses. The village is kept spotless for tourists who pay for the privilege with higher prices in hotels and restaurants.

Accommodation and food in Rochefort-en-Terre

Camping du Moulin Neuf €€ *Chemin de Bogeais; tel: 02 97 43 37 52; fax: 02 97 43 35 45.* Near town, the facilities at this attractive campsite include a swimming pool, children's room, tennis, fishing and a bar. 60 pitches.

Château de Talhouët €€€ *Turn off the D777a on the Molac road, Rochefort-en-Terre; tel: 02 97 43 34 72; fax: 02 97 43 35 04; e-mail: chateaudetalhouet@libertysurf.fr; www.chateaudetalhouet.com.* Classy *chambre d'hôte* set in its own park.

Cafe Du Puits *Place du Puits; tel: 02 97 43 30 43.* Homely spot that during July and August serves Breton dishes and an array of tempting desserts.

Le Menestrel € *Place du Champ de Foire; tel: 02 97 43 38 33.* Unassuming bar with good brasserie and *crêperie*; outside terrace.

St-Marcel

Musée de la Résistance Bretonne € *Tel: 02 97 75 16 90; fax: 02 97 75 16 92; www.resistance-bretonne.com. Open mid-June–mid-Sept, 1000–1900; mid-Sept–mid-June, Wed–Mon, 1000–1200, 1400–1800.*

In June 1944 St-Marcel was the site of a remarkable joint operation by members of the local French Resistance (the *Maquis*) and Free French parachutists, which successfully diverted German troops from defending the Normandy coast during the D-Day landings. Part of the forest is now an absorbing open-air **Musée de la Résistance Bretonne (Museum of Breton Resistance)**. In the main building montages, models, German propaganda posters and a reconstructed street scene all help to convey life under the German occupation, from rationing and the black market to collaboration and the activities of the local *Maquis*. Elsewhere in the park there is a collection of military vehicles, weapons and gas-run cars belonging to both German and Allied forces. There's even a guided tour in a US army half-truck. A brief explanatory leaflet in English is also available.

Suggested tour

Total distance: 193km (215km with detours).

Time: 4 hours' driving. Allow 11 hours for the main route, 14 hours with the detour to Lohéac. If you have children you might find yourself spending longer at the Parc de la Préhistoire (*see page 188*). Extra days should be allocated for boat excursions. Those with limited time should concentrate on the stretch between Rochefort-en-Terre and Malestroit via Redon.

Links: The N166 to Vannes (*see pages 134–41*) crosses the route, while the D177 links Redon to Rennes (*see pages 214–21*).

Leave **JOSSELIN ❶** on the D126 to **Guehenno** where the calvary, originally dating from 1550, was gamely restored by the parish priest and his assistant after it had been attacked by Revolutionary zealots,

ⓘ **Questembert** *15 rue des Halles; tel: 02 97 26 56 00; www. questembert.com*

Ploërmel *5 rue du Val; tel: 02 97 74 02 70; fax: 02 97 73 31 82; e-mail: ot.ploermel@wanadoo.fr; www.ploermel.com*

Malestroit *17 place du Bouffay; tel: 02 97 75 14 57; fax: 02 97 73 71 13; e-mail: tourisme@malestroit.com; www.malestroit.com*

ⓗ **Forteresse de Largoët** € *Elven; tel: 02 97 53 35 96; fax: 02 40 29 03 73. Open July and Aug, daily, 1030–1210, 1420–1830; June and Sept same hours but closed Tue; May Sat and Sun, 1420–1830.*

Parc de la Préhistoire €€ *Malansac, Redon; tel: 02 97 43 34 17; fax: 02 97 43 34 42; e-mail: contact@ prehistoire.com; www. prehistoire.com. Open Apr– mid-Oct, 1030–1930; mid-Oct–mid-Nov, Sun, 1330–1830.*

⊙ There is a good fruit and vegetable market on Thur in Malestroit.

⊙ Lizio Craft Festival – mid–late Aug.

ⓒ **Hôtel le Cobh** €€ *10 rue des Forges, Ploërmel; tel: 02 97 74 00 49; fax: 02 97 74 07 36.* Central hotel with excellent fish restaurant.

Hôtel de France €€ *15 rue Montauban, la Gacilly; tel: 02 99 08 11 15; fax: 02 99 08 25 88; e-mail: HOTEL.FRANCE.LAGACILLY @wanadoo.fr; www. hoteldefrancelagacilly.com.* Well-maintained *logis* with good restaurant.

saving his parishioners' pockets in the process but leaving some rather naive carvings to posterity. Look out for the crowing cockerel in the denial of Christ by St Peter. From Guehenno take the D160 through Cruguel, then after about 5km turn right to St-Aubin. Turn left opposite the church to **Callac**. As you enter the village, you'll see a modern copy of the Lourdes grotto. To the left a steep path lined by stations of the cross leads to a small calvary from where there are good views over the surrounding countryside.

Continue to Tredion and turn left on to the D1 through the Forest of Lanvaux. The Chouans established a short-lived independent kingdom here in the 1790s and during World War II these same wooded hills harboured members of the Resistance.

Take the D1 through **Elven**, then continue on the old road parallel to the N166. Take the right-hand turning signed 'Forteresse de Largoët'. The massive ivy-covered octagonal keep and watchtower of the ruined castle, known locally as Elven Towers, are a 30-minute walk through woodland from the car park by the gatehouse. The future King of England, Henry VII, was held captive here between 1474 and 1476, while the Duke of Brittany negotiated a ransom. Little more than a decade later the castle was abandoned after an attack by the French King Charles VIII.

Return in the direction of Elven, turning first right on to the D1. At the D775 crossing take the small detour into **la Vraie-Croix**, a pretty village where the church is built on a ribbed vault over the medieval road. Continue on the D1 to **Questembert**, a small town built around a superb 16th-century timbered market hall. From here take the D7, turning left on to the D777 to **ROCHEFORT-EN-TERRE** ❷.

Above
Malestroit: medieval carving

Opposite
Elven church and war memorial

① Tropical Parc €€
St-Jacut-les-Pins; tel: 02 99 71 91 98; fax: 02 99 71 87 80. Open July and Aug, daily, 0900–1900; Apr, May, Sept & Oct, 1000–1200, 1400–1900.

Le Végétarium €€ La Gacilly; tel: 02 99 08 35 84; Open mid-June–mid-Sept, 1030–1930.

Écomusée de Lizio €
Lizio; tel: 02 97 74 93 01; www.ecomuseelizio.com. Open Apr–Sept, 1000–1200, 1400–1900; Oct, Feb & Mar, 1400–1800.

Musée d'un Poète Ferrailleur € La Ville Stéphant, Lizio; tel: 06 77 81 11 44; e-mail: rocoudray@wanadoo.fr; www.poeteferrailleur.free.fr. Open May–Oct, daily, 1000–1800; Apr and Nov, Sun only.

① Château de Castellan €€€ St-Martin-sur-Oust; tel: 02 99 91 51 69. Traditional auberge with restaurant serving regional cuisine.

Le Bretagne €€€
Questembert; tel: 02 97 26 11 12; fax: 02 97 26 12 37; e-mail: lebretagne@ wanadoo.fr; www.paineaulebretagne.com. Popular hotel/restaurant serving nouvelle cuisine.

Leave Rochefort on the D21, turning sharp left on to the D134 to the **Parc de la Préhistoire**, where in a specially landscaped woodland setting, life-sized models are arranged to re-create daily life in prehistoric times. The 30 or so scenes include *Homo erectus* making fire and Cro-Magnon men organising a stag hunt. Dinosaurs emerge menacingly from the undergrowth – children beware!

Continue to Peillac, then turn right to **St-Jacut-les-Pins** and the **Tropical Parc** where the theme is the flora and fauna of the Far East and Australasia. Some of the animals, including emus and kangaroos, are tame enough to be approached. The park has only recently opened and is the result of over ten years of planning by enthusiast Michel Gicquel.

Take the D153, then the D764 to **REDON ❸**. Leave on the D177 to Renac, then take the left fork (the D65) to **St-Just**.

Detour: Turn right and take the D177 to **LOHEAC ❹**, a village devoted to cars. Return to St-Just.

Head westwards from the village through the **Cojoux Valley**, the second largest megalithic site in France. From the car park a signposted path threads its way through menhirs and dolmens to a granite outcrop popular with rock climbers; from here there are good views of lake le Val and the surrounding countryside.

Continue to the junction with the D777, then turn left to **la Gacilly**, a pretty, flower-bedecked town and the home of the Yves Rocher perfume factory, museum and **Végétarium** where you can learn all about the production of the famous natural beauty products. La Gacilly is also known for its craftsmen: glassblowers, carpenters, enamel workers, potters, weavers and others. A number of their workshops are open to the public. Alternatively you could take a boat trip down the River Aff to the local beauty spot, **Ile aux Pies** (Magpie Island).

In a region made for waterborne exploration there are copious opportunities for boat hire, and for lengthier cruises along rivers and lakes. Among many small locally-based companies are Day Boats, who offer river launches rentable by the hour; *tel: 02 99 08 05 02; www.bateaux-fluviaux-bretagne.com.* The bigger operation, Bretagne Plaisance, offers cruises ranging from one day to two weeks, departing from 12 quai Jean-Bart, Redon; *tel: 02 99 72 15 80; fax: 02 99 72 29 56; www.bretagne-plaisance.fr*

Above left
Josselin castle

Leave la Gacilly on the D777 through the New Forest to **St-Martin**, where the road crosses the River Oust – an ideal spot for a picnic. At St-Grave turn right on to the D764, a scenic road following the river valley to **Malestroit** on the Nantes-Brest Canal. The village has an attractive main square (place du Bouffay) – look out for the facetious wood carvings on the half-timbered houses.

Leave on the St-Marcel road, then continue past the **Musée de la Résistance** at St-Marcel and under the N166. Bear right on the D151 and drive through the chestnut forests to Sérent, then continue on the D151 to **Lizio**. Renowned for its local crafts, especially weaving, there's a lively artisan fair and folk festival here on the second Sunday in August. If you're interested in village crafts there's also a small museum, the **Ecomusée des Vieux Métiers** about 4km from Lizio on the D174. Further on you'll pass the **Musée d'un Poète Ferrailleur**, a unique collection of over 40 automated sculptures, each designed to reawaken the spirit of childhood.

Take the D174 back across the River Oust to **Ploërmel**, a busy market town but not as interesting as neighbouring Josselin. The main attraction is the largest natural lake in Brittany, the Etang du Duc, 2.5km to the north of town with fishing, watersports and walking. Take the N24 to Josselin.

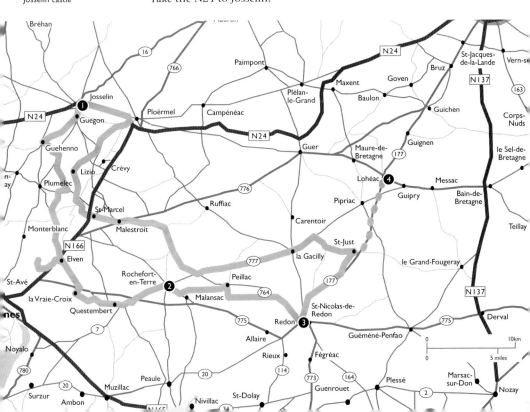

The Marais Salants

Ratings

Heritage	●●●●●
Scenery	●●●●●
Walking	●●●●●
Wildlife	●●●●●
Geology and landscape	●●●●○
Watersports	●●●●○
Beaches	●●●○○
Entertainment	●●●○○

Salt has been harvested in the Guérande Peninsula (the name means 'white country') since at least 700 BC. The saltpans extend over more than 1800 hectares as far as Guérande, Batz-sur-Mer and la Turballe. Bird and marine life flourish in the saline lagoons and shellfish farming is another local industry. If you're interested there are museums at Batz and Saillé.

Bordering the Marais Salants is the vast Brière Nature Park with its traditional communities of fishermen who ply the network of little rivers and canals in punts. The activities on offer here range from visiting craft museums to boat excursions, nature rambles and birdwatching.

For a complete contrast try la Baule, the largest seaside resort in Brittany with miles of golden sand and a night-life to challenge the most dedicated clubber. More sedate resorts include Pornichet, le Pouligen and le Croisic.

LA BAULE

ⓘ La Baule Tourist Information 8 place de la Victoire; tel: 02 40 24 34 44; fax: 02 40 11 08 10; e-mail: tourisme.la.baule@ wanadoo.fr; tourisme@ labaule.fr; www.labaule.fr

Ⓒ Casino de la Baule Esplanade L Barrière; tel: 02 40 11 48 28; www.lucienbarriere.com. English roulette, blackjack, stud poker, boule, 200 fruit machines, as well as a disco, restaurant and bars. Open, daily, 1000–0400.

Brittany's answer to Cannes and St-Tropéz, la Baule is as remote from the traditional Breton resort as it's possible to get. The place wasn't even on the map until 1879 when the little coastal town of Escoublac, already half buried under sand dunes whipped up by fierce Atlantic storms, was re-sited inland. The forest of pine trees planted at la-Baule-les-Pins stabilises the dunes and shelters the superb **beach** which extends for more than 7km in a vast arc around the bay. Most of the fashionable villas built for the French bourgeoisie in the 19th century have been elbowed out to make room for a seafront of humdrum hotels and apartment blocks with palm trees to complete the cliché. What la Baule lacks in character however, it more than makes up for in amenities – cinemas and casinos, as well as the usual assortment of restaurants, bars and discos. Sports enthusiasts are equally spoilt for choice with tennis, golf, horse riding and watersports on offer. If it's peace and quiet you're looking for there's the **Parc des Dryades**, or

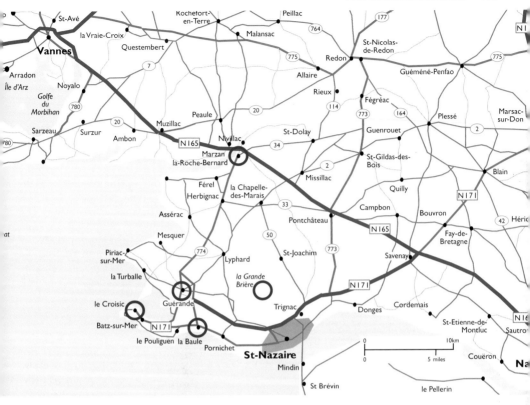

A lively daily market is held in the covered halls (*closed Monday from October to March*).

Pornichet also has a large daily market with an interesting, if smelly, fish hall.

you could head further afield to explore the caves of the **Côte Sauvage**. The mini-resorts of **Pornichet** and **le Pouligen**, connected to la Baule by tourist train, have a more authentic Breton flavour.

Accommodation and food in la Baule

Le Clemenceau €€ *42 avenue Georges Clemenceau; tel: 02 40 60 21 33; fax: 02 40 42 72 46; e-mail: hotel-le-clemenceau@wanadoo.fr; www.hotel-le-clemenceau.com.* Exceptional value *logis* with swimming pool and restaurant.

Le Lutétia €€ *13 avenue des Evens; tel: 02 40 60 25 81; fax: 02 40 42 73 52; e-mail: contact@lutetia-rossini.com; www.lutetia-rossini.com.* Comfortable family hotel near the beach.

La Mascotte €€€ *26 avenue Marie-Louise; tel: 0240 60 26 55; fax: 02 40 60 15 67; email: hotel.la.mascotte@wanadoo.fr; www.lamascotte.com.* Enclosed by pine trees but just 50m from the beach; also has a decent seafood restaurant.

La Roseraie € *20 avenue Jean Sohier; tel: 02 40 60 46 66; fax: 02 40 60 11 84; e-mail: camping@laroseraie.com; www.laroseraie.com. Open Apr–Sept.* Campsite towards the back of town.

LE CROISIC

Le Croisic Tourist Information *Place du 18 Juin; tel: 02 40 23 00 70; fax: 02 40 62 96 60; e-mail: bienvenue@ot-lecroisic.com; www.ot-lecroisic.com*

Océarium €€€ *Avenue de St-Goustan; tel: 02 40 23 02 44; fax: 02 40 23 22 93; e-mail: info@ocearium-croisic.fr; www.ocearium-croisic.fr. Open June, July & Aug, daily, 1000–1900; Sept–mid-Nov, Feb–May, 1000–1200, 1400–1800, mid-Nov–Dec, 1400–1800. Closed Jan. Shop, bar and crêperie.*

Market days are *Thursday and Saturday (also Tuesday in July and August).*

Below
Brière Nature Park

The old fishing port and seaside resort of le Croisic stands on a 5km-long headland with a lagoon on one side and the open sea on the other. More low-key (and therefore cheaper) than la Baule, it's a useful touring base for excursions to Batz, the Côte Sauvage, Parc Brière and the Guérande salt pans. Take an early morning stroll around the port to see the **fish auction** (the prawn catches rank among the best in France). There are sheltered **beaches** at Port-Lin, facing the Atlantic, and St-Goustan overlooking the harbour, although neither can compare with la Baule. The **Océarium** must rate as le Croisic's number-one attraction, especially if you have children in tow. The special feature here is a long see-through tunnel from where you can watch conger eels, rays, groupers and sharks swimming in the generous confines of a 300,000-litre tank. Labelling is in English and the amenities are first-rate. There are views of the salt marshes and the roadstead from two artificial hills formed from discarded ship's ballast, Mont-Esprit and Mont-Lénigo.

Accommodation and food in le Croisic

L'Estacade €€ *4–5 quai du Lénigo; tel: 02 40 23 03 77; fax: 02 40 23 24 32.* Popular, but noisy, hotel on the quay with bar and seafood restaurant.

Les Nids € *Plage de Port-Lin; tel: 02 40 23 00 63; fax: 02 40 23 09 79.* Traditional hotel with a large separate restaurant. Children's menus.

LA GRANDE BRIERE

ⓘ Maison du Tourisme de Brière *Rue de la Brière, la Chapelle-des-Marais; tel: 02 40 66 85 01; fax: 02 40 53 91 15; www.parc-naturel-briere.fr*

ⓝ Maison des Traditions € *La Chapelle-des-Marais; tel: 02 40 53 22 02. Open mid-June–mid-Sept, daily.*

Maison de l'Eclusier € *Rozé, St-Malo-de-Guersac; tel: 02 40 66 85 01. Open July–mid-Sept, daily, 1030–1300, 1430–1830; mid-Apr–June, daily, 1400–1800.*

Maison de la Mariée and Chaumière Brièronne € *St-Joachim; tel: 02 40 66 85 01. Open July–mid-Sept, daily, 1030–1300, 1430–1830; mid-Apr–June, daily, 1400–1800.*

Parc Animalier *Rozé, St-Malo-de-Guersac; tel: 02 40 91 17 80. Open June–Sept, 0900–1800.*

La Grande Brière forms the heart of the 40,000-hectare Brière Nature Park (Parc Naturel Régional de Brière), a mosaic of reedy marshes, peat bogs, grassy plains, canals and tiny rural communities known locally (for obvious reasons) as *îles*. A unique ecosystem has been preserved here since the 15th century when Francis II, Duke of Brittany, guaranteed the traditional rights and privileges of the inhabitants in perpetuity.

Learning about the Brièrons and their special environment is the main reason for coming here. Orientation is provided by the information centre at the **Chapelle-des-Marais**, where you will also find an exhibition on local crafts, the **Maison des Traditions**, and a little museum of clog-making, the **Maison du Sabotier**. There's more information on the flora and fauna of the region in the delightful lock-keeper's house at Rozé, the **Maison de l'Eclusier**. Moored outside is a reconstructed peat barge – peat is still cut for fuel but only on the nine days stipulated each year. The **Chaumière Brièronne** on the Ile de Fédrun (accessible by road bridge) is a traditional thatched cottage with furnishings typical of the region. You can learn all about local wedding customs in the nearby **Maison de la Mariée**. Wonderful bridal headdresses, ornamented with orange blossoms made from wax are on show here, the work of the women of St-Joachim.

South of Rozé is a 25-hectare protected zone known as the **Parc Animalier**. From hides placed at intervals along a 2km designated route visitors can observe the waterfowl (snipe, grey herons, harriers) and pond life. Information panels help with identification.

The most relaxing way of seeing Brière is by barge (*chaland*). Excursions leave from a number of places, including la Chaussée-Neuve, Port de Bréca and Ile de Fédrun and last anything from 45 minutes to four or five hours. Alternatively, you can hire a punt (the traditional way of getting about here) or travel overland in a horse-drawn carriage. Gastronomic specialities of the region include duck and eels.

Walks round the Brière Park

The footpath GR3 encircles the marsh. There is an information point at la Chapelle-des-Marais where you can pick up maps and route guides and a picnic area at la Chaussée Neuve.

Several local people offer guided walks round the park (in French). Try:

A Breca *Nicolas Legal; tel: 02 40 91 46 48.* Minimum 45-minute introduction to the migatory birds and native flora and fauna of the region. Also trips on a barque or calèche.

Briere Evasion *J.J Vilette; Port de la Pierre Fendue, St Lyphard; tel: 02 40 91 41 96; fax: 02 40 66 89 53; mobile: 06 75 23 58 58; e-mail: briere.evasion@wanadoo.fr; www.briere-evasion.com.* Guides trips by barge and caléche.

Les Calèches Brièronnes *Yannick Thual; Port de Bréca; tel: 02 40 91 32 02; e-mail: les-caleches-brieronnes@fr.st; www.les-caleches-brieronnes.fr.st.* Guided walks (*1900*) or boat trips.

La Chaussée Neuve *Anthony Mahé; tel: 02 40 91 59 36.* A 45-minute guided tour. Barge tours also.

GUERANDE

ℹ️ **Guérande Tourist Information** *I place du Marché au Bois; tel: 02 40 24 96 71; fax: 02 40 62 04 24; e-mail: contact@ot-guerande.fr; www.ot-guerande.fr*

🏛️ **La Château Musée** *€ Port St-Michel; tel: 02 40 42 96 52. Open Apr–Sept, 1000–1230, 1430–1900; Oct, 1000–1200, 1430–1800.*

🅿️ Outside the walls on boulevard du Nord.

🛒 Sunday morning market at Pradel in *July and August.* Main market *Wednesday and Saturday* by the church.

Guérande has a large selection of art and craft shops in the old town, for example on rue De Saillé and around place de la Psalette.

🎭 *August* – 3-day Interceltic Festival.

This fortified town, its **medieval walls** still completely intact after nearly six centuries, is a must see. You can't walk around the parapets but there are good views of the towers and gates from the little ring road encircling the walls. There's a museum of local history in the **Porte St-**

Right
La Roche-Bernard

Michel gatehouse, once the Governor's residence. The collection's modest size belies the past importance of Guerande when, rich on the proceeds of salt (a precious commodity in medieval times), it was a town of great importance. A colourful market takes place twice a week in front of the church of **St-Aubin**. The superb stained glass in the chancel depicts the coronation and assumption of the Virgin.

Accommodation and food in Guérande

Domaine de Leveno €€ *Guérande; tel: 02 40 24 79 30; fax: 02 40 62 01 23*. Camp and caravan site. Facilities include a swimming pool, tennis, mini-golf, games room, disco, restaurant and bar.

Roc-Maria €€ *1 rue des Halles; tel: 02 40 24 90 51*. Comfortable hotel in a 15th-century house in the walled town with a small *crêperie*.

La Roche-Bernard

ⓘ La Roche-Bernard Tourist Information *14 rue du Dr Cornudet; tel: 02 99 90 67 98*.

ⓑ Boats: Les Vedettes Jaunes *Armement Dréno; tel: 02 97 45 02 81; fax: 02 97 45 00 41; www.vedettesjaunes.com*. Pleasure cruises from the Arzal dam to la Roche-Bernard, Folleux and Redon.

ⓜ Musée de la Vilaine Maritime € *Château des Basses Fosses; tel: 02 99 90 83 47. Open June–Sept and Easter, daily, 1030–1230, 1430–1900; Apr, May & Oct, weekend afternoons*.

This enchanting river port was founded back in the 10th century on a rocky outcrop overlooking the Vilaine. Under the protection of its feudal overlords it flourished with the development of the salt trade in the Middle Ages. La Roche-Bernard was also the first town in Brittany to declare for Protestantism during the Wars of Religion. The history of the town is given the full treatment in the **Musée de la Vilaine Maritime**, located in the 17th-century castle. The focus here is on the maritime life of the port, notably shipbuilding: the *Couronne*, the first high-sided ship in the French navy was launched from la Roche-Bernard in 1638. Not far from the castle is place Bouffay and the heart of the **old quarter**. Here and in the picturesque streets leading down to the port are beautifully preserved half-timbered houses, artisans' dwellings, salt lofts and 17th-century warehouses with external staircases. Pleasure boats leave from the port for idyllic cruises on the Vilaine, journey's end being the Barrage d'Arzal or Redon.

Accommodation and food in la Roche-Bernard

Auberge Bretonne €€€ *2 place Duguesclin; tel: 02 99 90 60 28*. This classy restaurant, strong on regional fare, sits in an imaginatively restored hotel; an evocative if pricey place for an overnight stay.

Auberge des Deux Magots €€ *Place du Bouffay; tel: 02 99 90 60 75; fax: 02 99 90 87 87; www.auberge-les2magots.com. Closed for lunch Mon and Tue*. Delightful hotel in the old town which also boasts an excellent restaurant.

Les Vedettes Jaunes €€€ *Armement Dréno; tel: 02 97 45 02 81*. Food with a view. Cruise along the Vilaine river with lunch (*departs 1230, returns 1630*) or dinner (*departs 2000, returns 2400*).

Suggested tour

**ⓘ Batz Tourist
Information** 25 rue
de la Plage; tel: 02 40 23 92
36; fax: 02 40 23 74 10;
e-mail:
officetourismebatzsurmer@
wanadoo.fr;
www.mairie-batzsurmer.fr

**ⓒ Batz church clock
tower €** Tel: 02 40
23 94 12. Open mid-
May–mid-Sept, daily,
0900–1200, 1430–1800;
mid-Sept–mid-May, Wed
and Sun, afternoons
(address for key is pinned
to the door).

**Musée des Marais
Salants €€** 29 bis rue
Pasteur, Batz-sur-Mer; tel:
02 40 23 82 79; fax: 02 40
23 71 51. Open June–Sept,
daily, 1000–1200,
1500–1900; Oct–May, Sat
and Sun, 1500–1900.

Maison des Paludiers €
Rue des Prés Garnier; tel: 02
40 62 21 96. Open
Mar–Oct, 1000–1230,
1400–1700 (1830 in July
and Aug). Visit to saltpans
(€€€) 2-hour tour July
and Aug only.

**Guided tour of the
saltpans €€** Office de
Tourisme, place Charles de
Gaulle, la Turballe; tel: 02 40
23 39 87. July and Aug,
Mon, Tue, Thur & Sat, 1000.

Total distance: 145km (223km with detours).

Time: 3½ hours' driving. Allow 8 hours for the main route, 10 hours with detours. Those with limited time should concentrate on the area of the Brière Nature Park.

Links: The N165 links this route to the Gulf of Morbihan (*see pages 142–53*) in the north and Nantes (*see pages 202–7*) in the south.

Leave **LA BAULE ①** on the D45 coast road passing through the mini-resort of **le Pouliguen**. Continue past Rochers la Dilane and the edge of Batz-sur-Mer to **Pointe du Croisic** where you'll probably want to stop to admire the views of this dramatic stretch of the Côte Sauvage – two of the more prominent rocks have nicknames – the Bear and the Altar.

Follow the road back through **Batz-sur-Mer**, a pleasant resort with three sandy beaches. If you want to stretch your legs, follow the clifftop walk signposted '*Sentier des Douaniers*'. As you'd expect from a town close to the edge of the saltpans, Batz has a **Musée des Marais Salants** focusing on salt extraction and the lives of the workers. There are good views of the marshes from the **belfry** (182 steps) of the 'fishermen's church', St-Guénolé.

Take the left fork (D774) to **Saillé**. Call in at the **Maison des Paludiers**, a former chapel laid out as (another) museum of saltworkers. Tours of the saltpans are organised from here. Turn left on to the D92 – if you're here between June and September you'll probably see the salt being harvested on the **Marais Salants** as it has been for hundreds of years.

Parc de Branféré
€€€ (zoo) Le Guerno;
tel: 02 97 42 94 66;
fax: 02 97 42 81 22; e-mail:
contact@branfere.com;
www.branfere.com. Open
July and Aug, daily,
1000–1800; Apr–June and
Sept, daily, 1000–1700.

Hôtel la Poste €€
Piriac-sur-Mer; tel: 02
40 23 50 91. Comfortable,
welcoming hotel near the
beach.

Left
La Roche-Bernard

Above
Brière Nature Park

Continue to **la Turballe**, famous for the catches of anchovies and sardines which are auctioned on the quay and can be sampled in any one of an array of small restaurants. Take the D99 past **Pointe du Castelli**. A short walk from here to the cliffs gives fine views across the Rade du Croisic as far as the Rhuys Peninsula in the distance. Continue to **Piriac-sur-Mer**, a quieter, less commercialised resort than its neighbours to the south, but with a handful of hotels and restaurants. Leave on the D452 along a beautiful stretch of coast with beaches of sugary white sand, culminating at the **Pointe de Merquel**, just beyond Quimiac.

Take the D52 to the junction with the D774 then turn left to **LA ROCHE-BERNARD** ❷.

Detour: Follow the D774 north to Peaule. Leave on the D1, turning in the direction of le Guerno. You'll see **Branféré Zoo** signed to the right. This attractive park was originally laid out in the 18th century by an amateur botanist and some of the original trees, including a giant

ⓘ St-Nazaire Tourist Information

Boulevard de la Légion d'Honneur, Ville-Port; tel: 08 20 01 40 15; fax: 02 40 22 19 80; e-mail: contact@ saint-nazaire-tourisme.com; www.saint-nazaire-tourisme.com

ⓜ Sous Marin Espadon

€€€ The Port, St-Nazaire; tel: 08 10 88 84 44. Open 0930–1830.

Le Moulin de Pen Mur €

Muzillac; tel: 02 97 41 43 79; fax: 02 97 45 60 78; www.moulin-pen-mur.com. Open Apr–Sept, daily, 1000–1200, 1400–1800, closed Sun am; Oct–Mar, weekends and holidays, 1000–1200, 1400–1530.

Ecomusée de St-Nazaire

€€ The Port; tel: 02 51 10 03 03. Open June–Sept, 0930–1830.

St Lyphard Clock Tower €

Office de Tourisme, place de l'Eglise, St-Lyphard; tel: 02 40 91 41 34; fax: 02 40 91 34 96. Visits July and Aug, daily; Apr–June and Sept, Mon and Sat; Oct–Mar, Tue and Sat.

Château de Careil €€

Guerande; tel: 02 40 60 22 99. Open June–Aug, 1030–1200, 1430–1900 (guided tours ½ hour).

ⓐ Auberge de Kerhinet €€

Kerhinet; tel: 02 40 61 91 46. One of the thatched cottages has been converted into an attractive hotel with restaurant.

sequoia, have survived. Earlier this century Paul and Hélène Jourde added their own collection of exotic animals and birds including lemurs, ibises and wallabies before handing Branféré over to the nation. If you decide to make a visit, the amenities include a picnic area, café-bar and souvenir shop.

Leave Branféré and continue to le Guerno, then head south on the D139. At the junction with the D20 turn right to Muzillac. At the edge of the **Pen Mur** lake you'll find a restored 18th-century mill where paper is manufactured from natural fibres using machines and methods over 200 years old. Take the N165 back to la Roche-Bernard.

Leave on the D4, turning right at the junction with the D50 to **la Chapelle-des-Marais**, a small town at the edge of the **Parc Regional de Brière**.

Detour: Just outside the village turn left on to the D33. About 4km after St-Reine-de-Bretagne is the Pontchâteau calvary. In 1710 a local preacher commissioned this unusual Stations of the Cross in a garden overlooking the Brière. Leave your car in the car park and climb the hill for a closer look at the life-size white statues. Return to Chapelle des Marais.

Continue on the D50 to **St-Joachim** where the tall church spire is a local landmark against the low-lying marshland of the Brière. Take the small road to the right which leads to the thatched cottages of **Ile de Fedrun**. Return to the D50 through **Rozé**, a traditional boat-building centre, to Montoir-de-Bretagne.

Detour: Turn right on to the N171 to the port of **St-Nazaire** which, like Brest, suffered devastating bombing during World War II when it was used as a German submarine base. The story of the bombardment is graphically described in the local **history museum** in the port. Moored near the museum is the submarine *Espadon*, the first French sub to navigate beneath the ice at the North Pole. On the guided tour you'll be shown the cramped living quarters, the torpedo room and the engines. Access is through the covered lock – a secret entrance to the port.

To avoid the traffic congestion around St-Nazaire, take the country road from Montoir to Trignac. Cross the canal, then continue north of the main road via the hamlets of Bert, Aucard and Trembly to Brais. Join the D47 heading for **St-Lyphard** where from the top of the church belfry there are rewarding views of the Guérande saltpans, the Loire estuary and the Brière Nature Park.

Turn south on to the D51, detouring to the quaint hamlet of **Kerhinet** (signs to the left of the road). Accessible only on foot, several of the thatched cottages are open to the public and reveal the poor furnishings, dirt floors and primitive farming tools of the marsh workers. There is a small produce market on Thursdays in July and August.

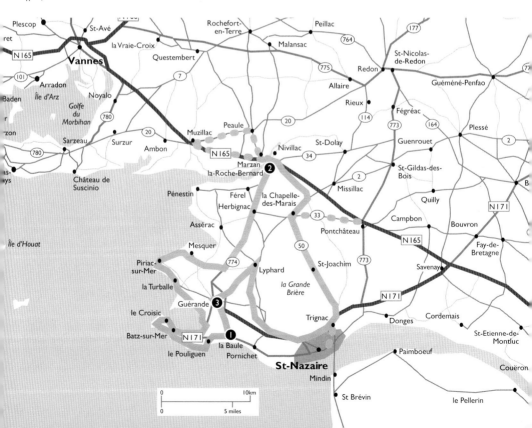

La Mare aux Oiseaux €€ *Ile de Fedrun; tel: 02 40 88 53 01.* Small hotel in a traditional village at the heart of the park, with restaurant serving mouthwatering local produce.

Musée Benoist € *Le Gâvre; tel: 02 40 51 25 14. Open Apr–Nov, Tue–Sun, 1400–1800 (guided tours 1 hour).*

Château de la Groulais € *Blain; tel: 02 40 79 07 81; fax: 02 40 79 94 79. Open Mar–Nov, Tue–Sun, 1000–1200, 1430–1830.*

Musée des Arts et Traditions Populaires € *Blain; details from tourist office, tel: 02 40 87 15 11.*

Continue on the D51 to **GUERANDE ❸**, leaving on the D92 from here. On the left is the **Château de Careil**, a 14th- to 16th-century castle, part of which is still inhabited.

Also worth exploring

East of the Brière Nature Park, the **Gâvre Forest** is a beautiful spot for walking, cycling, horse riding, canoeing, fishing or simply to take a picnic in the fresh air. To find out more about the forest and its inhabitants visit the **Musée Benoist** at le Gâvre, a quaint 17th-century house with a turret sprouting like a growth from one corner. The flora and fauna of the area is explained on the ground floor, while upstairs there are reconstructions of a typical domestic interior and several workshops including a clog maker's. **Blain**, the main town, lies on the Nantes-Brest Canal. The port is busy with visiting boats in summer and overlooking the river bank is the ruined **Château de la Groulais**. In Blain itself a local **museum** has a superb collection of crib figures from around the world, as well as reconstructed village shops and Roman remains.

Nantes

Ratings

Art	●●●●●
History	●●●●●
Architecture	●●●○○
Cathedrals and churches	●●●○○
Children	●●●○○
Food	●●●○○
Heritage	●●○○○
Castles and châteaux	●○○○○

Since 1962 this vibrant, energetic city of half a million people has been deemed to belong not to Brittany but to Pays de la Loire. Historically and culturally however, Nantes is unassailably Breton and there are still periodic calls for reintegration. During the Middle Ages Nantes alternated with Rennes as the capital and it was here that the Dukes of Brittany set up residence. Economically the town's prosperity came to rest increasingly on the slave trade and its abolition during the Revolution was a definite setback.

Traffic roars through the town centre incessantly, aided and abetted by a short-sighted decision in the 1930s to build over several channels of the Loire. Fortunately the River Erdre remains open for boat excursions and although there are few specific sights away from the château and the cathedral, there's no shortage of things to do. Night owls are also well catered for in this city with a large student population.

Getting around

ⓘ Nantes Tourist Information 3, cours Olivier de Clisson and 2, place Saint-Pierre; tel: 02 40 20 60 00; fax: 02 40 89 11 99; e-mail: office@nantes-tourisme.com; www.nantes-tourisme.com. Services include booking accommodation, guided tours, bureau de change and tickets sales.

ⓟ Place du Commerce, place de Bretagne, place St-Similien.

Nantes has an excellent public transport system comprising trams and buses (SEMITAM). All trams are fitted with ramps to take cycles and pushchairs. Tickets for bus and tram (valid one hour) are sold singly or in books of five or ten from TAN kiosks (day tickets are also available and good value). You must have a ticket from a machine before boarding. Most central attractions can be visited on foot.

A tourist train leaves from place St-Pierre (opposite the cathedral) *Apr–Sept, daily, 1015–1800.* **L'Omnibus de la Dame Blanche** (horse-drawn carriage tours) leave from outside the château *Apr–Sept, daily, 1100–1700.*

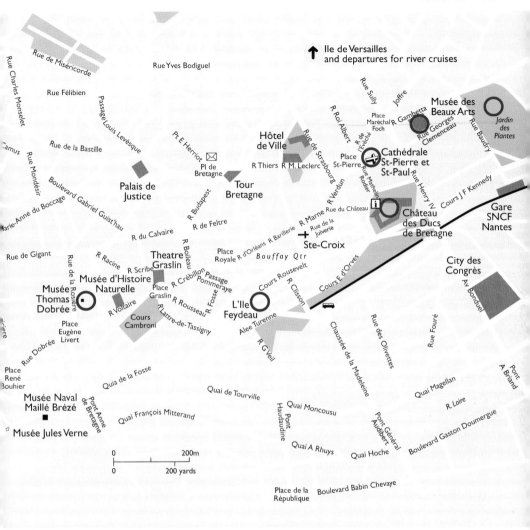

Sights

**Boats: Bateaux
Nantais** *Quai de la
Motte Rouge; tel: 02 40
14 51 14; e-mail:
commercial@bateaux-
nantais.fr;
www.bateaux-nantais.fr*

**Cathédrale St-
Pierre et St-Paul**
Open daily, 0830 until dusk.

Cathédrale St-Pierre et St-Paul

The 15th-century cathedral was admirably restored following a fire in 1971. Its most eye-catching feature is the vaulted nave of gleaming white stone which soars to a height of 37m. When you've had time to take it all in, head for the south transept where you'll find a matchless example of Renaissance sculpture. The marble tomb of Duke Francis II and Marguerite de Foix was commissioned by their daughter, Anne of Brittany, in 1502 and is the work of Michel Colombe. The stained-glass window which illuminates it so beautifully is modern.

Château *1 place Marc Elder; tel: 02 40 41 56 56. Open July and Aug, daily, 1000–1800; rest of year, Wed–Mon, 1000–1800. Due to re-open after renovation in 2007.*

Musée des Beaux Arts *€€ 10 rue Georges Clemenceau; tel: 02 51 17 45 00. Open Wed–Mon, 1000–1800; Fri until 2000.*

Musée Thomas Dobrée/Musée Archéologique €€ *Place Jean V, rue Voltaire; tel: 02 40 71 03 50. Open Tue–Fri, 1330–1730, Sat and Sun, 1430–1730.*

Château des Ducs de Bretagne

This formidable medieval château has been much restored and altered over the centuries yet for all that it's an impressive building steeped in history. Anne of Brittany was born here in 1477 and later added a couple of storeys to the main palace. King Henri IV came here in 1598 to sign the Edict of Nantes, granting toleration to Protestants, and it was here, too, that Bonnie Prince Charlie planned his disastrous invasion of England in 1745.

Visitors are allowed into the inner courtyard and up on to the ramparts for free. Temporary exhibitions are held in the castle museum while picnicking is possible on the grassy areas outside.

L'Ile Feydeau

No longer an island on the Loire, this is a district of finely constructed shipowners' houses of great character, mostly dating from the 18th century. Features to look out for include grotesques on the façades, wrought-iron balconies and the staircases in the inner courtyards. The 19th-century science fiction writer, Jules Verne, was born at No 4, Cours Olivier-de-Clisson. A good place to picnic is the small square, place Juillet XIV.

Musée des Beaux Arts

Make a visit to this fine arts museum, one of the best in the country, a priority, especially if you're a fan of modern art. There are canvases by Chagall and Picasso and a superb collection of works by Kandinsky dating from the 1920s and 1930s. Also featured are paintings by Perugino, Rubens, Georges de la Tour, Watteau, Monet, members of the Pont-Aven school and contemporary artists.

Musée Thomas Dobrée

The **Palais Dobrée** originally belonged to the wealthy Nantes shipowner, Thomas Dobrée (1810–95). Inside you can see his private

Above
Château des Ducs de Bretagne

❶ Musée d'Histoire Naturelle €€ *12 rue Voltaire; tel: 02 40 99 26 20. Open Tue–Sun, 1000–1800.*

Musée de l'Imprimerie €€ *24 quai de la Fosse; tel: 02 40 73 26 55. Open July and Aug, Mon–Fri, 1000–1200, 1400–1730; Sept and Jan, Tue–Sat, 1000–1200, 1400–1730. History of printing.*

Musée Jules Verne € *3 rue de l'Hermitage; tel: 02 40 69 72 52. Open Wed–Sat and Mon, 1000–1200, 1400–1700; Sun, 1400–1700. Documents, theatrical flyers, board games and ephemera based on his books and two re-created rooms. Verne's actual birthplace is elsewhere.*

Musée Maillé-Brézé € *33 quai de la Fosse; tel: 02 40 69 56 82. Open June–Sept, 1400–1800; rest of year, Wed, Sat & Sun, 1400–1700. Naval museum with tours of the ship, including the engine room.*

Musée Compagnonnique € *14 rue Guillon Verne; tel: 02 40 69 30 55. Open Sat, 1400–1800. Exhibition of masterpieces crafted by tradesmen of Nantes.*

collection of old manuscripts, ceramics, alabaster statues, jewellery, paintings and tapestries.

On the same ticket you can also visit two other museums: the 15th-century **Manoir Jean V** *18 rue Voltaire; tel: 02 40 48 23 87*, alternatively known as the Manoir de la Touche, for an exhibition on the Revolution and the Vendée rebellion of 1793–5, and the **Musée Archéologique**, focusing on the history of the Pays de Loire with an assortment of prehistoric, Gallo-Roman and medieval finds. If this doesn't take your fancy, further along the same street is the **Musée d'Histoire Naturelle**, an eclectic, sometimes bizarre exhibition of natural curiosities including rhinoceros toenails and the stretched human skin of a soldier whose dying wish was to be made into a drum!

Parks and gardens

Traffic flows heavily through the arteries of Nantes but the city is blessed with a number of attractive green spaces. The **Jardin des Plantes** (Botanical Garden) *tel: 02 40 41 90 09*, lies just east of the town centre (entrances opposite the railway station and on place Sophie Trébuchet). Covering an area of 18 hectares, the landscaped park contains collections of rare and medicinal plants, cactus houses and more. The greenhouses are open every day except Tuesday, (*1000–1200 and 1400–1700*), and there's a playground to amuse the kids. Guided tours are available; *tel: 02 40 41 98 67.*

Just north of the centre, near the boat station, is the **Ile de Versailles**, a man-made island created in the style of a Japanese garden and a good place for a picnic. The Maison de l'Erdre has an exhibition on the flora and fauna of the river. Further west, the **Parc Procé** runs along the banks of the tiny River Chézine. Amenities include a paddling pool and a children's garden.

Out of town, near the Parc des Expositions de la Beaujoire (*route de St-Joseph de Porterie*) is the **Parc Floral de la Beaujoire** with rockeries, rose and iris gardens and a play area for children.

River cruises

There are regular sailings on the rivers Erdre and Sèvre. The most popular excursion explores the Erdre as far as the junction with the Nantes-Brest Canal. It's a delightful journey which will introduce you to no less than ten châteaux along the way. From *June to August* **Bateaux Nantais** (the largest of several companies), operates two departures *daily at 1500 and 1700*, with an additional dinner sailing on *Saturdays at 2030*. Each cruise lasts for 1 hour 45 minutes and leaves from the Pont de la Motte Rouge at the far end of the Ile de Versailles (15 minutes' walk or tram stop, Motte-Rouge). Alternatively you can wine and dine on board the company's floating restaurant (lunch or dinner, cruise lasts approximately 3 hours), although it is expensive. Pedalo-type boats can be hired from **Ruban-Bleu** next to the cable footbridge. For details of Sèvre cruises, ask at the tourist information office.

Passage Pommeraye near place du Commerce is a gleaming 19th-century gallery on three levels worth seeing in its own right. A branch of the famous Paris department store **Galeries Lafayette** is at 2 à 20 rue de la Marne. There's a **Flower market** on place du Commerce, daily, 0830–2100. The covered food halls on **Rue de Talensac** are open Tue–Sun morning.

Fêtes de l'Eté (July) – open-air concerts, theatrical and other events around the château.

Hôtel St-Daniel € 4 rue du Bouffay; tel: 02 40 47 41 25; fax: 51 72 03 99; e-mail: hotel.st.daniel@wanadoo.fr. Fairly small hotel in the heart of the old town. Excellent value.

La Mangeoire €€ 16 rue des Petits Ecuries; tel: 02 40 48 70 83; fax: 02 40 35 11 03. Closed Sunday, Monday and for 10 days in May and one week in September. Excellent French cuisine with good-value set meals.

Accommodation and food

You shouldn't have a problem finding somewhere to stay in Nantes. If you've arrived late or are looking for a room on spec, focus your attention on place Graslin or in the area near the railway station (SNCF).

Brasserie La Cigalle €€ *Place Graslin; tel: 02 51 84 94 94; e-mail: lacigale@lacigalle.com.* A beautiful art-nouveau interior which some claim is the finest in France. Breton and Nantais specialities.

Hôtel l'Atlantique €€ *9 rue Maréchal de Lattre de Tassigny; tel: 02 40 73 85 33; fax: 02 40 73 89 33.* Pleasant hotel near the tourist office on place du Commerce. If full there's another hotel on the same street.

Hôtel des Colonies €€ *5 rue du Chapeau Rouge; tel: 02 40 48 79 76; fax: 02 40 12 49 25; e-mail: hoteldescolonies.com; www.hoteldescolonies.fr.* Tastefully-appointed rooms in subdued shades and centrally placed, with a ground-level art gallery.

La Mangeoire € *16 rue des Petites Écuries; tel: 02 40 48 70 83.* Excellent value set menus at lunch and dinner.

A walk round Nantes

Take rue Voltaire from **Palais Dobrée ❶** to **place Graslin ❷** and the 18th-century Grand Théâtre. Cross the square to **la Cigale ❸**, a delightful art nouveau café decorated with mosaics and mirrors. Take the narrow commercial street, rue Crébillon, to the junction with rue Santeuil then turn into **Passage Pommeraye ❹**, a palatial 19th-century shopping mall. At the end, turn left on to rue de la Fosse.

Detour: Cross rue de la Fosse into **place du Commerce ❺**, a pedestrianised square where you'll find a daily flower market and tourist information.

Take rue de la Fosse to **place Royale ❻**. The blue granite fountain is 19th-century – allegorical figures represent Nantes surrounded by the River Loire and its tributaries.

Leave on rue d'Orléans. Cross the Cours de 50-Otages and continue on rue de la Barillerie into the medieval city. At place du Champs, turn right on to rue de la Juiverie. The house at No 7 is one of several half-timbered buildings in the streets around **Eglise Ste-Croix ❼**. The eye-catching belfry of this 17th-century church once belonged to the old town castle. At rue de Verdun turn left to place du Pilori with its elegant 18th-century houses, then right on to rue du Château. Turn left at the end and walk past the **CHATEAU DES DUCS DE BRETAGNE ❽**. Continue in the direction of the cathedral then turn right on to Impasse

Le Petit Flore €€ | *rue des Vieilles Douves; tel: 02 40 48 24 88. Tempting range of fresh salads and other nutritious fare.*

St-Laurent. Cross the square and walk through the alleyway to **la Psalette** ❾, formerly the chapterhouse and choir school, a quaint 15th-century building with a polygonal turret. Follow the path round the front of the **CATHEDRALE** ❿. Turn right at place St-Pierre and pass a turreted 15th-century gateway; this was later incorporated into the bishop's residence (Porte St-Pierre). On your left, in the centre of place Maréchal Foche is a statue of Louis XVI, erected in 1790, just a few years before his execution.

Detour: Turn right along rue Henri IV then first left on rue Malherbe to the late Gothic **Chapelle de l'Immaculée** ⓫, given a face-lift in the 17th century along with many of the houses in the area.

Turn on to rue Georges Clémenceau for the **MUSEE DES BEAUX ARTS** ⓬ and the **JARDIN DES PLANTES** ⓭.

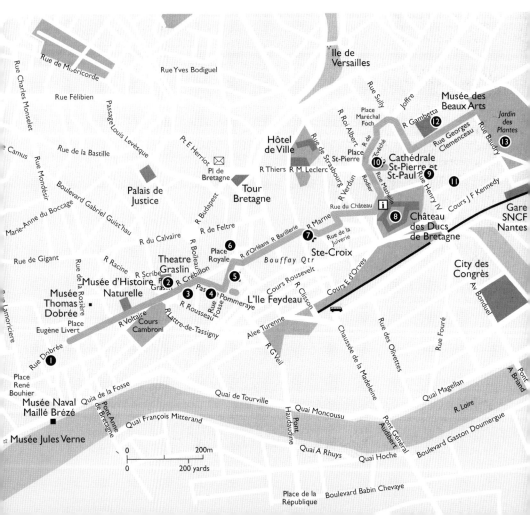

The Breton Marches

Ratings

Architecture	●●●●●
Castles and châteaux	●●●●●
Walking	●●●●●
History	●●●●○
Outdoor activities	●●●●○
Scenery	●●●●○
Cathedrals and churches	●●○○○
Children	●●○○○

Throughout the Hundred Years' War and the equally bloody War of Breton Succession, the Lusignans at Fougères, the la Trémoilles at Vitré and the Du Guesclins at Combourg used English ambitions to keep the French at bay and to preserve their own hard-won independence. These and other powerful baronial families who built the string of stupendous fortresses along the border between Brittany and France were, understandably, regarded by the local population as 'little dukes' in their own right. Built in what now seem like magical settings among sloping woodland, rocky escarpments and cascading waterfalls, the châteaux are hardly less impressive today than they were in the Middle Ages when the surrounding forests gave rise to innumerable legends about heroes, devils and enchantment. The area is also rich in literary associations. Both Victor Hugo and Honoré de Balzac wrote novels about the later stages of the Chouan rebellion in Fougères, while Vitré has close links with Madame de Sévigné, mistress of the Château de la Roche Sévigné and a letter writer of genius, famous for her *bon mots*.

CHÂTEAUBRIANT

ℹ **Tourist Information** 22 rue de Couéré; tel: 02 40 28 20 90; e-mail: tourisme-chateaubriant@fr.fm; www.tourisme-chateaubriant.fr.fm

🏰 **Castles €** **(Gardens free)** Tel: 02 40 28 20 20. Open mid-June–mid-Sept, Wed–Sat and Mon, 1000–1230, 1430–1930, Sun, 1430–1930. Guided tours (1 hour) Sat and Sun, 1500.

There's just enough here to keep you occupied for a couple of hours. To gain a sense of the history of this old border town, look no further than the château. The handsome Seigneurial Palace, with its finely sculpted arcades and dormer windows, was built for the first Governor of Brittany, Count Jean de Laval, around 1521. People were meant to live here in comfort and the contrast with the feudal keep on the other side of the courtyard, where the emphasis on military preparedness is total, couldn't be greater. If you take the guided tour you'll learn all about the unfortunate Françoise de Foix, Comtesse de Châteaubriant and sometime mistress of Francis I whom the Count is said to have murdered out of jealousy (although not until long after the king had finished with her). On the other side of town is the **Eglise St-Jean-de-Béré** where the Romanesque chancel and nave date from the 11th and 12th centuries respectively.

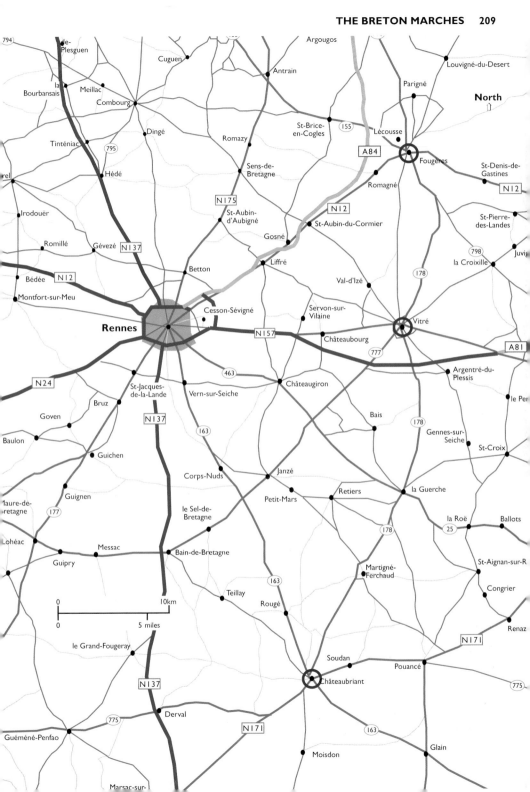

North

794

de-Plesguen

Cuguen

Antrain

Argougos

Louvigné-du-Desert

la Bourbansais

Meillac

Combourg

Parigné

St-Brice-en-Cogles

155

Lécousse

A84

Fougères

St-Denis-des-Gastines

N12

Tinténiac

Dingé

795

Romazy

Sens-de-Bretagne

Romagné

Hédé

N175

Romilly

St-Pierre-des-Landes

Irodouër

St-Aubin-d'Aubigné

St-Aubin-du-Cormier

798

la Croixille

Juvi

Romillé

Gévezé

N137

Gosné

Liffré

178

Bédée

N12

Betton

Val-d'Izé

Vitré

Montfort-sur-Meu

Rennes

Cesson-Sévigné

N157

Châteaubourg

777

A81

N24

463

Châteaugiron

Argentré-du-Plessis

St-Jacques-de-la-Lande

Vern-sur-Seiche

Bais

le Per

Bruz

Goven

N137

178

Gennes-sur-Seiche

St-Croix

Baulon

163

Guichen

Corps-Nuds

Janzé

Retiers

la Guerche

Guignen

Maure-de-Bretagne

177

Petit-Mars

la Roë

Ballots

le Sel-de-Bretagne

178

25

Lohéac

Messac

Guipry

Bain-de-Bretagne

Martigné-Ferchaud

St-Aignan-sur-R

163

Congrier

Teillay

Rougé

Renaz

N171

le Grand-Fougeray

Soudan

Pouancé

0   10km

0   5 miles

N137

Châteaubriant

775

N137

Derval

775

N171

163

Glain

Guémené-Penfao

Moisdon

Marsac-sur-

FOUGERES

ⓘ Fougères Tourist information *1 place Aristide Briand; tel: 02 99 94 12 20; fax: 02 99 94 77 30; e-mail: ot.fougeres@ wanadoo.fr; www.ot-fougeres.fr*

ⓟ There is a large car park at place Carnot; other spots are boulevard de Rennes, place de Lariboisière and place de la République by the station.

ⓗ Château Medieval *€€ Tel: 02 99 99 79 59. Open July and Aug, 0900– 1900; Apr and June, 0930– 1200, 1400–1800; Oct–Dec, Feb & Mar, 1000–1200, 1400–1700. Guided tours available (45 mins).*

Marché aux Bovins de l'Aumaillerie *€ rue Madame de Sevigné, then N12, 2km from town; tel: 02 99 99 25 50. Open Fri am.*

Musée Emmanuel de la Villéon *51 rue Nationale; tel: 02 99 99 19 98. Open mid-June–mid-Sept, daily, 1030–1230, 1430–1800; Easter–mid-June and mid-Sept–Nov, Wed and Sun, 1100–1230, 1430–1800.*

Parc Floral de Haute-Bretagne *€€ La Foltière, le Châtellier; tel: 02 99 95 48 32; fax: 02 99 95 47 74; www.parcfloralbretagne.com. Open July and Aug, 1030– 1830; Mar–June, Sept–mid-Nov & Sun, all year, 1400– 1800 (closed mid-Nov–Feb).*

ⓒ Centre Equestre *Ferme de Chênedet; tel: 02 99 97 35 46. Offers tours of the forest in horse-drawn carriages, pony trails and canoe and bike hire.*

One of the largest medieval fortresses in Europe, Fougères is still impressive. A combination of military stronghold and fairy-tale **castle**, its towers and turrets topped by witches' hat roofs, Fougères was used as a prison as late as the 19th century. You can walk around the ramparts and explore several of the towers, the most impressive being the 14th-century Tour Mélusine with walls 3.5m thick. Climb to the top (75 steps) for good views of the rest of the château.

Unusually, Fougères' castle is sited below the town, which straddles a rocky promontory formed by the winding River Nançon. **Place Marchix**, the former market square, is surrounded by the narrow, stepped streets of the medieval quarter. A slender steeple rises above the untidy cluster of 16th-century houses; it belongs to the Flamboyant Gothic church of **St-Suplice**. Take a look inside at the carved granite altarpieces and the treasured 12th-century statue of the Virgin suckling her child.

Across the Nançon, paths lead through a terraced garden up to the 'new town' and the church of St-Leonard where you can climb the belfry for views over the lower town and the forest beyond. Take a stroll down the main pedestrianised street, rue Nationale, past shops and market stalls to the **Musée Emmanuel de la Villéon**. This attractive half-timbered building is devoted to the drawings and water-colours of a minor Impressionist painter and native of Fougères, whose work was inspired by various aspects of Breton life.

It you're in the market for a new pair of shoes, you've come to the right place. The shoe industry flourished here after the production of the first handmade slippers in 1832 (you can see the old tanneries and mills along the river) and despite foreign competition women's footwear is still something of a local speciality.

The Friday **cattle market** (**Marché aux Bovins de l'Aumaillerie**), one of France's largest, handles over 100,000 animals a year. Signposts and audio-visual displays help explain the trade to the uninitiated. As the market has also become a shrine to French cuisine, you may be tempted to sample some of the beef in one of the local eateries.

Northeast of Fougères is one of Brittany's delightful **forests** where beech, spruce and chestnut trees shelter a scattering of megaliths and dolmens. The centre of activity is **Chênedet**, with horse riding, cycling and rambling trails. A short drive to the west, beyond **le Châtellier** is the **Parc Floral de Haute-Bretagne**, where a dozen gardens with evocative names such as 'the city of Knossos' and 'the Valley of the Poet' present a colourful floral pageant.

VITRE

🛈 **Vitré Tourist Information** *Place Général de Gaulle; tel: 02 99 75 04 46; fax: 02 99 74 02 01; e-mail: info@ot-vitre.fr; www.ot-vitre.fr*

🅿 Place de la République, place du Château, rue des Augustins.

🎫 One ticket allows entry to the museums below and to the Château des Rochers-Sevigné.

Castle Museum €€ *Place de Château; tel: 02 99 75 04 54.*

St-Nicholas Museum €€ *Rue Pasteur; tel: 02 99 75 04 54.* Both museums are open May–Sept, daily, 1000–1245, 1400–1800; Oct–Apr, daily, 1000–1215, 1400–1730.

📅 Monday markets are held on place Notre-Dame (in front of the church).

🎉 The **Fêtes du Bocage** are held in early July around Vitré – the villages of Ille-en-Vilaine come alive with night tours, illuminations, street theatre, music and other events.

🛏 **L'Espérance** € *Place du Champ de Foire; tel: 02 99 75 01 71; fax: 02 99 75 80 87.* Good-value hotel.

Le Minotel €€ *47 rue Poterie; tel: 02 99 75 11 11; fax: 02 99 75 81 26.* Modern hotel in the centre of town.

A market town with a beautifully preserved medieval core, Vitré is synonymous with its formidable **château**, founded in the 11th century on a rocky outcrop commanding the approaches to the Vilaine. It's the sort of castle you might see in a medieval illuminated manuscript with characteristic witches' hat towers and machicolations. Climb the Tour de Montafilant, next door to the Hôtel de Ville, for good views of the town and the river. The **museums** of natural and local history are unremarkable but don't miss the Renaissance tryptych, decorated with 32 Limoges panels, in the **fortress chapel** (Tour de l'Oratoire).

Spend the rest of your time wandering the twisting, cobbled streets of the old town, starting with **rue de la Baudrairie**, the old leather-workers' quarter. Many of Vitré's half-timbered granite mansions were built by wealthy cloth merchants and are worth closer inspection. Look out for more unusual features – balustraded wooden staircases and elaborate stone porches, for example. The **parish church** is a fine example of Flamboyant Gothic architecture and has some Renaissance stained glass, as well as a number of colourful altarpieces from the same period.

The weekly market takes place on Mondays on the square outside (place Notre-Dame). Only a short walk from here is **rue d'En Bas**, where you'll find a good selection of bars and restaurants. Rue des Augustins leads to the medieval suburb of **Rachapt**, meaning 'repurchase' – when the castle was under siege during the Hundred Years' War the defenders paid the English to go away. In the **Musée St-Nicolas**, the chapel of a former 15th-century hospital, you can see a small collection of precious religious objects and some of the original 15th- and 16th-century frescoes. The Promenade du Val follows the line of the 13th-century town walls to offer panoramic views of the Vilaine valley, including the **washerwomen's meadows** (Pré des Lavandières), a public garden decorated with flower beds and aquatic plants. Just south of the town centre the **Jardin du Parc** contains more than 50 different species of tree.

Suggested tour

Château des Rochers-Sévigné
€€ Route d'Argentré du Plessis; tel: 02 99 75 04 54. Open Apr–June, daily, 1000–1200, 1400–1730; July–Sept, daily, 1000–1800; Oct–Mar, Wed–Fri, 1000–1230, 1400–1730, Sat–Mon, 1400–1730.

Accommodation and food in Vitré
Accommodation is cheap and plentiful in Vitré, making it a good touring base. There's a variety of crêperies and restaurants on rue Notre-Dame and rue d'En Bas.

Hôtel du Château €€ 5 rue Rallon; tel: 02 99 74 68 59; fax: 02 99 75 35 47. Closed Sun in the winter. Traditional hotel with friendly staff in a good situation under the castle walls.

Total distance: 79km (224km with detours – 162km without Fougères).

Time: 2 hours' driving. Allow 4 hours for the main route (half a day in Vitré), 9 hours with detours. A visit to Fougères will take an extra day. Those with limited time should visit the area round Vitré.

Links: The northern end of this route is about 40km south of Mont-St-Michel (*see pages 222–31*).

Leave **VITRE ❶** on the D88, then follow the signs (left) to **Château des Rochers-Sévigné**, the home of the 17th-century Marquise, Madame de Sévigné whose witty, sometimes gossipy letters to her daughter provide a vivid insight into the goings-on in Breton high society. The château and formal gardens look much as they did when the Marquise was in residence and the chapel and two rooms containing manuscripts, documents and paintings are open to visitors.

Cross the N157 then take the D110 to the junction with the D178. Turn left and continue to **la Guerche de Bretagne**, where the Tuesday market has been going since 1121. If you've a penchant for witty medieval wood carvings, take a peek at the 16th-century misericords in the Basilica Notre-Dame.

Detour: Continue south on the D178 for 29km through forest and farmland to **CHATEAUBRIANT ❷**. Return to Martigne, then take the D94 westwards to Retiers.

Take the D47 to the small town of **Retiers**. Leave on the D41, then turn right on to the D341. After about 2km signs to the right point to **la Roche aux Fees**, a 20m-long covered alleyway which, according to legend, was built with the help of fairies – hence the name. It's said that if lovers visiting the site on the night of a full moon can agree on the number of stones in the dolmen, they're assured of a long and happy life together. Return on the D341 and turn left at the crossroads. At the junction with the D107 there are good views of the narrow Etang de Marcillé; follow the edge of the lake, turning right on to the D48 to Visseiche.

Detour: Take the D463 west to **Châteaugiron**, an attractive feudal town presided over by the remains of its 13th-century castle. As well as an impressive keep and a 15th-century clock tower, there are colourful half-timbered houses and a couple of *crêperies* in the main square. Follow the D34 back to Vitré.

From Visseiche take the D310 to the hillside town of **Bais**, where the Renaissance doorway of the church features decidedly secular carvings of King François I and the Greek goddess Aphrodite among the skulls and salamanders. Take the D110 to the junction with the D176 and turn left to return to Vitré.

Page 210
Half-timbered houses in Fougères

Previous page
Vitré château

Le Petit Billot €€
*5 place du Général
Leclerc; tel: 02 99 75 02 10;
fax: 02 99 74 72 96; e-mail:
petit-billot@worldonline.fr;
www.petit-billot.com.*
Comfortable hotel in town
centre, near château. No
restaurant, but plenty of
choice nearby.

Detour: Take the D178 northwards to the other fortress town of **FOUGERES ❸**.

Also worth exploring

Just west of Vitré take the D29 across the Cantache dam to the delightful town of **Champeaux**. There's a quaint town hall with large hipped roof, elegant canons' houses and a collegiate church, grouped round an ancient well. The 14th- to 15th-century church has some superb Renaissance features including canopied choir stalls and a stained-glass window in the apse which depicts the crucifixion.

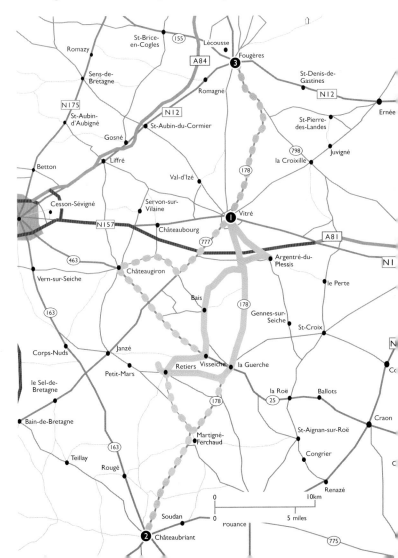

Rennes

Ratings

Architecture	●●●●●
Heritage	●●●●●
History	●●●●●
Food	●●●●
Art	●●●
Entertainment	●●●
Scenery	●●●
Cathedrals and churches	●●

The regional as well as the historic capital of Brittany, Rennes is a prosperous go-getting town of 200,000 people with an architectural heritage to rival Dinan and Vannes. A fire in 1720 led to the complete rebuilding of part of the city in an elegant, if restrained, classical style, a pleasing contrast with the chevron-patterned timber houses of the old town or *ville rouge*.

Rennes can also lay claim to be Brittany's most important cultural centre. Breton is still taught at the two universities and the separatist movement still has roots here. The presence of nearly 40,000 students gives Rennes an extra spark of vitality. The entertainment includes cultural festivals (the annual *Tombées de la Nuit* takes place in August) as well as exhibitions, concerts, opera, theatre and ballet. Almost every other building in the old town is an eatery of some kind while shopping addicts can get their fix at the Colombier Centre mall.

Sights

Cathédrale St-Pierre *Rue de la Monnaie; tel: 02 40 47 84 64. Open 0930–1200, 1500–1800.*

Musée des Beaux Arts *€€ 20 quai Emile Zola; tel: 02 23 62 17 45; e-mail: museebeauxarts.rennes@wanadoo.fr. Open Wed–Mon, 1000–1200, 1400–1800.*

Cathédrale St-Pierre
No expense was spared on the sumptuous interior of this 19th-century basilica and, although the project eventually ran out of money, there's more than enough paintings and gilded stucco here to satisfy most tastes. The finest art treasure in the cathedral is an exquisitely carved 15th-century Flemish retable containing scenes from the life of the Virgin and the child Jesus. You'll find it in the fifth chapel on the right-hand side. The impressive 18th-century façade belongs to an earlier building.

Musée des Beaux Arts
The fine arts museum's collection of paintings is arranged chronologically, from the Italian primitives to abstract art, and includes works by a number of big names – Veronese, Rubens,

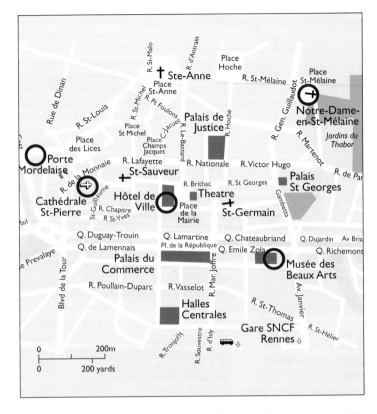

Gauguin and Picasso, to mention but a few. French artists of the 17th and 18th centuries are also well represented, especially Chardin, Greuze and Le Nain, but it's Georges de la Tour's haunting essay in chiaroscuro, *The Newly Born*, that lingers in the memory. Also on display are sculptures, drawings and archaeological treasures from the Egyptian, Greek and Roman civilisations.

Notre-Dame-en-St-Mélaine and the Jardin du Thabor

It's a short uphill walk from the river to the former Benedictine Abbey of St-Mélaine, dedicated to the advisor of Clovis, King of the Franks. The nave, now restored, dates from the 13th and 14th centuries and is lofty and spacious; the crossing belongs to an even older building. Look out for the remnants of medieval fresco painting in the south transept. The monastery became a hospital during the Revolution; the orchard was transformed in the 19th century into a splendid 10-hectare green space, part formal French garden, part English landscaped park, planted with roses, chrysanthemums, dahlias, camellias and rhododendrons. It's a great place for a stroll and there's plenty of shade but you're not allowed to picnic, or even to sit on the grass!

Above
Rennes: the Palais de Justice

Palaces of the New Quarter

The terrible fire that swept through Rennes in 1720 caused extensive damage to more than 30 streets and led to the complete rebuilding of part of the town. Two new squares were created. The focal point of **place de la Mairie** was the **Hôtel de Ville (Town Hall)**, designed by Jacques Gabriel in 1734. Two identical classical pavilions are linked by a slender clock tower known to locals as 'Le Gros'. A statue of Louis XV was to have filled the central niche but never materialised. The building on the opposite side of the square is the **Théâtre**, completed in 1846 to a neo-classical design by Charles Millardet. From the square you can see across the river to another monumental building, the **Palais du Commerce**, now the main post office and soon to be one of the stations on the new underground system. The **Vilaine** was not canalised until the 19th century but the elegant houses lining the quays date from the period after the fire. Following Paris fashions they were designed with granite arcades, limestone upper stories and mansard roofs, the classical frontages broken up by evenly placed pilasters. The arcades are now occupied by shops. Head in the opposite direction from place de la Mairie and you'll come to another of Gabriel's squares, **place du Palais**.

The magnificent **Palais de Justice** was the first building in Rennes to be made of stone and consequently one of the few to escape the fire. Completed in 1655 to a design by Salomon de Brosse, architect of the Palais de Luxembourg in Paris on which it is modelled, this was once the home of the Breton parliament. Ironically a mysterious fire in 1994 (attributed by some to the Breton fishermen's dispute) seriously damaged the roof but renovations are now complete. There are temporary exhibitions on diverse themes inside.

Portes Mordelaise
In medieval times the Duke of Brittany would have processed through this, the ceremonial gateway to the city, on the way to his coronation. The two machicolated towers – only recently restored – date from the 15th century and were once joined to the ramparts, a small stretch of which can be seen to the right, above third-century Roman foundations.

Accommodation and food

Hotel D'Angleterre €€ *19 rue du Maréchal Joffre; tel: 02 99 79 38 61; fax: 02 99 79 43 85.* Fairly spartan but good value in the heart of town.

Hotel MS Nemours €€ *5 rue de Nemours; tel: 02 99 78 26 26; fax: 02 99 78 25 40; e-mail: resa@hotelnemours.com.* Small but comfortable rooms in a modestly-sized hotel with a maritime theme.

Rennes offers a variety of dining experiences. For ambience it's hard to beat the half-timbered houses of the old town although the food doesn't always live up to expectations. Two dependable eateries are **L'Ouvrée** €€ *18 place de Lices; tel: 02 99 30 16 38* and **Auberge St-Sauveur** €€€ *6 rue St-Sauveur; tel: 02 99 79 32 56.* Both buildings date back to the Middle Ages and the restaurants specialise in classic French cooking.

Crêperies in equally good locations include **Maison de la Galette** € *6 place Ste-Anne; tel: 02 99 79 01 43* and **La Gavotte** € *41 rue St Georges; tel: 02 99 36 29 38, closed Sun,* the latter in a lively area popular with students. The pavement cafés and pizzerias on rue St-Michel and the adjoining square are good for people-watching after dark although you may encounter the odd wino. Follow the signs to le Prison St-Michel, a galleried courtyard with a selection of reasonably priced *crêperies* and restaurants, including **Pizzeria La Lupa** € *10 place de Rallier du Baty; tel: 02 99 79 31 15.*

Rennes is strong on ethnic restaurants with a choice of Spanish, Moroccan, Indian, even Turkish – **Le Temps d'Istanbul** €€ *21 rue de Penhoët; tel: 02 99 79 07 18.* For a comprehensive list of what's on offer, pick up the brochure *Accueil Hebergement et Restauration* from the tourist office.

A walk in Rennes

Leave from **place de la Mairie ❶**, passing the rotunda of the theatre and cross **place du Palais ❷** to the **Palais de Justice ❸**. Turn left on to rue Nationale which leads from the 'new town' into the 'ville rouge' where many of the buildings survived the fire of 1720.

Turn right into the triangular **place Champs Jacquet ❹** and you'll see an impressive line of five-storey 17th-century houses with distinctive timber patterning. Leave on rue Champs Jacquet to **place St-Anne ❺**, a shady square designed around the 19th-century neo-gothic church of St-Anne. Take **rue St-Michel ❻** for a complete change of atmosphere – overlooked by colourful half-timbered houses, diners and revellers spill out on to the pavements from the noisy bars and restaurants. To the right of **place St Michel ❼** is **place des Lices ❽**, a medieval jousting ground and now the site of the Saturday morning market. Cross the square, taking note of the art nouveau market halls, then turn left into rue de Juillet then right through the **PORTES MORDELAISE ❾**. Cross rue de la Monnaie to pass the **CATHEDRALE ST-PIERRE ❿**. Turn left on to **rue de la Psalette**, a quaint medieval street where the newly located tourist information office has recently opened in one of the timber houses. Continue on rue de Chapître, past the **Hôtel de Blossac** a grand 18th-century mansion, now home to the regional branch of the Ministry of Culture. If it's open, take a look at the entrance hall, a model of classical refinement with slender marble columns and a curving granite staircase. Continue to place du Calvaire.

Detour: Turn right on to **rue St-Yves** where a 15th-century Gothic chapel, once part of a medieval hospital, has been restored and is open to the public.

Turn left to the **Eglise St-Sauveur ⓫**, a rococo-style church with a popular shrine of 'Our Lady of Miracles' – the statue is said to have answered the prayers of the faithful in saving Rennes from depredation by English forces in 1357. From the church walk down rue du Guesclin to the **Hôtel de Ville ⓬**. Take rue d'Orléans and cross the elegant quays to place de la République and the **Palais du Commerce ⓭**. Walk along quai Emile Zola to the **MUSEE DES BEAUX ARTS ⓮**.

Re-cross the Vilaine and walk up rue Gambetta past the attractive gardens and massive 17th-century former **Palais St Georges ⓯** (now used by the city's administration). Beyond is an unusual art nouveau swimming pool, built between 1922 and 1925 on the site of the abbey church. The decorations include a mask of Neptune over the entrance.

Continue up rue Gambetta to **Notre-Dame-en-St-Mélaine ⓰**. Walk to the side of the church and into the **Jardin de Thabor ⓱**. Leave the garden by the path on the right which leads to rue de Paris and rue

Left
Rennes: Cathédrale St-Pierre

ℹ **Rennes Tourist Information** 11 rue St-Yves; tel: 02 99 67 11 11; fax: 02 99 67 11 10; e-mail: infos@tourisme-rennes.com; www.tourisme-rennes.com. Organises regular guided tours as well as providing information on festivals and other events. Will also help with accommodation.

🅿 Free parking spaces at place St-Mélaine and avenue A Briand; alternatively place Ste-Anne, place Hoche (maximum stay 2 hours). Long-stay car parks (24 hours) near the railway station.

Ⓐ All the main sights are accessible on foot. There is also a metro line with 15 stations. Trains run every few minutes, fares are €1.10 per hour or €3.20 for a day pass. Tel: 02 99 79 37 37; www.star.fr

Bikes are available for free (€76 deposit) from place de la République, daily, 0900–1900 for periods of up to 7 hours or 1 day. Tel: 02 99 79 65 88.

Ⓗ **Ecomusée du Pays de Rennes** €€ Ferme de la Bintinais (Route de Chatillon-sur-Seiche, 8km); tel: 02 99 51 38 15; fax: 02 99 50 68 35; e-mail: ecomusee.rennes@agglo-rennesmetropole.fr. Open Apr–Sept, Wed–Mon, 0900–1800; Oct–Mar, Wed–Fri and Mon, 0900–1200, 1400–1800; Sat, 1400–1800; Sun, 1400–1900. Leave Rennes on rue du Maréchal Joffre then follow the signs.

Victor Hugo. Cross rue Gambetta into **rue St-Georges**, a street of lively restaurants and fine 17th-century half-timbered buildings. Towards the end of the road, a turning to the left leads to **St-Germain** ⑱, a 15th- to 16th-century church in the Flamboyant Gothic style with many typical Breton features; note, for example, the fanciful sculpted ends to the wooden roof beams. Continue back to place de la Mairie.

Attractions outside Rennes

The theme of the **Ecomusée du Pays de Rennes** is five centuries of life on the farm. The open-air exhibition site extends over 15 hectares around the Ferme de la Bintinais where visitors learn all about agricultural customs and traditions. Apart from well-presented displays of costumes and farming implements there are reconstructed interiors, a livestock park with Breton draught horses, Pie Noire cows, Ushant sheep and other endangered breeds, as well as orchards, apiaries, botanical gardens and cultivated fields.

The **Parc Ornithologique de Bretagne** displays more than a thousand exotic birds, including toucans, parrots, hornbills and ibises in a colourful floral environment.

Also worth exploring

The Forest of Paimpont

A great forest, known as Brocéliande, once covered much of inland Brittany. It was an area rich in legend – the home of the magician Merlin, the fairy Viviene and her rival Morgan le Fay and, according to the medieval troubadour, Chrétien de Troyes, the focus of King Arthur's search for the Holy Grail.

At the centre of the present 7067-hectare forest is the former abbey and village of **Paimpont**. The 11th-century church by the lake is richly decorated with carved medallions, fruit and flowers. If the treasury is open, it is worth visiting to see the charming 15th-century statue of St Anne carrying the Virgin and Christ Child and a superb ivory crucifix which dates from the 18th century.

Other places to see in the forest include the picturesque hamlet **les Forges de Paimpont**, formerly forge-workers' houses; the **Church of Tréhorenteuc** – which cashes in on the tourism in the area by charging visitors to see the stained-glass window depicting the Holy Grail and post-war wall paintings of the knights of the round table; the **Château de Trécesson**, a 14th-century castle which has retained its original turreted appearance (the interior is not open to the public); and the **Château de Comper**, where the fairy Viviene was supposed to have been born and where the young Lancelot was raised. (The castle was rebuilt in the 19th century and is now Le Centre Arthurien, www.centre-arthurien.com – exhibitions are held here.)

Parc Ornithologique de Bretagne €€ 15
boulevard Pasteur, Bruz; tel:
02 99 52 68 57; fax: 02 99
52 95 48. Open daily,
1000–1200, 1400–1900;
Apr–June and Sept, daily,
1400–1900; Oct–mid-Nov
and mid-Feb–Mar, Sun,
1400–1800.

Abbey Church Paimpont;
tel: 02 99 07 81 37. Call for
hours.

Tréhorenteuc Church
€ details from Tourist Office.
Guided tours available.

**Château de Comper/Le
Centre Arthurien** €€
Tel: 02 97 22 79 96. Park
open Mar–Oct, 1000–1900.
Closed Tue, also Wed off
season.

**Paimpont Tourist
Information** Next to
the Abbey; tel: 02 99 07 84
23; fax: 02 99 07 84 27.
Open daily, 1000–1200,
1400–1700 or 1800.

**Tréhorenteuc Tourist
Information** Place Abbé
Gillard; tel: 02 97 93 05 12;
fax: 02 97 93 08 00.
Guided walks through
forest.

Getting out of the car

The various sites in the **Forest of Paimpont** that are linked to the
legends are not easy to find without detailed maps and route guides,
however, as you stroll through the woodland paths you might come
across the stone slabs known as Merlin's tomb or the Fontaine de
Barenton where Merlin fell in love with the beautiful Viviene. It is said
that if water from the fountain splashes on nearby Merlin's stone,
then a great storm will be unleashed on the land. Be cautious about
wandering into the Val Sans Retour (Valley of No Return). It is said
that the evil Morgan le Fay cast a spell at the Rocher des Faux Amants
(Rock of False Lovers) to entrap all unfaithful men. Only Lancelot, the
purest of knights was able to break the spell!

Various guided tours of the forest are available from the tourist
information centre in Tréhorenteuc, during the summer, including
some activities aimed at children.

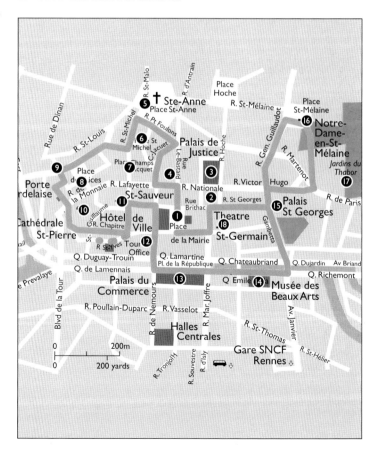

The Baie du Mont-St-Michel

Famous throughout France, Mont-St-Michel is the most popular tourist attraction outside Paris. Perched on the slopes of a remote granite rock, once isolated from the mainland (access today is via a causeway), are rising tiers of churches, cloisters, guest halls and fortified towers, founded on a labyrinthine system of crypts and cellars, which required remarkable expertise and ingenuity to design, let alone construct. Since the monastery was founded in the 8th century, the sea has retreated a long way, but travellers still need to be aware of quicksands, currents and tides. A project is underway to restore the site's island character by constructing a new barrage and replacing the causeway with a bridge.

The founder of the Abbey, St Aubert, was the bishop of Avranches and the monastic treasures are still preserved here. For that reason, the town museum is a 'must see' and there are wonderful views across the bay from the Botanical Gardens.

The pick of the local châteaux is romantic Combourg with beautiful lakeland scenery and a ghost in the guise of a black cat in one of the Gothic towers!

Ratings

Architecture	●●●●●
Castles and châteaux	●●●●●
Cathedrals and churches	●●●●●
Food	●●●●●
History	●●●●●
Children	●●●○○
Heritage	●●●○○
Scenery	●●●○○

AVRANCHES

First settled by the Celts in the 9th century BC Avranches is one of the oldest towns in Normandy and has had an unusually turbulent history: the salt-workers' revolt of 1639; bloody street battles between the 'blues' (republican troops) and the Chouans during the Revolution; and World War II have all left their mark.

Visitors with only a short time to spare should make the **Jardin des Plantes** a priority. This beautiful terraced garden once belonged to a Franciscan monastery, from where there are stunning views over the Baie du Mont-St-Michel. Concerts of music (with illuminations) are held in the evenings from June to September.

Another 'must see' is the collection of **illuminated manuscripts** and ancient books from the abbey of St-Michel, stored since the Revolution in the town hall. Around 30 items are on display at any one time in the **Bibliothèque du Fonds Ancien**, from classical works by Aristotle and Cicero to medieval histories, Books of Hours, treatises

ⓘ Avranches Tourist Information 2 rue du Gén. de Gaulle; tel: 02 33 58 00 22; www.ot-avranches.com

ⓜ Jardin des Plantes Open daily, 0800–dark.

Bibliothèque du Fonds Ancien €€ (combined ticket with the museum and Trésor St-Gervais) Mairie d'Avranches; tel: 02 33 89 29 50. Open July and Aug, daily, 1000–1900; May, June & Sept, Mon–Sat, 1000–1800; Oct and Apr, 1000–1230, 1400–1700 or 1800.

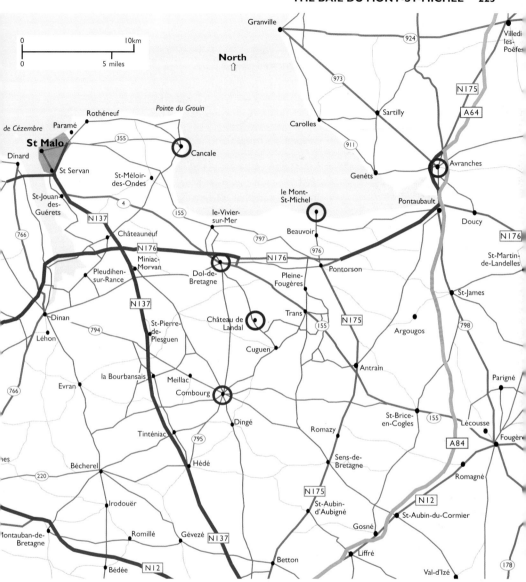

Musée Municipal €
*Place Jean de St-Avit;
tel: 02 33 58 00 22. Open
June–Sept, daily, 1000–
1230, 1400–1800;
Easter–May closed Tue.*

on astronomy, atlases etc – all outstanding examples of medieval calligraphy and illustration.

The **Musée Municipal** is housed in the former bishop's palace, a 15th-century building with a splendid vaulted ceiling in the main hall. Among the treasures on display is a reliquary containing the bones of Thomas Becket and an interesting collection of watercolours by Emile Sagot showing Mont-St-Michel in the 19th century. At the end of the bishop's garden, **place Thomas Becket** is the site of the old

Place Estouteville, rue Ormond (by the Church of St-Gervais).

Eglise St-Gervais *Place St-Gervais; tel: 02 33 89 29 50. Open June–Sept, daily, 0930–1200, 1400–1800 (June and Sept, Sun, 1400–1800 only).*

There is a market on *Tue and Fri mornings* in front of the Town Hall.

Flights: L'aero-club d'Avranches *Aerodrome du Val-St-Père; tel: 02 33 58 02 91.*

Horses: Château du Champ du Genêt *Route de Mortain, St-Senier-sous-Avranches; tel: 02 33 60 52 67; e-mail: info@cheval-plaisir.com; www.cheval-plaisir.com.* Half-day, weekend and longer pony trails.

La Croix d'Or €€ *83 rue de la Constitution; tel: 02 33 58 04 88; fax: 02 33 58 06 95.* Old-fashioned hotel with shady gardens. Superb restaurant. *Open Mar–Jan.*

Jardin des Plantes €€ *10 place Carnot; tel: 02 33 58 03 68; fax: 02 33 60 01 72; e-mail: jardin.des.plantes@ wanadoo.fr; www.le-jardin-des-plantes.fr.* Hotel and restaurant with great views.

La Renaissance € *17 rue de Fossés; tel: 02 33 58 03 71; fax: 02 33 60 86 12; e-mail: renaissance@ orange.fr.* Central, reasonably priced hotel with a brasserie.

cathedral which was allowed to collapse in 1794. A paving stone marks the spot where, in 1172, King Henry II of England publicly repented the murder of his erstwhile friend and chancellor.

Rue Challemel Lacour, with its quaint old houses, leads to the huge 19th-century church of **St-Gervais**. In the treasury (Trésor St-Gervais) is a reliquary containing the remains of St Aubert. According to legend, St Michael, infuriated by delays in the construction of Mont-St-Michel, jabbed his finger at Aubert the procrastinating abbot – you can still see the imprint on his skull!

Before leaving the town American visitors in particular might want to visit the small patch of US territory surrounding the monument to **General Patton**. The square marking the spot where he stayed in July 1944 before leading the crucial 3rd Army offensive has been filled with soil and trees imported from America.

CANCALE

ⓘ Cancale Tourist Information 44 rue du Port; tel: 02 99 89 63 72; fax: 02 99 89 75 08; e-mail: contact@ville-cancale.fr; www.ancale.-tourismef.fr

ⓡ La Ferme Marine €€ L'aurore, St-Kerber; tel: 02 99 89 69 99; fax: 02 99 89 82 74. Tours mid-June–mid-Sept, 1100, 1500 & 1700.

Musée des Arts et Traditions Populaires € Place St Méen; tel: 02 99 89 79 32. Open July and Aug, 1000–1200, 1430–1830 except Mon am; June and Sept, Fri–Sun, 1430–1830.

Famous for its oysters since ancient times (archaeologists have found shells in excavated Roman army camps), Cancale harbour is still as busy as ever, the fishermen unloading their catches, mending their nets and tinkering with boats. Six thousand tonnes of oysters, cultivated from year-old 'spats' brought in from the Belon estuary, are produced every year. You can sample them from a quayside stall or from one of many restaurants overlooking the sea. The Sentier des Douaniers, a clifftop walk to **Pointe de Grouin**, leaving from the steps at the end of rue de Port, offers views of the oyster beds at the foot of the cliffs. If you want to find out more about the industry visit the informative museum-cum-oyster farm, **la Ferme Marine**, where visitors can observe breeding techniques either in situ or via audiovisual presentations. There's also a huge display of shells.

A long, cobbled street leads from the port to the old town on the hill. Here, in the former **St-Méen Church**, is a museum of the art and traditions of Cancale, including an exhibition on the town's historic sailing school. On Sundays there is a lively produce market outside the church with local crafts also on sale.

COMBOURG

ⓘ Combourg Tourist Information Maison de la Lanterne, place Albert-Parent; tel: 02 99 73 13 93; www.combourg.org

ⓗ Hôtel du Château €€€ 1 place Chateaubriand; tel: 02 99 73 00 38; fax: 02 99 73 25 79; www.hotelduchateau.com. Ivy clings to the walls of this attractive hotel-restaurant with a large garden.

Rising above the shores of the aptly named 'lac Tranquille' and the grey-granite town of Combourg are the turreted towers of one of France's most impressive medieval fortresses. In 1761 the château became the family home of Combourg's most famous son, the Romantic writer François-René de Chateaubriand. It seems that not all his memories of this ostensibly idyllic home were happy ones. In his celebrated autobiography, Memoirs d'Outre Tombe (Memoirs from Beyond the Grave) he recounts how his morose father could not tolerate the noise of children and routinely banished François and his sister Lucile to their rooms. To make matters worse, François' bedroom was said to be haunted by a former owner of the château who assumed the form of a cat during his nightly wanderings. Visitors are shown round the chapel, the drawing room, the archive with its exhibition of manuscripts and portraits and, of course, the writer's bedroom in the Tour du Chat. From the crenellated parapet there are views of the town and the landscaped park.

DOL-DE-BRETAGNE

Now several miles inland, Dol was a craggy island much like Mont-St-Michel until the sea began to retreat in the 10th century. The self-

ⓘ **Dol-de-Bretagne Tourist Information** *Grand Rue; tel: 02 99 48 15 37; fax: 02 99 48 14 13; e-mail: office.dol@wanadoo.fr; www.pays-de-dol.com*

ⓝ **CathedralOscope** *€€ Place de la Cathedrale; tel: 02 99 48 35 30. Open Apr–Oct, 1000–1900. Special displays on Wed evenings in summer.*

styled 'capital of the marshes' was an important bishopric in the Middle Ages, hence the heavyweight 13th-century **cathedral**. Originally part of the town's defences, the parapet could be used for hurling missiles or for spying out the enemy.

The **Promenade des Douves** follows the line of the old walls and offers views of the marshes, now fully integrated into the landscape. The **CathedralOscope** museum, housed in a 19th-century former school building just along the road from Dol's own cathedral, shows how and why cathedrals were built as they are, with particular emphasis on the 'quest for light'. One of the houses on the **Grand Rue** (No 17) is 11th-century Romanesque and several have interesting architectural features.

Accommodation and food in Dol-de-Bretagne

Picturesque rue Ceinte has a good choice of reasonably priced restaurants.

Hôtel de Bretagne €€ *17 place Chateaubriand; tel: 02 99 48 02 03; fax: 02 99 48 25 75.* Reliable, centrally located *logis*.

CHATEAU DE LANDAL

ⓝ **Château de Landal** *€€ Broualan, Dol-de-Bretagne; contact Dol-de-Bretagne tourist office for details.*

The highlight of any visit to this imposing medieval castle must be the falconry displays. Visitors can see how these magnificent birds of prey are trained before watching them in flight. (An English language commentary is available on request.) Between shows you can take a guided tour of the château and its ramparts, go for a nature ramble in the grounds, or picnic near the trout lake.

LE MONT-ST-MICHEL

ⓘ **Mont-St-Michel Tourist Information** *Corps de Garde des Bourgeois; tel: 02 33 60 14 30; www.ot-montsaintmichel.com*

⊘ From St-Malo N176 (45km); from Avranches N176 (20km); from Rennes N175 (65km).

Hermits were living on the Mount as early as the 6th century but it was not until AD 708 that Bishop Aubert of Avranches (*see page 224*) built the first chapel – supposedly at the command of the Archangel Michael who had appeared to him in a dream. The abbey was founded in the 10th century by Benedictine monks under the special protection of the Dukes of Normandy. From that moment until 1897, when the statue of St Michael brandishing a golden sword was placed on the pinnacle of the church, buildings of unrivalled architectural splendour steadily accumulated to form the breathtaking ensemble visitors see today. Both the abbey and the town frequently came under attack but they never succumbed, not even during the Hundred Years' War when the English bombarded the island from a specially constructed wooden bastille,

Above
Le Mont-St-Michel

🏛 **Benedictine Abbey**
€€ *Tel: 02 33 89 80
00; fax: 02 33 70 83 08;
e-mail: anne.bernard@
monum.fr; www.abbaye-
montsaintmichel.com. Open
May–Aug, daily, 0900–
1900; Sept–Apr, daily,
0930–1800. Optional
guided tours, including
English.*

combining the assault with a sea blockade (you can still see two of the captured mortars near the information office). For much of the 18th and 19th centuries the abbey doubled as a prison for royalists, rebels and 'exiled gentlemen', even priests. It was designated an historic monument as long ago as 1874 but a token population of monks and nuns still serves the tiny local community of less than a hundred.

The Abbey
The focal point of the complex and its crowning glory is the **church**. The Romanesque nave, completed early in the 12th century, was constructed over an earlier chapel which now serves as a crypt (Our Lady Underground). The chancel collapsed in the 15th century; its sleek rib-vaulted replacement, Flamboyant Gothic in style, is supported by its own **Crypt of the Mighty Pillars**. The church also required plenty of external support in the form of flying buttresses and a spectacular chevet, a riot of pinnacles, finials and other decoration.

Early in the 13th century new accommodation for the monks was built on the north side of the mount. This stupendous structure, one of the finest examples of Gothic architecure in France, is known appropriately as **la Merveille** (The Marvel). The rooms open to the public include the **Almonry**, where the poorest pilgrims were looked after; the **Guest Hall**, a vaulted building with a double aisle, one side of which would have been curtained off to serve as a kitchen; the **Knights' Hall**, used as a workshop for copyists and illuminators; and the **Refectory**, where the monks ate their meals in silence as they listened to readings from the scriptures and where light flooded in not only from end windows, but from narrow apertures along the wall, partially concealed by slender columns. In the magnificent **Cloisters** the spaces between the arches are filled with ingenious limestone carvings of plants and other motifs. The Abbey's formidable **defences**, an elaborate network of ramparts, watchtowers, gatehouses and fortified courtyards are also impressive; the Guardroom is now the tourist information office.

The town
There's not much to the town besides the **Grande Rue** which winds tortuously around the base of the mount. A tourist trap crammed to bursting point with souvenir shops, *crêperies* and fast-food outlets, this is where medieval wayfarers would have bought their pilgrims'

Musée Logis
Tiphaine €
Tel: 02 33 89 01 85.
Open Feb–mid-Nov, tel for
hours.

L'Archéoscope *as Musée*
Logis Tiphaine.

badges before booking in at the Unicorn or one of the other hostelries. If you have time on your hands the pick of the small **museums** is the quaint old **Logis Tiphaine**, the house Bertrand du Guesclin built for his wife while he was away in Spain fighting the Infidel. It's furnished in period style. Also consider the **Archéoscope**, a multi-media show leading visitors on a whistle-stop tour of the island's history and legends.

Accommodation and food on Mont-St-Michel

La Mère Poulard €€€ *Grand Rue; tel: 02 33 89 68 68; fax: 02 33 89 68 69; e-mail: hotel.mere.poulard@wanadoo.fr; www.mere-poulard.fr.* Famous throughout the island for its (overpriced) omelettes. Rooms also available – again, mostly expensive.

St-Pierre €€ *Grande Rue; tel: 02 33 60 14 03; fax: 02 33 48 59 82; e-mail: aubergesaintpierre@wanadoo.fr; www.auberge-saint-pierre.fr.* Atmospheric half-timbered building with restaurant.

Suggested tour

Pontorson Tourist
Information *Place*
de l'Hôtel de Ville; tel: 02 33
60 20 65; fax: 02 33 60 85
67.

Maison de la Baie
€€ *Le Vivier-sur-mer;*
tel: 02 99 48 84 38. Open
July and Aug, daily,
0930–1230, 1400–1830;
rest of the year, Mon–Sat,
0730–1200, 1400–1730.

Port miniature de la
forêt de Villecartier €€
Tel: 02 99 48 55 49. Open
Apr–June, Sat, Sun &
holidays from 1400; July and
Aug, daily, from 1100.

Reptilarium du Mont-
St-Michel €€ *Beauvoir;*
tel: 02 33 68 11 18;
www.le-reptilarium.com.
Open daily, Apr–Oct, rest of
year, 1400–1800.

Total distance: 104km (138km with detours).

Time: 2 hours' driving. Allow 6 hours for the main route, 9 hours with detours. To explore Mont-St-Michel fully will require a day, at the very least a half-day. Those with limited time should concentrate on the section between Mont-St-Michel and Avranches.

Links: This route, which crosses the Brittany/Normandy border, links with St-Malo (*see pages 164–73*) and the Rance Valley (*see pages 174–81*).

Leave **CANCALE ❶** on the D76 and turn left on the D155, a lovely coast road with views over the Bay of St-Michel. (The rows of wooden posts jutting out of the shallow water are used for collecting mussels.) Continue to **le Vivier-sur-Mer**, a centre of leisure pursuits – sand-yachting is especially popular on the large expanse of flat sand left by the receding tide. For insights into mussel cultivation and collection, and general info on the natural life of the bay, visit Vivier-sur-mer's **Maison de la Baie** (one of several around the bay; see also Courtils, below) to view exhibtions and join a guided tour of a mussel farm. As you leave the town turn left on to the D282, then take the right fork to **Mont Dol**, a flat-topped granite outcrop rising abruptly from the plain. Once an island like Mont-St-Michel it shares legends of the titanic battle between Satan and the Archangel. Climb the steep footpath to the observation tower for panoramic seaward views of the 3000-hectare patchwork of polders, crisscrossed by dikes and dotted with abandoned windmills and grazing sheep.

Take the road from here to **DOL-DE-BRETAGNE ❷**.

ⓘ La Maison de la Baie du Mont-St-Michel €€ *Route de Roche Torin, Relais de Courtils; tel: 02 33 48 84 38; fax: 02 33 48 84 67. Open daily, 0900–1230, 1400–1730 (open until 1830 in summer; closed Sun in winter).*

Musée de la Seconde Guerre Mondiale €€€ *Le Val St-Père; tel: 02 33 68 35 83. Open Apr–Oct, daily, 0930–1830; Nov–Mar, Sun and holidays, 0930–1830.*

Ⓒ Hôtel Le Bretagne €€ *59 rue Couesnon, Pontorson; tel: 02 33 60 10 55; fax: 02 33 50 20 54; e-mail: debretagne@ destination-bretagne.com. Friendly staff here; restaurant with set menus.*

Hôtel Montgomery €€€ *13 rue Couesnon, Pontorson; tel: 02 33 60 00 09; fax: 02 33 60 37 66; e-mail: info@hotel-montgomery.com; www.hotel-montgomery.com. Closed between Nov and Mar. Central logis. Very good restaurant.*

🅟 Pontorson has a large market on Wednesday mornings.

ⓘ Details of both boat hire and horse riding tours from the tourist office in Pontorson.

Centre d'Animation de la Baie du Mont-St-Michel *Gare Maritime, Le Vivier-sur-Mer; tel: 02 99 48 84 38. Walking, cycling and horse riding tours along this beautiful stretch of coast.*

Detour: Take the D795 to the picturesque town of **COMBOURG ❸**. Return to Dol.

Take the D155 south to la Boussac. Leave on the D4 then turn left following the signs 'Les Aigles de Bretagne' to the splendid avenue of oak trees which leads to the **CHATEAU DE LANDAL ❹**. From here take the road through Broualan. At the junction with the D83, turn left, then right on to the D155 which passes through the **Forêt de Villecartier**. Signs to the right point to the **Port Miniature** where model boats – tugs, trawlers, ferries and paddle-steamers – can be hired to sail on the lake. There is also a restaurant and picnic area here.

Turn right to Antrain, then on to the D175 (N175) which crosses the border into Normandy. **Pontorson** offers a quieter alternative to Mont-St-Michel for an overnight stay. It's possible to walk to the abbey from here following the banks of the River Couesnon, a waterway depicted in the chancel window of the church of Notre-Dame, founded by William the Conqueror in gratitude to the Virgin who saved his army from quicksands here.

Leave on the D976 to Beauvoir where the 200 lizards, snakes and crocodiles in the **Reptilarium du Mont-St-Michel** *Route de Pontorson; tel: 02 33 68 11 18* may make your flesh creep. However, the tunnels, viewing frames, glass towers and tortoise garden make the experience fun for the kids. Continue to **LE MONT-ST-MICHEL ❺**. Return to the junction with the D275 then take the same road through the flat windswept salt marshes of the north coast. At Courtils look out for the **Maison de la Baie du Mont-St-Michel**, a museum which uses computer graphics, film and a recorded commentary (English available) to explain the evolution of the bay. Continue to Pontaubault, on the Sélune estuary, then take the N176 to **Ducey**, a tranquil 'ville fleurie' where a picturesque 17th-century bridge crosses the river. From here follow the scenic D78 to **AVRANCHES ❻**.

Detour: About 2.5km after St-Quentin on the D78, take the left turn to the junction with the D7. Turn left again and cross the N175 to the **Musée de la Seconde Guerre Mondiale**, where the liberation of France in June 1944 by General Patton's Allied forces is explained using film, model soldiers and a variety of artefacts and military hardware, including camouflaged motorbikes. Take the D7 to Avranches.

Also worth exploring

The coast beyond Avranches is pitted with small villages where the rhythm of the tides dictates the life of the people. If you're here in July and August, the tiny **Maison de la Pêche à Pied et des Anciennes Salines** at Vains documents the work of the fishermen and salt gatherers. Rounding le Grouin de Sud, the mud flats of the estuary

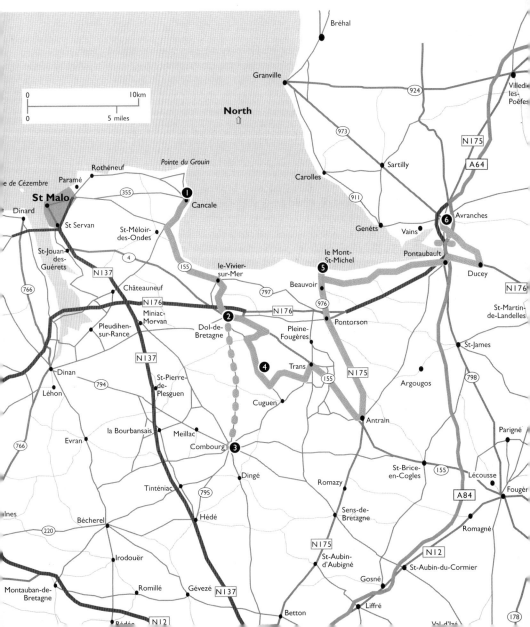

ⓘ Maison de la Pêche à Pied et des Anciennes Salines € *La Chaussée St-Léonard; tel: 02 33 58 16 16. Open July and Aug, daily, 1400–1800.*

give way to wide expanses of sand and dunes retreats into the bay. The best place for a swim From the village of **Genêts**, where the small 1 granite church was a popular stopover for pil views of Mont-St-Michel; for a panorama of the who the cliffs at Pointe de Champeaux.

La Manche

The majority of visitors to Normandy and Brittany see the Cotentin Peninsula (the northern end of la Manche) as little more than a way-station on the road to better things. This is a pity. While there's little to detain you in Cherbourg itself, the surrounding countryside has more to offer than you might expect, as well as several towns worth investigating. If you're into Norman architecture you should consider visiting Coutances, where the cathedral is the equal of any in the region. From here you could move on to the abbeys at Hambye (impressive ruins) and Lessay and Lucerne (both beautifully restored). Valognes was heavily bombed during World War II, but some of its magnificent architectural heritage of 18th-century mansions has survived.

The fishing ports of Granville and Barneville have a certain antiquated charm; both are now seaside resorts and with Barneville you get a second beach at Carteret thrown in. From Granville it's a short hop to the wild and rugged Iles Chausey, while Barneville offers good walks and even better views – you can see the Channel Islands in fine weather.

BARNEVILLE-CARTERET

ⓘ Barneville-Carteret Tourist Information
10 rue des Ecoles, Barneville; tel: 02 33 04 90 58; fax: 02 33 04 93 24; e-mail: tourisme.barneville-carteret.fr; www.barneville-carteret.fr; place Flandres Dunkerque, Carteret; tel: 02 33 04 94 54.

ⓟ On the quays in the port, place Flandre Dunkerque, behind the church in Barneville.

There are three distinct parts to this resort. Old Barneville is a typical Normandy market town with an 11th-century fortified church. Barneville Plage became a popular bathing resort in the 19th century – witness the smart villas clustering at the water's edge. A marina and watersports centre number among the more recent attractions here. Carteret lies on the other side of the harbour and has two beaches of its own: one tucked away in a small sheltered bay at the far end of the promenade; the other beyond the lighthouse, where the flat expanse of golden sand is popular with windsurfers. If you're after a change of scene, a tourist train runs twice a week to Portbail, 9km down the coast.

LA MANCH

North

Auderville
Urville
Nacqueville
St-Pierre-
Eglise
Cherbourg
Beaumont
Équerdreville-Hainneville
Octeville
Tourlaville
la Glacerie
Barfleur
901
901
904
Brix
N I3
Quettehou
Flamanville
St-Vaast-
la-Hougue
les Pieux
900
902
Valognes
Bricquebec
2
Montebourg
St-Sauveur-
le-Vicomte
Ste-Mère-
Eglise
14
Barneville-Carteret
Carteret
Picauville
N I3
Grandcamp
Maisy
Vierville-
sur-Mer
Portbail
903
900
St-Jores
903
la-Haye-
du-Puits
Carentan
Isigny
N I3
514
Trévières
Lessay
971
Tribehou
St-Jean-
de-Daye
le Molay-Littry
Créances
Périers
Pont-
Hérbert
Cerisy-la-
Forêt
572
650
St-Saveur-
Lendelin
900
N I74
2
Blainville-sur-Mer
St-Malo-de-
la-Lande
Marigny
Agneaux
St-Lô
Coutainville
44
Coutances
972
N I74
Montmartin-sur-Mer
Cerisy-sur-
Vire
Condé-
sur-Vire
Torigni
Quettreville-
sur-Seinne
Hambye
Tessy
Percy
A64
Cérences
Gavray
N I75
Pont-Farcy
Bréhal
N I74
Les Iles Chausey
Donville-les-Bains
St-Sever-
Calvados
Granville
924
Vire
924
Villedieu-les-Poêfes
St-Pair-sur-Mer
la Haye-Pesnel
Jullouville

he market is on Saturday.

Boats: Manche Iles Express runs a service to Jersey from the Gare Maritime; *tel: 08 25 13 30 50.*

Train: The Côte des Isles Train (with carriages from the 1930s and 1950s) runs along the coast from Carteret to Portbail (9km) in July and August. Regular services on *Sun (depart Carteret 1500, Portbail 1630)* and two market day specials: *Tue (depart Portbail at 1000 and Carteret at 1300)* and *Thur (depart Carteret at 0830 and 1000, return Portbail at 1300). Train Touristique du Contentin; tel: 02 04 94 54.*

Horses: Club Hippique Lypca *rue de la Corderie; tel: 02 33 04 93 63.* Pony trails along the beaches.

Accommodation and food in Barneville-Carteret

Hôtel le Cap €€ *Promenade Abbé Lebouteiller; tel: 02 33 53 85 89; fax: 02 33 53 08 19.* As the name suggests this beach-front hotel is sheltered by cliffs. The restaurant specialises in *fruits de mer.*

Hôtel des Ormes €€€ *Quai Barbey d'Aurevilly; tel: 02 33 52 23 50; fax: 02 33 52 91 65; e-mail: welcome@hoteldesormes.fr; www.hoteldesormes.fr.* Delightful hotel with character, overlooking the marina.

There are several campsites in the area including **Camping de la Gerfleur €** *tel: 02 33 04 38 41;* **L'Ermitage €** *tel: 02 33 04 78 90; fax: 02 33 04 06 62; www.campingermitage.com;* and **Camping Les Bosquets €** *tel: 02 33 04 73 62; fax: 02 33 04 35 82.*

A walk round Barneville-Carteret

Begin in Barneville at the **Eglise St-Germain**. Behind the church, an archway between two houses leads to Dessous le Bourg ('Below the town'). Follow this road into the lane through the hamlet of **le Tot**. Cross the footbridge over the River Gerfleur and walk up Chasse du Tot to the junction with rue des Ormes. Turn left and follow the road past a row of 18th-century shipowners' houses to the **marina**. Continue along the front to the **Gare Maritime**. At the end of the bay, the road follows the contours of the cliff before dipping to **Carteret beach**. From here follow the footpath, Sentier des Douaniers, over the **Corniche de Phare** to the dunes beyond. Turn right at the ruins of the old Romanesque church, then follow the path across rue du Phare to the **viewing table** (look for the Channel Islands of Jersey, Guernsey and Sark). Return to rue du Cap, then take the footpath to the left across the dunes – the highest on the Normandy coast and quite a climb in places. Continue to Hattainville, a hamlet of fishermen's houses. Pick up the GR223 footpath for les Moitiers d'Allonne, then walk along the small road parallel to the D904. Where the road crosses the D904, take the track opposite back to Barneville.

CHERBOURG

Cherbourg Tourist Information *Quai Alexandre III; tel: 02 33 93 52 02; fax: 02 33 53 66 97; e-mail: tourisme@ot-cherbourg-cotentin.fr; www.ot-cherbourg-cotentin.fr*

By the station, avenue Delaville, at the end of rue Fr. La-Vieille.

One of the busiest ports of entry for cross-Channel ferries, Cherbourg is also an important naval base. Visually, though, it's drab and unprepossessing and you'll probably be impatient to move on elsewhere. If you're looking for something to do you could take a stroll along the beach, calling in at the **Basilique de la Trinité**, a 14th- to 15th-century church with lurid medieval bas-reliefs depicting the Dance of Death. Alternatively, if you're feeling more energetic there are good views of the harbour and roadstead from the **Fort du Roule** where the **Musée de la Libération** takes a

Musée de la Libération €€ *Fort du Roule; tel: 02 33 20 14 12. Open May–Sept, Tue–Sat, 1000–1200, 1400–1800, Sun and Mon, 1400–1800; Oct–Apr, Wed–Sun, 1400–1800.*

Musée Thomas Henry *Centre Culturel, rue Vastel; tel: 02 33 23 39 30. Open May–Sept, Tue–Sat, 1000–1200, 1400–1800, Sun and Mon, 1400–1800; Oct–Apr, Wed–Sun, 1400–1800.*

5 August 'La Solitaire du Figaro' yacht race.

look at life in Cherbourg during World War II and the role played by the town in the Allied landings. If you're an art lover, the **Musée Thomas Henry** is a real find with more than 300 paintings and sculptures from the 13th to 19th centuries, including works by Fra Angelico, Murillo and the locally born French artist, Jean-François Millet.

Accommodation and food in Cherbourg

Mercure Cherbourg €€€ *Allée du President Menut; tel: 02 33 44 01 11; fax: 02 33 44 01 11.* Modern hotel with comfortable rooms, harbour views and quality restaurant.

La Régence €€ *42 quai de Caligny; tel: 02 33 43 05 16; fax: 02 33 43 98 37; www.laregence.com.* Most rooms have balconies overlooking the harbour and the restaurant is quite good value.

There's a cluster of restaurants on quai de Caligny. Alternatively, if you're in the mood to splash out, **Le Grandgousier €€€** *21 rue de l'Abbaye; tel: 02 33 53 19 43; fax: 02 33 53 04 74; e-mail: grandgousier2 @wanadoo.fr* serves quality French seafood and fish dishes in a warm ambience.

Coutances

Coutances Tourist Information *Place Georges Leclerc; tel: 02 33 19 08 10; fax: 02 33 19 08 19; e-mail: tourisme-coutances@wanadoo.fr*

Rue Tancrède, rue Gambetta.

Jardin des Plantes *Open July and Aug, 0900–2330; Apr–June and Sept, 0900–2000; Oct–Mar, 0900–1700.*

Musée Quesnel-Morinière € *2 rue Quesnel Morinière; tel: 02 33 45 11 92; fax: 02 33 76 55 76. Open daily except Tue, Sun am & hols, 1000–1200, 1400–1700 (1800 in July and Aug).*

Coutances is dominated by its Norman Gothic **cathedral**, which Victor Hugo rated second only to Chartres. Its a magnificent building, sited on a hill above two rivers. In 1218 the Romanesque cathedral was damaged by fire and the present structure was raised on its foundations, the twin towers on the façade moulded to fit the new style with spires added; but it's the exquisitely proportioned lantern tower, described by the great military engineer, Vauban, as 'the work of a sublime madman', that captures the heart and the imagination. Inside there's the nave to admire, as well as the stained-glass windows in the transepts – the 14th-century window on the south side depicts the Last Judgement. It's worth considering a guided tour of the cathedral: you get to climb the galleries and the lantern tower and there are superb views inside and out.

French, Italian and English influences are all apparent in the **Jardin des Plantes**, where the attractions include garden terraces, immaculately tended lawns and flower beds, 47,000 plants and rare trees and the **Musée Quesnel-Morinière**, and a beautiful 17th-century house with exhibitions of local costumes, ceramics and paintings, including works by Rubens, Vouet and le Soeur. If you're here in May, check out the **Jazz sous les Pommiers** (Jazz under the Apple Trees) festival. The Thursday **produce market** has everything from calvados to *foie gras*, butter, cream and oysters.

Market day is Thursday.

 Jazz sous les Pommiers May – international guest performances.
Municipal Theatre;
tel: 02 33 45 48 36;
www.jazzsouslespommiers.com

Summer in Coutances – July and August. Music and cinema events are staged in the cathedral and various châteaux. Contact Tourist Information for details.

Right
Coutances cathedral

Accommodation and food in Coutances

Hôtel Cositel €€ *Route de Coutainville; tel: 02 33 19 15 00; fax: 02 33 19 15 02; e-mail: hotelcositel@wanadoo.fr; www.hotelcositel.com.* A little out of town but definitely worth considering for the view. Prices in the restaurant are on the steep side.

Hôtel Le Normandie €€ *2 place du Général de Gaulle; tel: 02 33 45 01 40; fax: 02 33 46 74 54.* Reasonably priced rooms and restaurant.

GRANVILLE

 Boats: Mance Iles Express runs a service to Jersey from the Gare Maritime; *tel: (Jersey) 01534 888783; www. manche-iles-express.com*

Jolie France II takes foot passengers to Chausey, (Mar–Dec) *tel: 02 33 50 31 81.* The trip takes about an hour each way.

Granville presents two distinct faces to visitors. The severe-looking Upper Town (Haute Ville) is a smaller, less compelling version of St-Malo. It was fortified in the 15th century by Sir Thomas Scales who used it as a base for attacking Mont-St-Michel. The Lower Town (Basse Ville) looks more like a traditional fishing village although the 1000-berth yachting marina now overshadows the brightly painted trawlers and whelkers moored alongside the harbour wall. It's a lively place, congenial if you don't mind noise as well as bustle. The town beach is cramped while crowded. **Plage de Donville**, just north of town, on the other hand, has a generous expanse of soft sand and opportunities for watersports. There's also a thalassotherapy centre and that other standby of French seaside resorts, a casino.

Granville Tourist Information 4 cours Jonville; tel: 02 33 91 30 03; fax: 02 33 91 30 19; e-mail: office-tourisme@ ville-granville.fr; www.ville-granville.fr

P Place Marshal Foch, place aux Corsaire, Cours Jonville.

Musée du Vieux Granville € 2 rue le Carpentier; tel: 02 33 50 44 10. Open Apr–June, Wed–Mon, 1000–1200; July–Sept, 1000–1200, 1400–1800; Oct–Mar, Wed, Sat and Sun, 1400–1600.

Aquarium du Roc €€€ Tel: 02 33 50 19 83; e-mail: aquarium-du-roc@wanadoo.fr. Open daily, mid-Apr–mid-Sept, 1000–1230, 1400–1900.

Musée Christian Dior €€ Villa les Rhumbs; tel: 02 33 61 48 21; e-mail: museechristiandior@wanadoo.fr. Open mid-May–mid-Sept, daily, 1000–1230, 1430–1830.

Saturday is market day.

The entrance to the Upper Town is through a fortified gatehouse known as the Grand'Porte. Here, in the **Musée du Vieux Granville**, collections of regional costumes and furniture rub shoulders with rotating exhibitions on Granville's history as a cod fishing port, centre of piracy and bathing resort. The statue of Our Lady in the 15th- to 17th-century **Church of Notre-Dame** is venerated in the annual Grand Pardon at the end of July. It's just a short stroll from here to the lighthouse at **Pointe du Roc** where the attractions include an **Aquarium**, **La Féérie de Coquillages** (Shell Fairyland), **Palais Minéral** (compositions made from rocks and minerals) and **Jardin des Papillons** (Butterfly Garden). At the other end of town, near the beach, is the **Jardin Christian Dior**, designed by the famous couturier in 1920; his former home is now a **museum**. Boat excursions leave from Granville for the **Iles Chausey** (journey time one hour).

Accommodation and food in Granville

Hôtel des Bains €€€ 19 rue Georges Clémenceau; tel: 02 33 50 17 31; fax: 02 33 50 89 22; www.hoteldesbains-granville.com. Hotel looking out over the sea. Not all the rooms are expensive and there's a decent restaurant.

Hôtel Michelet €€ 5 bis rue Jules Michelet; tel: 02 33 50 06 55; fax: 02 33 50 12 55. Pleasant location between the casino and thalassotherapy centre, though the rooms are nothing special.

Le Phare €€ 11 rue du Port; tel: 02 33 50 12 94. Delicious fish and seafood dishes with panoramic views from the room on the first floor.

LES ILES CHAUSEY

There are several sailings a day from Granville to the Chausey archipelago, around 350 islands in all, some 50 of which may be visible at high tide. Many are little more than clumps of rock and only one, Grande Ile, is inhabited. The population increases from around half a dozen in the depths of winter to nearer a hundred during the tourist season. Don't expect much entertainment though – even Grande Ile is tiny; on foot it's possible to circuit the whole island, following the coastal footpath, in less than two hours. The scenery is of the wild and windswept variety – carpets of gorse, blue thistle and other rare plant species providing the dash of colour. Chausey granite was used not only in the construction of Mont-St-Michel abbey but for the embankments of London and Paris and there are abandoned stone quarries all over the place. Beaches are also in plentiful supply, at Port Marie, for example, or Port Homard where you'll also find the *vieux fort*, renovated by the motor magnate, Louis Renault, in the 1920s.

VALOGNES

ℹ **Valognes Tourist Information** 21 rue du Grand Moulin; tel: 02 33 95 01 26; fax: 02 33 95 23 23 and place du Château; tel: 02 33 40 11 55; fax: 02 33 40 00 04; e-mail: mairie.officetourisme. valognes@wanadoo.fr; www.mairie-valognes.fr

🏨 **Hôtel de Beaumont €€** 11 rue Barbey d'Aurevilly; tel: 02 33 40 12 30. Open July–mid-Sept, Wed–Mon, 1430–1830, Tue, 1030–1200, 1430–1830.

Musée Regional du Cidre €€ Rue du Petit Versailles; tel: 02 33 40 22 73. Open July and Aug, Mon–Sat, 1000–1200, 1400–1800, Sun, 1400–1800; Apr–June and Sept, Mon and Wed–Sat, 1000–1200, 1400–1800, Sun, 1400–1800.

ℹ **Bricquebec** 13 place Ste-Anne; tel: 02 33 52 21 65; e-mail: ot.bricquebec@wanadoo.fr; www.ville-bricquebec.fr

St-Sauveur-le-Vicomte Vieux Château; tel: 02 33 21 50 44; e-mail: ot.ssv@wanadoo.fr; www.saintsauveurlevicomte. fr.st

Portbail 26 rue Philippe Lebel; tel: 02 33 04 03 07; fax: 02 33 04 94 66; e-mail: tourisme.portbail@wanadoo. fr; http://tourisme.portbail. free.fr

🏰 **Bricquebec Castle €** Tel: 02 33 87 22 50. Open July and Aug, Wed–Mon, 1400–1830.

Sadly, Valognes no longer merits the description 'Versailles of Normandy', such was the extent of the wartime damage. Still, the tourist brochures are right to make the best of what there is, principally a cluster of 18th-century mansions, or *hôtels particuliers*. A tour of the **Hôtel de Beaumont**, with its splendid 50m-long façade of dressed stone, is certainly worthwhile for its insights into everyday life in the 18th century. You're shown the monumental staircase and half a dozen rooms, from the formal dining room and library to the children's nursery and the servants' quarters. The apartments are sumptuously decorated throughout and furnished in the styles of Louis XV and XVI. Just a street away is the 17th- to 18th-century **Hôtel de Grandval-Caligny**. The **Logis du Grand Quartier** is much older (1480). It now contains a **Cider Museum** with collections of apple presses and other equipment going back more than four centuries. Calvados is given similar treatment in another historic building, the **Hôtel de Thieuville** – a craft museum with nicely presented displays on shoemaking, cartwrighting and other trades. Flowers and agricultural produce are on sale in the weekly market (*Friday, place du Château*).

Suggested tour

Total distance: 152km (201km with detours).

Time: 3 hours' driving. Allow 6 hours for the main route, 8 hours with detours. Those with limited time should concentrate on the coast between Carteret and Granville, not missing Coutances.

Links: From this route the N175 heads into Brittany, while the N13 leads to the beaches of the Normandy landings (*see pages 242–55*).

Leave **CHERBOURG** ❶ on the D900 south to **Bricquebec**, where the traditional market is still held in the main square on Monday morning. Beside the 14th-century castle keep, the clock tower contains a small regional museum.

Detour: Take the D902 eastwards to **VALOGNES** ❷. Leave on the D2 to St-Sauveur.

Continue on the D900, heading south to the fortified town of **St-Sauveur-le-Vicomte**. The 11th-century castle saw action during the Hundred Years' War and again in 1944 when it suffered severe damage. The imposing keep and stretches of fortified wall have survived.

Take the D15, then turn right on the D130 to **BARNEVILLE** ❸ and **CARTERET** ❹. Follow the coast to **Portbail**, a picturesque resort at the end of a superb stretch of dune-strewn beaches. Reflected in the waters of the Ollonde estuary is the fortified tower of the early Romanesque

ℹ **Lessay** *11 place St-Cloud; tel: 02 33 45 14 34; e-mail: otlessay@voila.fr*

ⓟ **Portbail Church and Baptistery**
Open Easter–Sept, daily, 1000–1130, 1600–1830.

Lessay Abbey *Tel: 02 33 46 40 99. Open daily, 0900–1900. Guided tours twice daily in summer. A series of evening concerts takes place throughout July and Aug.*

Château du Pirou €
Tel: 02 33 46 34 71; www.chateau-pirou.org. Open July and Aug, Tue, 1000–1200, 1400–1830; Mar–June and Sept, daily, 1000–1200, 1400–1830; Nov–Feb, daily, 1000–1200, 1400–1700.

church. In the field behind, excavations have revealed the hexagonal walls of a Gallo-Roman **baptistery**. Take the D650 south along the coast.

Detour: Turn left on the D652 to **Lessay**, a small town with an 11th-century Benedictine **monastery** at its centre. Restored after World War II using original materials, tools and methods, the monastery church is an early example of the use of intersecting rib vaulting. In the atmospheric setting of the abbey, some of the best classical musicians

in the region, and indeed all of France, appear at the **Heures Musicales** festival: a series of evening concerts during July and August (details from the tourist office). If you're in town on the second weekend of September, you can enjoy the 700-year-old Holy Cross Fair, an animal market with produce stalls and a fairground.

Continue on the D650 to Pirou Plage. Turn left on to the D94. On your right, through three fortified gateways is the **Château du Pirou**. Built over a Viking settlement, the moated castle was begun in the 12th century and extended in the 14th and 18th. The chapel, assembly hall, guardroom, bakehouse and living quarters can all be visited. A tapestry (displayed between *mid-June and mid-Oct*) recounts the adventures of the medieval knight, Tancrede de Hauteville, who left the castle in 1036 to go to Italy where he founded the powerful and influential kingdom of Sicily.

Above
Coutances cathedral

Gratot Castle €
Tel: 02 31 27 97 40,
summer: 02 33 45 18 49.
Open daily, 1000–1230,
1400–1900.

Manoir de Saussey €€
Route de Villedieu; tel: 02 33
45 19 65. Open Sat and
Sun, 1400–1830.

Les Fours à Chaux du
Rey €€ *Regneville-sur-Mer;*
tel: 02 33 48 82 18. Open
July and Aug, 1100–1900;
June and Sept, 1100–1800;
Apr, May, Oct & school
holidays, 1400–1800.

Abbaye de la Lucerne
d'Outremer €€ *Tel: 02*
33 48 83 56;
www.abbaye-lucerne.fr.
Open mid-Feb–Dec,
1000–1200, 1400–1830.
Closed Mon Feb, Mar & Dec.

Ferme de l'Hermitière
€€ *St-Jean-des-Champs; tel:*
02 33 61 31 51; e-mail:
infos@ferme-hermitiere.com;
www.ferme-hermitiere.com.
Open Apr–June, Mon–Fri,
1400–1800; July and Aug,
Mon–Sat, 1000–1200,
1330–1800; Sept, Mon–Fri,
1000–1200, 1330–1800.
Visits 1 hr to 1¹/₂ hrs.

Champrepus Zoo €€€
Tel: 02 33 61 30 74; e-mail:
zoo.champrepus@wanadoo.
fr; www.zoo-champrepus.
com. Open July and Aug,
1000–1900; Apr–June and
Sept, 1000–1800; late Feb,
Oct & Nov, 1330–1800.

Abbaye de Hambye €€
Tel: 02 33 61 79 92; e-mail:
musee.hambye@cg50.fr.
Open Apr–Oct, 1000–1200,
1400–1800. Guided tours.

Return to the D650 and continue as far as **Coutainville**, a resort popular for its sand-sailing and windsurfing. Leave on the D44. As the road approaches Coutances, a left turn leads to the castle of **Gratot** with its distinctive four towers, all different shapes and sizes. The castle was in the hands of one family – the Argouges – for five centuries. Today it is a cultural centre with an exhibition on its history and restoration in one of the outbuildings. Return to the D44 and continue to **COUTANCES ❺**.

Detour: Take the D7 south to **Saussey** where, in the 17th-century **manor house**, you'll find one of the most impressive collections of glassware in France. There is also 20th-century pottery from Forges les Eaux in east Normandy and numerous cribs from France and Italy, including a fine example from 13th-century Naples. Return on the D7, then turn left on to the D437.

Leave Coutances on the D971 and turn right on the D20 to **Pont de la Roque** from where there are good views over the inlet. Turn right on to the D49 to Regneville-sur-Mer. **Les Fours à Chaux du Rey** is a museum of lime kilns dating from the 18th to 19th centuries when the local industry flourished. From here take the coast road (D156, D20 and D135) to **GRANVILLE ❻**.

Also worth exploring

Leave Granville on the D973 and head south for about 10km, turning left on the D580 through the Thar Valley to **Abbaye de la Lucerne d'Outremer**. Founded by the Premonstratensian order in the 12th century, the abbey was used as a spinning mill, then a sawmill after the Revolution. An extensive restoration programme is now complete and visitors can once again enjoy the sound of Gregorian chant at the Sun 1115 Mass.

Turn right on to the D105, then right again after St-Jean-des-Champs on to the D924. Signs to the left point to **la Ferme de l'Hermitière** where the production of cider, calvados etc is explained (English speaking guides and tastings). Turn left at the junction with the D7.

Detour: Continue on the D924: about 4km on is **Champrepus Zoo**, with more than 80 species of animals in a pleasantly landscaped environment. The attractive medieval town of **Villedieu-les-Poêles**, known as the 'city of copper' is now one large craft centre. To see the old skills demonstrated in the workshops of the stepped streets and alleyways, visit the **Bell Foundry**, **Copper** or **Pewter Workshops**, the **Museum of Copper and Lacemaking**, the **Museum of Norman Furniture** and **Clock Kingdom**.

Follow the scenic D7 across the Sienne Valley and through Gavray, then turn off on to the D198 to the majestic ruined monastery, **Abbaye de Hambye**. Set among trees on the banks of the river, the shell of the church, as well as the chapterhouse, refectory, library, monks' dormitory and kitchen still testify to its former wealth and glory.

The Normandy Beaches

Ratings

Architecture	●●●●●
Heritage	●●●●●
History	●●●●●
Cathedrals and churches	●●●●○
Children	●●●●○
Boats	●●●○○
Castles and châteaux	●●●○○
Watersports	●●●○○
Wildlife	●●●○○
Entertainment	●●○○○

Invasions have played an important part in the history of this stretch of coast. It is D-Day (J-Jour to the French) and the Normandy landings that immediately spring to mind, and if you're a military history buff you can explore the entire battlefield by following one or more of the eight signposted routes. Otherwise you can pick and choose from the dozens of monuments, cemeteries and museums, not forgetting the beaches themselves. Anyone who has seen Steven Spielberg's movie *Saving Private Ryan* (and American visitors of course) will probably want to make a beeline for Omaha beach and Pointe du Hoc where the fighting was most intense.

A little matter of nine centuries before D-Day, William the Conqueror launched his invasion of England from the little port of Dives-sur-Mer. Other towns associated with the Norman conquest are Falaise, where William was born, Caen, where he and his wife founded important abbeys, and Bayeux where the famous tapestry gives a blow-by-blow account of the events.

BAYEUX

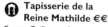
Tapisserie de la Reine Mathilde €€
Centre Guillaume le Conquérant, rue de Nesmond; tel: 02 31 51 25 50. Open May–Aug, daily, 0900–1900; mid-Mar–Apr, Sept & Oct, 0900–1830; Nov–mid-Mar, 0900–1230, 1400–1800.

The first French city to be liberated after D-Day, Bayeux alone survived World War II with its medieval core almost intact. Far and away the most popular tourist attraction is the **Tapisserie de la Reine Mathilde** (Bayeux Tapestry), exhibited in a former seminary now known as the William the Conqueror Centre. The tapestry is displayed in the Harold Room, under glass and with subdued lighting. But first the context is explained – admirably – with the help of slide shows and imaginative audio displays, in English as well as French. Despite the crowds, there's plenty of time to enjoy both the scenes themselves (wonderfully revealing about everyday life in the 11th century) and the border friezes with their exuberant depictions of fabulous beasts.

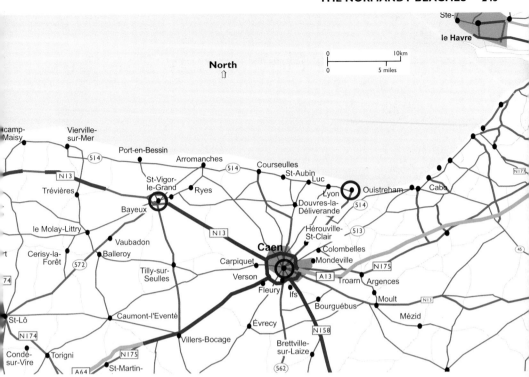

The Bayeux Tapestry

Perhaps the most famous piece of embroidery in the world – tapestry, is, strictly speaking, a misnomer – this remarkable work of art was produced by English nuns in the decade after the Conquest for William's half-brother, Bishop Odo of Bayeux. A roll of linen cloth 70m long, 50cm high and woven with strands of coloured wool, it was designed to hang in the apse of Odo's new cathedral on the feast of the holy relics.

Powerful propaganda, the carefully constructed narrative of 58 scenes is, first and foremost, a morality tale showing how divine retribution is exacted on Harold Earl of Wessex for going back on his solemn word. This portentous sequence of events begins after Harold has travelled to Normandy, at the behest of Edward the Confessor, to confirm William as the next king of England. When Harold's ship is blown off course, he is captured by the French and ransomed by William who persuades the earl to swear an oath of allegiance on the Bayeux relics. Edward dies, Harold retracts his oath and is crowned king. William is outraged. The tapestry depicts the military preparations for the invasion as William wins crucial diplomatic support from the pope, so turning the enterprise into a religious crusade. The appearance of Halley's comet is another positive augur as the Norman army embarks for England, landing at Pevensey, Sussex in September. The decisive battle is fought near Hastings on 14 October 1066. The Norman knights seize the initiative but appear to lose heart as rumours spread that William has been killed. He shows himself and, after rallying his troops, adopts the stratagem of feigning a retreat, tempting the Saxons to break ranks before turning on them mercilessly. When Harold is struck down by an arrow piercing his eye, defeat turns into rout and William emerges victorious.

ℹ️ **Bayeux Tourist Information** *Rue St-Jean; tel: 02 31 51 28 28; fax: 02 31 51 28 29; e-mail: info@bayeux-tourism.com; www.bayeux-tourism.com*

🅿️ Rue Franche, rue du Marche, place Charles de Gaulle.

🅷 **Cathedral** *Tel: 02 31 51 28 28. Open July–Sept, 0830–1900; Apr–June, 0800–1800; Oct–Dec, 0830–1800; Jan–Mar, 0900–1700.*

Musée Baron-Gérard €€ *Place de la Liberté; tel: 02 31 92 14 21. Open July and Aug, daily, 1000–1230, 1400–1900; Sept–June, 1000–1230, 1400–1800.*

Mémorial Général de Gaulle € *10 rue Bourbesneur; tel: 02 31 92 45 55. Open June and Aug, daily, 0930–1230, 1400–1830; Mar–May and Sept–Nov, 1000–1230, 1400–1800.*

Musée Mémorial 1944, Bataille de Normandie €€ *Boulevard Fabian Ware; tel: 02 31 92 93 41; museedelabataille@free.fr. Open May–mid-Sept, daily, 0930–1830; mid-Sept–Apr, 1000–1230, 1400–1800.*

🅜 Markets are held on Wednesday and Saturday.

The tapestry's original home was the breathtaking **Cathédrale Notre-Dame**. The crypt and the towers at the west end are all that survive of the building consecrated by Bishop Odo in 1077, but the transition from Romanesque to Norman Gothic is almost seamless, especially in the nave – note the stone carvings around the arches – and the chancel, one of the finest in France. The carved Renaissance choir stalls are also worth seeking out. The former bishop's palace, **Musée Baron-Gérard**, now houses valuable collections of lace and porcelain (Bayeux was an important centre of production in the 19th century) as well as paintings by the likes of Boucher, David and Corot. The 'saviour of France', General Charles de Gaulle, made his first speech on liberated soil at the 15th-century governor's house, later the French army HQ and now the **Musée Mémorial du Général de Gaulle**. For broader coverage of the events following D-Day, head for the **Musée Mémorial 1944, Bataille de Normandie** which tells the story with the help of life-size models, dioramas, memorabilia and large quantities of military hardware. There's a museum shop, a cinema and a picnic area outside, while directly opposite is the **British War Cemetery**. Just behind the cathedral is the place de la Liberté, a charming little square named after the plane tree known as **L'Arbre de la Liberté** (Liberty Tree), planted here during the Revolution. Many of Bayeux's well-preserved old houses (15th to 18th centuries) can be found between the cathedral and the main pedestrianised street, **rue St-Jean** (which continues as rue St-Martin). **Rue Franche** has some of the best examples. An equally enjoyable way of passing the time is to take a stroll along the banks of the canalised **River Aure** past the old Dyer's Mill.

Accommodation and food in Bayeux

Camping €€ *Boulevard Eindhoven; tel: 02 31 92 08 43; fax: 02 31 51 60 70*. Shaded municipal site near covered swimming pool.

Churchill Hotel €€€ *14–16 rue St-Jean; tel: 02 31 21 31 80; fax: 02 31 21 41 66; e-mail: hotel-churchill@wanadoo.fr; www.hotel-churchill.com*. Central location with quiet, comfortable rooms and excellent, if pricey restaurant.

Hôtel de la Gare € *26 place de la Gare; tel: 02 31 92 10 70; fax: 02 31 51 95 99*. Basic, but with all the necessary facilities, and a good value hotel – as its name suggests, by the railway station.

Le Petit Normand €€ *35 rue Larcher; tel: 02 31 22 88 66*. Restaurant with traditional Norman dishes such as *jambon à l'os au cidre*.

Le Pommier €€ *40 rue de Cuisiniers; tel: 02 31 21 52 10; fax: 02 31 21 06 01; e-mail: mailto:contact@restaurantlepommier.com; www.restaurantle pommier.com*. Classy, well-established provider of Norman fare; great value weekday lunch menu.

Left
The crypt at Bayeux's Cathédrale Notre-Dame

CAEN

ⓘ Caen Tourist Information *Place St-Pierre; tel: 02 31 27 14 14; fax: 02 31 27 14 18; e-mail: tourisminfo@ville-caen.fr; www.tourisme.caen.fr*

ⓟ Place St-Sauveur, quai Vendeuvre, rue G Lebret.

ⓜ Musée de Normandie € *Tel: 02 31 30 47 60. Open Wed–Mon, 0930–1800.*

Le Musée des Beaux Arts €€ *Enciente du Château; tel: 02 31 30 47 70; mba@ville-caen.fr. Open Wed–Mon, 0930–1800.*

Le Mémorial €€€ *Esplanade Eisenhower; tel: 02 31 06 06 44; www.memorial.fr. Open daily, 0900–1900. Reduced hours in winter.*

Abbaye-aux-Hommes *tel: 02 31 30 42 81;* **Abbaye-aux-Dames** *at the west end of rue des Chanoins; tel: 02 31 06 98 98. Open daily, 1400–1730. Guided tours to Abbaye aux Hommes at 0930, 1100, 1430, 1600, extra tours in July and Aug. Closed 1 Jan, 1 May & 25 Dec.*

Caen was heavily bombed during World War II but many of its historic buildings and architectural monuments have survived thanks to painstaking restoration. A regional capital and a lively university town, Caen can also offer excellent shopping, late-night bars, a yachting marina and river cruises, with more than 460 hectares of green space thrown in for good measure.

Caen was William the Conqueror's favourite town and you can still see the massive ramparts of the **Château**, the ducal castle founded in about 1060. Contained within the walls are a 12th-century chapel, the ruins of the keep (added by Henry I of England) and the Great Hall of the duke's palace, known as the **Salle d'Echiquier**. The 14th-century governor's residence is now the **Musée de Normandie**, a local history museum with archaeological finds, crafts, costumes and ceramics. The **Musée des Beaux Arts**, also within the confines of the castle, has an impressive collection of Flemish, Italian and French paintings. It is especially good on the French 19th-century schools (Géricault, Delacroix, Courbet, Bonnard). Allocate at least a couple of hours of your time to visiting le **Mémorial**, a museum dedicated to peace and human rights. Built on the site of the German command centre during the Battle of Normandy, it uses all the high-tech resources at its disposal, including lasers, computer graphics, and video screens to take visitors on a sombre but compelling journey through the history of Europe in the 20th century with the focus on World War II: the rise of Fascism, the German occupation of France, D-Day and the atomic bomb. The German commander's bunker is now used to tell the story of the Nobel peace prize. As well as a museum shop there's a self-service restaurant and a well-equipped play area for young children.

The **Abbaye-aux-Hommes** and the **Abbaye-aux-Dames**, founded by William the Conqueror and his consort Mathilda respectively, are also worth seeing if you're a fan of Norman architecture. The **Eglise St-Etienne**, completed in the 13th century, contains the tomb of the Conqueror and what's left of his mortal remains (perhaps only a thigh-bone after a succession of robberies and desecrations). The monastic buildings were reconstructed in the 18th century and are open to the public for guided tours (allow an hour). Mathilda is buried in the chancel of the **Eglise de la Trinité**, a magnificent Romanesque church with a spacious vaulted nave. Don't miss the decoration on the stone capitals, both here and in the **crypt**. The living quarters, including the grand staircase, Great Hall and cloisters – all 18th-century – are open to the public for guided tours (again allow an hour).

Caen has more than its fair share of fine churches: **Eglise St-Nicolas**, virtually unaltered since its completion in the 11th century; **Eglise St-Sauveur** with an unusual double nave; and the beautifully restored **Eglise St-Pierre** (16th-century). A number of medieval houses have survived on **rue St-Pierre**, notably the half-timbered buildings at

Le Boeuf Ferre €€
10 rue des Croisiers;
tel: 02 31 85 36 40;
e-mail: restaurant-le-boeuf-
ferre@boeuf-ferre.com;
www.boeuf-ferre.com.
Hearty traditional fare, as
the name suggests, strong
on beef dishes but with
plenty to choose from.
Closed Sun lunch in July
and Aug.

Markets are held at
various spots in Caen
including the square
outside St-Pierre on Sunday
and on place St-Sauveur on
Friday. A street art market
can be found in the
Quartiers des Quatrans on
the last Saturday of the
month.

Below
Caen: the Abbaye-aux-Hommes

No 52 (now the postal museum) and No 54, and the **Hôtel d'Escouville** (now the tourist office), the splendid courtyard, loggias and staircases are all influenced by the Italian Renaissance.

Accommodation and food in Caen

Alcide €€ *1 place Courtonne; tel: 02 31 44 18 06; fax: 02 31 94 47 45; e-mail: restaurant-alcide@wanadoo.fr.* Traditional French cooking. Good-value set menus.

Hôtel Ibis Doumer €€ *33 rue de Bras; tel: 02 31 50 00 00; fax: 02 31 86 85 91.* Unexceptional but convenient and reasonably priced.

Hôtel Moderne €€€ *116 boulevard Maréchal Leclerc; tel: 02 31 86 04 23; fax: 02 31 85 37 93.* Sound-proofed rooms with cable TV, sauna; restaurant.

L'Insolite €€ *16 rue du Vaugueux; tel: 02 31 43 83 87; fax: 02 31 93 43 76. Closed Sun pm and Mon.* Terrace restaurant serving fish and seafood specialities.

The Battle of Normandy

Preparations for the Allied invasion of Europe, known as Operation Overlord, began in the summer of 1943. To achieve the element of surprise it was decided to launch the offensive, not in the Pas de Calais, as the Germans expected, but on the Normandy coast, roughly between the River Orne and Dunes-de-Varreville. The invasion was preceded by months of sustained aerial bombardment of targets throughout Northern France, seriously weakening the German's lines of communication. Two artificial harbours, known as 'Mulberries' were constructed for the unloading of heavy equipment and specially adapted armoured vehicles were introduced to overcome obstacles and booby traps.

The D-Day landings began at 0630 on 6 June 1944. Around 135,000 Americans, British, Canadians, Free French, Poles and other nationalities were brought ashore in 7000 landing craft, along with more than 20,000 military vehicles. Casualties were heaviest on Omaha Beach, where US forces only won the day after displaying extraordinary tenacity and courage. (The full story is told graphically in Steven Spielberg's film *Saving Private Ryan*.) The beachheads at Sword, Juno and Gold on the other hand, were secured with much less difficulty although nowhere were the first-day objectives achieved.

The Battle of Normandy lasted 11 weeks in all. Bayeux fell to the British within 24 hours but they encountered fiercer resistance as they pressed on towards Caen. The capture of Cherbourg also took longer than expected. The decisive breakthrough came at the end of July when General Patton's 3rd Army used Avranches as the springboard for a lightning offensive into Brittany. A desperate but belated German counterattack was stopped in its tracks at Montormel before the 7th Army was finally caught in a pincer movement and forced to surrender at Tournai-sur-Dives on 21 August. Three days later the Allies were in Paris.

More than 100,000 servicemen lost their lives in the campaign as well as thousands of civilians. Six hundred towns and villages had meanwhile been reduced to rubble.

OUISTREHAM AND RIVA-BELLA

ⓘ Tourist Information *Jardin du Casino; tel: 02 31 97 18 63; fax: 02 31 96 87 33; e-mail: office.ouistreham@ wanadoo.fr; www.ville-ouistreham.fr*

Ⓩ Brittany Ferries *Gare Maritime Ouistreham; tel: 08 25 82 88 28; www.brittanyferries.com. Two services daily with extra sailings in the summer (6 hours).*

Ⓐ Riva-Bella Casino *Place Alfred-Thomas; tel: 02 31 36 30 00.*

Ouistreham is an international yachting centre, a fishing port with a large trawler fleet and a popular seaside resort. It gets very congested in the summer when the cars rolling off the Portsmouth ferry are disgorged on to the streets of what would otherwise be a picturesque old town. Life in **Riva-Bella** (Ouistreham's resort) revolves around the casino, the 'Queen Normandy' and the long sandy beach. This was where the first troops landed on D-Day; the **Musée No 4 Commando**, behind the casino, recounts the events from their perspective. Just up the hill is the **Musée du Mur de l'Atlantique**, a former German bunker and the communications centre commanding the Orne estuary.

Accommodation and food in Ouistreham and Riva-Bella

Le Channel €€ *79 avenue Michel-Cabieu; tel: 02 31 96 51 69; fax: 02 31 97 00 44.* Good-value fish restaurant.

Hôtel Mercure €€ *37 Rue des Dunes; tel: 02 31 96 20 20; fax: 02 31 97 10 10.* Comfortable rooms, handy both for the ferry and the beach.

Musée No 4 Commando €€
Place Alfred Thomas; tel: 02 31 96 63 10. Open Mar–Oct, daily, 1030–1800.

Musée du Mur de l'Atlantique €€ *Avenue du 6 Juin; tel: 02 31 97 28 69. Open Apr–Sept, daily, 0900–1900; Feb, Mar, Oct & Nov, daily, 1000–1800.*

Hôtel La Riva Bella €€€ *Avenue du Commandant Kieffer; tel: 02 31 96 40 40; fax: 02 31 96 45 45.* Large spa hotel with sea-water therapy centre.

Hôtel de la Plage €€ *39–41 avenue Pasteur; tel: 02 31 96 85 16; fax: 02 31 97 37 46; e-mail: hoteldelaplage@ aol.com; www.hotel-plageouistreham. com.* Pleasant hotel with a garden, near the beach.

Suggested tour

Total distance: 212km (247km with detours).

Time: 5½ hours' driving. Allow at least 12 hours for the main route; spread over two days if you intend to see all the D-Day museums and memorials, and two extra half days to see the towns of Caen and Bayeux. Those with limited time should concentrate on Bayeux and the coast between Courseulles and Port-en-Bessin.

Links: Just across the Pegasus Bridge in the east are the beaches of the Côte Fleurie (*see pages 256–67*), while to the west is la Manche (*see pages 232–41*).

Leave **BAYEUX ❶** on the N13 to **CAEN ❷**. Take the D514 north following the course of the River Orne. Turn off to Bénouville. Just beyond the town is the site of the **Pegasus Bridge** (free) (*Bénouville; tel: 02 31 44 62 01. Open Apr–Sept, daily, 0900–1830; Feb, Mar, Oct & Nov, 1000–1300, 1400–1700*). Of strategic importance to the Allies in their push towards Paris, the bridge was captured by the British 5th Parachute Brigade the night before the D-Day landings. *Son-et-lumières* recounting this action are performed in the summer (in English and French) near its modern replacement. Guided visits (€) available.

Below
Caen: le Mémorial Peace Museum

Return to the D514 and continue to **OUISTREHAM ❸** and **RIVA-BELLA ❹**, at the eastern edge of the Côte de Nacre, where the Allies launched Operation Overlord in 1944. This road takes you past the landing beaches codenamed Sword, Juno, Gold, Omaha and Utah. There are dozens of memorials to the troops who lost their lives here, but there's an equal emphasis on seaside pleasures on the 'Coast of Pearls', with the usual array of activity clubs,

ⓘ Arromanches *4 rue du Maréchal Joffre; tel: 02 31 22 36 45; fax: 02 31 22 92 06; e-mail: off-tour@ mail.cpod.fr; www.arromanches.com. Open all year.*

Grandcamp-Maisy *118 rue Aristide-Briand; tel: 02 31 22 62 44; e-mail: ot.grandcampmaisy@ wanadoo.fr*

Port-en-Bessin *2 rue du Croiseur-Montcalm; tel: 02 31 21 92 33; fax: 02 31 22 08 40.*

Courseulles *Rue de la Mer; tel: 02 31 37 46 80; fax: 02 31 37 29 25; e-mail: Tourisme.Courseulles@ wanadoo.fr*

Luc-sur-Mer *Rue du Dr-Charcot; tel: 02 31 97 33 25; fax: 02 31 96 65 09; e-mail: luc.sur.mer@wanadoo.fr; www.luc-sur-mer.fr*

◖ La Cremaillerie €€ *Courseulles-sur-Mer; tel: 02 31 37 46 73; e-mail: cremaillere@wanadoo.fr; www.la-cremaillere.com.* Beach-side *logis* with seafood restaurant.

Hôtel de la Marine €€ *5 quai Letourneur, Port-en-Bessin; tel: 02 31 21 70 08; fax: 02 31 21 90 36; e-mail: hoteldelamarine14@ wanadoo.fr; www.hoteldelamarine.fr. Closed Dec and Jan.* Comfortable hotel with rooms overlooking the sea and the port and an excellent restaurant.

Right
The Normandy coast

Mercure Omaha Beach €€€ *Chemin du Colombier; tel: 02 31 22 44 44; fax: 02 31 22 36 77. Out-of-town hotel with swimming pool and tennis courts; also close to a 27-hole golf course.*

Manoir de Cantepie €€€ *Aire de Cantepie, les Veys; tel: 02 33 71 19 55; fax: 02 33 71 22 23; www.cantepie.free.fr. Atmospheric restaurant in a manor house.*

Maison du Fossile € *2 place des Victimes du 2 Juillet 44, Lion-sur-Mer; tel: 02 31 96 88 00. Open May–Oct, Wed–Mon, 1000–1200, 1400–1800; Nov–Apr, Sat, Sun & holidays, 1400–1800.*

Maison de la Baleine € *45 rue de la Mer, Luc-sur-Mer; tel: 02 31 97 55 93; e-mail: mairie-luc-sur-mer@ wanadoo.fr; www.maisondelabaleine.com. Open June, daily, 1430–1800; July and Aug, daily, 1000–1200, 1400–1900; Apr, May & Sept, Sat and Sun, 1430–1800.*

Musée Radar €€ *Douvres–la Deliverande; tel: 02 31 37 74 43. Phone for hours.*

Château Fontaine-Henri €€ *Tel: 02 31 80 00 42; fax: 02 31 00 19 45; e-mail: contact@chateau-de-fontaine-henri.com; www.chateau-de-fontaine-henri.com. Hour-long guided tours only; several daily, with evening events during July and Aug. Closed Mon and weekdays off season.*

swimming pools, casinos, discothèques and hotels. In bad weather you can always turn to several small but interesting nature museums: the **Fossil Museum** at **Lion-sur-Mer** for example, or the **Maison de la Baleine** (an exhibition on whale conservation) at the genteel spa of **Luc-sur-Mer**.

Detour: Turn left on the D83 to la-Déliverande, a town dominated by the spires of the neo-Gothic basilica where a shrine to the Virgin Mary attracts pilgrims throughout the year. Continue through Douvres-la-Déliverande and follow the signs to the **Musée Radar**. This unique exhibition in a renovated blockhouse recounts the wartime uses of radar tracking and later developments.

Cross the D404 and continue through Basley, turning right on to the road that drops steeply towards the Mue Valley and **Fontaine-Henri**. This magnificent 15th-century château, set in a verdant landscaped park, is superbly decorated with elaborately carved friezes, mouldings and balustrades in the Renaissance style. The pavilion, added in the 16th century, has a huge, sloping, slate roof, taller than the house itself. There are guided tours of the interior.

Take the D141, turning right on the D22 to **Creully** where the 12th-century château was used by the BBC in 1944 to broadcast news of the invasion – one room is now a small museum. Take the D35 back to la Déliverande, then the D7 to **Langrune-sur-Mer**.

Continue along the coast, past a succession of sandy beaches ideal for children who will also enjoy shrimping and crabbing among the seaweed strewn rocks (**St-Aubin-sur-Mer** for example). Leave the coast road at **Bernières-sur-Mer** to make a brief visit to the 12th-century church – the spire on the belfry rises to a height of 67m and is one of the finest in Normandy. **Courseulles**, popular with yachters, is also renowned for its oysters which can be sampled at the daily fish market on quai des Alliés. The town's seafood heritage is on show at the **Maison de la Mer**.

The museum '**America-Gold Beach**' at **Ver-sur-Mer** commemorates D-Day and also the first transatlantic air-mail delivery from the US in 1927 (the plane was called *America*). As the road approaches Arromanches-des-Bains, it climbs to the edge of the Bessin plateau and a parking area where drivers can look down on the remains of the prefabricated 'Mulberry harbour' lying just off shore. Just beyond the viewing point is **Arromanches 360**, a cinema in the round showing 18 minutes of archive film of the Allied Landings at 10 and 40 minutes past the hour – an experience which brings home the events with a new immediacy. More information on the Mulberry harbour and its construction can be found in the **Musée de 6 Juin** on the seafront. **Arromanches** is also a good spot for lunch – head for the restaurants lining the pedestrianised street leading down to the small fishing port.

Château de Creully
€ *Tel: 02 31 80 67 08;
e-mail: tourisme.creully@
wanadoo.fr. Open July and
Aug, Tue–Fri, 1030–1230,
1430–1730. Guided tours.*

La Maison de la Mer €€
*Place Général-de-Gaulle,
Courseulles-sur-Mer; tel: 02
31 37 92 58. Open July and
Aug, 0930–1900; May and
June, 0930–1230,
1400–1900; Sept–Apr,
1000–1200, 1400–1800.
Closed mornings Oct–Jan.*

Arromanches 360 €€
*Chemin du Calvaire; tel: 02 31
22 30 30. Open June–Aug,
daily, 0940–1840; Apr, May &
Sept, daily, 1010–1740;
Oct–Dec, Feb & Mar, daily,
1010–1640.*

Musée de 6 Juin €€
*Arromanches; tel: 02 31 22 34
31. Open Mar–Aug, daily,
0900–1900; rest of year,
0900–1230, 1330–1730
(closed Jan).*

**Musée des Epaves Sous-
Marines** €€ *Route de
Bayeux à Commes, Port-en-
Bessin; tel: 02 31 21 17 06.
Open June–Sept, 1000–1200,
1400–1800, weekends and
holidays in May.*

Musée du Débarquement
€€ *La Madeleine; tel: 02 33
71 53 35; www.
normandy1944.com. Open
Mar–Aug, daily, 0900–1900;
rest of year, 0900–1230,
1330–1730 (closed Jan).*

Airborne Musée € *Place
du 6 Juin, St-Mère-Eglise; tel:
02 33 41 41 35. Open
Apr–Sept, daily, 0900–1845;
Feb, Mar, Oct & Nov, daily,
1000–1200, 1400–1800.*

Follow the D514 to **Port-en-Bessin**. This picturesque fishing harbour, lying in a sheltered hollow between two cliffs, is the subject of countless paintings (including works by Seurat and Signac). Novels by Flaubert and Georges Simenon are also set here. It's a pleasant spot for an overnight stay – in the morning make your way to the fish market on the quay where up to 12,000 tons of whiting, skate and mullet are handled every year. Just outside the town on the D60 is the **Musée des Epaves Sous-Marines**, a collection of D-Day wreckage salvaged from the sea.

Beyond Bessin the road passes the less-developed Omaha beaches, popular with windsurfers. The American Military cemetery on the cliffs at **St-Laurent-sur-Mer** is the last resting place of over 9000 men. The **Musée Omaha Beach** is on the other side of town, off the D517. More evidence of the ferocious battle can be seen at **Pointe du Hoc** where the 30m cliff is pitted with craters and shell holes. Several bunkers are open to the public and there are good views of the coast. Finally the road drops into **Grandcamp-Maisy**, a fishing harbour and small resort.

From Grandcamp the D514 turns south. At Cardonville turn right on the D197A through Isgny-sur-Mer (famous for dairy produce). Cross the N13 to **Carentan**, a market town at the head of the Taute estuary. The octagonal spire of the 12th-century church of Notre-Dame is a local landmark, while below are the 14th-century arcades of the former covered market. For nature lovers there are boat trips from Carentan exploring the various rivers which wind through the **Cotentin marshes**.

Leave on the D913. After Ste-Marie-du-Mont the road passes the monument to 800 Danish seamen who lost their lives in 1944. **La Madeleine** marks the beginning of **Utah Beach**. The huge stele commemorating the troops who died here was erected on the 40th anniversary of D-Day. A **museum** describes the action, *e-mail: museeutah-beach.com*

Turn left on the D67 to **Ste-Mère-Eglise** where an effigy of a US paratrooper hanging from the church tower recalls an episode from World War II which featured in the film of Cornelius Ryan's book *The Longest Day*. Ste-Mère Eglise was the first French community to be liberated on 6 June – the **Musée des Troupes Aéroportées**, under a parachute shaped dome, celebrates this action. Outside the town hall is Kilometre 0, marking the beginning of 'Liberty Way', the route forged through France by American forces.

Return on the N13 in the direction of Bayeux. The road passes through meadows and pastureland, but reminders of the war are never far away – at **la Cambe** for example where the 21,000 graves of the German Military Cemetery stretch into the distance. Continue to Bayeux.

ⓘ Ste-Mère-Église
6 rue Eisenhower;
tel: 02 33 21 00 33;
fax: 02 33 21 53 91;
e-mail: welcome@sainte-
mere-eglise.info;
www.sainte-mere-eglise.info

Falaise Tourist
Information *Forum; tel:*
02 31 90 17 26; fax: 02 31
90 98 70; e-mail:
info@otsifalaise.com;
www.otsifalaise.com

Ⓟ Parking By Tourist
Information.

ⓝ Château €€ *Falaise;*
tel: 02 31 41 61 44;
e-mail: chateau-falaise@
wanadoo.fr; www.chateau-
guillaume-leconquerant.fr.
Open July and Aug,
1000–1900; rest of the
year, 1000–1800 (closed
Jan).

Musée Août 1944 €€
Chemin des Roches; tel: 02
31 90 37 19. Open
June–Aug, daily, 1000–1200,
1400–1800; Apr, May &
Sept–11 Nov, Wed–Mon,
1000–1200, 1400–1800.

Previous page (p 252)
Bayeux: quai de L'Aure

Right
Sword Beach war memorial

Boat trips

Several companies offer boat excursions along the coast. Departure times vary according to the tides. Among them:

From Grandcamp-Maisy the *Colonel Rudder* departs for Omaha and Utah beaches (2½ hours) or for Pointe du Hoc (1 hour), *11 rue Aristide Briand; tel: 02 31 21 42 93.* Also birdwatching trips to the Baie des Veys (5 hours).

Trips from Carentan exploring the Parc Naturel des Marais du Cotentin depart from St-Hilaire, *Petit Ville (River Taute), tel: 02 33 55 18 07;* departures May–Sept, 0930 and 1430, or from Liesville-sur-Douve; *tel: 02 33 71 55 81; May–Sept* (3 hours).

ℹ **Musée des Automates €€**

Boulevard de la Liberation; tel: 02 31 90 02 43; e-mail: automates@ mail.cpod.fr; www.automates-avenue.com. Open Apr–Sept, daily, 1000–1230, 1330–1800, Oct–Mar, weekends, 1000–1230, 1330–1800.

Also worth exploring

Twenty-nine kilometres south of Caen is the historic town of **Falaise**, birthplace of William the Conqueror. The **château** was built on a rocky spur from which the town gets its name of 'cliff'. The impressive buttressed keep and circular tower are best viewed from the **Fontaine d'Arlette** beside the River Aute. According to legend the fountain marks the spot where the Conqueror's father, Robert, first set eyes on William's mother, the washerwoman Arlette.

Like the castle, much of the town was destroyed in 1944 when it was the focal point of German resistance. The **Musée Août 1944** recounts the events of 'the battle of the Falaise Pocket' during which the Allies surrounded the retreating German army. Parts of the old town have survived, including three ancient churches: **Eglise St-Trinité**, **Eglise Notre-Dame** and **Eglise St-Gervais** – an interesting mix of Romanesque and Gothic styles; note the fabulous carvings on the capitals in the south aisle.

Don't leave Falaise without calling in at '**Automates Avenue**'. This unique museum contains more than 300 automated models which first appeared in Parisian shop windows around the turn of the 20th century. They were made by the Ducamps company, which employed famous engineers such as Gustav Eiffel on the designs. The ingenious articulated figures, displayed in reconstructed shop fronts, will delight and amuse children and adults alike.

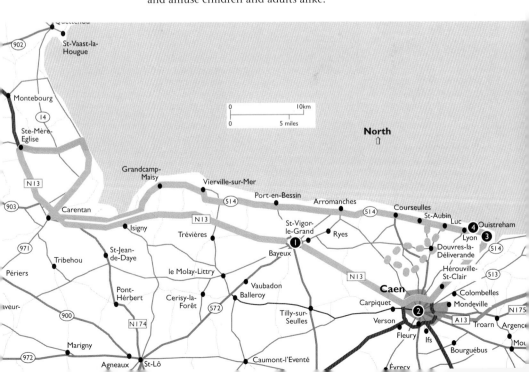

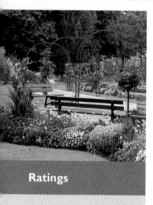

The Côte Fleurie

Ratings

Beaches	●●●●●
Children	●●●●●
Food	●●●●●
Outdoor activities	●●●●●
Scenery	●●●●●
Art	●●●●○
Heritage	●●●●○
Watersports	●●●●○
Entertainment	●●●○○
Cathedrals and churches	●●○○○

The 'Floral Coast' was first developed by sharp-eyed speculators back in the 19th century and most of the resorts, Cabourg and Trouville for example, are still characterised by stately seaside promenades and villas of a fading elegance. Trotters and racehorses are bred in the local stud farms and apart from attending a race meeting or showjumping competition (there are courses at Cabourg and Deauville), you can go pony trekking in the woods or take a gallop along the beach.

Lisieux has been an important centre of Catholic pilgrimage since the canonisation of St Thérèse in the 1950s. One of the largest basilicas in France was built in her honour, but this certainly doesn't overshadow the much nobler Gothic cathedral. The area around Lisieux is Camembert country and there are plenty of opportunities to sample the famous cheese either in one of the farmhouse museums or, even better, over lunch in one of the delightful roadside *auberges*. While you're at it, try one of the local ciders.

CABOURG

ⓘ Cabourg Tourist Information *Jardins du Casino; tel: 02 31 92 20 00; fax: 02 31 24 14 49; e-mail: office.tourisme@ cabourg.net; www.cabourg.net*

You wouldn't know to look at it but Cabourg is one of the oldest towns in Normandy – it was just along the coast at Dives-Sur-Mer that William the Conqueror set sail for England in 1066. The bathing resort dates only from the *belle époque*; Edith Piaf, Charles Aznavour and, latterly, the rock singer Sting have all stayed here, but Cabourg is most closely associated with the writer Marcel Proust – a regular visitor from the 1880s until 1914. Proust wrote part of his masterpiece *À la recherche du temps perdu* (*In search of lost time*) in his room in the **Grand Hôtel**. He was severely asthmatic and came to Cabourg (Balbec in the novel) mainly for health reasons. He rarely made it to the beach (there were too many draughts!) but he was familiar with the golf

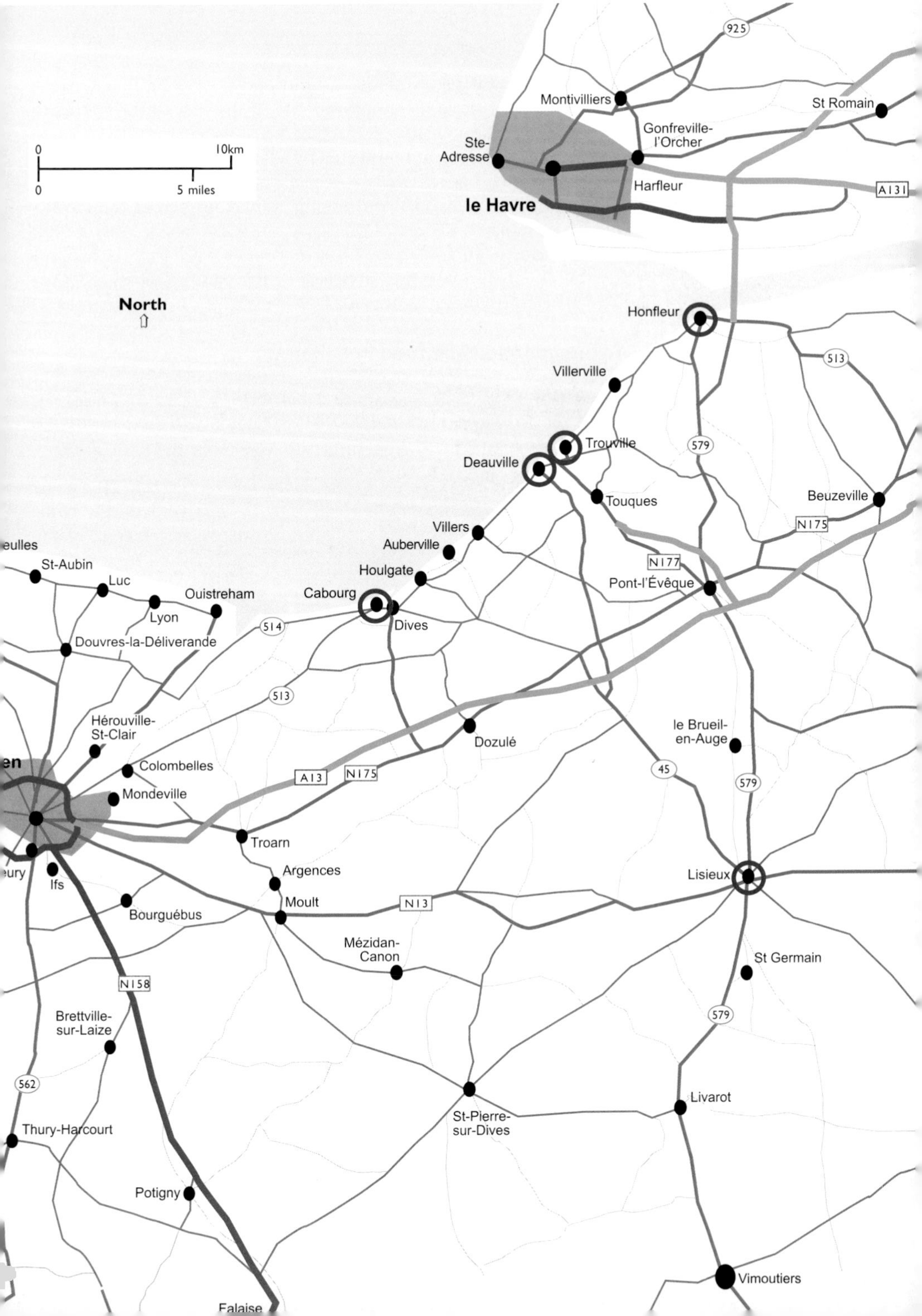

North

0 ___ 10km
0 ___ 5 miles

925

Montivilliers
St Romain

Gonfreville-
l'Orcher

Ste-
Adresse

le Havre

Harfleur

A131

Honfleur

513

Villerville

Trouville

579

Deauville

Touques

Beuzeville

N175

Villers

Auberville

N177

Houlgate

Pont-l'Évêque

Cabourg

Dives

le Brueil-
en-Auge

514

513

Dozulé

45

579

A13   N175

en

Hérouville-
St-Clair

Colombelles

Mondeville

Troarn

Lisieux

Argences

St Germain

Moult

N13

ury   Ifs

Bourguébus

Mézidan-
Canon

579

N158

Brettville-
sur-Laize

562

Livarot

Thury-Harcourt

St-Pierre-
sur-Dives

Potigny

Vimoutiers

Falaise

eulles

St-Aubin

Luc

Ouistreham

Lyon

Douvres-la-Délivrande

🐾 **Poney Club de Cabourg** 1 boulevard des Diablotins (opposite Champion); tel: 02 31 91 80 94 for treks along the sands and across country.

club, the baccarat tables of the Casino and the 'sumptuously ugly' villas. Unable to drive, he employed one of the first car-hire firms to chauffeur him through the Normandy countryside at reckless speeds, swaddled in overcoats and protected by a leather helmet.

The Grand has become a place of pilgrimage, and if you can't afford a room, it might be worth considering Sunday brunch in the dining-room overlooking the sea. Otherwise there's a beach with a 3km promenade, a golf course, trotting races and the casino for entertainment (formal dress *de rigueur* at the gaming tables). Despite these attractions, many visitors find Cabourg stuffy and pretentious.

Accommodation and food in Cabourg

Grand Hôtel €€€ *Promenade Marcel Proust; tel: 02 31 91 01 79; fax: 02 31 24 03 20.* Ostentatious luxury, sea views and rich Proustian associations are the main attractions; also piano bar and *salon de thè*.

L'Oie qui Fume €€ *18 avenue Brèche-Buhot; tel: 02 31 91 27 79; fax: 02 31 91 40 02. Closed Sun pm, Oct and Mar, Tue and Wed.* As the name implies, goose dishes are the speciality of this well-established hotel-restaurant.

Below
Ornate houses in Cabourg

DEAUVILLE

ℹ Deauville Tourist Information *Place de la Mairie; tel: 02 31 14 40 00; fax: 02 31 88 78 88; e-mail: info@deauville.org; www.deauville.org*

Ⓓ Duprat Concept, Circuit de Deauville *Route de Caen, St-Arnoult; tel: 02 31 81 31 31. Open all year.* Go-karting, quads, formula racing cars etc race round the five land tracks while speedboats and jet skis take to the lake.

Aeroclub de Deauville *Aéroport de St-Gatien-des-Bois; tel: 02 31 64 00 93.* Air trips over the coast.

Deauville was the brainchild of the Duc de Morny, Napoléon III's half-brother and an inveterate gambler who saw the possibilities of a racecourse across the river from Trouville. (Morny also built the Longchamps racetrack in Paris.) Deauville was created in just four years, between 1860 and 1864. Already popular before World War I, when the young Winston Churchill lost heavily at the casino, it was still thought chic in the 1930s. International *glitterati* now arrive only in the first week of September for the **American Film Festival** – Sylvester Stallone, Harrison Ford and Kim Basinger have all appeared in recent years. There are now two **racecourses**, Clairefontaine and la Touques (the flat season extends to July and August when showjumping competitions are also held). Deauville has a superb **beach** (generally crowded) and there's a Centre Nautique for watersports (kayaking, surf-boarding, speed-sailing, body-surfing). It's still fashionable – just – to take a stroll on the famous duckboard promenade (*planches*) behind the beach, but if you want to see more of the town, the tourist office has a leaflet with details of local **walks**, none of which should prove too exhausting. Alternatively, if you haven't already had your fill of World War II memorabilia, **Mont-Canisy** overlooking Deauville, is a restored subterranean bunker and command post built by the Germans – the guided tour is free of charge.

Accommodation and food in Deauville

As you might expect, it's more or less impossible to find reasonably priced accommodation in the centre of town. **Park Hôtel €€€** *81 avenue de la République; tel: 02 31 14 01 50; fax: 02 31 87 51 70 (closed Oct–Apr)* has a few moderately priced rooms and there are a couple of cheaper options (**Le Chantilly** and **Le Patio**) on the same road. Or you could try **Hôtel des Sports €€** *27 rue Gambetta; tel: 02 31 88 22 67* (no fax). Eating out is also expensive. **Restaurant Pizza Morny €€** *39 rue Olliffe; tel: 02 31 81 46 46* serves fish dishes as well as the usual pizza-pasta options.

HONFLEUR

ℹ Honfleur Tourist Information *Place Arthur Boudin; tel: 02 31 89 23 30; e-mail: office-du-tourisme-honfleur@ wanadoo.fr; www.ot-honfleur.fr*

Ⓟ Quai Lepaulmier, place A Normand, place J de Vienne.

The first sight to greet visitors to this famous port is **la Lieutenance**, the former Governor's House and gateway to the inner town. The eye is then drawn to the old harbour. The cobbled quays, twisting alleyways and brightly painted fishing boats proved inspirational to the Impressionists Monet, Sisley, Pissaro, Renoir and Cézanne who all made the pilgrimage to the Ferme St-Siméon (now a hotel) to learn from fellow artist **Eugène Boudin**. A museum in his name contains works by Courbet, Monet and Boudin himself, as well as Raoul Dufy. There's an accompanying exhibition on 19th-century rural life.

 Boat trips are available around the old port or in the Seine Estuary to the Pont de Normandie. Cruises leave from the quai des Passagers on the *Alphée* tel: 02 31 89 21 10, and *L'Evasion III* tel: 02 31 89 41 80.

 **Musée Eugène Boudin** €€ *Rue de l'Homme de Bois; tel: 02 31 89 54 00. Open mid-Mar–Sept, Wed–Mon, 1000–1200, 1400–1800; Oct–mid-Mar, Mon and Wed–Fri, 1430–1700, Sat and Sun 1000–1200, 1430–1700.*

One ticket €€ permits entry to the following two museums, *tel: 02 31 89 14 12. Open Apr–Sept, Wed–Sun, 1000–1200, 1400–1830; mid-Feb–Mar, and Oct–mid-Nov, weekends, 1000–1200, 1430–1730, Mon–Fri, 1430–1730.*

La Musée de la Marine *Quai St-Etienne.*

Le Musée d'Ethnographie et d'Art Populaire Normand *Rue de la Prison.*

Maison Satie €€ *67 boulevard Charles V; tel: 02 31 89 11 11; fax: 02 31 89 09 99. Open summer, Wed–Mon, 1000–1900; winter, Wed–Mon, 1000–1800.*

 A Saturday produce market is held on place St Catherine; also on Wednesdays there's a 'bio' market on place St-Leonard. Honfleur also has art galleries and antique shops.

Life revolves around the **Vieux Bassin**, the old port where restaurants and bars occupy the ground floors of the higgledy-piggledy, slate-hung houses. Behind them, on rue de la Ville, are the **Greniers à Sel**, huge 17th-century warehouses once used to store salt for the cod fleet and now home to temporary art exhibitions. The 14th-century Eglise St-Etienne is now a **Maritime Museum** with an exhibition on the navigator Samuel de Champlain who sailed from Honfleur to found the French colony of Quebec in 1608. Alongside, in the former prison, is the **Ethnographical Museum** with reconstructed rooms and furnishings in a variety of styles from a Norman manor house to a printer's workshop.

On the other side of the harbour is the old town and its focal point **place St Catherine** – there's a market here on Saturdays. The **church**, constructed largely of wood by local shipbuilders in the 15th century, is the most remarkable building on the square – note the unusual free-standing belfry, clad in chestnut weatherboarding.

If you're on the lookout for a refreshingly different experience, make a beeline for the **Maison Satie**, a museum celebrating the life of the eccentric French composer Erik Satie. The house where he was born in 1868 has been transformed into a Surrealist's playground inspired by Satie himself, his artistic collaborators (Picasso, Braque, Cocteau and Derain among others) and by fellow composers (Debussy, Ravel and Stravinsky). Visitors put on headphones to be guided through the exhibition which plays Satie's music as well as extracts from his writings and commentaries on his life and work.

Accommodation and food in Honfleur

Hotels in Honfleur tend to be on the expensive side.

L'Absinthe Hôtel €€ *1 rue de la Ville; tel: 02 31 89 23 23; fax: 02 31 89 53 60.* A 16th-century former presbytery in the old town – good value.

Le Cheval Blanc €€€ *2 quai des Passagers; tel: 02 31 81 65 00; fax: 02 31 89 52 80.* Hotel with superb views of the port.

La Diligence €€€ *53 rue de la République; tel: 02 31 14 47 47; fax: 02 31 98 83 87.* Timber-framed coaching inn near the Vieux Bassin.

L'Hippocampe €€ *44 quai St-Catherine; tel: 02 31 89 98 36.* Restaurant overlooking the Vieux Bassin, serving *fruits de mer* and fish specialities.

A walk to Mont-Jolie

Climb to the 90m-high **Plâteau de Grâce** from where there's a magnificent panorama of the Seine estuary, l'Havre, the cliffs of the Pays de Caux and the Normandy Bridge. The **Chapelle Notre-Dame-de-Grâce** dates from the 17th century, but is said to stand on the site of an earlier church erected by Duke Richard II and his son Robert (father of William the Conqueror) in thanksgiving for surviving a shipwreck. Follow the path to the left of the chapel, passing the **Pavillon 'Louis-Philippe'** where the king and his queen, Marie-Amélie stayed for several days en route to England and exile as they fled the revolution of 1848. From **Mont-Jolie** there are more views of Honfleur and the Seine Valley.

LISIEUX

ⓘ Lisieux Tourist Information *11 rue d'Alençon; tel: 02 31 48 18 10; e-mail: tourisme@cclisieuxpaysdauge.fr; www.ville-lisieux.fr*

ⓟ Place F Mitterand, place de la République.

ⓗ Maison des Buissonnets *Boulevard Herbet-Fournet. Open Apr–Sept, daily, 0900–1200, 1400–1800; Oct, Feb & Mar, 1000–1200, 1400–1700; Nov–Jan, 1000–1200, 1400–1600.*

ⓞ Le Nautile *Rue Joseph Guillonneau; tel: 02 31 48 66 67. Swimming baths with slide, water jets, several pools, saunas etc.*

The capital of the Pays d'Auge, Lisieux has been an important market town since Roman times. Sadly, though, it's only a shadow of its former self, most of the picturesque old houses having been destroyed by Allied bombing raids during World War II. A notable exception is the **Cathédrale St-Pierre**, a splendid Norman-Gothic building begun in 1170 and completed in the 14th century. Pierre Cauchon, the presiding judge at the trial of Joan of Arc, is buried in the main chapel.

It was Thérèse Martin (**St Theresa of Lisieux**) who brought international fame to the town. Born in Alençon in 1873, Thérèse joined the Carmelite order at the age of 15 after obtaining a special dispensation from the pope. 'A soul of such quality should not be treated as a child' was the verdict of the prioress. The 'little flower', as she afterwards became known, spent the remaining years of her short life in the local convent, dying of tuberculosis in 1897. Thérèse's claims to sanctity rested largely on her humility and the spiritual values set out in her testament, *The History of a Soul*. She was canonised by Pius XI in 1925. The vast **Basilique de Ste-Thérèse**, one of the largest churches to be built in the 20th century, was completed in 1954 and is now a place of pilgrimage. Anyone who has visited Sacré-Coeur in Paris will immediately recognise it as a model for the design. The nave is decorated with mosaics, while bones from the saint's right arm are on display in a reliquary in the south transept. Her shrine and the rest of her remains (also items of her clothing) can be found in the **Chapelle du Carmel**. Le Buissonnets, the house where Thérèse grew up, is also open to the public as a museum.

Accommodation and food in Lisieux

Hôtel des Arts € *26 rue Condorcet; tel: 02 31 62 00 02; fax: 02 31 32 23 26.* Reliable budget option near the cathedral. No restaurant.

Hôtel Mercure €€€ *Route de Paris; tel: 02 31 61 17 17; fax: 02 31 32 33 43.* Excellent garden restaurant, overlooking the swimming pool.

Terrasse-Hôtel €€ *25 avenue Ste-Thérèse; tel: 02 31 62 17 65; fax: 02 31 62 20 25.* Reasonably priced rooms on the hill leading to the basilica.

Au Vieux Normand €€ *14 rue Henry Chéron; tel: 02 31 62 03 35.* Traditional Norman cooking in a half-timbered house.

TROUVILLE

ⓘ Trouville Tourist Information *32 quai Fernand Moureaux; tel: 02 31 14 60 70; e-mail: o.t.trouville@wanadoo.fr; www.trouvillesurmer.org*

ⓗ Aquarium €€ *17 rue de Paris; tel: 02 31 88 46 04.* Open July and Aug, daily, 1000–1930; Easter–June, Sept & Oct, daily, 1000–1200, 1400–1900; Nov–Easter, 1400–1830.

Musée de Trouville € *Villa Montebello, 64 rue du Général Leclerc; tel: 02 31 88 51 33.* Open Mar–Sept, Wed–Mon, 1400–1830.

ⓐ Casino *Place du Maréchal Foch; tel: 02 31 87 75 00.*

Trouville has all the ingredients of a typical French seaside resort: golden sand, the famous boardwalk or *planches* that extends the length of the beach, an open-air swimming pool, an **aquarium**, a thalassotherapy centre and a casino. The town became fashionable in the 1860s when Napoléon III brought his court – witness the extravagant villas strung along the front. The delights of sea bathing through the ages are the theme of an exhibition in the **Villa Montebello** with paintings, engravings and a room of posters by the artist Ramond Sauvignac. On the other side of town is the **port**, with a traditional fish market every morning.

Accommodation and food in Trouville

Camping Caravaning de la Vallée €€ *Route de Beaumont, St-Arnoult; tel: 02 31 88 58 17; fax: 02 31 88 11 57.* Campsite with swimming pool, barbecue area and other facilities.

Hôtel Les Sablettes €€ *Rue P-Besson; tel: 02 31 88 10 66; fax: 02 31 88 59 06.* Comfortable hotel near the beach and casino.

Les Vapeurs €€ *160 boulevard Fernand Moureaux; tel: 02 31 88 15 24; fax: 02 31 88 20 58; www.lesvapeurs.fr.* Long established brasserie, reeking with atmosphere and serving top-notch seafood.

Suggested tour

Total distance: 130km (147km with detours).

Time: 2½ hours' driving. Allow 8 hours for the main route, 9 hours with detours. Those with limited time should concentrate on the section between Trouville and Lisieux.

Links: The A13 from Paris and Rouen (*see pages 276–81*) to Caen (*see pages 246–7*) crosses this route.

Leave **TROUVILLE ❶** on the D513 clifftop route with wonderful views back across Trouville and the Touques estuary. (There's a car park and viewing table at the Calvaire de Bon-Secours.) Continue to **Villerville**, a lively, if pricey, resort. Beyond is the picturesque 12th-

Le Bellvue €€€ *7 allée du Jardin Madame; tel: 02 31 87 20 22; fax: 02 31 87 20 56.* Traditional local and French fare served in a terrace restaurant with sea views.

Cambremer *Rue Pasteur; tel: 02 31 63 08 87; e-mail: cambremer.si@wanadoo.fr; www.cambremer.fr*

Houlgate *Boulevard des Belges; tel: 02 31 24 34 79; e-mail: houlgate@wanadoo.fr; www.ville-houlgate.fr*

Below
Trouville harbour

century church at **Criqueboeuf**, set among the woods and meadows so characteristic of the Côte Fleurie. As the road approaches **HONFLEUR ❷** and the **Côte de Grace** there are more superb views, this time of the Seine estuary towards le Havre.

From Honfleur follow the D279 to Barneville la Berton. Turn right at the airport perimeter on to the D288. On your left is **Bonneville-sur-Touques**, the ruins of an 11th-century castle with good views of the river mouth. Bonneville was one of the favourite castles of William the Conqueror, who installed his wife Mathilda as regent here when he set sail for England in 1066.

Turn left on to the N177. Just before the junction with the A932 the road passes Canapville and the charming 15th-century **Manoir des Evêques de Lisieux**, *open to the public on weekends and during the summer between June and August.* Continue in the direction of Pont-l'Evêque. The delightful **Domaine Coeur de Lion** at Coudray Rabut has timber-framed architecture typical of the 17th-century Augeronne

ⓘ Pont l'Evêque
*16 bis rue St-Michel;
tel: 02 31 64 12 77;
e-mail: contact@blangy-
pontleveque.com;
www.blangy-pontleveque.com*

Villerville *Rue du Général-
Leclerc; tel: 02 31 87 21 49;
e-mail: otvillerville@free.fr;
www.villerville.fr*

**ⓘ Bonneville-sur-
Touques** € *Near
Trouville; tel: 02 31 88 00
10. Open Easter–Oct, Sat
and Sun, 1400–1800.*

**Manoir des Evêques de
Lisieux** €€ *Tel: 02 31 65
24 75. Open mid-June–Aug,
daily, 1400–1800, Apr–mid-
June and Sept–Nov, Sat and
Sun, 1400–1800.*

**Domaine Coeur de
Lion** *Route de Trouville,
Coudray-Rabut; tel: 02 31
64 30 05; e-mail:
coudray@normandnet.fr;
www.coeur-de-lion.com.
Open Mon–Sat,
0900–1200, 1400–1800.*

**Atelier Fromager de
Pont l'Evêque** *Atelier
Fromage Parc Launay; tel: 02
31 64 61 96. Open
Mon–Sat, 0900–1200,
1400–1700.*

**Musée de la Belle
Époque de
l'Automobile** €€
*Château de Betteville; tel: 02
31 65 05 02. Open July and
Aug, 1000–1900;
Easter–June and Sept,
1000–1230, 1330–1900;
Oct–mid-Nov, 1400–1800.*

Château de Breuil *Le
Breuil-en-Auge; tel: 02 31 65
60 00; e-mail: info@chateau-
breuil.fr; www.chateau-
breuil.fr. Open daily,
0900–1200, 1400–1800.*

style. The farm has been producing cider since 1638 and visitors can still see the orchards, cider press, still and storeroom.

Pont-l'Evêque has been a centre of cheese-making since the 17th century. Pont-l'Evêque cheese is made from the milk of pure-bred Norman cows and can be sampled at the dairy east of the town on the D162. Pont-l'Evêque also has some splendid half-timbered houses in the neighbourhood of rue Vaucelles as well as an old Dominican convent with its original wooden balcony still intact. South of the town you'll find the Leisure Centre – an attractive lake with windsurfing, pedalos and camping facilities. (Horse riding is also available in the surrounding woodland.)

Follow the D48 along the Touques valley. Just after the bridge under the A13 is **Château de Betteville** *tel: 02 31 65 05 02* where the stables have become a **car museum** with over 100 vehicles dating from between 1898 and 1950, including a 1911 taxi cab and a 1912 model 30 Cadillac. There are also motorcycles, horse-drawn vehicles and, rather incongruously, a couple of reed organs.

Continue on the D48 to the **château** at **le Breuil-en-Auge**, a beautiful building with half-timbered walls and pink tiling in an attractive garden setting. The château produces calvados and the distillery and stills are open to the public – the brandy is left to mature in the pretty orangerie.

There's a larger distillery a few kilometres down the road at **Couquainvilliers** where the **Calvados Boulard Company** has been in business since 1825. Visitors can see the shiny copper distilling flasks while savouring the fumes from the oak casks. Tastings are held in the museum, the 'hall of ancient stills'.

Detour: Families might enjoy a visit to the unique farm at Norolles (on the D98) where, at the **Musée Vivant de la Basse-Cour**, more than 900 varieties of birds and animals native to the region are kept in paddocks on either side of

ⓘ Calvados Boulard Company € *Route de Manerbe, Coquainvilliers; tel: 02 31 48 24 00; www.calvados-boulard.com.* Open all year for tastings and guided tours.

Musée Vivant de la Basse-Cour €€€ *Norolles; tel: 02 31 62 78 78. Open Easter–Aug, daily, 0930–1800.*

Château de St-Germain-de-Livet €€ *Tel: 02 31 31 00 03. Open for guided visits Tues–Sun, 1100–1800; closed early Oct, Dec & Jan.*

St Loup-de-Fribois Dairy *Domaine de St-Loup; tel: 02 31 63 04 04. Open Mon–Sat, 0930–1230, 1330–1530.*

Chateau de Crèvecoeur € *Crèvecoeur-en-Auge; tel: 02 31 63 02 45; www.chateau-de-crevecoeur.com. Open July and Aug, daily 1100–1900; Apr–June and Sept, 1100–1800; Oct Sun, 1400–1800.*

Chapelle de Clermont Panorama *Open Easter–Nov, daily, 0900–1900.*

Musée de Paléontologique *TIC, place Jean Mermoz; tel: 02 31 87 01 18. Open July and Aug, 0900–1900; Mar–June, Sept & Oct, 0930–1230, 1430–1800; Nov–Feb, 1000–1230, 1430–1700.*

Opposite
Dives-sur-Mer

a 2.5km path. The 15th-century fortified farmhouse and the stables are open to the public.

Take the D48 to **LISIEUX ❸**.

Detour: Take the D579, turning left on to the D268 after crossing the Touques. **St-Germain-de-Livet**, a château straight out of a fairy-tale, dates back to the 15th century. The 16th-century extension has a number of attractive Renaissance features including a chequerboard façade in stone and glazed brick. The interiors are furnished in the styles of Louis XV and Louis XVI, while in the guardroom you can see some of the original frescoes.

From Lisieux take the N13 west. Turn left on the D101A through Monteille to **St-Loup-de-Fribois** where the **dairy** is still owned by a descendant of Marie Harel, creator of Camembert. Traditional methods of making cheese are explained. Turn right on the D16 to the **castle** at **Crèvecoeur-en-Auge**, a complex of buildings dating from the 11th to 16th centuries. Cross the moat to see the outer courtyard and farm buildings, the dovecote, the 12th-century chapel and the 15th-century manor house.

Take the D101 to **Cambremer** where the craft market, held on *Sunday mornings in July and August*, might be a good place to look for souvenirs. Continue on the D101.

Detour: Turn right to **Grandouet** where, among the apple orchards, you'll find a 12th-century church and a farm with a 16th-century half-timbered '*pressoir*' where you can sample and buy fruit juices, pommeau, cider and calvados.

Return to the D101 and continue to Montreuil-en-Auge, then turn on to the D117. At the junction with the D16 turn left, then right to Rumesnil where another left turn on to the D85 brings you to Clermont-en-Auge. Signs in the village point to the **Chapelle de Clermont Panorama**. An avenue of beech trees leads from the car park to the chapel from where there are superb views towards Caen and the network of rivers which crisscross the surrounding countryside.

Take the D146 to **Beuvron-en-Auge**, a beautifully preserved village where multi-coloured timber houses cluster around the central square. At the edge of the village is the Vieux Manoir, with wood carvings on the main beam – look for the Norman soldier.

Take the D49 passing under the N175 and A13 to **Dives-sur-Mer.** This historic town, once a major port on the Touques estuary, was where Duke William amassed his fleet before setting out for England in 1066. A list of the barons who sailed with him is carved on the west wall of the church of Notre-Dame. Don't miss the magnificent 15th-century market hall on place de la République, with its massive oak

ℹ Villers-sur-Mer
   Place Jean Mermoz;
tel: 02 31 87 01 18;
e-mail: villers14.
tourisme@wanadoo.fr;
www.mairie-villers-sur-mer.fr

**◯ Cambremer craft
   market –** *Sunday
morning in July and August.*

*Dives-sur-Mer – Saturday
morning market in the old
halls.*

*Pont l'Evêque – craft
market on place des
Dominicans, Sunday morning
in July and August.*

🏛 Musée municipal
   Vieux Manoir, Orbec;
*tel: 02 31 32 82 02. Open
July–Sept, Sun and Wed–Fri,
1400–1800, Sat
1000–1200.*

**Fromagerie
Graindorge** *42 rue du
Général Leclerc, Livarot;*
tel: 02 31 48 20 10;
*www.graindorge.fr. Open
Apr–Sept, Sun and Tue–Fri,
0900–1200, 1330–1700,
Mon and Sat, 0900–1200.*

Musée du Fromage €
*Manoir de l'Isle, 68 rue
Marcel Gambier, Livarot;
contact Livarot tourist office
for details: 1 place Georges
Bisson; tel: 02 31 63 47 39.*

Musée du Fromage €
*10 avenue du Général de
Gaulle (in tourist office in
Vimoutiers); tel: 02 33 39
30 29. Open May–Oct,
0900–1200, 1400–1800;
Nov–Apr, Tue–Fri,
0900–1200, 1400–1800,
Sat and Mon, 0900–1200.*

frame supporting a steep, tiled roof. There's an excellent produce market on Saturday mornings.

Cross the river to **CABOURG ❹**, then return to **Houlgate**, a typical French resort, popular with families who enjoy the fine sand as well as horse riding, rambling and cycling in the woodland behind the town. Leave Houlgate on the D163, climbing to the viewing table from where there are views over the estuaries of the Dives and Orne. Continue past the **Falaise des Vaches Noires** (Cliff of Black Cows), named after the seaweed-covered rocks strewn on the beach. The cliffs are rich in fossils; some of them are on show in the **Palaeontology Museum** in the tourist information office at Villers-sur-Mer. Turn left on the D513 to **Villers-sur-Mer**, an elegant resort where smart 19th-century villas line the 5km beach. Continue on the D513 to **DEAUVILLE ❺**.

Also worth exploring

South of Lisieux in cheese country you will also find several picturesque towns. Medieval **Orbec**, in the beautiful Orbiquet valley, has a picture-postcard main street with overhanging timber-framed houses dominated by the massive Renaissance tower of the church of Notre-Dame. The oldest and most impressive house in town is the **Vieux Manoir** dating from 1568. It was owned by a wealthy tanner who commissioned the geometric flint-and-tile patterns on the walls and carved figures on the beams. Inside is a small **museum** of local history.

The history of **St-Pierre-sur-Dives** is depicted in the modern stained glass in the **church**. Originally part of an 11th-century Benedictine abbey, the present Gothic structure has an elegant lantern tower and, inside, a copper strip crossing the floor of the nave. This is a form of sundial, tracing the line of the sun's rays at midday. The 11th-century timber **market hall** is also of interest. Destroyed in 1944, it was immediately rebuilt using traditional techniques – no nails or screws, just thousands of chestnut pegs.

Between the two towns lies **Livarot**, famous for its cheese. The **Musée du Fromage** can be found in the Manoir d'Isle, a mansion in attractive grounds near the Vie river, originally owned by cheese-maker Georges Bisson. To sample modern Livarot cheeses, head for the dairy of the Graindorge family, preferably in the morning when the process begins. English tours available.

The **Musée du Fromage** at **Vimoutiers** specialises in Camembert labels. In the main square of the town is a statue of Marie Harel who lived in the nearby village of Camembert. Credited with the creation of the famous Camembert cheese, she was actually given the recipe by a priest on the run from the revolutionaries.

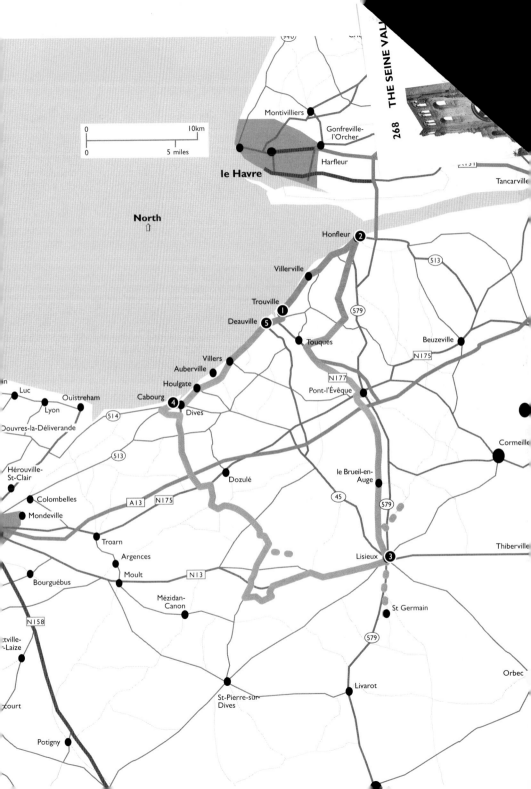

Montivilliers

Gonfreville-
l'Orcher

Harfleur

le Havre

Tancarville

A131

North
⇧

0   10km
0   5 miles

Honfleur **②**

513

Villerville

Trouville

Deauville **⑤** **①**

579

Touques

Beuzeville

N175

Villers

Auberville

Houlgate

N177

Pont-l'Évêque

Cabourg **④**

Dives

Luc

Ouistreham

Lyon

514

Douvres-la-Déliverande

513

Dozulé

le Breuil-en-
Auge

45

579

Cormeille

Hérouville-
St-Clair

Colombelles

Mondeville

A13   N175

Troarn

Argences

Moult

N13

Lisieux **③**

Thiberville

Bourguébus

N158

Mézidan-
Canon

St Germain

579

Orbec

Potigny

St-Pierre-sur-
Dives

Livarot

The Seine Valley

Ratings

Architecture	●●●●●
Art	●●●●●
Scenery	●●●●●
Castles and châteaux	●●●
Cathedrals and churches	●●●●
Heritage	●●●●
Outdoor activities	●●●●
Walking	●●●●
Children	●●
Wildlife	●●

More commonly associated with Paris, the Seine flows through a highly picturesque valley, past the historic town of Rouen to the sea. If you're arriving in le Havre, you will probably be anxious to move on, but art lovers should take the time to visit the Musée des Beaux Arts André Malraux. Some of Normandy's most evocative abbey ruins lie in this neck of the woods – Jumièges is probably the best of the bunch. Beyond Rouen there's Lyons-la-Forêt, a picture-postcard village which has appeared in numerous films. Dotted about the forest you'll also come across several fine châteaux. Vascoeuil is worthy of a detour, though you won't find anything to match the 'proper' castle – albeit ruined – at les Andelys. The views across the Seine Valley from Château Gaillard are equally unbeatable. Vernon is worth a short stopover en route to the bigger attraction at Giverny. This was where the artist Claude Monet spent the latter half of his life – he was brought up in le Havre.

LES ANDELYS

🛈 **Les Andelys Tourist Information** 24 rue Philippe-Auguste; tel: 02 32 54 41 93.

🛈 **Musée Nicolas Poussin** Rue Ste-Clothilde; tel: 02 32 54 31 78. Open Wed–Mon, 1400–1800. Free.

Perched on a rocky spur overlooking les Andelys is the main attraction. Now a magnificent ruin, **Château Gaillard** was built by Richard the Lionheart to defend the Seine and the approaches to Rouen. It was completed in little more than a year (1196–7). The state-of-the-art fortress was considered impregnable yet it fell to Richard's arch-rival, King Philippe Auguste of France, in 1204, after an eight-month siege (the advance party entered through the latrines). The castle was dismantled early in the 17th century but you're free to explore the remains and enjoy the superb views of the town and the river bend.

Les Andelys is actually two communities. **Petit Andely**, directly below the castle, has a tourist office, e-mail: contact@ville-andelys.fr;

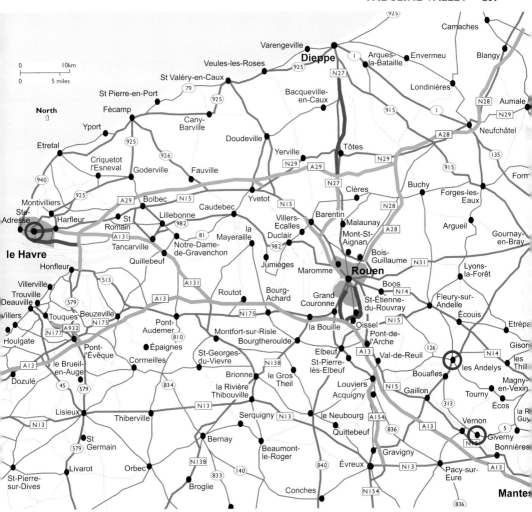

Hôtel de Normandie
€€ I rue Grande, Petit Andely (restaurant €€€); tel: 02 32 54 10 52; fax: 02 32 54 25 84. One of the best places to stay because of the terrace and the views of the Seine.

www.ville-andelys.fr, some half-timbered houses and the **Eglise St-Sauveur**, dating from the time of King Richard. **Grand Andely**, where most of the shops and bars are located, is a little further inland. The **Musée Nicolas Poussin** honours the famous 17th-century artist who was born in the town in 1594. You can see one of his great classical canvases, *Coriolan*, but most of the exhibition is devoted to local history. The **Eglise Nôtre-Dame** has some fine 16th-century stained glass.

GIVERNY

The village where the renowned Impressionist painter, Claude Monet, made his home for the last four decades of his life (1883–1926) is now a

ⓘ Fondation Claude Monet €€ *Rue Claude Monet; tel: 02 32 51 28 21; www.fondation-monet.com. Open Apr–Oct, Tue–Sun, 0930–1800.*

Musée Américain €€ *99 rue Claude Monet; tel: 02 32 51 94 65. Open Apr–Oct, Tue–Sun, 1000–1800.*

major tourist destination, notwithstanding the fact that there isn't a single original canvas by the artist in sight. **Monet's house and gardens** are open to the public as a museum. It's disappointing to find at the outset that the artist's studio is now a gift shop and reception centre with little to evoke him besides books, videos and reproductions of his paintings. Still, the rest of the house is more atmospheric, especially the rooms decorated with Monet's wonderful collection of Japanese prints. The **gardens** will bowl you over. The walled garden to the rear of the house, known as the *clos Normand*, is a riot of colour, its shrubs and archways of climbing plants designed by Monet himself. From here a tunnel leads to the *jardin d'eau* and the water lilies which were such a great source of inspiration to the artist. The famous Japanese bridge casts shadows on the pond as wistarias, azaleas, rhododendrons and weeping willows bewitch and dazzle.

If you have time on your hands it's only a short stroll from Monet's house to the **Musée Américain** which exhibits works by leading American disciples of the French master, including Whistler, Mary Cassatt, Theodore Robinson and John Singer Sargent.

LE HAVRE

ⓘ le Havre Tourist Information *186 boulevard Clemenceau; tel: 02 32 74 04 04; fax: 02 32 42 38 39; e-mail: contact@lehavretourisme.fr; www.lehavretourisme.com*

France's second port after Marseille, le Havre was founded in 1517 to replace the silted harbours at Honfleur and Harfleur. It was almost totally destroyed during World War II, allowing the architect Auguste Perret to indulge freely in his appetite for concrete! The most impressive examples of his work are the **Hôtel de Ville** *tel: 02 35 19 45 45*, set in a vast square ornamented with fountains, pools and lawns, and the **Eglise St-Joseph** *François 1er Avenue* with its 106m-high central tower. A more recent, though no less controversial project is the **Espace Oscar Niemeyer** *tel: 02 35 19 10 10*, a cultural centre designed by the well-known Brazilian architect and nicknamed 'the Volcano' on account of its shape.

Many visitors to le Havre see little more than the ferry port at the beginning or end of their holiday, but art lovers should try to find time for the **Musée des Beaux Arts André Malraux** which occupies a superb site overlooking the sea. The collection of European Art from the 17th to 20th centuries is strongest on French Impressionism – there are works by Boudin, Pissaro and Sisley among others – as well as canvases by the great 20th-century artist, Raoul Dufy, who was born in le Havre in 1877.

A few reminders of the old town remain. The **Cathedral** *rue de Paris*, dating from 1575–1630, has been restored along with the organ, a gift from Cardinal Richelieu in 1637. The **Musée de l'Ancien Havre** occupies one of the oldest houses in the city and recaptures the past with engravings and other memorabilia. There's also an exhibition on the history of French shipping lines in **Espace Maritime et Portuaire des docks Vauban.**

Air: The **Aéroport du Havre-Octeville** *tel: 02 35 54 65 00* has flights from London City Airport.

Car: Most drivers arrive on the A131 (E5) from Paris or on the D929 across the Normandy Bridge from Western France.

Ferry: LD Lines Ferries run boats from Portsmouth all year round *(tel: 08 25 30 43 04)*.

P Chausée du 24th Territorial, Cours de la République.

Musée des Beaux Arts André Malraux € *2 boulevard Clémenceau; tel: 02 35 19 62 62. Open Wed–Mon, 1100–1800; Sat and Sun, until 1900.*

Musée de l'Ancien Havre € *1 rue Jérôme Bellarmato; tel: 02 35 42 27 90. Open Wed–Sun, 1000–1200, 1400–1800.*

Espace Maritime et Portuaire des docks Vauban €€ *Dock Vauban, quai Frissard; tel: 02 35 24 51 00. Open Wed–Mon, 1000–1200, 1400–1800. Naval artefacts.*

Accommodation and food in le Havre

Hotel Celtic €€ *106 rue Voltaire; tel: 02 35 42 39 77; fax: 02 35 21 67 65; e-mail: postmaster@celtic.com; www.hotel-celtic.com.* Well-appointed and reasonably-priced option within easy reach of the ferry terminal.

Hôtel le Richelieu €€ *132 rue de Paris; tel: 02 35 42 38 71; fax: 02 35 21 07 28; e-mail: hotel.lerichelieu@wanadoo.fr.* Good value rooms in a promising location.

Suggested tour

Total distance: 219km (305km with detours, plus 42km to le Havre).

Time: 6½ hours' driving. Allow at least 14 hours for the main route and an extra couple of hours to see Giverny. Those with limited time should concentrate on the stretch between Rouen and les Andelys.

Links: The A13 from Paris to Caen *(see pages 246–7)* follows the Seine Valley, while the beaches of the Côte Fleurie *(see pages 256–67)* are just to the west.

Above right
le Havre at dawn

Shopping

Shopping areas include place de l'Hôtel de Ville, around rue de Paris, and avenue René Coty, where there's also a market on Monday Wednesday and Friday. Cours de la République is the venue for the market on Tuesday, Thursday and Saturday. There's a second-hand and antiques market on the second Saturday of the month on rue Racine, by the Espace Oscar Niemeyer.

ⓘ Vernon Tourist Information 36 rue Carnot; tel: 02 32 51 39 60; e-mail: of.vernon27@wanadoo.fr; www.ville-vernon27.fr

Lyons-la-Fôret Tourist Information 20 rue de l'Hôtel de Ville; tel: 02 32 49 31 65.

ⓗ Abbaye de Mortemer € (grounds) €€ (grounds and museum) Lisors; tel: 02 32 49 54 34. Open Easter–Sept, daily, 1400–1830; Oct–Easter, Sat, Sun & hols, 1400–1800. Grounds open all year.

Abbaye de Fontaine-Guérard € Armée du Salut; tel: 02 32 49 03 82. Open Apr–Oct, Tue–Sun, 1400–1800.

Château de Fleury-la-Fôret €€ (combined ticket with Abbaye de Mortemer) Tel: 02 32 49 63 91. Open Easter–Sept, daily, 1400–1830; Oct–Easter, Sun and hols 1400–1800.

Leave **LES ANDELYS ❶** on the D1, taking the right fork (the D2) to the village of **Ecouis** and the early 14th-century church of Notre-Dame. This large, austere building is a treasure trove of religious art, from the 14th-century stained glass in the chapel of St John to the original carved wooden choir stalls and a plethora of statues dating from the 14th to 17th centuries.

Continue on the D2 to **Forêt de Lyons**, a dense wood of beech and oak trees that was once a favourite hunting ground of the dukes of Normandy. Henry I of England died here in 1135 after a day in the saddle. Today the forest is still popular but for more peaceful leisure pursuits (cycling, walking). As the road bends through le Coisel and Lisors, turn on to the D175 for the ruined 12th- to 13th-century **Abbaye de Mortemer**. The 18th-century convent buildings are now a museum on the history of the abbey with models, audio-visual reconstructions of monastic life and illuminated manuscripts. A tourist train runs through the attractively landscaped deer park.

On leaving the abbey take the turning opposite which climbs steeply back to the D2, before continuing to flower-bedecked **Lyons-la-Forêt**. The centre square with its old market attracts numerous visitors including film directors – scenes from the 1990 version of Madame Bovary were set here. The composer Maurice Ravel was inspired to write the piano suite le Tombeau de Couperin while staying in a house on rue d'Enfer.

Detour 1: Take the D321, turning right at the signs to **Abbaye de Fontaine-Guérard**. The ruins occupy a peaceful spot on the banks of the River Andelle. Part of the nave of the 13th-century church is still visible as well as the chapterhouse – a more impressive building with delicately moulded columns and carved capitals revealing Norman architecture at its best. Return to Lyons-la-Forêt.

Detour 2: Take the D15, following the left fork (D14) through **Beauficel-en-Lyons** where the church contains an unusual 14th-century statue of the Virgin made from stone inlaid with glass. An avenue of limes leads to the 17th-century **Château de Fleury-la-Forêt**. As well as furnished rooms, including a pristine kitchen and reconstructed wash house, there is a diverting collection of toys and dolls. Return to Lyons-la-Forêt.

Take the D2 northwards, turning on to the D115 at le Tronquay. Continue to **Vascoeuil** where you'll find an elegant red brick château dating from the 14th century. In the 19th century this was the home of the eminent historian, Jules Michelet; there's a documentation of his life and regular art exhibitions. Other sights include a huge 17th-century brick dovecot, several restored farm cottages and, in the courtyard, a superb collection of modern sculptures and mosaics by Braque, Dalì, Léger and Cocteau among others. The shady riverside restaurant is an attractive spot for lunch.

Château de Vascoeuil €€ *Tel: 02 35 23 62 35. Open July and Aug, daily, 1100–1900; Easter–June and Sept, Mon–Sat, 1430–1830, Sun and holidays, 1100–1900.*

Château de Martainville €€ *Tel: 02 35 23 44 70. Open summer, Wed–Mon, 1000–1230, 1400–1800 (winter until 1700).*

Ancienne Abbatiale St-Georges €€ *St-Martin-de-Bouscherville; tel: 02 35 32 10 82; e-mail: ass_atar@club-internet.fr; www.abbaye-saint-georges.com. Open Apr–Oct, 0900–1830; Nov–Mar, 1400–1700.*

Abbaye de Jumièges €€ *Tel: 02 35 37 24 02. Open mid-Apr–mid-Sept, daily, 0930–1900; mid-Sept–mid-Apr, 0930–1300, 1430–1730.*

Above right
Wandrille:
Abbaye de St-Wandrille

Join the N31 heading west to **Martainville**. The 15th-century château with massive round towers, brick chimney stacks and a tall grey slate roof, is a complete contrast to the château at Vascoeuil. On display are period costumes and furnishings. From Martainville take the N31 to Rouen. Leave on the D982 through the Forêt de Roumare to **St-Martin-de-Bouscherville**, a Benedictine abbey founded in 1144 by William of Tancarville. The church, which survived the Revolution, has a beautifully proportioned Romanesque nave with elaborately carved capitals on the pillars.

Continue on the D982, turning left at Yainville to the impressive ruins of **Abbaye de Jumièges**. Consecrated in 1067 in the presence of William the Conqueror, the abbey was destroyed and used as a quarry during the Revolution. However, the walls of the nave and chancel have survived together with the distinctive twin towers. The small church of St-Pierre is even older (10th century) although the east end

Place Benserade in Lyons-la-Forêt has several good souvenir and postcard shops.

Au Pâté de Lyons (No 32) does a nice line in picnic fare (*closed Wed*).

Camping St-Paul €€ *Lyons-la-Forêt; tel: 02 32 49 42 02. Closed Nov–Mar. Campsite in attractive setting between the river and the forest. .*

Hostellerie du Domaine St-Paul €€ *Route de Forges-des-Eaux, Lyons-la-Forêt; tel: 02 32 49 60 57; fax: 02 32 49 56 05. Comfortable logis with expensive restaurant.*

La Halle €€ *Place Benserade, Lyons-la-Forêt; tel: 02 32 49 49 92. Terrace restaurant with good-value set menus.*

Abbaye de St-Wandrille € *Tel: 02 35 96 23 11; www.st-wandrille.com. Open at various times daily for services and tours.*

Moulin d'Hauville € *Tel: 02 32 56 57 32. Open July and Aug, daily, 1330–1830; Apr–June and Sept, Sat and Sun, 1400–1830; Mar, Oct & Nov, Sun and holidays, 1400–1800.*

was reworked in the 14th century. An ancient yew tree is all that remains of the cloisters but the Abbot's lodging in the gardens beyond is a magnificent 17th-century building, definitely worth a detour.

Return to the D982 and follow the Seine to the Fontenelle Valley and the turning to **Abbaye de St-Wandrille**. Founded back in the 7th century by Wandrille, a count who famously renounced his worldly wealth to become a hermit, the abbey was rebuilt by the Benedictine Order in the 10th century. Thereafter the complex had a chequered history. The church was destroyed during the Revolution while the convent was used as a mill, then as a private home – the monumental gateway was erected by a 19th-century resident, the English Marquis of Stacpoole. The site was returned to the Benedictines in 1930 and the programme of restoration is well under way. A 13th-century tithe barn (transported from la Neuville du Bosc) now serves as a church. The modern shrine nearby contains the head of St Wandrille.

Detour: Architect buffs may like to visit the 14th-century **Eglise Notre-Dame** in Caudebec-en-Caux, a splendid example of the Flamboyant Gothic style. Continue to Tancarville where the road passes under the Pont de Tancarville before it joins the E5 to **LE HAVRE ❷** .

Take the D490 to the Pont de Brotonne, a humpback toll bridge with superb views from the 50m high platform. About 11km into the **Forêt de Brotonne** a road to the left (look for the signs – port Jumièges) leads to a picnic area with viewing table overlooking the Seine towards Jumièges forest and abbey. Turn right at the D101 to the **Moulin d'Hauville**, a 13th-century mill which once belonged to the abbey. It has since been restored and, if the wind is up, you can see the sails turning.

Take the D101 across the D313, then the D712. Turn left at the junction with the D91, then right on to the D265 to la Ronce. Take the D93 following the Seine to **la Bouille**, a pretty village on a river bend.

From la Bouille follow the signs to the ruined 11th-century **Château de Robert-le-Diable**. The ruins looming above the Seine make for a great spectacle but the viking museum once operating inside has closed, leaving no current public entry to the interior.

To avoid the tolls, take the small road under the autoroute, turning left on to the D64. Turn right on to the D938 then, at the junction with the D321, turn left and continue to Pont-de-l'Arche. Cross the Seine on the N15, turning right on to the D321. Take another right turn on to the D19 to **Amfreville**, passing the locks and dam (1-hour tours available). On reaching Amfreville-sous-les-Monts turn on to the D20, then left on to the side road that climbs to the **Côte des Deux Amants** and superb views of the Seine Valley. Return to the D19 and follow the river to Andé. As you enter the village, take a sharp left on to the D313, a scenic route running along the foot of the cliffs to les Andelys.

Château de Bizy
€€ *Vernon; tel: 02 32 51 00 82. Open Apr–Nov, Tue–Sun, 1000–1200, 1400–1800; Mar, Sat and Sun, 1400–1700.*

Also worth exploring

The D313 heads south from les Andelys to the picturesque town of **Vernon**, founded by Rollo, the first Duke of Normandy, in the 9th century. The main attraction is the timber-framed cottage balanced precariously on the remaining span of the medieval bridge. Just outside Vernon is the imposing 18th-century **Château de Bizy** where the famous stables now contain a collection of horse-drawn carriages.

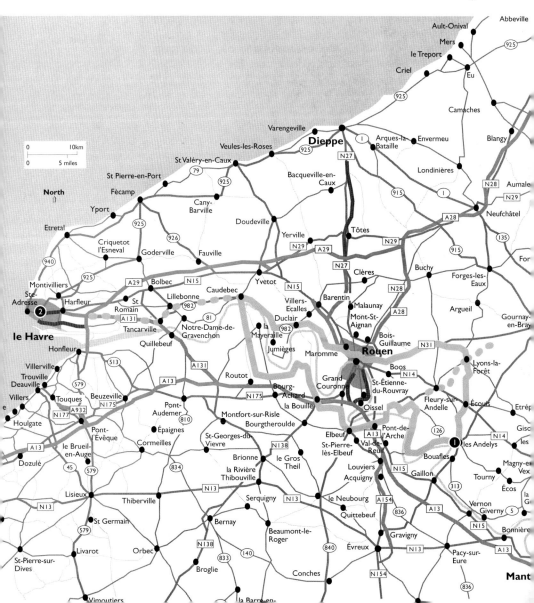

Rouen

Ratings

Architecture	●●●●●
Art	●●●●●
Cathedrals and churches	●●●●○
Food	●●●●○
Heritage	●●●●○
History	●●●●○
Markets	●●●●○
Children	●●●○○
Entertainment	●●●○○

Originally founded by the Romans, Rouen is a delightful town, famous as the place where Joan of Arc was tried for witchcraft and later burnt at the stake. During World War II, Allied bombing raids destroyed more than 40 per cent of the town centre as well as the bridges over the Seine but you'd hardly notice were it not for the restoration which appears almost too complete. Improvements continue, targeted for 'Rouen 2005'.

Today Rouen is an industrial city and an important inland port. For the tourist it's the agreeably manageable old town with its tortuous streets, cheery, half-timbered houses and ethereal towers and spires that's the source of Rouen's appeal. Apart from some of the finest church architecture in France, there's a polychrome clock dating from the Middle Ages, an old plague cemetery and the tower where St Joan was shown the rack, not forgetting the Impressionist paintings in the Musée des Beaux-Arts, the Sunday flea market and the mouthwatering duck pâté.

Sights

ⓘ Eglise Ste-Jeanne-d'Arc *Place du Vieux Marché. Open Sat, Mon–Thur, 1000–1215, 1400–1800.*

Musée Jeanne d'Arc €€ *33 place du Vieux; tel: 02 35 88 02 70. Open daily, mid-Apr–Sept, 0930–1900; Oct–mid-Apr, 1000–1200, 1400–1800.*

Sights associated with Joan of Arc

On 30 May, 1431 Joan was burned at the stake on **place de Vieux-Marché** (Old Market Square) after being proclaimed a heretic and excommunicated. A large plain cross, known as the **Croix de la Réhabilitation** (Cross of Rehabilitation) marks the site of her martyrdom. The square itself was redesigned by Louis Arretche in the 1960s, although the half-timbered houses are authentic. The **Eglise Ste-Jeanne-d'Arc**, also by Arretche, was completed in 1979 and is starkly modern. It contains 16th-century stained glass taken from another church, destroyed in World War II. The **Musée Jeanne d'Arc** has little to recommend it unless you're a fan of waxworks. It does, however, contain a model of the 13th-century castle of Phillippe-Auguste, where Joan was imprisoned. She was first held in the **Tour de la Pucelle**

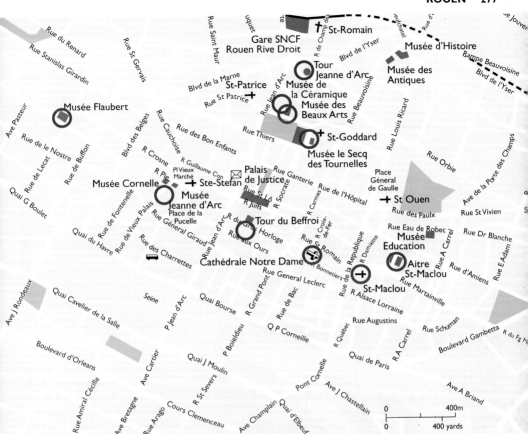

(Maid's Tower), the remains of which can still be seen at 102 rue Jeanne d'Arc. The **Tour Jeanne d'Arc**, where she was taken for interrogation but refused to confess, despite being shown the implements of torture, has been preserved intact and contains a small exhibition.

After her trial, Joan was led to the cemetery of the **Abbatiale St-Ouen** to make a public recantation of her heresy. Don't be put off by the blackened exterior – this church, dating from the 14th to 16th centuries is one of France's finest Gothic monuments and should not be missed. When you have finished marvelling at the sublime symmetry of the nave, check out the 14th-century stained glass at the chancel end. Come here on a Sunday and you may get a chance to hear the magnificent organ, rebuilt in the 19th century by the renowned Cavaillé-Coll.

The grim ruins of the **Archevêché** (Archbishop's Palace) is where Joan was sentenced to death by an ecclesiastical court after being tricked by Bishop Cauchon into relapsing into heresy, and it can be seen on **rue St-Romain**, next to the cathedral. (This was also where she would eventually be rehabilitated.) After her death, Joan's heart and ashes were cast into the Seine near the **Pont Boïeldieu**.

Cathedral *Place de la Cathédrale. Open Tue–Sun 0800–1800; Mon, 1400–1800. Guided tours of the crypt etc hourly, 1000–1700.*

Eglise St-Maclou *Place Barthélemy. Open Mon–Sat, 1000–1700; Sun, 1030–1700.*

Cathédrale de Notre-Dame

This venerable ensemble, dating mainly from the 12th and 13th centuries might be described as a Gothic theme and variations. Art lovers will have no difficulty recognising the magnificent **west front**, made famous by Monet's timeless studies of changing light, most of which can now be seen in the Musée d'Orsay in Paris. An ambitious restoration programme is currently under way, making viewing difficult; all the same, it's worth taking a tour of the exterior before venturing inside. The spire on the **lantern tower** is the tallest in France, soaring to a height of 151m. Equally impressive is the stone filigree of the portals: the **portail de la Calende** (south, rue du Change) and the **portail des Libraires** (north, rue St-Romain), the latter surmounted by an exquisite rose window. (You'll get a better impression of the 14th-century stained glass from inside.) To see the **ambulatory**, **Lady Chapel** and **crypt** (*closed Sundays and during services*) you'll have to sign up for the 40-minute guided tour. The highlights are the effigies of Duke Rollo of Normandy and King Richard the Lionheart – the said heart is actually buried here – and the sumptuous 16th-century tomb of the Cardinals of Amboise.

Below
Cathédrale de Nôtre-Dame

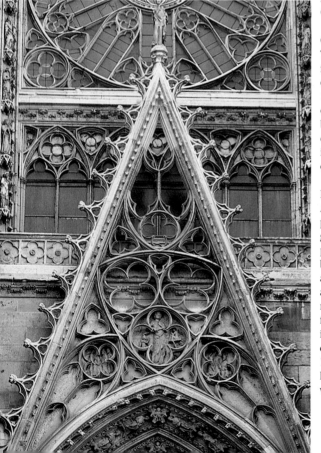

Gros-Horloge

The decorated stone arch beneath this famous gateway (note the magnificent carvings on the underside) dates from 1527, at which point the medieval clock was moved from the adjoining belfry. Go inside to see the collection of bells, including Cache-Ribaud, cast in 1260, which still tolls the 2100 curfew (opening times vary).

Eglise St-Maclou, Aître St-Maclou

Aître St-Maclou is a 16th-century **plague cemetery**, though at first glance you wouldn't realise – the pleasant cloister-like garden, fringed by sedate, half-timbered houses is almost too peaceful. Look more closely at the timbers, however, and you'll see macabre carvings of skulls and figures from the Dance of Death. The **church** is yet another Gothic masterpiece, completed in the Flamboyant style in 1517. Before going inside, take a closer look at the elaborate portal and the wood panelling on the doors.

⚑ Musée des Beaux Arts €€ *Square Verdrel; tel: 02 35 71 28 40. Open Wed–Mon, 1000–1800.*

Musée de la Céramique € *1 rue Faucon; tel: 02 35 07 31 74. Open Wed–Mon, 1000–1300, 1400–1800.*

Musée le Secq des Tournelles € *Rue Jacques Villon; tel: 02 35 88 42 92. Open Wed–Mon, 1000–1300, 1400–1800.*

Musée Flaubert et d'Histoire de la Médecine € *51 rue Lecat; tel: 02 35 15 59 95. Open Tue, 1000–1800, Wed–Sat, 1000–1200, 1400–1800.*

Museums

The strong suit of the **Musée des Beaux Arts** is its collection of 19th-century French painting. Géricault, David, Ingres and Corot all feature, as do several Impressionists: Degas, Renoir and Monet, the latter represented by three works, including one of the celebrated Rouen Cathedral studies. You'll also find plenty of Old Masters – Veronese, Caravaggio, Velázquez and Rubens, they're all here.

The **Musée de la Céramique** is devoted to Rouen faïence which flourished in the workshops of the 17th and 18th centuries. The collection is comprehensive; many of the items are decorated with animal and floral motifs and there's a wide variety of styles to admire.

The **Musée le Secq des Tournelles** presents an unusual exhibition of ironwork. Wander round the old church premises and you'll encounter everything from locks and door knockers to signs, clasps, tools, kitchen utensils and manufacturing implements. The oldest items in the collection go back to Roman times.

Rouen was the birthplace of the 19th-century novelist, Gustave Flaubert, and aficionados of his writing should not miss the **Musée Flaubert et d'Histoire de la Médecine**. Flaubert lived with his family in a wing of the Hôtel-Dieu, the hospital where his father was a surgeon. The surgical paraphernalia, pharmaceutical cabinets and demonstration models would certainly have been familiar to the creator of *Madame Bovary*. Also on display is Flaubert's parrot, as featured in the novel by Julian Barnes.

Accommodation and food

Hôtel Alive €€ *18–24 rue de Québec; tel: 02 35 70 09 38; fax: 02 35 15 80 15.* Warm welcome and reasonably priced rooms not far from the Cathedral. On-site parking but no restaurant.

Hotel de la Cathedrale €€€ *rue St Romaine; tel: 02 31 71 57 95; fax: 02 35 70 15 54; www.hotel-de-la-cathedrale.fr.* Immaculately presented option in the heart of the old town; perfect for cosy stay after a day exploring on foot.

Hôtel Frantour Rouen Vieux-Marché €€€ *15 rue de la Pie; tel: 02 35 71 00 88; fax: 02 35 70 75 94; e-mail: hotelduvieuxmarche@wanadoo.fr; www.hotelduvieuxmarche.com.* Not too bad price-wise, bearing in mind the location – almost on top of place du Vieux Marché. Other advantages include well-appointed rooms and garage parking. No restaurant.

Place du Vieux Marché is the best place for **restaurants**. Duckling (*caneton*) is the local speciality. If you're in the mood to splash out, **La Couronne €€€** *31 place du Vieux-Marché; tel: 02 35 71 40 90* claims to be the oldest hostelry in France (1343), with traditional Norman cooking. For somewhere steeped in local history, try **Brasserie Paul €€** *1 Place de la Cathédrale; tel: 02 35 71 86 07*; popular since 1911.

ⓘ **Rouen Tourist Information** 25 *place de la Cathédrale; tel: 02 32 08 32 40; fax: 02 32 08 32 44; e-mail: tourisme@rouen.fr; www.rouentourisme.com.* Services include a bureau de change, guided tours and help with booking accommodation.

Ⓟ Place du Vieux Marché, square Verdrel, place du Général de Gaulle.

Ⓖ All the main sights are accessible on foot. To hire a taxi, call Radio-Taxis (*tel: 02 35 88 50 50*).

Ⓐ **Aux 100 Souvenirs** *3 place de la Calende.* Gifts and souvenirs, including calvados and regional produce.

Ma Normandie 48 *rue St-Nicolas* (faïence).

Alternatively, for general shopping, the **St-Sever shopping mall** is a little way south of the river on the street of the same name. The best of the **markets** is on *place St-Marc: flea market Sunday mornings, fruit and veg other days.*

A walk around Rouen

Begin in the **place du Vieux Marché** ❶ with its half-timbered houses and plentiful restaurants. On one side of the square is the **Musée Jeanne d'Arc** ❷; opposite is the modern **church** built in her honour and the **cross** which marks the site of her martyrdom.

Detour: Take rue G. Flaubert, turning left on to rue de Lecat, then rue de Crosne to the **Musée Flaubert et d'Histoire de la Médecine** ❸. Return via rue du Contrat Social. At boulevard des Belges turn right, then left on to rue Racine. Turn left, crossing place Martin Luther King and **place de la Pucelle** ❹, where the **Hôtel de Bourgtheroulde** ❺ (No 15) is a blend of Gothic and Renaissance styles. A bas-relief in the courtyard depicts the 'Field of the Cloth of Gold', the celebrated meeting between François I and Henry VIII of England in 1520.

Leave place du Vieux Marché by **rue du Gros Horloge** ❻, a lively shopping street. On your right you'll pass beneath the clock which gives the road its name. At the end is the **Cathédrale de Notre-Dame** ❼. Turn left past the west end, then turn right, taking the pedestrianised **rue St-Romain** ❽ past the ruined **Bishop's palace** ❾ and half-timbered houses dating from the 15th to 18th centuries. Cross rue de la République to place Barthélémy and the handsome Gothic **Eglise St-Maclou** ❿. Follow the path to the left of the church, past the attractive Renaissance fountain at the corner of the north wall, then cross rue Martainville and take the alleyway to the cloisters (**Aître St-Maclou** ⓫). Return to rue Damiette with more superb timber-framed houses, many with antique shops on the ground floor. **Rue Eau de Robec** ⓬, off to the right, has a canalised stream running beside the houses. Continue on rue Boucheries St-Ouen into place du Général de Gaulle and the **Eglise St-Ouen** ⓭. From here take rue de l'Hôpital to the junction with rue des Carmes where you'll see a restored Gothic fountain.

Turn right on to rue Beauvoisine, then left on to rue J Lecanuet. On your right is the **Musée le Secq des Tournelles** ⓮. Continue to square Verdrel and the **Musée des Beaux Arts** ⓯. Also facing the square, in the 17th-century Hôtel d'Hocqueville is the **Musée de la Céramique** ⓰. Take rue Fauçon at the side of the museum. At the end turn left, then right on to rue Philippe Auguste and the **Tour Jeanne d'Arc** ⓱. Take rue du Donjon to rue Jeanne d'Arc and turn left, pass the ruins of the **Tour de la Pucelle** ⓲. At the end of square Verdrel turn left on to rue J Lecanuet, then right on to Allée Eugène Delacroix. Turn left on to rue Ganterie. At rue des Carmes turn right, then right again on to rue aux Juifs. This will take you past the **Palais de Justice** ⓳, a fabulous building with Renaissance mouldings and rounded windows and a profusion of Gothic spires and intricate stone tracery. Take rue Rollon to return to place du Vieux Marché.

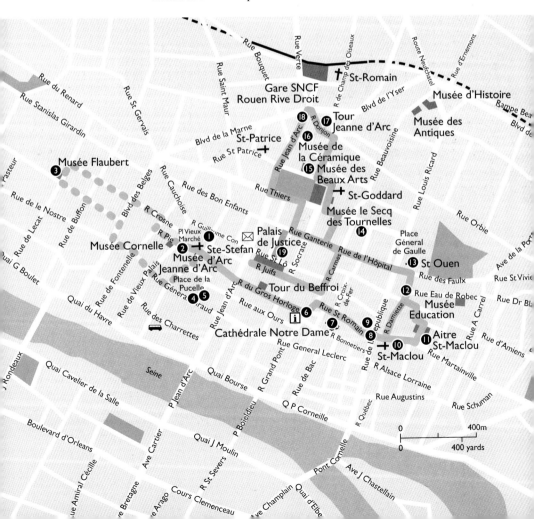

Language

Although English is spoken in most tourist locations it is courteous to attempt to speak some French. The effort is generally appreciated, and may even elicit a reply in perfect English! The following is a very brief list of some useful words and phrases, with approximate pronunciation guides.

- **Hello/Goodbye**
  Bonjour/Au revoir *Bawngzhoor/Ohrervwahr*
- **Good evening/Goodnight**
  Bonsoir/Bonne nuit *Bawngswahr/Bon nwee*
- **Yes/No**
  Oui/Non *Wee/Nawng*
- **Please/Thank you (very much)**
  S'il vous plaît/Merci (beaucoup) *Seelvooplay/Mehrsee (bohkoo)*
- **Excuse me, can you help me please?**
  Excusez-moi, pouvez vous m'aider, s'il vous plaît?
  Ekskewzaymwah, poovay voo mahyday seelvooplay?
- **Do you speak English?**
  Parlez-vous anglais? *Pahrlay voo ahnglay?*
- **I'm sorry, I don't understand.**
  Pardon, je ne comprends pas. *Pahrdawng, zher ner kawngprawng pah.*
- **I am looking for the tourist information office.**
  Je cherche l'office de tourisme. *Zher shaersh lohfeece de tooreezm.*
- **Do you have a map of the town/area?**
  Avez-vous une carte de la ville/région? *Ahveh-voo ewn cart der lah veel/rehzhawng?*
- **Do you have a list of hotels?**
  Avez-vous une liste d'hôtels? *Ahveh voo ewn leesst dohtehl?*
- **Do you have any rooms free?**
  Avez vous des chambres disponibles? *Ahveh voo deh shahngbr deesspohneebl?*
- **I would like to reserve a single/double room with/without bath/shower.**
  Je voudrais réserver une chambre pour une personne/pour deux personnes avec/sans salle de bain/douche. *Zher voodray rehsehrveh ewn shahngbr poor ewn pehrson/poor der pehrson avek/sawns sal der banne/doosh.*

- **I would like bed and breakfast/(room and) half board/(room and) full board.**
  Je voudrais le petit-déjeuner/la demi-pension/la pension complète. *Zher voodray ler pewtee-dehjewneh/lah dermee-pahngsyawng/lah pahngsyawng kawngplait.*
- **How much is it per night?**
  Quel est le prix pour une nuit? *Khel eh ler pree poor ewn nuwy?*
- **I would like to stay for . . . nights.**
  Je voudrais rester . . . nuits. *Zhe voodray resteh . . . newyh.*
- **Do you accept traveller's cheques/credit cards?**
  Acceptez-vous les chèques de voyages/les cartes de crédit? *Aksepteh voo leh sheck der vwoyazh/leh kart der krehdee?*
- **I would like a table for two.**
  Je voudrais une table pour deux personnes. *Zher voodray ewn tabl poor der pehrson.*
- **I would like a cup of/two cups of/another coffee/tea.**
  Je voudrais une tasse de/deux tasses de/encore une tasse de café/thé. *Zher voodray ewn tahss der/der tahss der/oncaw ewn tahss der kafeh/teh.*
- **I would like a bottle/glass/two glasses of mineral water/red wine/white wine, please.**
  Je voudrais une bouteille/un verre/deux verres d'eau minérale/de vin rouge/de vin blanc, s'il vous plaît. *Zher voodray ewn bootayy/ang vair/der vair doh mynehral/der vang roozh/der vang blahng, seelvooplay.*
- **Could I have it well-cooked/ medium/rare, please?**
  Je le voudrais bien cuit/à point/saignant, s'il vous plaît. *Zher ler voodray beeang kwee/ah pwahng/saynyang, seelvooplay?*
- **May I have the bill, please?**
  L'addition, s'il vous plaît? *Laddyssyawng, seelvooplay?*
- **Where is the toilet (restroom), please?**
  Où sont les toilettes, s'il vous plaît? *Oo sawng leh twahlaitt, seelvooplay?*
- **How much does it/this cost?**
  Quel est le prix? *Kehl eh ler pree?*
- **A (half-) kilo of . . . please.**
  Un (demi-) kilo de . . . s'il vous plaît. *Ang (dermee) keelo der . . . seelvooplay.*

Index

Acknowledgements

Project management: Cambridge Publishing Management Limited
Project editor: Karen Beaulah
Series design: Fox Design
Cover design: Liz Lyons Design
Layout and map work: Concept 5D/Cambridge Publishing Management Limited
Repro and image setting: Z2 Repro/PDQ Digital Media Solutions Ltd/Cambridge Publishing
Management Limited
Printed and bound in India by: Replika Press Pvt Ltd

We would like to thank Image Select International/Chris Fairclough Colour Library for the
photographs used in this book, to whom the copyright in the photograph belongs, except for
the following:

Comité Régional du Tourisme de Bretagne: pages 75, 106, 171
Pictures Colour Library: pages 244, 250
Spectrum Colour Library: page 16

Front cover: Street in Dinan, Roland Gerth/zefa/Corbis
Back cover: Breton cake, photocuisine/Corbis

Honfleur
Le Manoir De Poterie

Feedback form

We're committed to providing the very best up-to-date information in our travel guides and constantly strive to make them as useful as they can be. You can help us to improve future editions by letting us have your feedback. Just take a few minutes to complete and return this form to us. And, as an extra 'thank you' from Thomas Cook Publishing, you'll be automatically entered into our exciting monthly prize draw.

When did you buy this book? ....
....

Where did you buy it? (Please give town/city and, if possible, name of retailer)
....
....

When did you/do you intend to travel in Brittany and Normandy? ....
....

For how long (approx)? ....

How many people in your party? ....

Which cities, national parks and other locations did you/do you intend mainly to visit?
....
....
....
....

Did you/will you:
❑ Make all your travel arrangements independently?
❑ Travel on a fly-drive package?
Please give brief details: ....
....

Did you/do you intend to use this book:
❑ For planning your trip?   ❑ Both?
❑ During the trip itself?

Did you/do you intend also to purchase any of the following travel publications for your trip?
Thomas Cook Travellers: Brittany and Normandy ....
A road map/atlas (please specify) ....
Other guidebooks (please specify) ....

Have you used any other Thomas Cook guidebooks in the past? If so, which?

....

....

Please rate the following features of *Drive Around Brittany and Normandy* for their value to you (circle VU for 'very useful', U for 'useful', NU for 'little or no use'):

The *Travel facts* section on pages 14–23	VU	U	NU
The *Driver's guide* section on pages 24–29	VU	U	NU
The *Touring itineraries* on pages 40–41	VU	U	NU
The recommended driving routes throughout the book	VU	U	NU
Information on towns and cities, National Parks, etc	VU	U	NU
The maps of towns and cities, parks, etc	VU	U	NU

Please use this space to tell us about any features that in your opinion could be changed, improved, or added in future editions of the book, or any other comments you would like to make concerning the book:

....

....

....

....

....

....

....

....

Your age category: ❑ 21–30   ❑ 31–40   ❑ 41–50   ❑ over 50

Your name: Mr/Mrs/Miss/Ms ....

(First name or initials) ....

(Last name) ....

Your full address (please include postal or zip code):

....

....

....

....

....

Your daytime telephone number: ....

Please detach this page and send it to: Drive Around Project Editor, Thomas Cook Publishing, PO Box 227, Unit 18, Coningsby Road, Peterborough PE3 8SB.

Alternatively, you can e-mail us at: *books@thomascook.com*